Religion and the American University

Religion and the American University

James W. Fraser

Johns Hopkins University Press

Baltimore

Johns Hopkins University Press
2715 North Charles Street
Baltimore, Maryland 21218
www.press.jhu.edu

Library of Congress Cataloging-in-Publication Data

Names: Fraser, James W., 1944– author.
Title: Religion and the American university / James W. Fraser.
Description: Baltimore : Johns Hopkins University Press, 2025. | Includes
    bibliographical references and index.
Identifiers: LCCN 2024038670 | ISBN 9781421451732 (hardcover) | ISBN
    9781421451749 (ebook)
Subjects: LCSH: Universities and colleges—United States—Religion—
    History. | Church and college—United States—History.
Classification: LCC LC383 .F73 2025 | DDC 200.71/173--dc23/eng/20241227
LC record available at https://lccn.loc.gov/2024038670

A catalog record for this book is available from the British Library.

*Special discounts are available for bulk purchases of this book. For more
information, please contact Special Sales at specialsales@jh.edu.*

EU GPSR Authorized Representative
LOGOS EUROPE, 9 rue Nicolas Poussin
17000, La Rochelle, France
E-mail: Contact@logoseurope.eu

For Katherine

Contents

Preface

As a historian of American education and also a Protestant minister, I have long been interested in, and care deeply about, the interplay between religion, education, and society in the United States. College students of every generation also care deeply about meaning and purpose—and some, spirituality—in their lives and in the society in which they live. The words they use to describe this concern and the forms that their spirituality takes have changed greatly over time. Tracing the place of religion—a word that means many different things to different people—at American colleges and universities is a project that I find both fascinating and important.

A summary perspective of this volume on the place of religion in American higher education over the past 220 years might look something like "secularization, but . . ." Without a doubt, most colleges and universities in the United States, with the exception of a few institutions, appear to be much more secular places than they were 100 or 200 years ago when matters of religious faith, nearly always in a Protestant Christian form, were central to all aspects of the student experience. But if the institutions as a whole are more secular, religion and religious interest keep popping up in the cracks and crevices at the edges of colleges, often led by students; sometimes, but less often, by faculty; occasionally by outside religious communities. They are rarely central to the self-described priorities of colleges themselves. But in every decade, from 1800 to the present, religion has been alive and well in American higher education, sometimes at the center and sometimes on the distant margins. Even as most schools become more secular over time, new religious expressions seem to pop up in unofficial ways. This volume will examine religion when it is central and when it is on the distant margins of campus life.

Gone are the days of presidents—most of whom were once ordained Protestant ministers—teaching moral philosophy, preaching in daily chapel, and hoping for the salvation of their students' souls. Gone also are required or institutionally sponsored chapel services. In public universities, and even in most private universities, any links to religious communities are, at most, symbolic of past partnerships, not active or vibrant partnerships. One of the most prominent symbols of a religious presence on many campuses—the large chapels at the center of campus in schools such as at Stanford, the University of Chicago, Princeton, and Yale—stand mostly empty or are used for activities that its early twentieth-century donors would see as far from the intended purpose. In many higher education institutions today, the majority of faculty are probably suspicious of any mention of religion, seeing it as a conservative force at war with academic freedom and the disinterested approach that they view as essential to serious scholarly inquiry. At the very least religion is—and has been for some time—something to keep private and out of the class-room or official student programming. Indeed, it is often vaguely embarrassing to be religious or overly interested in things of the spirit in the modern university.

And yet any standard theory of secularization that assumes sure and relatively steady progress toward a diminished role for religion hardly helps us understand the many ways religion, spirituality, and questions of deeper meaning keep crop-ping up around the edges of the modern campus. At the beginning of the twenty-first century there are significant signs of a resurgence of religion on campus. This new religious vitality can be found in a number of different places. While many small religiously affiliated colleges may have felt embattled or faced closure be-cause of low enrollment, a few are maintaining deep religious roots, while also embracing the modern academic world. The academic study of religion, with deep roots in the nineteenth century, has attracted students, often resulting in interest-ing conflicts between faculty committed to a focus on religion as an objective of study from a social science or humanities perspective, and students who want to use courses offered by religious studies departments to pursue their own religious quests. On some campuses—even if far from all—interest in matters of religion can be found in other departments, notably history but also anthropology, sociology, and occasionally philosophy.

There are also more chaplains, some volunteer and some paid, across American higher education than there were twenty years ago even if still fewer than might have been on campus in the 1950s as student service administrators and off-campus religious organizations seek to respond to renewed student interest. From the days of the 1806 Haystack Prayer Meeting at Williams College and the growth of the YMCA and YWCA in the later nineteenth century to the expansion of Muslim and Hindu student associations in the twenty-first century, students have often been ahead of preachers and professors in launching their own religious movements on campus without waiting for leadership or authorization from their elders.

Finally, and most intriguing, John Schmalzbauer and Kathleen A. Mahoney describe a new and unique resurgence of student interest in religion in the twenty-first century:

> For the most part, religion's return to campus is not a restoration project. . . . While some have evinced a strong propensity for traditional religious expression, "spirituality," with all its diverse meanings and forms, has made strong headway on campus and sometimes vies with religion. Today's campuses are diverse, with Baha'is, Buddhists, Muslims, and Wiccans joining Protestants, Catholics, Jews, and the religiously unaffiliated.[1]

This is not the religious energy of 1960s or the 1920s, the student-led prayer meetings of the 1870s, the pre–Civil War birth of Catholic colleges, evangelical Protestant-supported women's colleges, or the first colleges for African Americans—all topics of concern in this book. But it is religious. It is vibrant. It is fascinating. It is also sometimes deeply divisive. And it is the final topic of concern in this volume as chapter 8 and the afterword will show.

In the nineteenth century, most American colleges were deeply Protestant in curriculum and culture. The few emerging Catholic colleges were equally Catholic in curriculum and culture. By the late nineteenth century and into much of the twentieth century, the so-called old-time college with its obvious religious orientation was replaced by something new: the research university, which emerged along with the Industrial Revolution. It did not appear overnight but slowly in the decades between the Civil War and World War II, sooner in Protestant and state schools and a bit later in Catholic ones; the research university became the dominant and certainly the most prestigious structure for American higher education. Research universities have long been described as secular institutions, but if a modern visitor were to time travel to most research universities prior to the middle of the twentieth century, they would find fairly religious places. Many state universities held chapel services into the 1920s and private universities for far longer. Their presidents often described them as strongly religious places, sometimes to placate a critical state legislature or donor but also sometimes out of their own deeply held religious convictions.[2]

Nevertheless, in the early twentieth century, many saw higher education becoming more detached from religion, and especially from the active life of the nation's religious communities. Religious leaders, in and out of universities, tried a number of creative experiments to reverse course. It is also important to note that several hundred American colleges, out of a total of several thousand, have maintained their status as religious schools directly linked in one way or another to a single denomination, or are nondenominational but still very religious colleges. The vast majority of colleges, however, took a different route, slowly becoming more secular.

In spite of the growing secularization, three developments in particular have exhibited tenacious staying power: college chaplaincy, the academic study of religion, and student voluntary associations. The advent of college chaplaincy meant that religious leaders, mostly ordained clergy sometimes funded by the colleges and more often by religious communities, were appointed to serve on a college campus. The parallel development of religious studies as an academic discipline was often begun to maintain religious sensibilities among students, but in most places, it soon developed into its own academic discipline purposefully divorced from any faith-based commitments. Finally, student voluntary associations, sometimes supported by adults outside of the university, have continued in importance, including the modern Muslim and Hindu student associations. Together these developments have been hallmarks of college religion for more than a century.

Since around 1990 and especially since 2001, universities have seen an extraordinary broadening of what is meant by religion. Whereas for much of the twentieth century religion was seen in its Protestant/Catholic/Jewish forms, the religion of the new century includes a new interest in Islam, and in Eastern religions—Hindu, Buddhist, Bahá'í—and what many students simply call "spirituality." Some of this religious diversity has been fueled by new and broader immigration rules established in the United States in 1965, which have resulted in immigrants and the children of immigrants attending college in large numbers. The rise of Islamophobia after September 2001 has led many universities to take seriously their need to support the growing numbers of Muslim students who have been on their campuses, often unseen, for some time. It has also led to a growing need to understand Islam in all of its diversity so as to avoid easy and often hostile stereotyping.

In addition, many students whose grandparents or great-grandparents were active in the older religious communities, but who themselves learned little about religion during childhood, come to college with a curiosity that is not limited to the faith of their family of origin. They want to know more about many religious traditions—Western and Eastern. Some of these students arrive with a curious and open mind, others with deep hostility and wounds. Some call themselves "just curious," but large numbers also identify as "spiritual-but-not-religious," or "nones" (not to be confused with women religious *nuns*). All of them make up the American student body of the twenty-first century: a challenging and fascinating mix of people and ideas for anyone—professor of religious studies, college chaplain, or curious historian—who is interested in making sense of the current scene.

Religion and the American University is not the first volume to trace aspects of this story. Indeed, this work is deeply indebted to some scholarly giants who have looked at aspects of this history before. Among my intellectual predecessors I especially want to note a few. D. G. Hart's *The University Gets Religion: Religious Studies in American Higher Education* (1999) traces the rise of the academic study of religion in the new research universities of the 1870s and 1880s up to the end of the twentieth century with a critical yet thoughtful eye. James Turner's *Religion Enters the Academy: The Origins of the Scholarly Study of Religion in America* (2011) also reminds us that what we now think of as the academic discipline of religious studies has roots that go back to the very early 1800s. George M. Marsden's *The Soul of the American University: From Protestant Establishment to Established Nonbelief* (1994) and Julie A. Reuben's *The Making of the Modern University: Intellectual Transformation and the Marginalization of Morality* (1996) have rightly long been the dominant books on the place of religion in American higher education since their publication in the 1990s. Both books begin with the role of religion in early American colleges but focus primarily on the changes wrought by the growth of the research university and the marginalization of religion alongside any discussion of morality, which has too frequently disappeared in the "objective" and "disinterested" modern university.

Happily, Marsden published an updated version of his work in 2021 as I was first working on this volume. His new edition, now subtitled *From Protestant to Postsecular*, not only brings the work up to the second decade of the twenty-first century but in its examination of developments in recent decades also casts a wider net. The last two chapters of the revised volume look far beyond the Ivy League focus of the earlier chapters to consider sometimes marginalized institutions and campus ministry organizations like the InterVarsity Christian Fellowship and the Cru. Perhaps most intriguingly, he also looks carefully at the role of the humanities in providing some students a new venue to discuss issues of meaning and purpose in their lives. I have greatly valued Reuben's and Marsden's work, as a careful read of the back notes of this book will show, and readers will note similarities especially in my interests and those addressed in Marsden's 2021 work.[3]

John Schmalzbauer and Kathleen A. Mahoney's revealing examination of recent developments in *The Resilience of Religion in American Higher Education* (2018) has already been noted. Looking at an earlier era, Andrea L. Turpin reminds us that gender has played a major role in the shifting place of religion or more broadly in discussions of purpose in American universities in *A New Moral Vision: Gender, Religion, and the Changing Purposes of American Higher Education, 1837–1917* (2016). In *The Sacred and the Secular University* (2000), Jon H. Roberts and James Turner offer an in-depth look at the way secularization and the parallel turn away from an earlier Protestant ethos worked in many American universities as the research university emerged as the dominant North American model of higher education. In recent years Adam Laats has emerged as a new voice in the history of education to remind us that secularization is not the whole story. Beginning with his 2015 *The Other School Reformers: Conservative Activism in American Education* and then his 2018 *Fundamentalist U: Keeping Faith in American Higher Education*, Laats helps us hear the conservative voices that sought a different future for higher education in the United States.

More focused works include Margaret M. Grubiak, *White Elephant on Campus: The Decline of the University Chapel in America, 1920–1960* (2014) and Philip Gleason, *Contending with Modernity: Catholic Higher Education in the Twentieth Century* (1995), while William C. Ringenberg also reminds us in *The Christian College: A History of Protestant Higher Education in America* (2006) that there are dozens of schools all across the United States that happily and proudly continue to reaffirm the Protestant nature of their curriculum. The list could go on, and many scholars have contributed to—and are contributing to—our understanding of the changing place of religion in American colleges and universities in the last decades.[4]

The current volume builds on the prior work noted above, and I am deeply indebted to the scholars who have gone before me. At the same time, my work differs from others in some important ways. With the exception of Marsden's recent updates, many of the above books were written in the 1990s or early 2000s, and much has happened in the intervening decades. Along with Marsden, and echoing Schmalzbauer and Mahoney, I argue that religion is more robust in the 2020s than it was in 1999, although we may need to look in different places to find it. Even more obviously, religion is different—much more diverse and much more contentious— than some have recognized. New religious traditions have made themselves heard on college campuses—many that were barely noticed in the 1990s if at all. Religious questioning and pondering is much stronger. The older binary of religious / not religious simply does not apply when large numbers of college students call themselves "spiritual-but-not-religious" and many others are alienated from traditional religious communities but anxious to find new ways to find meaning and purpose in their own lives and in the larger society. Among the "nones" there are many who mean "none of the above" when asked about religious traditions but who remain very curious, even if others specifically mean none as in no interest in matters religious.[5]

In addition, I have consciously cast a broader net than Hart, Marsden, or Reuben. The primary focus of their work has been on the nation's leading universities, the best-known private universities, and the major state universities that constitute the elite and usually the trend-setters of higher education. As Marsden argues, "when doing cultural history there are advantages in looking at the most influential leaders and institutions." And there are. But those schools, as important as they are, are not where most Americans go to college. Indeed, as Marsden himself notes, "one must always bear in mind that, given America's bewildering religious and ethnic diversity and opportunities for local initiatives, there are many alternative stories that are important in their own right."[6] Regional or lesser-known public universities; smaller private colleges, some of which maintain religious commitments of a stronger or weaker intensity and some of which don't; historically Black colleges and universities; and other kinds of schools—when taken together—educate far more Americans and employ far more faculty than the major research universities do. There is, therefore, much to be learned by looking at other, different schools which may or may not follow the trends set by the elite. Some may quarrel with my selection of schools. Among several thousand institutions of higher education in the United States, far more are left out of this study than those included. But I hope that the variety of schools reported here represents a useful snapshot, perhaps a more accurate snapshot, than another review of the place of religion in the best-known schools alone would offer.

A book on religion and the American university demands that terms be defined. In this volume, what does the author mean by "religion," "American," and "university," since all three terms have more than one meaning and different people hear different things when the words are used? For this study, when I use these terms, I try to remain as consistent as possible. The reader can decide the degree to which I have succeeded.

Religion means many different things to different people at different times in history. As we will see, in the nineteenth century at most institutions of higher education in the United States, religion meant Protestant Christianity. Beyond that, it also meant a deep personal commitment to the Christian faith usually including a life-changing personal conversion. Not every student had this sort of cathartic experience, but most college leaders tried hard to make sure that as many of their students as possible did. In addition to conversion, religion meant a fairly detailed understanding of the Bible and the Christian faith. Finally, religion meant ethical living, although as we will also see, different people defined ethics differently, especially in the antebellum era on the ethics of slavery.

Toward the end of the nineteenth century and for much of the early twentieth century, the emphasis on conversion declined. For more and more college faculty and students, religion came to mean maintaining a level of loyalty to one's religious tradition—Methodist, Baptist, Presbyterian, Catholic, or later Jewish—or some version of the so-called Social Gospel. Saving your own soul received less attention, while maintaining links to the faith of one's family of origin while saving the whole society, especially the poor and marginalized, received much more. In some ways the religious inspiration of some participants in the civil rights and anti-war movements of the late 1960s and early 1970s could be seen as a culmination of the Social Gospel. At the same time, of course, like many faculty, some students in every generation drifted far away from anything recognizably religious.

By the coming of the twentieth century, whether or not to accept the implications of evolution—whether or not to agree with the discoveries of biblical criticism—took on a new and more divisive role than in the nineteenth century. The fundamentalist–liberal split meant that some deeply religious people found themselves alienated from other deeply religious people and even considered those in the opposite camp to have lost their religion. New institutions were born favoring one side or the other. Protestants in the United States were joined by more and more Catholics and Jews. At the same time, far more people lost interest in religion, and secularization of intuitions and individuals proceeded apace.

By the twenty-first century, while all of these differing definitions of religion continued, new definitions emerged with the growth of Muslim, Hindu, Buddhist, and other religious communities that were large enough to make themselves felt. Various centering and mindfulness practices grew often with or without traditional religious connotations. By the 2020s, religion might or might not involve certain ritual practices, it might or might not involve prayer or meditation, and it might or might not involve holding certain beliefs. Whether religion is being affirmed or denied, the definition of the word has often become increasingly broad and unclear, though often linked in one way or another to that other vague term: spirituality.

American is also a term with different meanings, often depending on where one finds oneself. Many in Central and South America rightly resent the tendency of those in the United States to presume to own the term. As a pastor in Cuba once said to me, "I'm an American too." Nevertheless, the term has come to mean what is happening in the Unites States, not so much in the rest of the Americas. And with apology, that is the meaning here. Religion and the American university refers to religion at colleges and universities in the United States. By using the word American, I confess that I have chosen what I see as a less clunky title over one that might be more accurate.

University may, surprisingly, be the least specific term in the title of this book. For some, especially those steeped in the British tradition, a university is a gathering, more or less tightly, of different colleges. The term sometimes has that meaning in the United States: New York University, where I teach, includes the College of Business, the College of Medicine, the College of Arts and Sciences, and my own School of Culture, Education and Human Development. But in many places, the terms are less clear. The difference between Boston University and Boston College is not one of inclusion of one in the other. They are quite separate institutions, both of which function as modern universities with constituent schools, but with Protestant and Catholic origins, respectively.

In the nineteenth century, college meant many different things. Often what was called a college a hundred or more years ago would be seen as a glorified high school or even an elementary school today. Differentiating a college from an academy often had more to do with a founder's choice than with one offering more advanced work than the other. At the beginning of the twentieth century, there was a major effort to regularize American secondary and postsecondary education. Most colleges shed their academies and their precollege programs and regularized their efforts at the postsecondary level in a way that required a level of attainment to enter college and some clear—if often ignored—standards for the meaning of a college degree. But such twentieth-century usage should not be read back into nineteenth-century institutions. It is fair to say that the meaning of college in the twentieth century is quite a bit clearer than the meaning of the term before that, if still not as clear as some would wish. But after the early 1900s, college generally did not mean a secondary school as it might once have.

At the same time, for all the well-intentioned efforts to differentiate between the word *college* and the word *university*, the reality is that the terms are practically interchangeable even though both now clearly mean postsecondary. They are used interchangeably in this volume. It is worth noting, however, that while the word *college* often brings to mind a four-year residential community, only a small minority of college students experience such an education. Far more often, college students live at home, go to school part-time, attend multiple intuitions (from community colleges to traditional colleges to for-profit online colleges), and complete their college experience at a very different school than the one where they began. Graduate schools, especially those offering a master's and doctoral degree, generally require an undergraduate degree, and students at this level are somewhat less likely to move around between institutions. Yet all of these diverse students are college students and contribute to the large cohort of young people who attend colleges—sometimes called universities and sometimes not—in the United States today.

Finally, in this volume I focus primarily on the undergraduate experience. There are a few references to master's and doctoral programs that continue undergraduate majors, especially in religious studies. There is virtually no mention of graduate professional schools. This means that there is no study of the growing interest in the impact of spirituality in medical schools and little study of one of the major places where religion is studied today—the graduate theological seminaries—either those at research universities like the Divinity schools at Harvard or Chicago or the many independent seminaries such as the many Baptist schools. The one exception is my case study of New York's Union Theological Seminary, which I felt was an essential case study to understand the growing contention over biblical criticism at the beginning of the twentieth century. To include seminaries or other professional schools would have created a much longer volume, interesting perhaps but certainly unwieldy.

A word on the structure of this volume. The eight chapters that follow are arranged chronologically. Many things change in different eras, and some key terms, such as "Christian college," "the study of religion," or "college chaplain," mean different things at different times. But new developments almost always have roots in the past, and a chronological approach helps understand the origins of any given change more clearly than a topical history. Within each chapter, the discussion of an era opens with a broad overview of the major themes and developments regarding the place of religion in American higher education in the decades under consideration. Often this is done through multiple specific examples. All chapters then shift to individual college case studies. The case studies are by no means representative (whatever that might mean in this context), but they do offer as diverse a view as possible at the changing place of religion on many different campuses, large and small, public and private, committed to one religious tradition or none, serving one constituency or many. The goal of each chapter, in the overview and the individual campus case studies, is to give the reader as clear a sense as possible of what is happening to religious faith and practice in as many colleges and universities in the United States in different decades as possible.

Acknowledgments

This book would never have appeared without the enthusiastic support but also wise prodding of my long-time editor, Greg Britton, at Johns Hopkins University Press who urged me—strongly—to expand an initial plan for a narrower book into the present one, and then championed this book through to publication. It would also not have appeared in its current form without the support of Jonathan Van-Antwerpen of the Henry Luce Foundation, who saw promise in this project and backed the research at an essential moment in its early stages. New York University provided a much-needed sabbatical that allowed me essential time to finish this book. Two anonymous reviewers were exceedingly helpful with the encouragement, critique, and wise suggestions.

Many academic colleagues have been generous with their time, discussed various aspects of the book, and offered encouragement, including Dorothy Bass, Robby Cohen, Hasia Diner, Steven Diner, Carl W. Ernst, Paula Fass, Warren Goldstein, Arthur Levine, John Rogers, Norman Samuels, Troy Smith, Catharine Stimpson, Jonathan Zimmerman, and Angela Zito. As with so many other efforts, Amy Wilson has provided extraordinary research assistance and editorial advice for every chapter of this book as did Brittney Lewer earlier in my work. I am especially grateful to John Schmalzbauer of Missouri State University for his enthusiastic support for this project, and to Andrea Turpin of Baylor University for sharing research in religion and higher education and for several discussions of this work.

Students in my seminar on religion at the American university and my doctoral students in the NYU Steinhardt college chaplaincy program were very helpful in both their feedback and their willingness to share their own research, especially Sara Aeder, Melissa Carter, Vineet Chander, Faiyaz Jaffer, Lawrence James King, J. Cody Nielsen, Jacob Pankow, Erika V. Reyes, Jonathan Schwab, and Anna Zinko.

Much of the research and writing for this book was done at a time when the normal travel to archives was not possible because of the COVID-19 pandemic. A number of university archivists went out of their way to share material from archives that were closed at the time that I wanted to use them. I am especially grateful to Sister Janet Gilligan, SP, of the Sisters of Providence Archives and several of her colleagues without whose help the case study on Saint Mary-of-the-Woods College would not have been written. A big thank-you also to Denise D. Monbarren, special collections librarian at the College of Wooster who sent me key archival material. Kate Siebert Medicus of the special collections at Kent State University shared old catalog material and also recent oral histories about Kent with me. And a big thank-you to Angela Lawrence, archivist at Rutgers University–Newark, who found key data that allowed me to flesh out the material on her school. The archivist at my own school, New York University, Janet Bunde, also called my attention to University Christian Fellowship material in our own archives while always encouraging me in my research and our co-teaching. Many other archives have digitized some of their records and have them accessible online to researchers, making research in higher education much easier than it was just a few years ago. Late in the book's development, Terri Lee Paulsen did an extraordinary job of carefully editing the full manuscript as did Charles Dibble and Devon Thomas.

Finally, the very idea of writing a book would not be possible without the constant support of my wife, Katherine Hanson, who has read and critiqued every word but much more has been ready with encouragement and wisdom. I owe Katherine more than I can express.

CHAPTER ONE

Religion at the "Old Time College," 1800–1870

Yale College was established in 1701, the third college in British North America after Harvard and William & Mary. Like its predecessors, Yale was modeled on the British universities at Oxford and Cambridge, which in the 1600s and 1700s had a strong classical curriculum in Latin and Greek literature considered essential to the preparation of a "learned gentleman," whether he entered the clergy or a more secular profession like law. For the next quarter century, Yale admitted only men to its student body. According to its founders, Yale's purpose was to provide Congregational Connecticut with new generations "fitted for public employment both in church and civil state."

At the time that Yale was founded, the Congregational Church and the civil state in Connecticut were one and the same. Prior to the Civil War, the US Constitution's prohibition of "an establishment of religion" applied only to the federal government and not individual states, and Connecticut was one of the last states to vote to apply the "separation of church and state" to its internal policies, doing so only in 1817. Thus, throughout the 1700s, Yale remained small but important to the colony as a source of leaders—ministers and magistrates. The college was a religious institution, and the college's president was expected to be its spiritual as well as academic leader.[1]

The Antebellum Protestant Christian College

In 1795 Congregational minister Timothy Dwight became the eighth president of Yale College, serving until his death in 1817. Dwight expanded and exemplified the college's religious focus. He saw his role as ensuring the orthodoxy and salvation of its student body and leading the academic work of the institution, mostly in that order. Like nearly all college presidents of his day—and as the role model for most college presidents of the next three decades—Dwight preached every Sunday morning and evening, and he taught the senior capstone Moral Philosophy course. Dwight could not imagine delegating the leadership of religion at Yale to anyone else. Religious leadership and fostering a religious conversion experience for students was as much a part of the presidency, as he understood it, as hiring new faculty or tracking the budget.[2]

For Dwight, orthodox theology—but also a sense of personal salvation—were key to everything he wanted to accomplish in a student's education. Dwight hoped that some students would decide to become Congregational ministers like himself. But he was absolutely committed to ensuring that every student was a devout Christian. In one of his graduation sermons, Dwight said that without religious belief, what he called infidel philosophy, "presents no efficacious means of restraining Vice, or promoting Virtue; but on the contrary encourages Vice and discourages Virtue."[3] For Dwight and many other college leaders of his day, restraining vice and promoting virtue were essential elements—perhaps the essential elements—of a college education.

Lyman Beecher, one of Dwight's most well-known students, remembered his college experience with his president. According to Beecher, Dwight left the students on their own for much of their studies, but "Dwight was, however, a revival preacher and a new era of revivals was commencing," not only at Yale but across the country. The so-called second Great Awakening was just beginning to turn America's revolutionary era secularism into the huge growth of Protestantism in the United States over the next thirty years.[4]

It was not only through the president's preaching and counseling of students or his teaching that Yale, and the colleges that followed in its wake, centered the curriculum around religion and religious issues, however. As historian Julie Reuben has argued, "In the first half of the nineteenth century the broad conception of . . . the 'unity of truth' was institutionalized into the structures of higher education."

Even as the college curriculum broadened beyond the Latin and Greek classics, this meant that colleges had a unifying focus, and different courses in ancient and modern literature, mathematics and the sciences, and religion were assumed to point to one unified version of truth. This curriculum was brought together by the capstone Moral Philosophy course, to make the point that faith, knowledge, and morality were inseparable, and that faith was the key to their unity.[5]

Yale served as a role model for many of the new colleges founded in the rapidly expanding United States, especially within the Atlantic states and later the newer communities of the Midwest. Most other pre–Civil War college presidents saw themselves with a similar role to Dwight's, and they kept their college's—usually Protestant—religious ethos strong. (Other than Georgetown College, founded in 1789, there were no Catholic colleges in the United States until the 1840s, while the first Jewish colleges were established in the mid-twentieth century and Muslim and Buddhist schools only much later.) Few, however, could match the financial support or draw on the number of students who were ready and able to start college-level work that Yale did. Yet in 1800 Yale only enrolled slightly over 200 students. In its first century, from 1701 to 1801, Yale awarded college degrees to 2,333 men, an average of 23 per year. Yale may have been one of the largest colleges, but it was still very small.[6]

Most of the new colleges founded after 1800 were much more colleges in the hopes and dreams of their founders than in reality. Most had preparatory departments to get students ready for college that were larger, sometimes much larger, than the collegiate department. Nevertheless, the blueprint for what constituted a college and a college-level curriculum was clear, even though in many cases it took decades for some schools to grow into their names and shed their preparatory departments to nearby academies or later to high schools.

Various Protestant denominations—Congregationalists, Presbyterians, Lutherans, Baptists, Methodists, and Disciples of Christ—all competed to build colleges. In colleges that were started by specific Protestant denominations—as most were in this era—the denominations seldom exercised control once a school was launched. Colleges did, however, maintain a deeply pan-Protestant commitment to maintaining a religious and generically Protestant culture. The result was schools that were not church controlled but were deeply religious nonetheless.

It may be difficult for a twenty-first-century observer to understand the confidence of most college founders and leaders that colleges could be solidly Christian institutions without some level of church control, but in the nineteenth century Protestant Christianity so dominated the culture that denominational leaders did

Figure 1.1. Yale College, founded in 1701, represents an important model for the place of religion in American higher education from the 1700s to the present. The Yale chapel pictured here was built in 1761 and demolished in 1893. From Library of Congress—Yale

not feel the need to worry about the future direction of the colleges they were founding. Thus, in 1830 Julian Sturtevant, a Presbyterian minister, college teacher, and soon to be the long-time president of the Presbyterian-affiliated Illinois College, described the ideal of a college that was not denominational but that was deeply Christian:

> We never sought for Illinois College any ecclesiastical control, and would never have submitted to it.... It was never intended to be a Presbyterian or a Congregational institution, but a Christian institution sacredly devoted to the interests of the Christian faith, universal freedom and social order.[7]

Sturtevant spoke for the majority of nineteenth-century college leaders: Colleges of his day did not need denominational control to be carriers of a broadly Protestant Christian culture.

The small size of the colleges made it much easier, and indeed necessary, for the president to have multiple roles—religious, academic, and administrative. In most pre–Civil War colleges, the multiple roles would have been hard to separate. Yale never had more than a few hundred students—all White men—during Dwight's tenure, and it remained one of the largest colleges in the country before the Civil War. It is important to remember how few Americans attended college in these years. At no time prior to the Civil War did college enrollment top 1 percent of the young adults in the college-going age cohort. The colleges that served these young men were small. Everyone associated with these small schools had many roles.

College students were sometimes ahead of presidents and faculty in terms of religious commitments. In the famous Haystack Prayer Meeting in 1806, students at Williams College initiated an event that influenced nineteenth-century student religious life—and quickly the work of the major Protestant churches in the United States—in a far more lasting way than most college presidents. In the summer of 1806, five Williams College students—Samuel J. Mills, James Richards, Francis L. Robbins, Harvey Loomis, and Byram Green—were together in a field talking about the possibility of becoming missionaries to bring their faith to foreign lands. At this time, there were almost no American foreign missionaries, though missionaries from England were role models. When a thunderstorm passed over the five took shelter in a nearby haystack and as they remembered it, "The brevity of the shower, the strangeness of the place of refuge, and the peculiarity of their topic of prayer and conference all took hold of their imaginations and memories." As a result of a deeply emotional, religious experience that day, the five made a commitment to missionary service, a decision resonated among Protestants across the United States.[8]

According to Mills's biography, by that fall "religion had become a vital thing in college and was finding what it had most of all needed—an outlet, an expression in work and life for others" in the new focus on foreign missions. Later, these same students helped create the Society of Brethren to foster foreign missions, one of the first such organizations in the United States.[9]

After graduating from Williams, Mills attended Andover Seminary, where he met Adoniram Judson. Mills and Judson convinced the Congregational churches of Massachusetts and Connecticut to establish the American Board of Commissioners for Foreign Missions (ABCFM), which quickly began to send American missionaries to India, Burma, and beyond. The ABCFM that Mills founded lasted until 1961 when it merged with the missionary boards of the United Church of Christ, which continue its work in the twenty-first century and celebrated the bicentennial of the Haystack Prayer Meeting in 2006. Few college student movements have had such a 200-year-long influence.[10]

The Moral Philosophy Course

While much of college religious life took place outside of the classroom, whether in faculty-led chapel services or in student-led voluntary gatherings like the one at Williams College, the antebellum college curriculum was also deeply suffused with Christianity. Most colleges followed the basic outline of a college curriculum that was prescribed by the famous Yale Report of 1828. In response to a proposal to make the curriculum more practical and to drop the "dead" languages, the Yale faculty voted that the core should remain the study of Greek and Roman classical literature in the original languages, and they voted to retain "the ancient languages as an essential part of our course of instruction." After all, the faculty insisted, "in ancient literature, [a college student] finds some of the most finished models of taste."

Yale saw its curriculum not as an immediately practical one but rather a way to help students develop "the discipline and furniture of the mind; expanding its powers, and storing it with knowledge," for whatever role in church or civil society the graduates might pursue. In addition to the ancient classics, students needed to learn "pure mathematics," the physical sciences, and some English literature. Given the religious nature of Yale and the many colleges that adopted its curriculum, it may be surprising that there was so much of the so-called pagan classics and so little Bible in the curriculum. But the faculty was confident that all subjects could be made to reinforce the student's faith. The most important course in the college curriculum, Moral Philosophy, was taught usually in the senior year and nearly always by the college president, with a view to ensuring that students understood the intellectual and moral unity of what they had been learning.[11]

As Julie Reuben reminds us, most of those associated with the antebellum college believed in what they called "the unity of truth." Thus, the *Veritas* on the Harvard seal meant all truth for all the truths of literature, the sciences, and religion were and had to be compatible. As Reuben said, "The term truth encompassed all 'correct' knowledge; religious doctrines, common-sense beliefs, and scientific theories were all judged by the same cognitive standards." Nevertheless, religious truth "was the most important and valuable form of knowledge because it gave meaning to mundane knowledge." While this sense of the "unity of truth" pervaded the curriculum, allowing a Christian to learn from the non-Christian classical literature and the sciences, it was the Moral Philosophy course that was "designed to draw together all higher learning."[12]

There are surprisingly few modern studies of the antebellum college that actually discuss what was taught in Moral Philosophy or how. An earlier book did. In 1879, a young G. Stanley Hall—destined in later life to bring psychology to the American college curriculum and the American public—wrote a survey of what he saw being taught under the heading of philosophy in American colleges. Hall was an astute observer if not a very happy one. He visited some thirty schools and consulted the catalogues of more to see what was being taught in courses labeled as philosophy. In most of the colleges he studied in 1879, Moral Philosophy still reigned supreme. Hall himself was an advocate of what he saw as a much more scholarly and secular approach to philosophy and what at the time was its subdiscipline of psychology. He had little use for the traditional Moral Philosophy course.[13]

Nevertheless, Hall's survey and critique sheds light on what was actually being taught in Moral Philosophy in the United States in the 1870s, much as it had been in 1800 or 1840. Hall wrote, "There are nearly 300 non-Catholic colleges in the United States . . . conferring the degree of A.B. upon their students at the end of a four years' course. . . . In nearly all of these institutions certain studies, aesthetical, logical, historical, most commonly ethical, most rarely psychological, are roughly classed as philosophy and taught during the last year almost invariably by the president." Hall made it clear that he had little use for these courses which he called "strictly denominational" (read religious).

As Hall noted, from his perspective the courses offered at most institutions represented "semi-theological philosophy," which included a review of "recent discoveries in science . . . the very kernel of truth [that] has been shelled from books and nature by a master-hand. Then, with much liberality of interpretation, scriptural doctrines are compared with these results, all in a conciliatory spirit: but whenever teachings of science or philosophy are judged to vary from those of Scripture, the supreme authority of the latter is urged with all the intensity of a fervid and magnetic personality which makes dogmatism impressive and often even sublime."[14]

Finally, Hall analyzed the pedagogy that he observed in moral philosophy:

> The practical questions of daily life are often discussed in the class-room with the professor with great freedom and interest. Current social or political topics are sometime introduced, and formal debates by students appointed beforehand by the professor and followed by his comments, may occasionally take the place of regular recitations and lectures.[15]

This description of the pedagogy of the moral philosophy course seems surprisingly progressive and open for the nineteenth century. Nevertheless, it seemed to Hall that the pedagogy often masked the basic role of the course being to convince students that religious truth reigned supreme. Whether it succeeded in doing so for nineteenth-century students remains an open question.

If we turn to the textbooks themselves, there is another perspective on the issues taught in Moral Philosophy. In his 1873 best-selling *A Manuel of Moral Philosophy: Designed for Colleges and High Schools*, Harvard's Andrew Peabody reports that he "has endeavored in this treatise to comprehend all that is essential in a manual of ethics . . . to give emphasis to his view of the ground of Right, as consisting in intrinsic fitness, independent of any will or arbitrary law human or divine, and essential as furnishing the only standard by which we can attain a knowledge of the Divine attributes." Peabody did this through a detailed examination of what he considered the sources of knowledge as to right and wrong, which in his book included conscience, observation, experience, tradition, law, and finally Christianity.[16] Cultivating moral action and right belief were the twin goals of moral philosophy.

Noah Porter, Princeton's more conservative president, also wrote a textbook for his own course and for use by others. Porter's *The Human Intellect With an Introduction Upon Psychology and the Soul* (1868) might have made Hall happy with his attention to psychology but not so happy with his discussion of the soul. When Porter looked at the "mutual relations of material and spiritual substances," he insisted that the mind can know matter by sense-perception but "we can by no means have an adequate and exhaustive, or what is often called an absolute knowledge," although humans can know that the absolute exists.[17]

While the Moral Philosophy course in almost every college in the United States concluded that Christian religious faith was a necessary and correct way of understanding all other knowledge, they were not especially denominational but described a broadly Protestant faith. Courses differed—sometimes greatly—however, when it came to a discussion of the ethical issue of slavery in the United States. Oberlin president Asa Mahan and Wilberforce's Daniel Payne, both staunch abolitionists, and Randolph-Macon's president William Andrew Smith, a defender of slavery, all taught Moral Philosophy in their respective schools, but they could not have been further apart. (See below in the discussion of Moral Philosophy in sections on Randolph-Macon, Oberlin, and Wilberforce.) In most other colleges, the ethics discussed in Moral Philosophy came somewhere in between these polls, but the issue remained impossible to avoid in any discussion of ethics.[18]

In 1881, very soon after publishing his critique of the older Moral Philosophy course, Hall took a position at the new Johns Hopkins University, the model for the research university that was replacing the "old time college." At Johns Hopkins, Hall taught the "L.E.P." course—short for Logic, Ethics, and Psychology—that was replacing Moral Philosophy in some colleges and universities even as it replicated it in many ways. For all of his commitment to free philosophy from theology, Hall retained deeply religious commitments that he sought to balance with his scientific ones. And Daniel Coit Gilman, the liberal president of Johns Hopkins for its first quarter century, went further: "Religion has nothing to fear from science. . . . Religion claims to interpret the word of God, and science to reveal the laws of God."[19] Religion remained alive and well within the culture and the curriculum, not only at the "old time" colleges but also the new research universities as they began to take shape.

Nonetheless, moral philosophy courses began to disappear by the 1880s and 1890s, most quickly in the new research universities, replaced by the more scientific approach or more inclusive one that a new generation that included Hall had advocated. But moral philosophy's disappearance was gradual, well into the twentieth century in many schools. In time, the belief in the "unity of truth"—that there was only one truth and it was always consistent with the Christian faith—disappeared from American higher education. But the change did not happen quickly, nor completely, and attention to faith and morality remains a part of the twenty-first-century curriculum in some colleges, even if significantly less central than it once was at others.[20]

College Competition: Denominational, Regional, and Personal—The Example of Randolph-Macon

Early nineteenth-century Methodists saw themselves in competition with other more established branches of Protestantism. By the 1840s they had won the membership contest, having grown from a tiny group at the time of the American Revolution to the largest denomination in the United States before the Civil War. In this period, the Methodist Episcopal Church* in the United States developed very much as a church by and for the common people—which nearly always meant members and ministers without a college education.[21]

Peter Cartwright began preaching at seventeen and never had much in the way of a formal education, but he was highly successful at converting people to Christianity in its Methodist form. Cartwright focused his preaching on others like himself without much formal education. But such people were by far the largest number of White Americans—and more than a few Black Americans—and they transformed the Methodist Church. Cartwright relished his approach to ministry as one of the traveling itinerant Methodist ministers. In 1856 Cartwright, then retired, wrote:

> The Presbyterians, and other Calvinistic branches of the Protestant Church, used to contend for an educated ministry, for pews, for instrumental music, for congregational or stated salaried ministers. The Methodists universally opposed these ideas; and the illiterate Methodist preachers actually set the world on fire, (the American world at least,) while they were lighting their matches![22]

Cartwright was obviously pleased and proud of the work of these "illiterate Methodist preachers."

Nevertheless, even as Cartwright was at his prime, in the 1820s and 1830s, other Methodists were beginning to have their doubts about the educational level of their ministers. Few questioned the highly successful Methodist approach with its itinerant ministers who did not lead parishes but traveled from community to community to preach and gather converts. But some began to question whether those

---

* The Methodist churches in the United States were called "Methodist Episcopal" in the nineteenth and much of the twentieth century, and the African American branches of Methodism—the AME, AME Zion, and CME churches—still are. The "Episcopal" in the name refers to churches governed by bishops, which Methodism in the United States was, but these Methodist denominations have nothing to do with the Episcopal, formerly Protestant Episcopal, Church in the United States.

itinerant ministers might not do a much better job if they were able to receive more education—specifically go to college.

In late 1824, three prominent Methodist ministers, Hezekiah Leigh, Gabriel P. Disosway, and John Early, appealed for a Methodist college "to afford young men, who give evidence of their being called by the Lord Jesus Christ to preach the Gospel . . . an opportunity to obtain important qualification for the Ministry."[23] They persuaded the Virginia Conference of Methodists to make application for a charter for a college and the Virginia Legislature to grant it, in 1830. After assembling funding and a small faculty, Randolph-Macon College opened in 1832. Stephen Olin, the school's first president, proudly wrote, "nothing can save us but an able ministry, and this can not be had but through education."[24] Some Methodists, like John Cartwright, might not have agreed about the link between education and an able ministry, but enough did to found and fund Randolph-Macon and a number of other Methodist colleges in quick succession.

Future ministers were not ever the only students at Randolph-Macon. Keeping Methodists Methodist—whether as ministers or lay members—was a high priority for the denomination's leaders. While serving as Randolph-Macon's president, Olin said of the school's potential students:

> They mean to do good—to teach or preach, or neither as God wills. They are just such men as the Church wants and must have—men who will be educated somewhere . . . the Methodist Episcopal Church can not dispense with such an instrument. She must educate her own youth, and those of her adherents, or prove false to her trust, and lose them—and generally they will be lost to others.[25]

Hezekiah Leigh's biographer wrote that Leigh "saw the disastrous effects of educating our young people in college of other denominations, or, worse than that, of educating them in colleges where religion is ignored."[26] Competition among American Protestants was keen, and Methodists like Olin and Leigh had no intention of losing their membership to others.

When Randolph-Macon's founders talked about "men who would be educated somewhere," they meant men, and as with nearly all colleges of the day they meant White men. Randolph-Macon remained a men's college until 1971 when the college admitted women. However, the school's leaders did create Randolph-Macon Women's College as a parallel institution in 1891, and the women's college itself admitted men in 2007, changing its name to Randolph College. It is not clear when the college began accepting African American students. It is clearly racially integrated today, and it was clearly not in the era of its founding.

While their school served White men, the Methodist college founders did not mind poaching these men from other denominations—in fact, it needed them. Symbolically, the school was named for John Randolph of Virginia and Nathaniel Macon of North Carolina—neither of whom was a Methodist—and the school welcomed Methodist and non-Methodists and students from Virginia and beyond. In part the goal was to win converts, but another basic goal was just to have enough students to keep the doors open and pay the faculty. Thus, when the college advertised for students in 1845 there was no mention of the ministry or indeed even of the school's Methodist affiliation, just that attending Randolph-Macon "should form very strong inducements to such young men to prosecute their studies here" and a note about how inexpensive the college was with tuition at $40 per year and board at $77.

In spite of the efforts, there were days when the goal of a sufficient number of students seemed illusive, but the college survived. So-called market forces trumped specific commitment to a religious tradition in assembling a student body for most schools. Only later did many colleges consider admitting White women or African Americans who might also add their tuition dollars to the budget. These admissions might have been the ethical thing to do, but they also helped the schools support their almost always precarious finances.[27]

The competition to have a college was not only between Methodists and other Protestants, it was also between one town and another for the prestige of hosting a college. Many different towns wanted a college of their own to show the world— or at least their region—that they had reached a new status as a "college town," and whatever the religious interests of the town's citizens. The town of Boydton, Virginia, originally won the competition for Randolph-Macon, but after the Civil War the school sought better opportunities in Ashland, Virginia, where it remains today. Towns thus poached colleges just as colleges poached students from each other. In his 1967 work, Daniel Boorstein coined the term "booster college" to describe the ways colleges were sought to boost a town's reputation. As a result, there were too many colleges, and they always were in competition for too few students.[28]

Methodists not only competed with other Protestant bodies but also with other Methodists. Virtually every Methodist state conference wanted its own school. In 1834, Randolph-Macon president Stephen Olin went to Georgia to ask the Georgia Methodists to support his college as they had originally promised to do. But the Georgia Methodists had changed their minds. George Pierce—later a Methodist bishop—remembered that for the Georgians, "a new idea had been thrown into our midst": Georgia meant to have a college for itself.[29] Olin protested sharply, writing in 1835, "I regret to hear of the Georgia Conference College. It is said they propose to take the endowment pledged to this college. This I think impossible as it would be a breach of faith to us and the donors."[30] But impossible though it might be, and plead as Olin might, the direction was set, "that Georgia needed a college of her own—ought to have it, must have it, would have it."[31] And they did. Emory University opened in Atlanta in 1836.

By the 1830s, a denomination that had originally undervalued a college education had founded several. Wesleyan University opened its doors in 1831 in Connecticut, and Indiana Asbury (later DePauw) in Indiana, Allegheny and Dickinson colleges in Pennsylvania, McKendree in Illinois, and of course Emory all followed quickly. Many more would follow, and not just among Methodists. The Baptists, the Presbyterians, the Congregationalists, the Lutherans, and many smaller religious bodies all meant to have their own college and usually many of them succeeded.[32]

Some worried about the broad diffusion of colleges that was taking place in the United States in the antebellum era, fearing that the result was that no school would have enough students or money to offer a quality education. It was a valid worry. Illinois College's Julian Sturtevant complained about the "new obstacle to the progress of collegiate education in this state . . . in the excessive multiplication of institutions of learning." Sturtevant seemed to warn about the role of boosterism in college development when he noted the "mania for college building, which was the combined result of the prevalent speculation in land and the zeal for denominational aggrandizement."[33] Nevertheless, when a Methodist committee on education declared in 1840 that the "advantages of education are most wisely diffused and the certainty secured, by multiplying institutions of learning," they accurately summarized the American reality, however much they went against the wisdom of those like Sturtevant who hoped for ensuring quality by limiting the number of schools.[34]

For all the focus on college creation, the founders of most schools did not put a lot of thought into the curriculum. They simply adopted the core of the classical curriculum as it was taught at older schools, especially Yale. Thus, an 1845 advertisement for Randolph-Macon reflected the commitment to the Latin and Greek classics, noting that for a student to begin, "they must stand an approved examination on English Grammar, Geography, Arithmetic, Latin Reader, Caesar, Sallust, Virgil, Cicero's Orations, Greek Reader, and Xenophon's Anabasis." And, of course, students took a version of Moral Philosophy. It seems a very ambitious list and one wonders how many students were admitted who knew a bit less than expected by the official publications.

The college made allowances for the limitations of some students, adding a note,

"There are many young men who desire to acquire an extensive English and scientific education, without prosecuting the ancient Languages. Our course of study is so arranged as to meet the wants of all such." All students would have "the benefits to be derived from the use of the Libraries and from attendance upon the Literary Societies which are attached to the College." Having very high standards was well and good but having a sufficient student body was even more important for small, struggling schools.[35]

There was also another reason that Methodists, and others, began so many colleges in the early 1800s. Colleges conferred prestige on individuals as well as denominations, towns, and regions. Creating a Methodist college elevated the status of Methodism but also of specific Methodists. The founding of a Methodist college offered a new professional identity and created a new career option for Methodist ministers—that of college professor and president. Thus, when Stephen Olin first began teaching, he wrote, "It will give me opportunity to preach as often, probably, as my health will admit under any circumstances; it will secure me a comfortable support, a useful and respectable station in society, and it will restore me to friends whom I love, and habits which I reverence."[36] It is hard to imagine Olin—committed Methodist as he was—being happy as a lone circuit rider. He was an academic by taste and he liked social status, a good salary, and stability. Leading a Methodist college let him have it all.

Other Methodist ministers gained status by becoming college trustees. Hezekiah Leigh and John Early, two of Randolph-Macon's founders, became trustees of the school even though they remained itinerant preachers throughout their lives. The honor of serving on a college board of trustees was especially useful when it led the same board to confer the coveted if honorary DD degree—a high mark of status indeed in the leveling world of the United States and the culture of the Methodist ministry.

As the nation became more and more divided between North and South, and between antislavery and proslavery camps, many colleges joined one side or the other. Some colleges also reflected a deafening silence on the issue of slavery. But some college leaders also spoke out—a lot on both sides of the issue. The Methodist Church itself split over slavery in 1844.[37]

The issue of slavery had made its way firmly into the Randolph-Macon curriculum. William Andrew Smith, president of Randolph-Macon from 1846 to 1863, lectured his students in Moral Philosophy on "the philosophy and practice of slavery." In these lectures, which Smith developed in his Moral Science course and later published, he focused on the moral question, "is the institution of domestic slavery sinful?" And his conclusion was that "slavery per se, is right . . . and is fully justified by the condition and circumstances of the African race in this country." Smith also concluded that he could not "imagine that any public movement, having for its object the instruction of the blacks in reading and writing, could be made without involving the most disastrous results." Smith was far from alone in these beliefs. Every antebellum college may have taught ethics, but different colleges taught very different ethics.[38]

There were many good reasons for every religious group to start colleges, including keeping some of the future leaders of the next generation both Christian and loyal to a specific denomination of Protestant Christianity and increasingly to a region and viewpoint; competing for status with other religious bodies and other regions of the country and one's own tradition; and raising the status of its leaders. In the three decades before the Civil War, virtually every denomination of Christians did so.

Evangelicalism, Abolitionism, Student Activism—New Life for Oberlin Collegiate Institute

If most pre–Civil War colleges were founded by ministers and their lay supporters, Oberlin was born—or really reborn—out of students' religiously inspired protest. While many schools were founded because of the religious zeal of ordinary ministers to embrace higher education—and to ensure the spread their unique approach to the Protestant Christian faith—the story of Oberlin illustrates the zeal of a generation of deeply religious students to spread their religious beliefs about justice to a divided nation.

The student protest that effectively launched Oberlin took place 200 miles to the south of Oberlin, in Cincinnati, Ohio, at Lane Theological Seminary. In the fall of 1834, the majority of the students at Lane withdrew from the school. They left because Lane's trustees had grown nervous about the student antislavery activity in a city just across the Ohio River from slaveholding Kentucky and had placed strict limitations on the sorts of abolitionist work that the students could do. The students refused to abide by the restrictions and instead sought to get away from the "soul chilling atmosphere of a popular institution where to gain the art of pleasing rather than saving men is the standard of excellence." They wanted a place that was focused on "not parleying with wrong, but calling it to repentance; not flattering the proud but pleading the cause of the poor." Lane, they concluded, was not going to be such a place. The Lane rebels, as they were called, found a very different school that was just what they were looking for at the Oberlin Collegiate Institute, a struggling school that had many reasons to welcome the student radicals with open arms.[39]

The Oberlin Collegiate Institute was founded in 1832 by John J. Shipherd, a Presbyterian missionary recently arrived from the East, and Philo P. Stewart. From the beginning, Shipherd and Stewart wanted their college to be "distinctive in its character." Their design for the college said:

> Its grand object is the diffusion of useful science, sound morality, and pure religion . . . For this purpose it proposes as its primary object, the thorough education of ministers and pious School teachers. As a secondary object, the elevation of the female character. And as a third general design the education of the common people with the higher classics in such a manner as suits the nature of Republican institutions.[40]

Oberlin was the first college in the nation to admit women along with men and was vaguely Presbyterian, although without the formal church ties that would hamstring Lane.

In his study of Oberlin's history, Geoffrey Blodgett noted that the decision to admit women to the college was surprisingly uncontroversial at a time when no other college allowed women and men to study together. Blodgett said that "coeducation in nineteenth century Oberlin," developed as part of an "odd atmosphere of conservativism that surrounded the experiment for decades." Women did take a different course of study than men in the first years at Oberlin, though before long both genders were pursuing the same curriculum in the same classrooms, eating their meals in the same dining rooms, and receiving the same degrees. The *Oberlin Evangelist* (a newspaper of evangelical revivalists) reported "The idea that the young lady is a toy or a plaything is very thoroughly exploded by the practical workings of intellectual competition."[41]

Oberlin was far from flourishing in its early years, with only two teachers, eleven students, and no endowment. Then Shipherd and Stewart heard about what was happening in Cincinnati. Anxious to be of help and more anxious to save their floundering school, Shipherd reached out to the estranged Lane students in early 1835, and also their New York benefactors, the Tappan brothers, who had supported the students at Lane and who were among the major financial supporters of abolitionist causes in the nation. Tight agreements were negotiated, which in the end looked more like a student takeover than the usual effort to recruit students or benefactors. The abolitionists—students and benefactors—insisted that Asa Mahan—

the only Lane trustee to back the students—must be elected president at Oberlin and that the nation's best-known evangelist, who was also an ardent abolitionist, Charles Grandison Finney, be elected professor of theology. They also insisted that African Americans be admitted to the student body, making Oberlin not only the first college to admit women and men together but also Blacks and Whites.

Shipherd met initial resistance to the package from his own trustees who were happy about the new students, the money, and the prestige that Finney would bring to Oberlin but could not imagine a racially integrated student body. But the students, Mahan, and Finney would not come without an ironclad promise of racial integration nor would the Tappans contribute without it. In the end, Shipherd had to threaten "that if the injured brother of color, and consequently brother Finney, Mahan and Morgan, with eight professorships and $10,000 must be rejected, I must join them." The majority of the trustees understood the threat and voted to accept the package. The prospect of students, money, and national recognition was more than a struggling school could reject.[42]

The arriving Lane students established a new theology department at Oberlin that reflected Finney's theology and abolitionism. It can be hard for the twenty-first-century reader to imagine the link, but the political and religious atmosphere was not the same in the 1830s as in the 2020s, and evangelical fervor was often a driving fuel for abolitionism—certainly the Finney brand of evangelicalism—even if other evangelicals used their faith to espouse quite different views.

While the theology department was new, the undergraduate college remained as it had been but with renewed energy and increased student enrollment. It thrived on the institution's commitment to evangelical theology and social justice. It was also for a time the only place in the nation where males studied along with females and Whites alongside of Blacks. By the early 1840s it was the first to award degrees across the lines of race and gender, although it would be another twenty years before Mary Jane Patterson became the first African American woman to receive her BA from the school. More women eventually followed in Patterson's footsteps.[43]

Finney taught in the theology department from 1835–1875. He also served as Oberlin's president from 1850 to 1866, while continuing his revival campaigns around the country. Finney preached at the college chapel, where students across the institution encountered his beliefs on a regular basis.[44] Finney warned his audience, future ministers but also all other students, that the "church has in many cases been made to think that religion consists in feelings," but for Finney action was the test of true religion. Especially regarding slavery, it was clear to everyone who heard Finney that action meant political action and organizing.[45] No one who attended Oberlin over that forty-year span escaped Finney's influence. Oberlin historian Robert Fletcher said that because Finney traveled so much to conduct his own revivals, he was in many ways a figurehead, but "he was a very impressive figurehead."[46]

The commitment to abolitionism made Oberlin anathema to colleges that were proslavery. But admitting women and men, Blacks and Whites, and embracing abolitionism, feminism, and Finney's emotional perfectionism were all part of why Oberlin prospered. Sixty-three men and thirty-seven women entered Oberlin in the year after the new leaders arrived. Between its founding in 1833 and 1866, Oberlin educated over eleven thousand students or over 300 each year, making it one of the larger colleges in the United States.[47]

Oberlin also embraced what was called manual labor education—a popular if far from universal approach to college education in the 1830s in which students divided their time between work, often on a college farm, and study. Manual labor was designed to help college students cover part of the cost of their education, but it was also a way of modeling a more egalitarian society, which their evangelical faith demanded. Letters from early candidates for admission make it clear that Oberlin's uniqueness was also its appeal. Mary Lyon, herself the founder of Mount Holyoke College, wrote an endorsement for a nephew of hers who had "nothing of his own," and would not get "anything from his father," but was an "able, skillful laborer on the farm" and wanted to go to college. Susan Hooker wrote in an 1839 application that she was "fond of domestic labor."[48]

Sometimes the financial and the religious aspects of Oberlin merged, as when Marcus W. Fay gave his reasons in an 1841 application, saying "First to obtain an education by my own exertions without involving myself in debt. Secondly the religious character of the institution. My object is seeking an education, is a preparation for the gospel ministry." Many others said simply, "I want to prepare for the ministry." Women also talked about the religious nature of Oberlin. So, Cornelia Barnes was studying "to prepare for Foreign Miss. Labor, Teaching, Translating, Scriptures etc."

For others, the religious aspect of Oberlin was important whether or not it led to ministry or missionary work. Flora Brown, the sister of John Brown, who led the antislavery raid on Harper's Ferry, simply said she wanted to study "to prepare myself for usefulness in whatever field the Lord [might] see fit to place her." And another student, Elam J. Comings, transferred from the University of Vermont because "I wish to go to where more prominence is given to religious education. It is a notorious fact that while the officers of the University [of Vermont] are diligent and unsparing in their efforts to thoroughly discipline the intellectual powers, they woefully neglect the moral training of their Students." Comings expected something much better at Oberlin.[49]

Perhaps Oberlin's most famous student, Anthony Burns, arrived at the campus in 1855. Burns had come to national, even international attention, a year before when he was arrested under the Fugitive Slave Act while working in a store in Boston after having run away from slavery. After federal marshals arrested him in May 1854, he was marched in chains through the streets of Boston to a Coast Guard ship that took him back to slavery. The anger at the public spectacle in Boston fueled abolitionism as nothing beforehand.

Burns did not, however, remain enslaved for long. Members of Boston's African American Twelfth Baptist Church raised the funds to purchase Burns and set him free. Burns then enrolled in Oberlin and after graduation became the minister of the Zion Baptist Church in St. Catharines, Canada, where he served until his premature death in 1862.[50]

There were many other African American students at Oberlin, though they were always a minority of the student body. And not a few of them were like Burns, born in slavery. Oneda Eselle Dubois escaped from slavery in Alabama in the 1840s and came to Oberlin. In 1846 Elias Poston wrote to President Mahan, "I succeeded in walking out of Slavery on the 22nd of April last. I am now in Marion County, Ohio where I have worked five months. . . . I understand that you are a lover of liberty not for the white man alone but for all of every Clime and of every Color . . . And therefor I feel emboldened to address you and to request admission as a student." Oberlin's first African American student was James Bradley, one of the Lane Rebels who came in 1836. George Vashon was the first to receive an AB degree, in 1844, before going on to a career as a lawyer, and Lucy Stanton was elected president of the Young Ladies' Literary Society while an Oberlin student.[51]

In an 1851 graduation speech, Finney reminded the graduates, "You are not only educated, but educated in *God's College*—a College reared under God, and for God, by the faith, the prayers, the toils and the sacrifices of God's people. You cannot but know that it has been the sole purpose of the founder and patrons of this College to educate here men and women *for God and for God's cause*."[52] To attend Oberlin in the early years was to breathe this religious atmosphere, which was the foundation of all else, including the racial and gender inclusivity and the militant abolitionism.

Religious services were a steady part of life at Oberlin. In 1850 one student wrote to a friend, "There is preaching every morning at half past ten. At six in the evening there is an inquiry meeting held at the music hall and a prayer meeting. At seven those at the music hall come to the chapel where we have preaching." So the days went except for seasons of revival when even classes were canceled and services lasted all day. Between services, faculty visited students in their dorm to inquire about the state of their souls. It was a strong-willed student who was not led to embrace the faith that was so pervasive.[53]

The curriculum at Oberlin reflected the same religious commitment. Study of the Bible, surprisingly limited in so many schools, was essential at Oberlin as was acquisition of Hebrew. The Greek and Latin classics, so important in most antebellum colleges, was far less important in Oberlin's earliest years, "on the ground that the poetry of God's inspired prophets is better for the heart and at least as good for the head as that of Pagans," and so the college substituted Hebrew and English literature for the Latin and Greek classics. In time, criticism from other schools led the Oberlin faculty to add more Latin and Greek to the curriculum. If Oberlin would never conform to the standard mold on abolitionism or its inclusive student body, there was more willingness to conform on curricular issues. As a result, within a decade Oberlin students, like their counterparts at more traditional colleges, were studying Cicero (always the most popular), Tacitus, and poetry in Latin, and Xenophon's Memorabilia, Demosthenes, and Homer in Greek. As they progressed through the four years of undergraduate study, they also studied mathematics, algebra, astronomy, and in the junior year chemistry and what was then called natural philosophy and now called physics. Like almost all colleges before the Civil War, there were no electives at Oberlin and everyone took the same classes.[54]

Up until at least 1870, the senior Moral Philosophy capstone course was taught by the president. As elsewhere, Moral Philosophy was wide ranging, including ethics, religion, a little psychology, and a fair measure of logic, aesthetics, politics, law, and political economy. What was different at Oberlin—and it was a significant difference—was that the students were taught by Asa Mahan (1835–1850) and Charles Grandison Finney (1851–1866), though when Finney's travels kept him away from campus the course was taught by James Fairchild, who later became the third Oberlin president (1866–1889) and who continued teaching the course. Mahan, Finney, and Fairchild were all ordained ministers and passionate exponents of their beliefs. Notes from Mahan's lectures include such topics as "the Idea of right and wrong," "reason," "the soul," "God," and "Moral Obligation." Students learned their duties as members of a civil society but most of all they learned that the "will of God was supreme authority," and that slavery was "the perfection of tyranny." It was quite a diffcrent Moral Philosophy course than that taught elsewhere, and to study at Oberlin was to study in a heady time and place.[55]

Women, Catholics, and Religious Community: Catholic Sisters Begin Saint Mary-of-the-Woods College

In July 1840, six Catholic sisters left Ruille, France, for a small settlement a few miles from Terre Haute, Indiana, and after a difficult trip they arrived in what they later described as a desolate spot in the forest. They had taught and led schools before but in urban France. They spoke only French and had little idea of what they were in for. Nevertheless, within a few months the sisters had learned English, opened an academy that would become a college, and attracted their first students.[56]

In 1834, Pope Gregory XVI had approved a plan to divide the United States into several new dioceses and to appoint Simon Gabriel Bruté as the first bishop of the new Catholic diocese of Vincennes, Indiana, which included all of Indiana and a large portion of Illinois. One of the new bishop's top priorities was to improve the educational opportunities for Catholics in this far-flung region. He sent one of his priests, Célestin de la Hailandière, to France to find men and women in religious orders who were operating schools in France, where the Catholic church was still recovering from the French Revolution, to come to Indiana. Soon after Father de la Hailandière's arrival in France, he learned of the death of Bishop Bruté and his own appointment as his successor bishop.

While still on his mission, the new bishop first approached the male Congregation of the Holy Cross, which agreed to send six brothers who became the founders of Notre Dame University. He also approached the Sisters of Providence, who agreed to send a group of nuns led by one of their own, Sister Théodore Guérin (originally Anne-Thérèse Guérin) who, as leader of the group became Mother Théodore. In June 1840 then-Sister Théodore received instructions from the Mother Superior of her order to "conduct the Sister to Vincennes . . . be the Superior [and] open a school amongst a small Congregation of Catholics." The nuns left France a month later, in July 1840. After a long sea voyage—and a fair amount of seasickness—and then a journey to Indiana that included an overturned stagecoach, they arrived in late fall of 1840 at the small farm house that had been arranged for them by the diocese of Vincennes.

The determined sisters planned an academy for women that opened in June

1841, less than a year after their arrival. The sisters began simply with advertisements in newspapers in Terre Haute, Springfield, and Indianapolis that read:

> Situated in Sugar Creek Township, Vigo County, 4 miles northwest of Terre Haute, St Mary's Academy for Young Ladies will open the second of July. Branches taught are as follows: Reading, Writing, Arithmetic, Geography and History, both Ancient and Modern, English Composition, Natural Philosophy, Chemistry, Botany, Mythology, Biography, Astronomy, Rhetoric, Plain and Fancy Needlework, Bead Work, Tapestry, and Lace Work. . . .
>
> Those who wish to learn the Latin, German, and Italian languages can do so Terms the same for French. For further particulars, application must be made to the Mother Superior. All letters directed to the institution must be postpaid. A Prospectus will be published in a few weeks. Mother St. Theodore.[57]

While the advertisement did not mention the religious nature of the school—and was probably designed for as broad an audience as possible—the core religious values were hard to miss with the name and references to the Mother Superior. And the students came.[58]

The first student, Mary Lenoble, arrived at Saint Mary-of-the-Woods on the fourth of July and only three days later there were thirteen students, Protestants and Catholics, including the daughters of some of the most prominent families in the region. The Midwest did not offer nearly as many educational opportunities for women as for men, and so a new opportunity to learn appealed to many young women and their parents, Catholic or not. The sisters had already made the decision, similar to most Protestant-founded colleges, that they would accept both Protestant and Catholic students. As one early history of the Catholic diocese reported, the sisters agreed to accept all young women of any denomination "on the sole condition that they would conform to the customs of the house [and] hence it was that several Protestants placed their daughters under the care of the sisters." A more recent historian of the college adds, "Mother Theodore [was] always concerned about keeping numbers up," while many Catholic immigrants couldn't pay the tuition. She was pleased to report that by the 1850s, the school had seventy-eight students, among them thirty Catholics. When Mother Théodore complained "we are as poor as Job," she wanted to remedy the situation with increased revenue from all who could pay and if that meant taking Protestants, so be it. Mother Théodore and her colleagues may have come to Indiana to educate young Catholic girls, but as with most other colleges, there were bills to be paid and classrooms to fill. A student who could pay the minimal tuition was always welcome.[59]

Mother Théodore worried about the growth of competition. In 1842, she complained to the bishop of Le Mans in France, whom she saw as her protector, that other Catholics had opened a school for girls at Terre Haute, only a few miles away and "they are succeeding [so that] we shall have very few pupils next year." The competing school did not last long.[60] Mother Théodore and her sisters also ended up in a running battle with Bishop de la Hailandière, their local bishop, over their ownership of the school's real estate that was only resolved when de la Hailandière returned to France and a new and much more generous bishop was appointed in 1847.[61]

Like the Methodist men at Randolph-Macon and religious leaders at many other schools, the Catholic women at Saint Mary's wanted to serve and protect young people of their own faith but also convert a few others to their version of the Christian faith. And when one of the new Protestant students "conforming to the customs of the house" asked for a rosary, she was first told that rosaries were only for Catholics but she responded that if she wore one the Blessed Virgin would love her. That sentiment must have pleased the sisters. It was not a sentiment that the student had learned in her Protestant home.[62]

The Prospectus (catalog) for 1865 described not only the curriculum and the tuition but the religious tone of the school:

> The principle that animates the mode of instruction tends to form the heart to virtue, as well as to cultivate the mind; the lessons imparted are calculated to develop virtuous sentiments and the powers of intellect. The Preceptresses of St. Mary's direct their teachings to establish the well-being of their pupils on the basis of moral and mental culture closely united.[63]

The "unity of truth" that Julie Reuben describes as "encompassing both knowledge and morality" at Harvard also represented the heart of a small college for women operating in an isolated corner of Indiana in those same years.[64]

Maintaining an institution's moral character may have been easier in a remote part of the Midwest than in Harvard's urban environment. The same Prospectus that described the moral character at St. Mary's also included a list of regulations and notices that said:

- The Institute is open to visitors only on the first Thursday of every month. No visits are permitted except by parents and guardians. Calls on the Sabbath are an intrusion that allows of no exception but in favor of sickness or of urgent business.

- Parents have the privilege to send a box of sweetmeats to their children at Christmas and Easter.[65]

These rules created a closed—essentially cloistered—community in which the students and their teachers could successfully focus on their studies and on the moral—and religious—culture that the school aimed to create for all who studied there. Of course, human nature being what it is, there were various escape routes. One 1845 student writing to a friend in Washington, DC, was being perhaps a bit snarky when she reported on another student: "Mary Ann Caldwell is going to marry old Judge Moore. You have often heard Mary Ann speak of Mr. Moore. They say he is an old gentleman of some sixty years of age, but he is rich." How Mary Ann managed to meet a rich, old man is not recorded.[66]

As most antebellum colleges, Saint Mary's took students at multiple levels and there were those at the elementary, high school, and college levels while the curriculum was sometimes quite mingled. Nevertheless, by the 1860s, the curriculum of the senior department (closer to college-level work than the larger preparatory program) quickly came to reflect some of the same subjects as most other antebellum colleges, including history, rhetoric, logic, mental philosophy, and the ever-present moral philosophy.[67] The academic year was capped by public exams which seem to have been both daunting and celebratory. A *History of the Sisters of Providence* reported, "Public examinations to which parents and friends were invited, established during the first years, had now become an institution and weeks of hard study and drill by the teachers preceded the final oral tests in all branches of study as far as each class had gone." While most official accounts of the school describe the pride and celebratory nature of these exams, one 1845 student, Phoebe Ann Dowling, was perhaps more honest when she wrote to a friend, "the examinations came off as most examinations do; some were satisfied and delighted, others not so pleased."[68]

It should not be surprising that a school in which the leader and all the teachers belonged to a religious order tried hard to recreate a cloistered religious life for their charges, whether those charges were Catholic or not. The language of the official history of the nuns' order reported, "The convent wardrobe was very simple, three dark calico dresses, plainly made for the week days and a wool dress for Sundays." Whether the use of the word *convent* in the report is intentional, it is clear that simple living in a religious community was part of life at Saint Mary's.[69]

In 1850 Mother Théodore wrote a long letter to the bishop of Le Mans outlining the growth of Saint Mary's and the religious life of the school:

There are always from six to seven hundred pupils in our school. About two-thirds are Catholics. We might almost say that the other third are also Catholics, at least in their heart. . . . Several of the pupils are taking instruction and have already received permission to be baptized, but there are others who cannot obtain permission. One who desires to be baptized before leaving, is seventeen or eighteen years old and belongs to a family remarkable as to high morality, but much opposed to Catholicism. The young girl is a model in every sense. Must we see her leave without being regenerated in the holy waters of Baptism?[70]

Whatever the fate of this student—Mother Théodore did not say—the tight nature of the community at Saint Mary's created an emotional draw for the non-Catholics.

Of course, Saint Mary's was never completely isolated from the larger world. Not only did some students manage to develop romantic relationships with men in surrounding towns, but in a letter to the bishop, Mother Théodore wrote, "Our schools have suffered much this year from Protestant opposition." Nevertheless, she said that God gives their community, "as much peace as a work of this kind can have in the midst of a Protestant people."[71]

For all the problems faced by the founding generation—Protestant nativism, constant worries about money and enrollment, troubles with their religious authorities, or a rebellious student—the core of Saint Mary-of-the-Woods College in the middle years of the nineteenth century was the same as most other colleges: "the unity of truth" in which scholarship, morality, and religious faith were inextricably tied. In the case of Saint Mary's, it was a unity inextricably tied to the Catholic faith that inspired the founders and many of their students.

A Quest for Faith, Education, and Self-Determination for African Americans—Wilberforce University

Wilberforce University was the first college in the country to not only serve African American students but also be led by African Americans. It also admitted women and men. Wilberforce was like many other antebellum colleges in that it was founded by and for religious organizations, but it was also unique in at least two ways: It opened before the Emancipation Proclamation when around 90 percent of African Americans were still enslaved, but it was committed to the education of African Americans; and Wilberforce was created by an all-too-rare cooperative effort of Black and White Christians, specifically by the (Black) Cincinnati Conferences of the African Methodist Episcopal (AME) Church and the (White) Methodist Episcopal Church. Both groups had been in their own separate discussions

WILBERFORCE UNIVERSITY, XENIA, OHIO.

Figure 1.2. Wilberforce University in Ohio opened decades before the end of slavery but was led by and served African Americans, providing a quality education and deeply religious community context. From Library of Congress—Wilberforce

of the need for a school for African Americans since the 1840s. To be sure, such efforts made sense for Methodists, since as early as 1800 an estimated 20 percent of all Methodists in the United States were people of African origin and by the 1840s the Methodists had a number of colleges for their White members.[72] But the realities of race and racism meant that a joint White–Black enterprise and, indeed, any school for African Americans was something very few Whites considered. Nevertheless, by 1855 representatives of the Black and the White Cincinnati conferences began to talk about combining their efforts. The result, three years later, was the creation of something unique in the United States at the time: a school with a racially integrated board of trustees and faculty that served over 200 African American students, though most were in precollege programs.

Religion and race were both equally at the heart of Wilberforce. As the school's second president, Daniel Payne, remembered:

> The founding of Wilberforce University opened a new chapter in the history of the Church. [It] clearly shows that the hand of God was leading these two branches of the Methodist family in the same direction, at the same time, for the accomplishment of the same great end—the Christian education of a race, a race then enslaved and ostracized by Christians in a so-called Christian land; and that, too, in the name of Christianity.[73]

Christianity and the education of a race went hand in hand for Payne and for all those who supported Wilberforce.

Addressing the religious nature of the school, the first (and only White) president of the school, Richard S. Rust, happily reported that in its first years, "the school has been visited with a gracious revival of religion and many of the pupils have been made the happy subjects of a work of grace," which was as important to their futures as the academic offerings of the school. As the historian Yolanda Pierce said of Wilberforce and other historically Black colleges and universities founded soon after it, "These schools understood themselves to be religious organizations, that they had a calling and a value higher and beyond just the individual. They understood themselves to be doing the work of God." The sense of doing the work of God was never far from Wilberforce.[74]

Wilberforce was also committed to the education of "a race then enslaved and ostracized by Christians," as Payne said. Over a century later, Henry Lewis Gates said these schools existed to promote "Black self-representation and pride." John F. Wright, one of the White founders of the school, said:

> The mission of Methodism, like that of the gospel, is to every human being. All classes have engaged her attention, especially the poor; and the colored people of this and other lands have shared of her sympathy and labors.[75]

Not all Methodists shared Wright's understanding of their faith's response to every human being, but before long Payne and other African American founders were in a position where they did not depend on sympathy but on their own leadership and management skills. From 1863 to the present, Wilberforce's leaders have been proud of the fact that theirs is a Black-led institution serving Black students.[76]

While the founders—White and Black—thought they were creating a school for free Blacks, that is not what happened. In fact, Wilberforce secured the majority of its students in its first years because some number of southern slaveholder fathers broke with the standard pattern of the day and sent their own children by enslaved Black women to the school to receive an education that was illegal in southern states (and probably to ensure some distance between them and their White half-siblings).[77]

The coming of the Civil War so soon after Wilberforce opened cut off the students from the South while many from the North also joined the war effort. The war seemed to be a devastating blow, and the school suspended its operations. However, the temporary closing of Wilberforce opened a new opportunity for the AME. In the spring of 1863, AME Bishop Daniel Payne, who had been part of the Black minority on the original integrated board of trustees, was approached by Richard Rust, then still the school's president, who told him that the White Methodist Episcopal trustees—the majority of the board—wanted to sell the currently unused property. The state of Ohio was willing to offer a good price for the land and buildings for a state asylum, but the board wanted to give the AME the first option at a greatly reduced price. Rust said, "Bishop Payne, if your Church will purchase it, we will let you have if for its indebtedness, which is ten thousand dollars; but no other party can obtain it for that sum." Payne was intrigued and ultimately took a risk and bought the property in the name of the AME, although the church had not authorized him to do that. But the church rallied around the idea of owning the college outright; over the next two years, gifts of $100 or $500 and conference support of $1,000 began arriving and the mortgage was successfully paid off. Starting in 1863, even as the Civil War continued, the school reopened as an entirely Black-owned and Black-led institution, although it continued, as it had before, to have an integrated faculty.[78]

Daniel Payne had moved to the campus in 1856 and taken charge of the operation in the summer when others were away. After the AME purchase, Payne led the school's reorganization and the new board elected Payne as the school's president, making him the first African American in the United States to hold the title of college president.

When Daniel Payne became president of Wilberforce, William Andrew Smith at Randolph-Macon was his fellow Methodist college president and was using his position to lecture his students and the country on "the philosophy and practice of slavery" (see p. 18). At the same time, Payne preached both the sinfulness of slavery and the absolute religious necessity of freedom, education, equality, and the advancement of African Americans. The institution that he led meant to make sure that the educational advancement that he preached actually happened.[79]

It was in a country at war over these issues that Payne made sure that Wilberforce was both a very religious institution and one dedicated to the African American community. The new incorporation document, which he likely authored, stated that "the institution shall be and forever remain under the management, direction, and control of the African Methodist Episcopal Church." The new Wilberforce was meant to last as both a church college and an African American college.[80]

Payne was born to free parents in 1811 in the slave state of South Carolina. As he remembered it, his family was deeply religious, with regular family prayer and church attendance. They were also highly committed to education, and Payne described his teen years as a time when he devoured as many books as he could find. While still in his teens, Payne joined the Methodists and opened a school in Charleston in 1829, when he was eighteen. But in 1834, South Carolina joined most other slave states in making it illegal, subject to imprisonment and public lashing (if one was Black), for a person to teach a slave to read or write. Rather than tempt fate, Payne left Charleston for New York City, where he taught and became a minister, later attending Gettysburg College and helping to found the AME after a break with the White Methodists. He quickly rose to the rank of bishop in the AME, and it was as one of the bishops of his church that Payne began his long association with Wilberforce, first as a resident trustee from 1856 to 1862 and then as president from 1863 to 1876.[81]

Payne's autobiography, *Recollections of Seventy Years*, provides a sense of what life was like for Payne during his years as president. He never stopped being an active bishop of his church, and much of his time was filled with visits to churches, regional and annual conferences, and travel, including three trips to Europe and after the Civil War travel to the American South to set up AME churches among the previously enslaved. He was also consumed with fundraising for his college. *Recollections of Seventy Years* reports on the school's finances:

> In 1867–8 the Society for the Promotion of Collegiate and Theological Education in the West aided the institution in the sum of eighteen hundred dollars. . . . Chief Justice Chase induced an English gentleman to send us three hundred dollars, and in his own last will and testament he left us ten thousand dollars. In 1869 we received through General Howard from the Freedman's Bureau three thousand dollars.[82]

Except for the amounts, it seems very much like what many a twenty-first-century college president might report as one of their primary activities.

Like Finney at Oberlin, Payne seems to have been away from the school as much as he was there; but, also like Finney, if he was a figurehead, he was a very impressive one. Not every college president, Black or White, could go to Washington, DC, and solicit funds from the chief justice of the Supreme Court and the head of the Freedman's Bureau and then convince both of them to solicit funds from yet others.

At the General Conference of his denomination in 1872, there was a discussion of whether Payne could or should continue as both a college president and an active bishop, but the AME needed him in both places for "the whole American people are looking toward our university; it is the only thing which is really testing the capabilities of the race, and we cannot give too much attention to it." Thus, it was resolved that Payne should remain the college's president and that he would also continue to preside over Methodist districts as an active bishop. He continued in both roles until 1876, when he resigned as president to focus on his writing and take on expanded roles as a bishop. His two successors who served Wilberforce until 1900 expanded the school but continued its twin focus on religious and racial uplift.[83]

Payne was proud of what the school accomplished. He wrote of the opening of Wilberforce in 1856 that the "studies were elementary English studies therefore the institution was improperly called a university" by "our zealous white friends who projected it and took out its charter." He insisted a "more modest title would have been better suited to such a humble beginning." But before he stepped down as president, Payne was delighted that the school had grown into its name. "From a school of one Principal and assistant, with only primary work, it has been developed with power to send out its graduates yearly with degrees conferred. It has now a working faculty consisting of six members." And he added that up to 1886–1887, "it has sent out graduates from the different departments—theological (for ministers), collegiate (scientific and classical) and normal (for teachers). Hundreds of its under-graduates have become successful teachers and preachers, and others are to be found in various fields of usefulness." Reflecting on his long experience with Wilberforce, Payne advised those who wanted to start a college: "The founding of a college requires a great deal of forethought and preparation. This is true of those who can command a deep, long, and wide purse." Few who started or led any college would disagree.[84]

Payne recruited and urged African American Methodist churches to recruit young men whom they saw as destined for the ministry, young women who could be either in Christian education or serve as teachers in public schools, and people of both sexes for work among the freedmen (gender stereotypes did remain real at Wilberforce as most other places, well beyond the nineteenth century). Half a century later, Horace Talbert, an early graduate of the school and later a member of the faculty, reported of the early years that the "religious influence of the school has been phenomenal, for hundreds of the students had entered the Christian life," as ministers and teachers. Payne wanted to be sure that the ministers and teachers who went out from Wilberforce had both the religious zeal and the proper training to do the work that was needed.[85]

From the beginning, some Wilberforce students sought to subvert the tight rules and heavy religious emphasis that they encountered. Payne and his successors were strict moralists as well as deeply religious. But the large revivals, with their passionate intensity, swept students in many directions. Revivals were a time when the normal prohibition of too much talk between male and female students were relaxed so that they could discuss the state of their souls, and the faculty had to discuss what to do when students were "fondly holding hands or whispering words of love in willing ears" during a revival meeting. Earlier, in 1874, Payne recorded "our school was thrown into confusion and received a severe blow from the circumstances connected with the expulsion of one of our leading students and events following it." Payne never elaborated and there is no further record of what happened, but it seems that not all students quite agreed with Payne's strict rules and religious focus.[86]

Students at Wilberforce studied much the same curriculum as at other schools. At the collegiate level, there was the usual mix of Greek and Latin classics including the ever-present Cicero and Livy poetry, the sciences including chemistry and geology and physics, and the normal capstone in moral philosophy. Payne was committed to ensuring that the school offered "Christianity and Culture." Under Payne, all students were expected to attend religious services twice a day—a practice that continued long after Payne was gone. There were also regular prayer meetings every week and religious revivals that stopped all other activity. In 1888 another religious revival led the faculty to pass a resolution that "all class work of the institution be suspended on the following day in view of the religious interest manifested." Also similar to other colleges, the student-led Young Men's Christian Association (YMCA) and Young Women's Christian Association (YWCA) were an important part of the college's religious and social life. (See chapter 2 for a more detailed look at the nineteenth-century Y as a religious force.)[87]

One wonders what went on in the mind of a Wilberforce student in the nineteenth century as they attended classes, chapel services, and prayer meetings and followed—or violated—the strict rules set up by the college's ministerial leaders. We do, however, know more about the school's graduates who reflected the college's goals by becoming AME ministers, teachers, and leaders in other fields.

One such student was Richard Harvey Cain, who graduated before the school closed for the Civil War. Cain was born to free Black parents in 1825 in what is now West Virginia. Cain was ordained well before his college education began. He started out in the White Methodist church but finding it unwelcoming he transferred to the AME and soon began to study at Wilberforce. Cain remembered the beginning of the Civil War when he and 115 fellow Wilberforce students sought to enlist in the Union Army but the army was not yet accepting African Americans, as it later enthusiastically did, and they were all rejected. At the end of the war, Cain became the pastor of the Emanuel AME Church in Charleston, South Carolina, and was very active in both the church and Reconstruction politics. Cain led an effort to rebuild Emanuel, a church that had been destroyed by a White mob decades earlier and proudly reported that for the new building, "every nail hammered in Emanuel was driven in by a Black hand." He saw the building as a sign that the "sun has lit up the horizon."

During Reconstruction, Cain was elected to the state legislature and represented South Carolina in Congress between 1873–1875 and 1877–1879, where one of his major accomplishments was to help shepherd the stalled Civil Rights Bill through the chamber. When some representatives objected that a Civil Rights Bill would damage Black–White relations in the post–Civil War South, Cain responded, "Now I am at a loss to see how the friendship of our white friends can be lost to us by simply saying we should be permitted to enjoy the rights enjoyed by other citizens. . . . We do not want any discrimination. I do not ask for any legislation for colored people of the country that is not applied to the white people. All that we ask is equal laws, equal legislation, and equal rights."

After his influential political career, Cain again focused on church issues and served as bishop of the AME Texas-Louisiana Conference and then the Mid-Atlantic and New England Conference. He also lived long enough to see "much of what he worked for become unraveled and that's the tragedy of this story." It was a tragedy for Cain and for the nation. At the same time, for Cain his faith—fortified by the years at Wilberforce—gave the strength to carry on.[88]

In an era of strict gender stereotyping, the assumption was that Wilberforce women would become teachers. Yet preparing teachers ranked equally with preparing ministers at Wilberforce. One of the many women to do just that was Hallie Quinn Brown, who graduated in 1873. Brown's parents had escaped from slavery and lived in Chatham, Ontario, where they were active in the Underground Railroad, bringing other slaves to freedom, and in the AME church. After her studies at Wilberforce, Brown moved to the South and taught recently freed slaves in rural schools in Mississippi and South Carolina, and later at Tuskegee Institute. In 1893 she returned to Wilberforce to teach elocution, and Wilberforce remained her home until she died there at the age of 100 in 1949.

Brown was also active on a broader stage. In 1893 she helped found the Colored Woman's League, which became part of the National Association of Colored Women, and served as the national president from 1920 to 1924. She lectured on women's rights and for the importance of education, especially proper elocution. In 1889 she told an AME conference to stop its sexism, adding "I believe there are as great possibilities in women as there are in men. . . . There is a great vanguard of scholars and teachers of our sex . . . all over the country." She documented this vanguard in one of her books, *Homespun Heroines and Other Women of Distinction*. She did not want the stories of "many mothers who were loyal in tense and trying times" lost to history.

Brown's lectures took her to Europe, where she met Queen Victoria, and also to the 1893 World's Congress of Representative Women in Chicago, which had initially excluded African American women but after a protest by Brown and others, invited six Black women including Frances Harper, Anna Julia Cooper, Fannie Jackson Coppin, and Brown herself to speak. Brown reminded her mostly White audience that African American women had established their own organizations while also making "greater progress in education than in any other direction." It was to mark Black women's success in education that allowed Brown to point with pride to Frances Harper's *Iola Leroy*, while Anna Cooper gives 'no uncertain sound' in *A Voice from the South*. And all of this had happened, she noted, in just thirty years since the Emancipation Proclamation. If Payne could say at the end of his presidency that "hundreds of its under-graduates have become successful teachers and preachers," he certainly could claim Hallie Brown and Richard Cain among them.[89]

Randolph-Macon, Saint Mary-of-the-Woods, Oberlin, and Wilberforce were very different schools. Protestant and Catholic, proslavery and antislavery, segregated and integrated, single sex and coeducational, they may be taken as a reasonable sample of the hundreds of other colleges dotting the different states of the United States in the antebellum era. Yet in one way they were very similar, as were the majority of their contemporaries: Religion was at the very center of college life. In the moral philosophy course, revival services, and individual counseling, president and professors sought to ensure that college was an experience in which every student was deeply engaged in a strongly religious community. It was a reality that would soon change—and quickly so—after the Civil War, and to those changes we turn in the chapters that follow.

CHAPTER TWO

From Moral Philosophy to a Research University, 1870–1905

In 1859, a former medical student turned naturalist, Charles Darwin, published *On the Origin of Species*, the book with perhaps the greatest impact of any in the nineteenth century. Higher education was never the same again, although it took several decades for the full impact of Darwin's work to be felt. As a much younger man, Darwin had sailed on a British mapping expedition to the remote Galapagos Islands in the Pacific. When Darwin reflected on the different species he had seen on different islands he concluded that the differences were part of a larger battle for survival and that the species that thrived did so because of minor adaptions in their makeup that gave them a head start in the never-ending war for survival. Darwin called the process "natural selection." As the present-day Oxford historian of religion, Diarmaid MacCulloch, commented, "There was nothing benevolent about the providence which watched over the process. Reason was served her notice as the handmaid of Christian revelation." Or to put it another way, once Darwin's ideas sunk in—and if they were accepted—the "unity of truth" that held reason and faith, literature, science, and religion together in a unified college curriculum simply collapsed.[1]

Multiple Truths: New Challenges, Less Unity

While the ideal of a single, unified truth in all fields dominated the curriculum of most antebellum colleges in the United States—uniting classical literature, instruction in the sciences and mathematics, and especially Christian ethics and theology—such a tight unity could not withstand the changes, structural and intellectual, that came to American higher education after the Civil War. Most of all, two intellectual developments fractured the old unity, the increasingly wide understanding and acceptance of biological evolution and a growing acceptance of higher criticism, the belief that the Bible might not be historically accurate in every case. While many Americans ignored both developments, within institutions of higher education both ideas gained wide acceptance however much they led away from unity toward a world of multiple—and often conflicting—truths.

Evolution

While Darwin's work was known in the United States soon after its publication in England, it was close to 1890 before it began to have a significant impact on the relationship between religion and science in American higher education. A large part of the delay was due to the work of America's leading botanist, Asa Gray, who was convinced that there was no conflict between religion and evolutionary theory, and who did an impressive job of convincing Americans of his generation (though not so much people in England) that he was right. Gray and Darwin first met over lunch in Kew Gardens in 1839 and continued a close and always respectful relationship until Darwin's death in 1882. When *Origin of Species* was first published, a US copyright could only be obtained by an American citizen so Gray secured the copyright for Darwin and made sure that his friend got royalties for the American edition, with a 5 percent fee for himself.

Darwin was forever grateful for Gray's protection of his most famous book, and the two shared over 300 letters during the course of their long friendship. Darwin had previously considered himself a Christian—and had once considered the ministry as a profession—but as he thought through the implications of natural selection he sadly wrote that "I cannot see as plainly as others do, and as I should wish to do, evidence of design and beneficence on all sides of us." For Darwin, the losers in the selection process outnumbered the winners, and they often suffered greatly as a mouse might when played with by a cat. A loving God would not have made the world that way.[2]

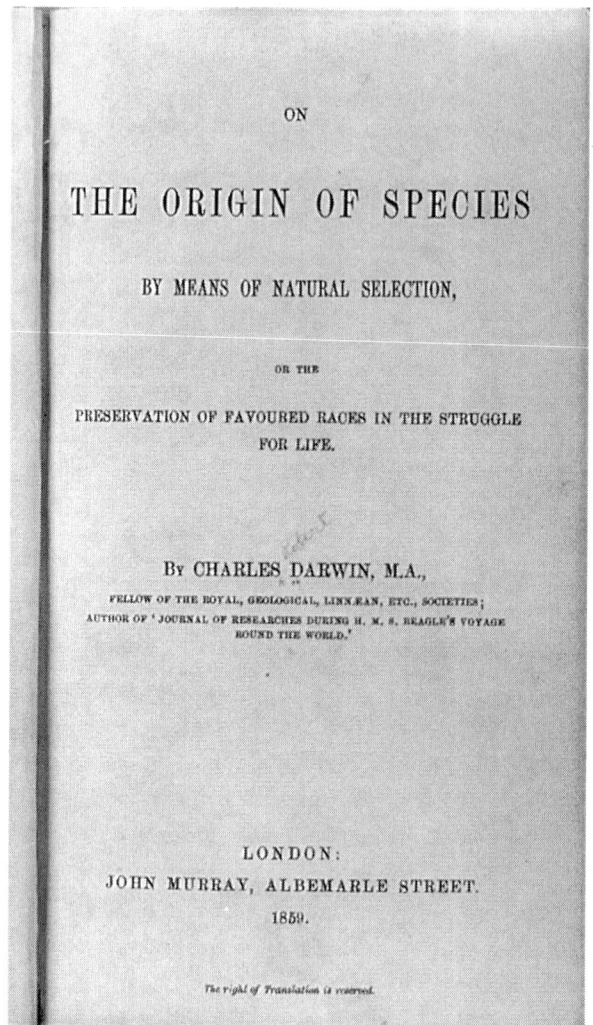

Figure 2.1. No single book broke the "unity of truth"—the assumption that all knowledge must be in agreement—to the degree that Charles Darwin's 1859 *On the Origin of Species* did. From Library of Congress

Gray, a devout Presbyterian, never gave up trying to convince Darwin to return to his old faith. He argued with his friend that he believed that God was the source of all evolutionary change and, indeed, that God's design could be seen in all forms of life. Gray never succeeded with Darwin, as hard as he tried, but Gray's prestige allowed him to convince both scientists and much of the general public in America that there was at best only minimal conflict between evolution and religion. Gray wrote not only for scientists. His popular textbook for use in the relatively few high schools that existed at that time said that evolution showed that all forms of life "are all part of one system . . . the conception of One Mind." It was not far at all from the unity of truth shared by most of Gray's contemporaries.[3] Most other scientists of the 1870s and 1880s agreed. Any conflict of science and faith lay in the future.[4]

In the United States, most of the best-known religious leaders of the day also aligned with Gray's perspective. Schools like Oberlin and Andover Theological Seminary established chairs in the Harmony of Science and Revelation, and Andover's George Harris wrote that "Evolution has won . . . it has won us so completely that we do not think of it, as we do not think of gravitation." For Harris, that victory did not create any conflict with religion. Princeton's conservative president, James McCosh, also became convinced that evolution simply described the ways that God worked in nature. Finally, in an essay in *The Fundamentals*, a 1910–1915 publication that is considered the bedrock of fundamentalism, Princeton's B. B. Warfield wrote that evolution simply described the "divine procedure in creating man." For those already open to a more liberal interpretation of religion and revelation, acceptance of a new approach to the *how* of creation was even easier.[5]

The comfortable coexistence of religious belief and the scientific study of evolution was not to last, however. If both scientists and religious people were so comfortable with evolution, why was it so disruptive to educational institutions—colleges and high schools—after about 1890? Several things changed.

Andrew Dickson White, a historian and also the founding president of Cornell University, was one person who challenged any comfortable agreement between faith and science. When Cornell opened, White announced that it would be a place where science was safe from religion and he would protect the freedom of scientific inquiry from religious dogma. He never mentioned anything religion might fear from science. After he left the Cornell presidency in 1885, White wrote the two-volume *A History of the Warfare of Science with Theology in Christendom*, published in 1896. White considered talk of harmony to be a mere coverup for an unbridgeable gulf. He convinced many that religion had been at war with science for centuries and that the role of wise leaders like himself was to protect science from oppression by those with a religious worldview.[6]

A younger generation of American scientists also began to see what Darwin and many of his English friends had seen since 1859, that natural selection and traditional Christianity might be harder to reconcile than their predecessors had believed. But while evolution itself was without challenges from most scientists, religion in general, and especially the reigning Protestantism, found itself under siege. By 1900, while many retained both their faith and their commitment to science, many others did not, and for more and more people within the academy (still a very small subset of the American people) the idea that there was one truth that encompassed all ways of knowing simply no longer made sense.

Finally, the sheer growth of both secondary and postsecondary education at the turn of the twentieth century meant that there were many more battlefields where potential hostilities could explode. For most of the nineteenth century, while the number of colleges was growing rapidly, most were still very small. In addition, there were only a handful of high schools to be found in the United States, and a high school diploma was not required to attend college. In the first years of the twentieth century, high schools spread rapidly to most of the nation. Dayton, Tennessee—destined to be the home of the Scopes Trial in which evolution dominated international headlines in the summer of 1925—only opened its first high school in 1906. High school enrollment grew from 200,000 students in 1890 to two million by 1920 in the United States. College enrollment also grew, from 156,756 in 1890 to 597,880 in 1920. There were simply a lot more people prepared to fight about the curriculum, whether at the secondary or postsecondary level. And fight they did. We will explore some of the college-based explosions that followed in the next chapters.[7]

Higher Criticism of the Bible

Along with evolution, the issue of higher criticism of the Bible—using traditional academic research norms for studying ancient documents to examine the Christian Bible itself—hit very close to home for many Christians. After all, higher criticism involved the use of some of the university's most valued tools—research, historical analysis, and a critical eye—and challenged the faith of many believers. The field of biblical criticism had begun to develop earlier in the nineteenth century in German universities. As early as 1835, David Friedrich Strauss, of the University of Tubingen, published a book translated into English as *The Life of Jesus Critically Examined* in which he argued that Jesus needed to be seen as a great Jewish teacher and the New Testament as a telling of his life by people who were drawing themes from Jewish scriptures and symbolism more than trying for historical accuracy. Other German scholars expanded on Strauss's work. By the 1870s and 1880s, higher criticism was well known among those ministers and scholars in the United States who were interested in such matters. The implications of higher criticism included an assumption that the Bible was a human construct like any other book and that Jesus was a very human teacher, more than divine.[8]

Some of the first American scholars to pay attention to biblical criticism were teachers at theology schools, especially Andover Seminary and Harvard Divinity School, both in Massachusetts. Like other developments in higher education in the late nineteenth century, the German origins of this approach gave it extra cache among scholars who believed that the German universities represented the model of scholarship that all of American higher education should follow. The German connection also generated greater distrust among many outside of the academy.[9]

For its exponents, biblical criticism was a way to strengthen faith and find a more sophisticated approach to religion. But for others, any challenge to the literal truth of the Bible was a betrayal in which scholars seemed to turn against them and their most cherished beliefs. The Savannah, Georgia, *News* reported that, "The great majority of Christians regard the Bible as the inspired work of God, and, therefore it cannot contain errors." The paper continued that the ideas "may be entirely satisfactory to those who clearly understand them, but it is about impossible to make them understood by the masses. To the average mind, the whole Bible is true, or it is not the inspired work of God." The scholarship that developed in the higher criticism of the Bible split Protestants among themselves and in their relationship with higher education.[10]

The gulf between those who embraced higher criticism and those who rejected it only widened in the years that followed. Many conservatives, including the leading thinkers of the new fundamentalist movement, might have found ways to accommodate biological evolution (they certainly tried for years) but they simply could not accommodate biblical criticism and remain true to their most cherished convictions. If conflicts between science and religion were no longer to be resolved in favor of religion, as many people, including most academics, believed that they should be up to about 1870, then there was no unified reality to be taught in college and each field was left to go its own separate way.[11]

The Birth of the Research University Challenges the Christian College

The arguments about both evolution and biblical criticism happened within a larger context of a rapidly changing world of American higher education. While small colleges had been the American model of higher education until after the Civil War, by 1900 something new on the horizon—the research university—quickly came to be the dominant mode of higher education, even if many colleges continued in older models well into the twentieth century.

Most historians of American higher education describe a major transformation that took place starting in the 1870s from colleges that transmitted knowledge to the new universities that created new knowledge. No clear or absolute change took place, but American higher education did experience a fundamental transition in the late nineteenth century. The shift began with a few schools, spread to more, and over time came to represent the ideal for most. Three college presidents, Charles W. Eliot at Harvard, Andrew Dickson White at Cornell, and Daniel Coit Gilman at the new Johns Hopkins University, were among the early leaders of the movement.

When Eliot began his long tenure as the president of Harvard at the age of thirty-four in 1869, he began a campaign to modernize what he saw as a fairly sleepy and self-satisfied place. The innovation for which he is most famous was to move from a single unified undergraduate curriculum to an elective system that gave students virtually complete choice in what to study; equally important is that it allowed the faculty to teach advanced courses in their fields, which both allowed and required increased faculty specialization and research.

White had the advantage of starting with a brand-new university, serving as the first president of Cornell University, founded with federal land grant support and the wealth of Ezra Cornell. Cornell also stressed electives but also practical studies especially in modern literature and history. The "Cornell Idea" made the university a place that focused on technical expertise and the free range of scientific and technical inquiry.

The most important development in the early history of the research university occurred in 1876 after the Quaker benefactor Johns Hopkins left his fortune of a then astounding $7 million to start a new university. At the same time, Daniel Coit Gilman, seeking a fresh start, accepted the presidency of the new school and set it on its course toward becoming the national model for a research university. Undergraduate education interested Gilman less than graduate education and faculty research. Young scholars, some fresh from PhD programs in Germany or the few US schools offering the doctorate, found the opportunity to do research and work with graduate students much more appealing than teaching at a traditional college. By 1889 Johns Hopkins had awarded 151 PhDs, far more than any other school.

Many scholars note the important influence of German universities, which had been focusing on advanced research since the early nineteenth century and where many of the new American scholars got their doctoral training. Historian Emily Levine notes that "the modern university's origins can be traced, then, to institutions in early nineteenth-century Germany . . . [and] an American nation on the cusp of industrialization." But while there was much romanticization of the German model in the United States, academics and administrators in the United States and in Germany developed different institutions for different reasons.

For the United States the industrial revolution also played a key role in the development of the research university. Arthur Levine and Scott Van Pelt argue that the Industrial Revolution, far more than the impact of a German model, led to the creation of the American research university. An agrarian nation might be happy with the transmission of knowledge from generation to generation with few challenges to the reigning ideas. Industrialism, however, demanded something more experimental and more standardized. American university presidents like Eliot, White, and Gilman were creating a model that placed the emphasis on new subjects and an openness to new ideas, and indeed what some called the "religion of research," in place of teaching ancient truths—sacred or secular.[12]

The new model came of age in 1891 when William Rainey Harper, supported by seemingly unlimited—if sometimes reluctant—gifts from John D. Rockefeller, led the creation of the University of Chicago, perhaps surpassing Johns Hopkins as the nation's premier early twentieth-century research university. (See University of Chicago case study later in this chapter.) In spite of Chicago's deeply Baptist origins, the religion of research—and the freedom to follow research and new ideas wherever they led—trumped all else at Chicago. Very quickly more and more schools, from older colleges to the new growing state universities, found in Johns Hopkins and Chicago a model to emulate. If the nineteenth century was the age of the college, the twentieth century was the age of the university in higher education.[13]

While debates about the relationship of religion, evolution, and higher criticism created huge splits across the American educational landscape, these were not the only issues to end earlier harmonies. Most historians of American higher education view the decades immediately after the Civil War as the time when American colleges became significantly more secular as they were more enthralled with developing the research university and less committed to—indeed, less able to comprehend—the unity of scientific truth and religious truth as it had been taught in the antebellum college. While most academics of Timothy Dwight's generation could not have imagined a conflict between scientific discoveries and the Bible, by the 1870s many could not imagine how to reconcile the two, hard as some others tried.

The term "secularization" has been widely debated, but for the purposes of this volume the historian George Marsden provides a useful definition when he writes, "Our subject is the transformation from an era when organized Christianity and explicitly Christian ideals had a major role in the leading institutions of higher education to an era when they have almost none."[14] As Marsden also reminds us, this process was slower than some have recognized. While the time up to the 1870s when the majority of college presidents were clergy with a specific mandate to set a religious tone were long gone, religion was a much more powerful presence in campuses through much of the twentieth century than often recognized. As late as 1939, nearly a fourth of state universities still had chapel services and accepted course work offered by denominational campus ministries toward their degrees.

It was in the 1960s that liberal Protestantism faded most significantly in higher education. Challenged by the dual forces of new religious diversities and the dissatisfaction of a new generation with liberalism in all its forms, liberal religion on campus was staggering. As the liberal ideals of so-called value-free scientific inquiry and individual freedom, which was in fact "never as free from political, commercial, class, and gender interests as their rhetoric implied" faded, so did liberal Protestantism.[15]

The research university challenged the earlier college model steeped in religion. Religion did not disappear, but religious topics and matters of religious faith did migrate. Religion remained alive and well in many corners of most universities, but its place on campus evolved significantly. Less and less did religion retain the central role that it once held, even as it thrived in new ways in unexplored margins.[16] Change, and resistance to change, took place across the breadth of higher education from the most elite to the smaller often religious private colleges, and especially at the growing public universities that educated more and more students.

In 1886, Harvard president Charles Eliot, who believed the emerging university should be a place where both students and faculty were free to explore new ideas and new knowledge wherever it took them, and Princeton president James Mc-Cosh, who would have none of it, held a debate in New York. McCosh insisted on required daily chapel and continued the Moral Philosophy course and other courses in the evidence of Christianity. McCosh and Eliot differed about religion, but they also differed about the purpose of a college—should a school, as McCosh thought, transmit the knowledge and faith of the past to a new generation or as Eliot argued should it give students and faculty the freedom to pursue knowledge wherever it could be found? Neither president convinced the other but in the next two decades Princeton, like Harvard, moved in the university direction.[17]

The changing place of religion in American higher education can also be found in other places. In 1883, one of the first practicing Hindu students, Anandibai Joshi, traveled with two English missionaries to the United States from Kolkata (Calcutta) in India and was admitted to the Women's Medical College of Pennsylvania (now part of Drexel University). The dean of the college, Rachael Bodley, personally arranged Joshi's admission and invited her to live in the dean's home and arranged for her to prepare her own meals "which her religious convictions prescribed for her." Dean Bodley, a devout Protestant, struggled with her sense that she should try to convert Joshi to Christianity and her responsibility to extend hospitality and respect to Joshi's Hindu beliefs. The demands of hospitality won and Bodley supported Joshi, who graduated in 1886. Joshi returned to India to practice but sadly died soon after. At the time of her Hindu cremation ceremony, she was recognized as the first Hindu woman to receive a medical degree abroad—a high honor to her and her hosts.[18]

One of the biggest challenges to the denominational college came in 1905 when Andrew Carnegie founded the Carnegie Foundation for the Advancement of Teaching. Carnegie was one of the handful of nineteenth-century capitalists who had made huge fortunes in the rapidly industrializing United States. Indeed, Carnegie may have been the richest man in the United States when he began giving his fortune away after 1901. Where John D. Rockefeller, the staunch Baptist, had made his fortune by monopolizing oil, Carnegie, who monopolized the production of steel, believed mostly in a religion of science that revealed "the divine law of his [God's] being which leads man ever steadily upward." But both Rockefeller and Carnegie had a passion to organize and regularize industry, and also education. While Rockefeller sought a way to regularize education through founding a new model in the University of Chicago, Carnegie poured some of his wealth into the new Carnegie Foundations.

One of the new foundations sought to standardize higher education through the creation of a new pension system for college faculty (a pension system that became TIAA-CREF, much appreciated by many faculty today). In part, the pensions were designed to encourage some of the most able and research-oriented young people in the nation to become college professors but also encourage an older generation of faculty to comfortably get out of the way and let the new research-focused generation move in.

The hand-picked Carnegie board also made the pensions available only to private colleges that were completely free of denominational ties, which they saw as inevitably undermining standards and academic freedom. Colleges with a board appointed by or accountable to a religious body were ineligible for the pensions. When the pension system started, only fifty-one colleges were fully qualified. Almost immediately, twenty more schools cut their denominational ties in order to qualify for the Carnegie funding. Some schools like Methodist-affiliated Syracuse University were furious at being left out. But Carnegie money—a lot of money—mattered, and in time more and more schools jettisoned the last remaining vestiges of denominational control, becoming more secular in governance if not in spirit. In the long run, however, changes in governance also led to changes in spirit in American higher education, which was quickly finding many reasons to put some distance between the research university and much that was overtly religious. Carnegie money significantly speeded the process.[19]

New Roles for a (Marginalized) Religion in Higher Education
Chapels and Chapel Services: Significant and Marginal

Ironically, some of the places where the research university idea first took off were also places that went on a building spree to ensure that religion had a visible, physical presence on campus even while ebbing elsewhere. In the case of the relatively new Stanford University, the Stanford family made it a condition of the founding grant that the university "prohibit sectarian instruction, but to have taught in the University the immortality of the soul and the existence of an all-wise and benevolent Creator." They also established a church at the center of the campus. After her husband's death, Jane Stanford personally supervised the construction of what became the elegant Memorial Church still today at the center of the Stanford campus. She also selected a young clergyman, Rev. David Charles Gardner, to be chaplain of Memorial Church. Rev. Gardner stayed on at Stanford until 1936, and the position continues to be filled and paid for out of the university budget.[20]

Around 1900 several very well-known private universities, including Duke, Syracuse, Princeton, Harvard, Williams, and Notre Dame, also built large and impressive new chapels at the center of the campus, often funded by wealthy patrons as Jane Stanford had done. As late as 1930, Yale had an older chapel but a huge and beautiful new library and what some called a "cathedral-like gymnasium." President James Angell argued that the campus reflected a "somewhat distorted" picture of the place of religion and championed the building of a new Yale chapel as a "natural completion to a scale of values." On some campuses, including Harvard, Yale, and Cornell, the chapel services had their own endowment while at others such as Vassar, Wellesley, Mount Holyoke, and the University of Missouri they were (and often still are) part of the regular college budget.

Attendance at chapel was high. Most universities, including state universities, offered regular if not daily chapel services through the nineteenth century. As late as 1906, one study reported chapel services at seventeen of nineteen state universities, including required attendance at nine.[21] In 1885 a student was expelled from the University of Illinois for not attending chapel, but chapel did decline at state universities soon thereafter. Illinois ended its chapel services in 1894 and neighboring Purdue in 1901. The University of Michigan ended compulsory chapel in 1871 though daily prayers were offered until 1895. In 1907 voluntary services at the University of Minnesota had an average student attendance of 500 while at Kansas the average was 800.

Charles Eliot abolished required chapel at Harvard in the 1880s. Throughout his tenure, however, Eliot made sure that some of the best preaching in New England continued to draw students to voluntary daily chapel services. Many elite and non-elite private nondenominational colleges followed the pattern if more slowly. A 1907 report on college chapels noted the example of New York University where chapel attendance was required and a student who missed fifteen or more services had to write an 800- to 1,000-word paper on a religious subject.[22] Columbia ended required chapel in 1891. Religious services at Dartmouth were made voluntary in 1925 and at Yale in 1926.

The newer universities—Johns Hopkins, Stanford, and the University of Chicago—made religious services optional but available from the beginning. In 1892, University of Chicago president William Rainy Harper happily reported that chapel services, "though voluntary, are well attended, the room being practically filled and some days many being compelled to stand." He did not say, however, how large the room was. Harper later instituted required chapel attendance for students in many of the university's programs. Whether these chapel services made much impact on the majority of the school's students or had anything to do with what was taught in the classrooms after the end of the chapel service remains a different question.[23]

What all the construction of chapels and religious life centers means raises interesting questions. Commenting on the 1920s-era construction of the large and impressive Rockefeller Chapel that still dominates the University of Chicago campus today, George Marsden noted that it was "one of the clearest cases of a building erected in memory of a fading religious spirit." At Princeton in 1927, as the new elegant Gothic chapel was nearing completion, the editors of the campus newspaper, the *Princeton Tiger*, asked "is that thing a white elephant?" It was not an irrelevant question as chapel attendance kept dropping even as the buildings got larger.[24]

Student-Led Religious Activity—The YMCA/YWCA

As higher education changed, students lived increasingly separate lives from the faculty. The pre–Civil War notion that faculty supervised the student body—inquiring into the state of their souls and monitoring their personal behavior—slowly disappeared. While university officials led chapel services, some students often found other ways to assert their faith. Advances in transportation also gave students much more choice, and many could travel farther from home to a school whose culture, religious beliefs, and focus they liked. Indeed, it could be said that the railroad changed the nature of the student body on many campuses as much as the growing regard for research changed faculty life. Many students now selected a school farther from home that had a more acceptable religious tradition for them or simply offered the right courses at lower tuition.

For some late-nineteenth-century students, even as resistance to required courses and chapel attendance grew, student life included a large measure of interest in religion—but on the students' own terms. By the 1850s, and especially after the Civil War, new student-led religious organizations appeared in the United States. During a pan-Protestant religious revival that swept the nation, including many college campuses in 1857–1858, two organizations became very popular in the United States. The Young Men's Christian Association (YMCA)—recently imported from England in 1851—grew rapidly among young urban male converts, especially those working in the expanding middle-class world of business. A parallel, but quite separate, women's organization had less connection to any English activities, but in 1858 church women in New York established the Ladies' Christian Association to provide for the many unaccompanied working girls who were moving to the city. The association rented rooms on University Place for religious and social activity. A decade later, a group of well-to-do church women established the Boston Young Women's Christian Association and the idea of providing safe and inexpensive boarding houses with accompanying Bible study classes for working girls soon spread. Throughout its history, the YWCA, more than its male counterpart, was identified with safe and inexpensive housing.

While the birth of the YMCA and YWCA was outside of higher education, students at the University of Virginia and the University of Michigan sought a structure that could bridge (or more often ignore) their denominational differences yet keep their religious enthusiasm intact. They found it in the Young Men's Christian Association. In these years, YMCA chapters on college campuses often included women as well as men. The YWCA's leaders also built women-only chapters that could empower women, first at women's colleges and the mostly female teacher preparation Normal Schools, but quickly on other campuses. The first recorded YWCA college chapter was organized at the Normal University in Normal, Illinois, in 1873 but by 1877 there was a chapter at the coeducational Olivet College in Michigan and by 1881 student delegations were being welcomed into the YMCA board meetings.

By the 1880s, the national YMCA adopted a policy of strict separation by gender. Since the YWCA was already engaged in campus work, it was happy to pick up the women. While national organizations set clear—and strict—policy, there was resistance on some campuses over gender segregation. The University of Michigan YMCA withdrew from the national organization from 1886 to 1897 rather than segregate by gender. Throughout the late 1800s, staff from the two organizations often met together and coordinated their efforts, but the two organizations also went their separate ways, serving different students and holding different policies on some issues.[25]

Both of the early Ys were Protestant Christian evangelistic associations that grew when a religious revival sparked renewed religious interest on a college campus. These revivals could sweep up an entire student body as they had for generations in the Protestant world of higher education. At Amherst, the president, perhaps with some exaggeration, reported that "the entire college community was brought under the influence." President Arthur Tappan at the University of Michigan saw similar effects of "a deep and solemn thoughtfulness among students of the State University." In a time of such intense emotion, an organization that could channel and maintain the fervor was in the right place at the right time.[26]

Well into the 1880s, the YMCA maintained a primary focus on evangelism and personal conversion, Bible study, and individual morality. YWCA student members sought to create a more inclusive organization. When in 1885 the YWCA's board considered a motion to limit leadership roles "to young women who are members in good standing of an evangelical church," the YWCA split and nearly all college chapters went with the faction that put no such restriction on membership or leadership.[27]

From the beginning, the YMCA and the YWCA both kept their distance from specific denominational connections—sometimes to the frustration of church leaders but to the delight of college administrators, who recognized that even the most religiously connected college drew students from many Protestant groups and did not want to get embroiled in denominational rivalry. In 1870, Adam K. Spence, a founding member of the University of Michigan Y and by then a professor at the university, insisted that "children of today" would "grasp hands over walls of sectarian separation . . . [ignoring] minor distinctions and focusing on essentials." In this way, the Ys could create a unified religious community for students while they were at college.[28]

One of the big differences between the men's and women's organizations had to do with racial segregation. Early in the YWCA's history it began work on Black campuses as well as White and quickly created a staff position for this work. By the 1920s, at a time when the Ku Klux Klan was strong and strict racial segregation seemed permanent in the United States, a report of the YWCA's student division noted, "we began with the active participation of colored students in . . . commissions of the national movement." White and Black staff visited "mixed campuses in the interest of interracial understanding" between "students from white and colored colleges." There is a tone of condescension and level of comfort with the prevailing segregation by Whites in the YWCA reports, but the outreach was real; real enough that critics claimed the YWCA was a front for "inter-racial propaganda . . . social intercourse and interbreeding . . . between Negroes and whites."[29]

The men's organization seemed to be more comfortable with racial segregation. Black YMCA chapters were formed at Fisk and Howard in the 1870s and in 1879 the (White) national organization also hired a traveling secretary to create more such chapters. By 1888, there were twenty-seven associations at African American schools, with 1,093 student members. As late as 1914, the Y's Negro Christian Student Conference in Atlanta urged chapter members to "give the present generation of Negro students in the United States a strong spiritual and moral impulse" toward the end of building individual character and motivating some to become missionaries to Africa. The conference did criticize "habitual injustice and unkindness" in the treatment of Black Americans, but leaders argued that too early a challenge of segregation would fail. The aging Booker T. Washington attended the 1914 conference, and his blessing spoke to the direction of the YMCA in racial matters.[30]

In the decades after the Civil War, the focus of religious life—and Y activities— changed. In its early years, the Y work focused on religious conversions and fostering study groups, spiritual reflection, and a commitment to missionary work. After the election of the charismatic John R. Mott as the new national leader for the YMCA in 1888, the emphasis migrated to a focus on social reform movements. As Mott told the 1906 YWCA national convention, it was time for "great advances" of "Christian civilization." Amanda Izzo explains that by the early years of the twentieth century this new emphasis "tipped the balance away from the evangelical concerns of piety, social morality, and personal salvation. Instead an emphasis on the 'social principles of Jesus' and Progressive coalition politics prevailed." These shifts were part of something much larger than the Y alone. Much of American Protestantism was embracing the Social Gospel—a widespread movement across Protestantism that shifted the primary focus from saving individual souls to saving society from poverty, corruption, and injustice. Under Mott's national leadership from 1888 to 1915, the YMCA became a student arm of the Social Gospel.[31]

The YMCA's religious emphasis did not disappear, but under Mott it did acquire a new focus that often overwhelmed the old. Mott championed a kind of "muscular Christianity," popular especially among men in the progressive Social Gospel era. Nevertheless, the core of the Y's work became a focus on ethical Christian living and action in Christian service rather than concern with personal salvation.

The growing new focus on service made the Y extremely popular among many faculty and administrators as well as students. In an era before universities considered a robust program of campus-based student services their responsibility, more than a few were happy to see an external organization take on work that was very important to student lives but not necessarily a university priority.

The YMCA and YWCA both spanned Protestant denominational differences. They were student led and quickly became the institution that led campus-based religious life—and often social life—for the remainder of the nineteenth century and beyond. From 40 campus chapters in 1877, the YMCA grew to 559 local chapters and 31,901 college student members in 1900, and to 764 institutional chapters serving 80,649 students by 1920. At the time the different factions of the YWCA united in 1906, the combined organization included 469 student associations with 41,688 members. Some of this growth was not surprising at a time of incredible growth in college attendance, from 62,839 students in 1870 to 355,430 students in 1910, or from 3 percent of college-age Americans in 1870 to over 5 percent in 1910. But there was fervent energy to be found in the Ys, and happily for the organizations, they managed to capture an extraordinarily high percentage of this enrollment growth.[32]

Beginning at Cornell, Princeton, and Yale in 1886, the YMCA began to appoint paid campus field secretaries to support the work of local chapters and often to manage the Y buildings that were starting to dot many campuses. Before the end of the 1880s, the YWCA followed the same model, especially at women's colleges. The campus secretaries were also expected to be a kind of "campus pastor" and spiritual leader. They were not distant clergy but rather often recent graduates and key players in the Y's expansion. The secretaries supported and mentored the students, and the Y was a student-led organization. Yale's 1887 decision not to replace the chaplain but to appoint the YMCA secretary to care for student religious life and be the superintendent of Dwight Hall, the building for religious life at Yale, was a sign of the Y's status. Students and most of the professional staff of field secretaries in the Y savored their lay status, reflecting something close to an anticlerical view of what interdenominational Christianity ought to be.[33]

Although welcomed by most college administrators and existing alongside the major denominations, the Y depended on neither for its finances. Money was raised from individual contributions. As a report to the 1891 New York YWCA conference recommended, "Go to people whose hearts are in sympathy with the work . . . who do and give for the cause of Christ in every other direction."

Though the organization appreciated supportive college leaders, it also did not depend on them nor ask permission for its right to do its work. Late nineteenth- and early twentieth-century college campuses did not have the kinds of security measures seen in many places a century later. It was not odd for field secretaries and students to move back and forth between classroom buildings and Y buildings several times in a normal day. Before 1870, colleges as diverse as the University of Rochester, the University of Mississippi, Grinnell College, Olivet College, the College of the City of New York (now City College or CCNY), and the newly created African American Howard University had YMCA chapters that quickly became the heart of campus religious life.[34]

After World War I, the place of the YMCA and YWCA in campus religious life began to falter. David P. Setran, the foremost recent historian of the campus-based YMCA, gives three interconnected reasons for this shift. As he describes it, first there was the growing religious diversity of the student bodies at many schools; second, the movement by many universities to reengage with student life and provide student centers and supervise students themselves; and third, a growing sense among individual denominations that they wanted to foster student loyalty to their own tradition, not to a generalized and separate kind of broad Protestantism.

By 1920, the college-going population expanded dramatically. Included in that expansion were growing numbers who did not share the Protestant culture of the campus and the Y. As John Whitney Evans, a historian of Catholic student movements, wrote, "Roman Catholics, Unitarians, Jews, and Universalists complained about official university sponsorship of an organization so fully in the tradition of evangelical Protestantism."[35] If the Y shared the basic theological outlook of most Protestants, Catholics or others were left out. And there were more "others" on college campuses. And why, some of the "others" asked, were the state-funded and tuition-funded universities giving special preference to the obviously Protestant Y when it clearly did not support them?[36]

Higher education as it developed in the late nineteenth and early twentieth century is often seen as increasingly secular—and compared with the antebellum college it was—but in comparison with the modern student today, the so-called secular college of a century ago was actually a place alive with religious influences. This was true of state universities almost as much private institutions.[37] But in the twentieth century, Protestant students were joined by growing numbers of Catholic, Jewish, or unaffiliated students. The Y's failure to embrace the growing religious diversity of the nation's college student body meant it could no longer be seen as offering support for the spiritual lives of many students.

As the Y took on the role of serving the student body on campus—providing everything from dorms to space for relaxation and counseling services—many college leaders were initially happy to shed the responsibility. However, in the early twentieth century, many colleges began to take some of these roles back, building dormitories, erecting student unions, and beginning the creation of what became a whole cadre of student service personnel where none had previously existed. In doing so, university leaders, intentionally or unintentionally, entered into direct competition with the Y. As early as 1911, the Michigan student newspaper, the *Daily*, reported a survey that found that the majority of students thought the YMCA "overstepped its bounds" in competing with the student union and should stick to religious activities—a far cry from the role the Y had played at Michigan in past generations.

Many campuses also began offering more courses in religion and establishing religion departments. For the curious student, the religion courses covered much of the same ground as Y study groups. If the large, new YMCA/YWCA buildings near many campuses were no longer needed for student residences or student social activities, or for their own religion classes, what were they for? And who would pay for the upkeep? These were questions that would consume a great deal of attention in the Ys of the post–World War I years.[38]

Clergy-Led Religious Activity—Guilds, Chairs, Affiliated Colleges, and Chaplains

The most significant competition for the Y, however, did not come from within the university. Churches and especially denominational church leaders had their own worries about an organization that was entirely lay led, almost to the point of being anticlerical, and that also went out of its way to ignore denominational differences. Creedal issues, important to many church leaders, never mattered much to the Y. As a result, some church leaders became more and more uncomfortable with the Y. Some clergy also felt that the Y also fostered a sense of arrogance among student members who saw its nonsectarian approach an advance over outdated church theology and the worship life of most churches.[39]

In the nineteenth century, many people in the churches had seen the ecumenical Y as serving students well, and keeping a religious spark alive among them, when traditional parish churches could not find a way to do it. By the turn of the twentieth century, however, what had once been a strong alliance was coming apart. Some pastors and denominational leaders saw the Y as creating loyalty to a different ecclesiastical organization—itself—and building a sense of superiority in students that made them unlikely to return to parish churches as adults. As it evolved from evangelism to a focus on Christian living and social justice, a popular move with students and college administrators, the Y risked losing its theological edge, which clergy thought they themselves, not recent-graduate lay field secretaries, could address. As a result, in the last two decades of the nineteenth century, some Protestant ministers and Catholic priests began to question the Y's place in college student religious life, even though in that long-before-Vatican II era, they never spoke to each other about it. (Convened by Pope John XXIII in October 1962, Vatican II was important in ending the isolation of the Catholic Church and beginning Catholic–Protestant dialogue or as the Pope said, to "open the windows and let in some fresh air" for Catholics but also Protestants. But in the early 1900s that was far in the future.)[40]

By the 1880s, the fastest growth in college enrollment took place on the campuses of public universities. Even though Protestant and Catholic religious leaders might complain that the students really should attend denominational schools, they had to recognize where the students—and future congregational members and clergy—actually were and then respond accordingly. Catholics and Protestants worried greatly about who was winning the fight for the souls of college students. They distrusted each other. But when it came to college students, they distrusted the winds of secularism, simple disinterest, and specifically the work of the seemingly anti-institutional Y even more. As early as the 1880s, some religious leaders were sharply questioning the Y's role.[41] Something new was needed, many church leaders were convinced, something that would link college students not merely to Protestantism in general but to a specific denomination and tradition, be it Presbyterian, Episcopal, Baptist, or others, or for Catholics—who never quite trusted the Y's ecumenical Protestantism—the Catholic Church. They all explored multiple ways to make sure the specific churches played a larger role in the lives of college students.

Denominational Guilds

The first steps away from denominational support for the Y came with denominational support for the guild movement. Like the YMCA, the guilds that sprang up on college campuses in the 1880s and 1890s were student led and focused on the students' quest for religious meaning. But quite unlike the nondenominational Y, the guilds were strictly denominational and created by denominational bodies—local churches or national agencies—and meant to foster denominational loyalty. A university might have an Episcopal, a Presbyterian, and a Methodist guild, and later a Catholic club on campus, and the Protestant guilds might work together on many matters, but each guild was strictly separate and loyal to its own denomination. The local church of that denomination may play a significant role, providing funds and staff support, or most support might come from higher levels in the denomination. But the guilds were student-led affairs but with clear denominational loyalty.[42]

In the case of the University of Michigan, the guild work was relatively extensive. The Episcopal guild there began in 1887. An 1889 article in an Episcopal journal described the work of Hobart Guild as having as its objective "to bring the Episcopal and other students of the university into acquaintance with one another by social and other gatherings; to promote the spiritual welfare of its members by stated meetings for worship, for the study of Holy Scripture, of Church history, of Christian literature, and by mutual counsel and encouragement in the performance of Christian duties." The article also described the building—which the article called Hobart Hall, as "on the most eligible site" at Huron and State Streets three blocks from the campus. It included three stories, with a gymnasium, bowling-alley, parlors, a library, reading rooms, a dining room, and an auditorium that could seat 400. The center also had a staff minister, Rev. William Galpin, apparently connected to the nearby Episcopal St. Andrew's Parish. After two years of operation, the author was pleased to report that as a result of constant pastoral care of the clergy of St. Andrew's parish, the guild had led to an increase in students attending services at the parish, growing interest in church matters, and a "missionary spirit" among the students. The Hobart Guild was clearly under the control of the nearby parish. The parish rector served as president of the board, and the church owned the building.[43]

The Episcopal work at Ann Arbor may have been the most impressive, but other Protestants were not far behind. When Presbyterian MacMillan Hall, including a

4,000-volume library, a gymnasium, auditorium, and social and study rooms, was dedicated in 1891, the Presbyterian General Assembly—the church's national governing body—was meeting in Detroit and adjourned for a day to take a special train to Ann Arbor for the dedication ceremonies. The Presbyterians described their goal in quite similar terms to the Episcopalians, saying it was "to bring the Presbyterian students of the University of Michigan into closer acquaintance and more intimate communion with each other, to confirm the faith of students coming from Presbyterian families, to promote the spiritual welfare of members of the Association, and increase their influence in advancing the cause of Christianity." While the MacMillan Hall building was a specific gift to the association from wealthy patrons, the guild itself was, like that of the Episcopalians, under the oversight and care of the local Presbyterian church, whose pastor was at the core of its work.[44]

Michigan Methodists established their own Wesleyan guild at the university. As Alexander Winchell, a professor at the university and an active Methodist, described it in 1890, "With the growth of other guilds, it became more distinctly apparent that the Methodist organization required a larger and more imposing form, more ample provisions, and a furnished home or hall in which its peculiar work could be done." As of 1890, funds were still being raised to build a structure, but meetings of the Wesleyan guild included "social, musical and minor literary entertainments" as well as sermons and lectures. The object of the organization was, not surprisingly, "the religious and denominational care of students entering the University from Methodist families and families under Methodist influence." Though the guild did not try to draw students from other groups, "every student is welcomed." And while, at the date of Winchell's publication the local Methodist church carried the expense of the guild, it was clear by 1890 that continuing the work and building a hall required commitment from other Methodists far beyond Ann Arbor.[45]

While the work of the guilds at the University of Michigan was early and well documented, the guild movement spread to many other campuses, urged on by local congregations and denominational agencies. At the University of Illinois, a small church was built and a separate congregation was organized for Methodists there in 1892. In 1898, the Episcopalians organized a chapel and multipurpose building at the University of Texas at Austin, and the Presbyterians began work at the University of Colorado, including supporting a part-time student pastor.[46]

Among Catholics, the earliest known guild work was more informal. According to the memoirs of several Catholic students, the idea of a Catholic student organization at the University of Wisconsin began in the fall of 1883 when a law student, John J. McAnaw, accused his professor, William Francis Allen, of derogatory remarks about Catholicism. While no record is known of what the remarks were, Allen was a Unitarian with a known dislike of Catholicism. In any case, McAnaw described his complaints at a Thanksgiving dinner hosted for Catholic students at the home of Mr. and Mrs. John Melvin. Mrs. Melvin proposed a society to "study Irish and Catholic history and literature" and thus was born the so-called Melvin Club, named after the hosts of the dinner where it was proposed, and considered to be the forerunner of the hundreds of Newman Clubs still serving Catholic students to this day.

The Melvin Club continued to meet through the 1880s. One active early member of the Melvin Club, Timothy Harrington, described it as the place for "much of the social life of the Catholic students," at Madison and the source of "most of the intellectual food on Catholic subjects." In addition to discussions, Melvin Club members went on sleigh rides; shared oysters, cider, and cigars; and enjoyed their meeting in welcoming homes. Another Melvin Club member, Sidney Dean Townley, described the club in 1890 as the place at the university that taught him "to think well and hard . . . to speak fluently and correctly." Townley wished the university itself could have offered a course in Bible, about which he wanted to learn more.

After Timothy Harrington graduated from Madison, he went on to study medicine at the University of Pennsylvania, where he carried his Melvin Club memories with him and organized a "Catholic club on the pattern of the Melvin Club." In addition to discussions, the Pennsylvania Catholic Club was able to end the ban on Catholic clergy speaking at the university chapel, and later hosted the archbishop of Philadelphia and the eminent Catholic leader Cardinal Gibbons as chapel preachers. Nevertheless, the Catholic club at the University of Pennsylvania seems to have disbanded after Harrington and its other founders graduated.

By 1900, the Melvin Club at Madison was in decline. The Wisconsin Catholic students were ready, however, to use their experience in the club as a springboard to something more. They sought help and quickly got it from a young priest at the nearby Catholic church that ultimately resulted in the appointment of that priest as the first Catholic chaplain at a public university (see chapter 3). In its own way, the Melvin Club was a forerunner of the Newman Catholic student organizations that grew in the twentieth century. Institutionally there was a gap, but the Melvin Club did play a role in giving voice to the concerns that later led to both the founding of the Newman Clubs and the appointment of full-time Catholic chaplains.[47]

Affiliated Colleges

In 1906, North Dakota Methodists took a very different course of action to attend to Methodist students in that state. They created an institution they called an affiliated college. Known as Wesley College, it was created to operate in parallel to the state University of North Dakota. The two colleges were completely separate, with their own faculty, but they negotiated full exchange of credit for classes. As Wesley College's president, Edward P. Robertson, wrote, "religious education and religious service are clearly not within the organic purpose of the state university . . . due to the fundamental principle of the separation of church and state." Robertson was clear that this was "simply a fact to be recognized and is not a basis for accusation."[48]

The issue of the separation of church and state emerges often as an issue in discussions of the place of religion on a college campus, especially at state schools. In 1791, the First Amendment to the federal Constitution made it clear that "Congress shall make no law respecting an establishment of religion, or prohibiting the free exercise thereof." And over the next forty years, every state adopted a somewhat similar rule. But there was a more recent and stronger reason to be careful. In 1875, Republican Congressman James G. Blaine proposed a further amendment to the federal Constitution that would prohibit any state or federal tax money from ever being "under the control of any religious sect." The amendment barely failed in Congress, but so-called Baby Blaine amendments were added to the state constitutions in the majority of states; when North Dakota entered the Union in 1889, the new state constitution included the prohibition. Blaine himself, and most Baby Blaine supporters, primarily wanted to ensure that no tax money went to the support of Catholic schools, which were growing in competition with the (then culturally Protestant) public schools. But the amendment cut both ways, and the decades immediately after the amendments proved so popular was no time for Dakota Methodists, or any other religious group, to push their luck with the state-funded university.[49]

Robertson's solution was to establish and lead a legally and financially separate but parallel institution that could offer courses in religion, the Bible, and related subjects specifically from a Methodist perspective. Through the transfer policy, he could ensure that the courses were "suited to be taken as a part of the regular college course." The president insisted that the affiliated college was not a theological school, though he proudly claimed that the college's undergraduate preparation could surely help students who wanted further study for the Methodist ministry.

As an agent of the church, the affiliated college could be expected to stand for the faith as it was taught and preached by Methodists. However, as an accepted partner of the state university, it could also ensure university credit for its Methodist courses. Believing they had solved the twin problems of a passion for religious instruction following their own traditions and the American belief in the separation of church and state, the Methodists of North Dakota publicized their plan proudly. Although the plan seems to have been modeled on similar affiliated colleges at the University of Toronto, no other American institution adopted the arrangement, though it may have been considered briefly in Missouri. Other lines of religious programming seemed more promising to those in other states.[50]

Bible Chairs

A much more successful or at least widespread effort to bring religious instruction into state universities was introduced by the Disciples of Christ (Christian) churches. Beginning in 1893 at the University of Michigan, site of so many firsts in bringing religion to a state university, the Disciples of Christ supported the academic teaching of religion for the campus. They committed serious financial resources to support Bible chairs at state schools, with 100 percent of funding coming from the denomination, which also picked the incumbent based on both their academic credentials and their faith. A number of state universities permitted those holding Bible chairs to teach regular university classes, allowed students to receive credit, and otherwise treated the chair-holders as full faculty members, though ones who did not cost the university budget anything (a part of the arrangement much appreciated by college presidents).

Unlike other religious groups of the time, Protestant or Catholic, the Disciples of Christ's effort to create Bible chairs was led by women, specifically the Christian Women's Board of Missions. Anna R. Atwater, president of the board, insisted that:

> We look upon Bible work in state universities as offering one of the best opportunities for the enlisting of strong and capable leaders in Christian activity. The time will come, if it is not now here, when all will admit that religion must be given as full and fair consideration as is given to science, art, law and literature.

Recognizing as did the Methodists that the separation of church and state meant that taxpayer funds could not easily be used for "full and fair consideration" of religion, at least from the perspective she wanted, Atwater also said that such efforts "must come from some organized force of the church."

The arrangement that Atwater pioneered was the appointment of top-flight academics, who were also active Disciples adherents, to Bible chairs that would be funded privately but would allow the incumbent to offer academic courses for credit at state schools. After its start at Michigan in 1893, Disciples-funded Bible chairs were created at state universities in Missouri, California, Oregon, Virginia, Georgia, Texas, and Kansas.

In a 1910 report, W. C. Payne, the occupant of the Disciples Bible chair at the University of Kansas, argued:

> The Bible is the book for religious education. Systematic Bible study will result in: 1. A growing acquaintance with the facts and truth of the Bible. 2. A keener appreciation of the personal good derivable from such knowledge. 3. A more vital and forceful life. Pastoral oversight and social activities are considered necessary accessories for accomplishing the desired results, but the teaching function should be primary.

Like the Methodist affiliated college, the occupant of the Bible chair received no salary from the state and was thus free to teach the Bible from their own faith-based perspective. On the other hand, organizers of Bible chairs insisted that the quality of the instruction "should measure up well to university ideals" and "must be scientific." Payne also wrote that since the college student is busy, the Bible courses must not lead to neglect of other courses, and therefore the university must allow students to count the courses and not treat such study as a non-academic add on. Especially with the non-burdensome financial arrangements, most universities were happy to do just that.[51]

In the 1930s, under the national leadership of Lura E. Aspinwall, another lone woman in a male world, many of the holders of Bible chairs began encouraging other Protestant denominations to add their own Bible chairs and expand their work to create schools of religion or Bible colleges a bit like the older Methodist affiliated college. She also encouraged the Disciples of Christ's Bible chair holders to broaden their work by adding more pastoral attention to Disciples's students on their campus, even while maintaining a primary focus on the academic instruction in religion that was their primary purpose.[52]

A New Idea Emerges: College Chaplains

In 1907, the Religious Education Association (a mostly Protestant ecumenical body) created a prestigious "committee of six," including four college presidents, to report on religious activities on American college campuses. The committee surveyed a total of 144 colleges and universities—state, private, and religiously affiliated. The committee noted the many activities of denominational guilds, some with well-funded buildings, but also affiliated colleges, and Bible chairs. Nevertheless, the committee said of the YMCA and YWCA that, "Of all the various student agencies the Christian Associations are by far the largest and most influential." Indeed, they found that a total of 28.8 percent of all the students enrolled in the 144 schools they surveyed were active in Y programs.[53]

The report also noted that "local churches, occasionally supported by the controlling denomination as a body, are interesting themselves in the religious work of the universities and colleges." At the University of Iowa, the Congregational State Missionary Society supported staff and a special student membership in the local Congregational church in Iowa City, while at the University of Illinois, Trinity Methodist Episcopal Church notified the pastors of Illinois to report the names of any Methodist men or women entering the university and then welcomed these students to the church. This sort of effort to link all college students of one denomination to the nearby parish would also long be a hallmark of the Episcopal approach to campus work.[54] The committee also found a growing number of Bible and religious history courses, some offered by university faculty and some by nearby pastors, including a plan at the University of Kansas for a University of Kansas Bible Institute that offered four days of intensive summer courses taught by local clergy in Lawrence from Baptist, Christian, Congregational, Episcopal, Lutheran, Methodist, Presbyterian, United Presbyterian, German Methodist, United Brethren, Friends, Catholic, and Unitarian churches. Finally, the committee noted that university chapel services were still common on many a campus in 1907, often required but popular if not, and not only at religious colleges but many private and public universities.[55]

Between the YMCA and YWCA and the many denominational and university initiatives, it might seem that the first decade of the twentieth century was one of intense student religious involvement. And in some ways, it was. But many pastors and church leaders were far from satisfied. Too many students seemed adrift. Too many programs were still dominated by the Y, which many in the denominations saw as a competing body. And there was too much drift in student-led organizations, where each new generation of students might take the group in a quite different—and perhaps less orthodox—direction, or simply let it become a mere social club or even disband. Certainly, the professional leaders of the churches were beginning to feel that they had far too little influence with current college students. Something more permanent was needed.

In 1911 Joseph Wilson Cochran, secretary of the board of education of the Presbyterian Church (U.S.A.), wrote:

> The Christian Associations have wrought a notable work in our colleges. The World's Student Union [World's Student Christian Federation; linked to the Y] is the most powerful organization of college men in existence. The far-sighted leaders of the Y.M.C.A. have been a generation ahead of the churches in their address to the religious needs of college men.

Nevertheless, given the author, there was a "but" coming:

> The question is often raised whether the Associations are real extensions of the Church or actually separate denominations supported by the Church. . . . They are charged with a policy that tends to wean the student away from his old time religious affiliations; when he returns to the world of affairs, he finds himself detached from any organized form of religion.

Cochran added that the Ys did "not assist the churches in securing attendance upon public worship; that they fail to encourage students to unite with the church of their choice; that they are largely occupied with building up their own membership."[56]

If the Y was a separate denomination, Cochran argued, then it was in direct competition with the other denominations in which students had been raised. Both Ys always had about them a whiff of anticlericalism, which would turn graduates against the clergy and clergy-led churches. If the Y's model of student leadership supported by a few field secretaries was to be the model of church leadership, where was the place of the clergy—on campuses or in the post-college life of graduates? Finally, Cochran said, he believed that the YMCA left students "unpastored and unchurched" at a time when they needed more "parental influence."[57]

For the indomitable Cochran, the response to these concerns seemed clear: clergy would have to become campus-based pastors and the churches would have to find the funds to support them and the new campus centers from which they would work. The work was simply too important to be left to the students, the Ys, and a few friendly faculty advisers. Clergy needed to assert their leadership.

Cochran argued that the church had special reason to care about college students. If, he said, less than 2 percent of the nation's youth attended college but 73 percent of the men listed in *Who's Who* were college graduates, then it was obvious that if the church cared about future leaders, clergy and lay, it needed to give special attention to those who attended college. In his view, a college education that did not attend to character development and faith, that taught only the scientific method and vocational preparation, was insufficient. So, Cochran asked, "are we turning out real world helpers?" For him, the essential step was to produce "a healthy, moral and religious atmosphere." And campus-based clergy were the people to do that.

The Y was not the only problem that concerned Cochran. He also dismissed the efforts of local churches near campuses, noting in surprisingly harsh terms that "state universities are located in small towns whose churches do not appeal to the average college student. Generally the buildings are inadequate, the welcome perfunctory, the preaching indifferent." How local pastors responded to these remarks would be interesting to know, but Cochran was driving home his point.

What was needed, Cochran argued, was something new: "The Church has, until now, failed to demonstrate the vitality of religion in university centers, but she now proposes to move up." For him, this meant full-time pastors at university centers. In another article, he added that this required statewide denominational funding—more than any one congregation could afford—and most of all the kind of work he sought required support from a few wealthy and far-sighted donors. The key was "the securing of a student pastor, an ordained man who shall devote his energies entirely to the work among university students."[58] Who was this "student minister" and what did he (in the early stages it was always *he*) actually do? To that question we turn in chapter 3.

Biblical Criticism and Liberal Evangelism—Union Theological Seminary in New York City

On May 31, 1893, the New York Presbytery, a convening of all the Presbyterian churches in the then very Presbyterian city of New York, voted overwhelmingly to convict Union Theological Seminary Professor Charles A. Briggs of heresy, suspending him from the Presbyterian ministry and indirectly from his chair at the city's Union Theological Seminary. They did so, the majority said, because they saw his embrace of higher criticism of the Bible—the belief that modern scholarship led to the conclusion that the Bible was a human construct that included religious truths and lovely poetry but was far from infallible or historically accurate—as a significant departure from their faith. By the time of the church trial, Briggs had become the best-known national symbol of the debates about the Bible. The move by the Presbytery brought the debate about higher criticism to a much broader audience in the United States. If many church people and indeed most academics did not pay much attention to the issue earlier, after the trial it was hard to ignore.

Briggs's suspension from the ministry by an overwhelming vote was a huge victory for a growing conservative movement in the churches that saw Briggs as the symbol of an attack on all that was sacred, and therefore that his exclusion from the ministry was essential.

Briggs was no agnostic, but he talked freely about errors he saw in the Bible. In looking at the Bible he insisted, "The divine authority is not in the style of the words but in the concept," and indeed, taking every word literally was a kind of superstition or "Bibliolatry." He argued that Moses could not possibly have written the first five books of the Bible, that there were at least two authors for the book of Isaiah, and he saw Jesus as a historical figure. To many, such claims were an attack on their faith. As one critic said, "We are struck . . . with the hypocrisy and treachery of these attacks on Christianity. . . . Is a theological seminary an appropriate place for a general massacre of Christian doctrine?" This critic went on to condemn teachers like Briggs, calling them "infidels masquerading as men of God and Christian teachers."[59]

The long saga of the Briggs trial, which moved back and forth between local and national church bodies between 1891 and 1893, generated national interest in biblical criticism. Nationally recognized newspapers, not just religious periodicals, ran headlines like "Priming Their Guns for the Briggs Fight." Briggs's willingness to wage a scorched-earth campaign did not always help his cause. Even his Union Seminary colleagues had qualms. In their formal statement of support for him, his faculty colleagues at Union added that they "recognize and deprecate the dogmatic and irritating character of certain of Dr. Briggs' utterances." One of his students, Henry Ranck, wrote, "We all think he is right in his higher criticism ideas but as a teacher & prof. we don't like him very well. . . . In fact he is no teacher." In spite of the efforts to remove him, Briggs stayed on the Union faculty for another two decades and remained a Union hero for far longer. But the trial symbolized that for many people their traditional faith was no longer welcome in the most sophisticated circles of American higher education, including seminaries, even if people like Briggs insisted that they were merely defending Christianity in a new intellectual context.[60]

The Briggs trial changed Union Seminary and American theological education in significant ways. It also changed American Protestantism. Some of the changes would probably have come in time anyway and were simply hastened by the trial. Without question, the trial significantly widened the general public's and the church's understanding of what biblical criticism meant. It also hardened the divide between liberals and conservatives among Protestants—those who accepted biblical criticism (and usually also evolution) and those who did not. Only a few years earlier, many had found ways to bridge—or ignore—the differences between those who took the Bible literally and those with a more flexible approach to Scripture. Speaking at a conference of New York ministers in the 1890s, Dwight L. Moody, the most famous evangelist of the second half of the nineteenth century, said "I don't see why you men are talking about 'two Isaiahs, half the people in the country do not know that there is one Isaiah yet."[61] After Briggs's conviction on a 379 to 116 vote, there was not to be such harmony again. Neither the 379 nor the 116 would agree to it. The split was deepest in the Presbyterian church, but it was widely felt and the hostility lasted for generations. Within many universities where the new research focus led to an easy acceptance of both evolution and higher criticism, more faculty also found themselves simply dismissing any religious belief even as many in the more conservative churches came to dismiss and distrust universities that they saw as bastions of unbelief.

Union Seminary itself cut its ties to the Presbyterian Church rather than fire Briggs. Union had been founded as an independent school, although all nine of its founders were Presbyterians. However, in 1870, the seminary had tightened its ties to the Presbyterian Church in an effort to attract more students. With the decision to end the Presbyterian affiliation in 1892, Union regained its independence.[62]

In the decade after the trial, the Union faculty made several changes. As many colleges had done or were doing, Union shifted from a completely prescribed curriculum to offering electives and even the option for Union students to take courses elsewhere. They shifted from oral to written exams. They also added a degree in place of a diploma, awarding the BD (Bachelor of Divinity) after 1897. Significantly, the school also began to admit women, an action accelerated by the first female applicant, Emilie Grace Briggs, daughter of the heretical professor. Emilie Briggs was an academic star, and many women followed. The school also became more engaged in the Social Gospel and encouraged students to work outside of its academic walls with New York's growing but impoverished immigrant communities.

Similar to what was happening elsewhere, the daily 8:30 a.m. chapel services at Union were made voluntary in 1898. Attendance remained high though some professors, Briggs among them, objected when chapel ran long and 9:00 a.m. lectures were disrupted by what Briggs called an "excess of devotion." Within a decade after the failure of Charles Briggs to win at trial in the Presbyterian church, his ideas were far better known than ever before and even taught at seminaries affiliated with the

Presbyterian Church. For Union and a good many other seminaries, the research model became more important to seminary faculty who sought freedom and academic status, even as the role of church bodies declined.[63]

Prayer Meetings, the YWCA/YMCA, and Missions— The Religious Atmosphere at Hampton Institute

In October 1895, Henry Mayberry, an African American student at Hampton Institute in Virginia, wrote to one of the school's White benefactors, Alice Mary Longfellow, in Massachusetts, to thank her for her financial support. Every Hampton student was expected to write to one of the benefactors each year. In his letter Mayberry described his days at Hampton:

> I know you would be glad to know of the many good societies with our school. We have the Young Men's Christian Association, the Young People's Society of Christian Endeavor, and the Young Ladies Missionary Society. The YMCA does missionary work. Young men go out in the country and help the poor by reading the Bible to them, or cutting wood in winter. We sometimes fix up their houses.

In a separate letter, also to Alice Mary Longfellow, another student, Della Stodghill, added:

> There are many inducements to cause students to flock here; for an example, we have a number of religious associations, which every student may attend. I attend the Christian Endeavor and the YWCA. This Young Women's Christian Association is held only for the young women, and has a large attendance every Sunday after noon. These meetings have helped me spiritually and socially; they are held every Sunday at different hours of the day, which gives one an opportunity of attending all.

Other similar letters round out the picture of prayer meetings, church and chapel services, the Ys, and missionary associations, many of which were student led. These meetings dominated Sunday and were an important part of the other six days. Hampton, as the school was portrayed—or idealized—in these student letters, was a very religious place. Certainly, the student letters were tailored to please donors, but they also spoke to a vibrant religious life that seems to have been real.[64]

Hampton was not the only historically Black school to have active Y chapters. By 1888, there were twenty-seven YMCAs in African American colleges, with a combined membership of over 1,000 students, and there were Y chapters on as many as 150 out of 200 Black colleges in the early twentieth century. Blacks were drawn to the Y in larger percentages than Whites, even though only three African American schools—Hampton being one of them—could afford full-time campus secretaries as did many White schools. Even when the Y attendance declined among Whites after World War I, it kept growing on Black campuses. On Black campuses from the 1880s until well into the twentieth century, the YMCA and YWCA were important driving forces in the lives of many students.[65]

Another window into the religious atmosphere at Hampton comes from a graduate who became the first African American appointed as a missionary by the Southern Presbyterian Church. William Sheppard spent twenty years in the Congo, arriving with plans to preach, teach, and convert as many Africans as he could to Christianity in its Presbyterian form. Sheppard arrived in the Congo just as the Belgian King Leopold II was expanding his reign of terror in a search for wealth through ever more rubber production. Leopold's policies were forcing the people of the Congo into slavery to gather rubber that enriched White Belgians.

In 1898, Sheppard began his exposé of the horror of the Congo with an article about discovering eighty-one severed hands being smoked over a fire. Historian Adam Hochschild described the importance of Sheppard's work: "His eyewitness account was cited by almost every American reformer, black or white." Sheppard continued speaking out over the next decade and more. Describing the fate of the Kuba people of the Kasaï region of the Congo in a January 1908 article for American supporters, Sheppard wrote:

> Only a few years ago, travelers through this region found them living in large homes, having one to four rooms in each house, loving and living happily with their wives and children, one of the most prosperous and intelligent of all the African tribes. . . .
>
> But within these last three years how changed they are! Their farms are growing up in weeds and jungle, their king is practically a slave, their houses now are mostly only half-built single rooms and are much neglected. . . .
>
> Why this change? You have it in a few words. There are armed sentries of chartered trading companies who force the men and women to spend most of their days and nights in the forests making rubber, and the price they receive is so meager that they cannot live upon it.

The article made a significant impact on public opinion in the United States and in Europe, a fact that did not go unnoticed in Brussels.

In his book *King Leopold's Ghost*, Hochschild adds, "Sheppard and Morrison [a White fellow Presbyterian missionary] were the most outspoken of any of the American Congo missionaries, whose protests had long nettled Leopold." The king was nettled enough, and the missionaries were outspoken enough, that Sheppard and Morrison were indicted by the Belgian authorities. Sheppard was tried in the Congo, but the court found him innocent and Sheppard was welcomed back to his home in the Congo by his American wife and hundreds of Kuba Christians who were shouting and singing Christian hymns in his honor. The Congolese court may have experienced US pressure to find this American citizen innocent. Although none of the records mention it, the fact that William Howard Taft was both president of the United States and a member of the Hampton Board may have had something to do with the government's support for a distant African American citizen—something the United States was not known for doing for Black citizens in the early 1900s.[66]

Within two years of his trial, Sheppard was back in the United States speaking about the Congo to Black and White audiences and demanding that the Belgian oppression end. In 1911, Sheppard and Booker T. Washington both spoke at Hampton Institute fundraisers in New York and the next day in Boston, where Sheppard's fame was such that he got top billing ahead of the famous Washington.

In 1915, Sheppard spoke at Hampton about why he decided to become a missionary, calling Hampton his birthplace, "not natural birth, but the place where I was born in instruction and inspiration and vision." In an article published later that year in the Hampton newsletter, *Southern Workman*, Sheppard added:

> One Sabbath, at the close of the afternoon Sabbath school, Dr. Frissell [then chaplain at Hampton Institute] came to me and said, "We are going to a village near by to hold divine service: won't you bring along some Bibles and hymn books?" I was delighted. . . . This, through this great man's kindness and influence, was my first missionary work. Later it was the pleasure of my life to do more missionary work—twenty years' service in the Congo in Central Africa.

Sheppard knew his spiritual roots and where those roots led.[67]

Hampton traces its roots to the early days of the Civil War when Union Army forces under the command of Major General Benjamin Butler took control of Fort Monroe in Hampton, Virginia. In September 1861, Butler recruited Mary Peake, a free Black, to open a school for runaways from slavery who were flocking to the fort. After the war, Samuel Armstrong, another Union General and a child of missionaries in Hawaii, arranged both federal and church funding from the Congregational American Missionary Association to expand Peake's school into the Hampton Normal and Agricultural Institute "to train selected Negro youth who should go out and teach and lead their people." By the 1870s, Armstrong had become the school's president and Hampton became a model for many other schools, including Tuskegee Institute in Alabama, founded in 1881, and at Armstrong's recommendation, led by Hampton graduate Booker T. Washington.[68]

While Hampton's focus was the education of African Americans, the federal government transferred some seventy Native American prisoners from the Red River War to Hampton. The Native American program continued until 1923 and sought to teach the Indians "to read, count, about God, about justice and truth." William H. Robinson, writing in a history of Hampton, described efforts to Christianize Indian students at Hampton as based on ignoring "the obvious fact that they were profoundly religious although they were not followers of Christ." But few anywhere in nineteenth-century American education could imagine being religious without being Christian, and Hampton under Armstrong was more Christian than most colleges.[69]

Armstrong's successor was the school's chaplain and vice president, Hollis B. Frissell, who served until 1917. Frissell was not as well-known nor as charismatic as Armstrong, but as historian Troy Smith has shown, Frissell was a genius at fundraising. He recruited northern White Protestants to provide financial support for Hampton. As Smith notes, 200 northern White churches gave a total of $9,000 a year to Hampton—a lot of money at the time—and their members sometimes gave further support based on a connection solidified by the letters with which this section opens. Frissell expected the Hampton graduates to be teachers or missionaries like Shepperd, and to bring job skills, culture, and the Christian faith to their own students. In an 1890 graduation speech, Frissell reminded the graduates that they had a "high and holy calling." It was Frissell's way of reminding the Hampton graduates to share their faith widely and to be advocates for the rights of all African Americans.[70]

Baptist Ministers, a Baptist Millionaire, and a Baptist Commitment to Freedom—The University of Chicago

When the board of trustees of the newly reorganized University of Chicago met in September 1890, they were responsible for what was a very Baptist school. One of the trustees' first actions was to invite Yale professor William Rainey Harper to assume the presidency of the school. Harper was the best-known Baptist educator in the nation, mostly because of his popular Bible commentaries, and he had helped draft early plans for the university. The trustees had no real second choice for the job. Harper, both a good Baptist and an imaginative and ambitious educator, was destined to be not only the first but the most influential leader in shaping the university.

Initially, Harper was hesitant about taking the presidency. In January 1891, Harper wrote to John D. Rockefeller, who was bankrolling the new enterprise, stating that he worried that his views on higher criticism of the Bible might hurt the new school even though, "I cannot but believe from the results connected with my teaching of the Bible, that it is the will of God that I should teach it in the way in which I have been teaching it."[71]

Harper had reason to worry. When word spread that he had been offered the Chicago position, many conservative Baptists, knowing his views of biblical criticism, raised questions. The aging president of the Southern Baptist Theological Seminary in Louisville, Kentucky, John Broadus, one of the best-known Baptist preachers and educators of an earlier generation, wrote to Harper, his fellow Baptist educator, to congratulate him on his pending appointment but also to urge him to prefer faculty who "incline to conservative views about biblical inquiries and about the relation between Christianity and critical science." Harper intended no such thing. He was also well aware of the storm clouds gathering around Charles A. Briggs in New York, and Harper considered Briggs one of the "brightest lights in the liberal firmament." Pushback from more conservative Baptists was a real concern, much more of a concern for a soon-to-be university president than if he remained a well-known but protected professor at Yale.

On the other hand, the Rockefeller funds that would underwrite the university were not at risk. Rockefeller was a fan of Harper, and though a deeply devout Baptist, he could not care less about the battles over higher criticism one way or the other. Rockefeller was not to be deterred by indignation in his philanthropy any more than he had been by the widespread indignation about his monopolistic business practices. And Harper was no Briggs. Whereas Briggs seemed to relish offending any who disagreed with him, Harper, while not compromising his views, was committed to engaging as many people, and especially as many Baptists, as possible. He possessed a generally irenic spirit that was foreign to someone like Briggs. A month after his exchange with Rockefeller, Harper took the job leading Chicago and is rightly credited with launching the University of Chicago into its twentieth-century future as one of the nation's leading academic institutions and as a place that initially took religion very seriously.[72]

Harper was not, however, Chicago's first president. The University of Chicago opened its doors in 1857 as a small Baptist school, much like many other small Midwestern denominational colleges, but in the rising city of Chicago, Illinois. Much of the initial impetus for starting the school came from Illinois's senator Stephen A. Douglas (of the Lincoln–Douglas debates). While not a Baptist, Douglas thought it was important for Chicago, where he had many business interests, to have a college just as other college boosters thought every town in the Midwest needed a college. John Burroughs, pastor of the First Baptist Church of Chicago, was chosen as the school's first president. The University of Chicago, like most similar denominational schools, was open to students of any denomination. And like most similar schools, its position was always precarious.

The new university suffered from several problems. It was small and enrollment did not increase with the growth of the city of Chicago. After the Civil War, the association with Douglas hurt more than it helped, since Douglas was seen as the proslavery antagonist of Lincoln. Its board was always divided within itself and never able to build a partnership with the Chicago Baptist Union Theological Seminary. The divisions made some donors—John D. Rockefeller among them—very wary, and the split of university and seminary diluted Baptist funding for both. Finally, and perhaps most seriously, the school got deeper and deeper into debt as its grand plans and building programs far outran available funds. John Boyer, the University of Chicago historian, commented, "Most colleges in mid-nineteenth-century America hovered between genial penury and unmitigated fiscal disaster." The Chicago school moved further and further toward the latter, until it collapsed in 1886 when the Union Mutual Life Insurance Company, which held most of the debt, foreclosed on the campus. The school, as did so many other small colleges of the nineteenth century, simply ceased to exist.[73]

Unlike most colleges that went out of business, however, the University of Chicago was fairly quickly resurrected in a new and much improved form. Thomas Goodspeed, financial secretary of the Baptist Seminary, along with several Baptist ministers, including a new and gifted recruit named Frederick Taylor Gates, began working to recreate a school that would be free of the divisiveness of the old one, and also free of its debt. In 1888, a Baptist convention created a new American Baptist Education Society specifically to raise funds to strengthen Baptist education in the Midwest. Slowly Goodspeed, Gates, and the others began to pull the pieces—and the money—together and create a much more unified plan than anything the old university had ever witnessed. In time they recruited Rockefeller, the richest Baptist in the United States, to their cause.

Initially very skeptical, John D. Rockefeller became convinced that the new plan was free of the weaknesses of the old university and that a strong Baptist school in the Midwest would be an important contribution to his faith community. At the outset, Rockefeller pledged $600,000 if the local leaders could raise a matching $400,000, which they did in short order, including a substantial gift of land in Hyde Park from the department store owner Marshall Field. The school thus started with a campus, free of debt and with $1 million—more money than the old university had ever imagined.

The trustees had their first meetings in the summer of 1890, formally electing Harper as president, effective July 1, 1891; Rockefeller helped persuade him to take the job. A new enterprise in American higher education had begun. Even before he took office, Harper had done what the old university leaders could not do: convinced the Baptist Seminary to move to Hyde Park and become the core of the new university's graduate school. He also persuaded Rockefeller to give an additional $1 million to launch the graduate school. Over the years, Rockefeller contributed several million more, including a final capstone gift of $10 million to the new university.[74]

The university that Harper presided over from 1891 until his premature death in 1906 was something new in American higher education: an undergraduate college and a diverse graduate school with a commitment to academic excellence and academic freedom throughout. Although the fact is now often forgotten, in its early years Chicago was also a deeply Baptist school. While welcoming students and faculty of many persuasions and none, the initial bylaws did require that two-thirds of the trustees and the president needed to be Baptist, and Baptists felt a strong commitment to—and ownership of—the school.

The mix of academic freedom, academic excellence, and Baptist culture was made possible, in part, by two forces. The Rockefeller money helped the school attract some of the best faculty in the world, and Harper and his successor president, Harry Pratt Judson, regularly asked for and received additional Rockefeller funds. There is also something deep in the Baptist tradition—a core belief in "soul freedom"—that can make Baptist churches and Baptist colleges internally contentious places but also free of hierarchy and cherishing their freedom. Until long after Harper's time, there was no central Baptist authority to set limits on individual freedom. (Sadly, in the late twentieth century, the Southern Baptist Convention seems to have forgotten that commitment to soul freedom.)[75]

While Harper was proud of his role in founding and leading the University of Chicago, he personally considered his work as a biblical scholar most important. At the height of his presidency at Chicago, Harper wrote to his friend J. M. Taylor that he thought his own "special business in the world is stirring up people on the

English Bible." To this Harper added, "The University of Chicago is entirely second hand matter."[76]

Harper had received his PhD from Yale at the age of 19 and began his academic career teaching Bible at the Baptist Denison University in Ohio, then at the Baptist Seminary in Chicago, and later back at Yale where he was a popular teacher and scholar. Harper's intellectual interest was in biblical linguistics more than theology, but he was also a devout Christian who wanted as many people as possible to know the Bible. He taught Hebrew for the interested public at the Chautauqua summer education programs starting in 1883, ran correspondence courses in the Bible from his position at Yale, published a steady stream of material on the Bible for the general public, and became highly popular with a wide range of Baptist ministers. Harper was committed to applying the highest level of academic scholarship to the study of the Bible even when it got him in trouble with some other Baptists.

Harper never retreated into the ivory tower. He also believed higher criticism was essential to converting a new generation to the Christian faith, for he feared that without biblical criticism a time would come "when intelligent men of all classes will say 'if this is your Bible we will have none of it.'" (Harper was also deeply sexist.) Harper's whole career, including his presidency, can be understood as an effort to ensure that the day when people would have nothing to do with his faith never came for men or women.[77]

Harper is remembered today for his successful presidency of what became one of the leading research universities in the world. But his plans had a religious element to them that is too easily forgotten, even if few contemporaries could forget it. Harper's commitment to scholarship was never in doubt, and for his first faculty he hired people he considered the best scholars—whether they were Baptists, or indeed Christians, or not. The Rockefeller money let him attract great scholars with higher salaries than anyone else offered. Nevertheless, his own deep beliefs were visible in many parts of the university.

In March 1891, after accepting the presidency at Chicago but before taking up his formal duties, Harper wrote an article for the *Chicago Tribune* saying:

> To be sure it will be a Baptist institution, under Baptist control, because we are Baptists. But we are also men and men desirous of adding to the store of knowledge and for this we shall make the University of Chicago broad and Christian in the fullest sense.[78]

A *Tribune* reader might assume the new university was not much different than dozens of other denominational colleges still focused on the "unity of truth" and broadly Christian in orientation. But from the beginning, Harper was also leading a subtle shift at Chicago, and soon in much of American higher education, whether for secular or—in Harper's case—deeply religious reasons.

Just two months after he wrote the *Tribune* article, Harper gave a speech to a Baptist convention in which he said:

> There is but one thing in the Universe sacred aside from God; that thing is truth. Searching for truth is searching for God. Investigation must not be hampered. It should be honest and sincere, cautious and reverent, but it should also be broad; and the truth wherever and however found must be accepted at any cost.[79]

The embrace of "investigation" changed everything. For Harper, the search for truth was a divine mission, and if the search ended up in conflict with any revealed religious matter, the truth, not fidelity to orthodoxy, had to prevail. Perhaps this was Harper's Baptist soul freedom at work. Perhaps it was what his own embrace of biblical scholarship had taught him. Perhaps it was his longstanding devotion to higher education that had been honed carefully at Yale. Whatever the source, it meant that the university he presided over would have no limits on academic freedom even if the research exploded the unity that was at the heart of the older style college. Something new was indeed being born in American higher education, even if the quest for truth was always for Harper a quest for God.

The new sociology department at Chicago illustrated what the Chicago approach to religious commitment and academic freedom meant. As Harper assembled his initial faculty, he focused on people—mostly men but sometimes women—whom he respected. He did not care as much about strengthening specific academic fields or disciplines. He also did the hiring himself. There were no search committees, just generous offers from the new president. Among the early offers was one to Albion W. Small, who at the time was president of Colby College, a small Baptist college in Maine. Small was an ordained Baptist minister who had studied social issues at Berlin and Leipzig and who held a PhD from Johns Hopkins University. Small's research and his faith led him to a commitment to improving the world in which people lived and to using the best of social science research to find ways to do it.

Small responded to Harper's offer that he would consider coming to Chicago if he could lead a department of sociology that would focus on "the actual conditions of American economic problems," as a way to find concrete solutions to pressing social issues in Chicago and the nation. Harper agreed. As Steven Diner said in his study of sociology at Chicago, Small believed that "sociology should study contemporary society; that the study of modern society should be conducted at first-hand, as well as through the study of documents; that it should be centered upon practical problems; and that it must be an intellectual discipline." Thus was born the first sociology department in the United States.

Small's approach to sociology was very similar to Harper's approach to the study of the Bible. Ever the Baptist minister, Small's faith was what led him to sociology. Small's academic preparation also led him to believe that rigorous academic research, in-person direct conversations with the poor and marginalized, along with careful statistical research was what was most needed to alleviate inequality. And it was essential that those pursuing the research be free of both ideological and religious limitations. Under Small, the University of Chicago's sociology department was beginning a very new kind of university research, even if the reason for that research had been inspired by a very traditional religious faith.

Harper made a number of other hires in sociology. One of Harper's last appointments was Alice Freeman Palmer, former president of Wellesley College, to join the sociology department and also serve as dean of women students. Sometime later, Edith Abbott, who had lived at Jane Addams's Hull House and studied the place of women in industry and the state of housing conditions in Chicago, also joined the department. While mostly male, sociology at Chicago had a gender mix that was unusual for any university department until much later.

Harper made other appointments that shaped the approach to sociology at Chicago. Frederick Starr, from the American Museum of Natural History, came to lead work in anthropology. Harper also invited another Baptist minister, Charles R. Henderson, to Chicago. Harper's initial offer to Henderson was to be the university chaplain, which Henderson found intriguing, but only if he could also have an academic appointment. Henderson believed that simply being a college pastor would marginalize him—an issue of concern to generations of chaplains after him—and besides, Henderson believed that Christianity needed a broad intellectual approach and that a minister needed the intellectual foundations that hands-on social science research would give him. As he wrote in 1899, "God has providentially wrought out for us the social sciences and placed them at our disposal." It was as a sociology professor more than as college chaplain that Henderson made his greatest mark.

Harper also recruited Graham Taylor, one of the leading theologians in the Social Gospel movement, to come to the Chicago Theological Seminary—soon the Divinity School of the university—to teach "Christian sociology" in the Divinity School with a cross-appointment in sociology. Taylor also led a major Chicago settlement house, the Chicago Commons, that linked the Social Gospel, the study of sociology, and direct work with some of the poorest citizens of Chicago in one unit. Other professors came and went in the sociology department, and together they created a new academic field close to Harper's heart—inspired by religious faith but free to search for truth and a better society wherever that search took them.

The sociology department had a wide reach. Some faculty gave lectures at Tuskegee Institute and corresponded with Booker T. Washington. They also included African American communities in the Jim Crow–era South and in Chicago in their research and reform efforts, and they recruited some African American students to their own doctoral program. In 1927 the *Who's Who in Colored America* listed thirty-five African American sociologists. Nine of them were Chicago graduates, far more than those from any other school.[80]

The rebirth of the University of Chicago in 1892, along with the earlier foundation of Johns Hopkins University in 1876, constituted the real beginning of the modern research university in the United States. Older schools, including eventually Yale and Harvard and the great public universities like Michigan, Wisconsin, and California and in time many other schools, followed. If the college was the nineteenth-century norm for higher education, the research university was the norm for the twentieth century. It took the creation of new universities such as Johns Hopkins and Chicago to give the research model the opportunity to fully mature, even as others followed.

In looking at the shift from college to university—from teaching the "unity of truth" to the free pursuit of truth wherever it was to be found, universities can be seen as quickly secularizing. But Chicago's founding years also tell a different story. Religion in its Baptist form was the motivating spirit behind the early efforts to make academic research, academic freedom, and community service untrammeled by restraints the key element in what it meant to be part of a community of scholars as a student or a teacher. Understanding that religious motivation—whether at Chicago or very different places like Hampton—adds important complexity to any understanding of the place of religion at the American university at a crucial moment in the history of American higher education.[81]

CHAPTER THREE

Chaplains, Professors, and Their Students, 1905–1925

At the University of Michigan in the spring of 1905, a Presbyterian minister, J. Leslie French, became the first Presbyterian, and one of the first Protestants, to be a full-time college chaplain at a public university in the United States.[1] A little over a year later, as a new academic year began in September 1906, the Archbishop of Milwaukee reassigned Father Henry C. Hengell, an assistant at Madison's Holy Redeemer Church, to be the full-time Catholic chaplain at the University of Wisconsin in Madison. Hengell was the first Catholic chaplain assigned at any public university in the United States.[2] Appointed within eighteen months of each other, French and Hengell were among the early few of what quickly became a growing number of clergy appointed to a new kind of professional position, that of campus minister or chaplain at public universities in the United States.[3]

Chaplains: Protestant and Catholic

For decades, private schools sometimes appointed chaplains, as in the case of Hollis Frissell at Hampton. However, the idea of having full-time clergy assigned to a public campus and paid by their respective denominations to minister to students at state universities was new in 1905–1906.

Appointing clergy to minister on college campuses, whether paid by the school (in the case of some private colleges) or by the sending denominations (nearly always the case at public schools and increasingly common at private ones), represented a new strategy to strengthen religion in American higher education in the twentieth century. Of course, the increasing tendency toward chaplains funded by denominations meant that only those religious bodies with sufficient funding and interest to support a chaplain were represented on campus, since denominational bodies made the decision whether to fund chaplains or not, as well as who to appoint. It was also the case that in the early years of the twentieth century that the culture of campuses, like the culture of the United States, was overwhelmingly Protestant. Individual Protestant bodies—Methodists, Presbyterians, Baptists, and others—nevertheless competed for the allegiance of college students. After 1900, there were also sufficient numbers of Catholic students, though sometimes a besieged minority, for them to demand attention. In these years, the numbers of Jews, Muslims, and Hindus were so small that the thought of a non-Christian chaplain occurred to virtually no one.

There are also quite different ways to view just what the appointment of college chaplains actually meant for the place of religion in the life of the universities. On the one hand, the growing numbers of college chaplains was a continuation of the antebellum assumption that matters of spirituality, morality, and faith should be central to the life of a college. The chaplain, or a team of chaplains representing different Christian groups, was the major representative of religious belief on a college campus.

On the other hand, the very same appointments were a sure sign of the continuing marginalization of religion in college life. Saying "let the chaplain take care of religious concerns" could mean that the president, most of the faculty, and the growing ranks of student service personnel could be free to devote all of their time and attention to other matters even if they could still assure funders that, of course, the school remained religious since there were one or several chaplains. Individual students who sought a faith-based home could find one with the chaplain. And the majority of students, faculty, and administrators could turn their attention elsewhere.

Perhaps college chaplains represented both: a new resilience of religious energy in an institution that was growing less religious, and a way in which a long-term trend toward the marginalization of religion continued. Perhaps they offered a pathway for matters of faith to find a powerful place on the margins, which is often where religious passions thrive.

The First College Chaplains

College enrollment grew by close to 300 percent between 1869 and 1900. While it still accounted for only some 2 percent of the age cohort—mostly male and overwhelmingly White—that 2 percent received an outsized level of attention from society in general and the churches in particular. The new generations of college students also shifted the location of their studies. Where the relatively small, mostly denominationally affiliated college had been the pre–Civil War norm, in the latter decades of the nineteenth century the secular state universities grew much more rapidly than the denominational colleges. By the turn of the twentieth century, they dominated American higher education. It was to serve the students at the growing public universities that a new form of ministry was born, that of college chaplain at a state school.

J. Leslie French was formally appointed as student pastor at the University of Michigan by the Presbyterian Synod of Michigan on March 20, 1905. The title "student pastor" in this case meant ordained pastor to students, not a student-held position. Initially, a variety of terms were used for chaplains until in 1910 a group of them agreed to use the term "university pastor" and later "chaplain."[4] This specific position was different from any ministerial assignment authorized by the Presbyterian church in the past. French was not to be part of the staff of a specific church nor a missionary nor a denominational official. He was the full-time, church-funded minister serving students at the University of Michigan. With French's well-publicized appointment, a new form of the leadership of religious life in American universities and a new kind of professional work for American clergy began to emerge.[5]

Looking back a quarter century later, French wrote of the growing sense among many pastors and denominational leaders that the nineteenth-century forms of campus religious leadership—the YMCA and YWCA, voluntary extracurricular work by faculty, denominational guilds, or outreach work by local churches—were not sufficient. He said, "The feeling seemed to grow that if churches put full-time men of ecclesiastical standing and adequate academic preparation at the various [university] centers solutions of the problems would be worked out first hand."[6]

French clearly met his own criteria for the assignment. He held a baccalaureate and master's degree from the University of Michigan with majors in Hebrew, philosophy, and ethics and a Bachelor of Divinity graduate degree—from Hartford Theological Seminary. He had spent two years studying in Europe at the University of Berlin, the Sorbonne, and the University of Marburg, and received a PhD in church history just at the time of his appointment. He had already been ordained to the ministry. French entered his new role well positioned to win the respect of both church and university authorities. As generally expected of a Protestant pastor, French was married. He had met and married Edna Cumming, who had previously taught history at the Port Huron, Michigan High School. She left her teaching career and became an unpaid assistant to the chaplain.[7]

The university offered French an appointment in the Department of Semitics teaching courses in Greek and English Bible. Some of French's successor chaplains would have similar academic appointments. Others were not offered academic positions or chose to keep a bit more distance even if the appointment was offered. The local Presbyterian pastor promised to back French to the limit. A well-organized Christian Endeavor Society—one of the early twentieth century's major ecumenical student movements—provided an initial constituency. Perhaps most importantly, the student-led but church-sponsored guild, the Tappan Association, had been active at Michigan since the 1890s and had its own buildings, although French did complain about a lack of funds to properly run the building. French was thus provided with a ready-made Presbyterian student group, a home contiguous to the campus, and an office in a building belonging to the Presbyterian Church but very close to the campus and already known to several generations of students as a welcoming gathering place. With his new full-time appointment, French had the opportunity to design a new kind of ministerial job.

French quickly conducted a census to find out how many Presbyterian students were at the University of Michigan. He found 768 Presbyterian students, of whom 122 were enrolled in his Bible and Mission classes, 200 were active in Christian Endeavor, and 65 held affiliate membership in local churches. Despite the competition, he built ties with the YMCA's Student Volunteer group. He also organized and taught Bible classes, and his wife taught a Bible class for nearly thirty nurses at the University Hospital. French made it a point to meet a number of local pastors, as well as students and graduates of the university. He loved his one-on-one meetings counseling and getting to know students.[8]

On one occasion French described what he considered the most important element in his ministry—one that many generations of future college chaplains would recognize. Because of the house that came with his job, he was able to provide "home life and a home atmosphere for students" in the chaplain's house. He described "a scene in the home that has been furnished us; the dining room with the table shoved back in the corner with a sheet and a lot of sofa cushions spread along the floor, and a body of young men and women sitting around before an open grate fire, coming into closer fellowship and relationship . . . than they can in any other way." French explained that he held such dinners almost every Friday or Saturday night throughout the university year for eighteen to twenty-five students at a time. "It dignifies the whole relationship of the pastor in the university to have a manse of that kind," he insisted.[9]

French continued his work until the fall of 1913, when he took a full-time appointment in the Michigan's Semitics department and following that a stint as a local pastor in Ohio. After French resigned, Michigan Presbyterians appointed Rev. Roy Hamilton as chaplain at Ann Arbor. French later returned to his first love, campus ministry, and served as the Presbyterian chaplain at the University of West Virginia, 1925 to 1935.[10]

While Henry C. Hengell's formal appointment as the first Catholic chaplain at a non-Catholic university came after French's, Hengell actually began working with students at the University of Wisconsin earlier than French and seems to have lobbied for the position of full-time chaplain. Informal religious support for Catholic students at Madison began when the so-called Melvin Club first met in 1883. By 1903, however, new generations of Catholic students wanted something more than a social club and asked for help from the curate (assistant priest) at the local Holy Redeemer (Catholic) Church. Father Hengell, who was in his mid-twenties at the time, had recently returned from study in Europe and ordination there. He had grown up in nearby Waukesha, Wisconsin. He was young and worldly enough to relate well to the Madison students and enthusiastically agreed to teach informal classes for the college students based on his belief that religion was "not an emotion or sentiment . . . but a postulate of the intellect." Hengell's classes, offered at Holy Redeemer, were very popular and soon he was teaching Bible and Christian doctrine to large groups.[11]

Father Hengell, along with some of the students and their supporters, among both alumni and the Catholic hierarchy, wanted more. Like French, Hengell conducted a census and found that there were some 300 Catholics out of the 2,600 students at the university. Working closely with his religious superior, Archbishop Sebastian Messmer of Milwaukee, Hengell organized a student petition to the archdiocese to authorize "the organization of a Catholic Students' Association, the appointment of a Chaplain, and the eventual erection of a suitably located chapel." Messmer, who liked Hengell and knew the petition was coming, responded quickly. The petition was sent in January 1906 and in February the Archbishop visited the university and promised to act positively. He reassigned Hengell from Holy Redeemer parish to be full-time Catholic chaplain at the University of Wisconsin, with instructions to establish "a Catholic college attached by the Church to the University of Wisconsin." Just what the bishop meant by a Catholic college has been debated, but Hengell took it as a charge to raise funds for a chapel and multipurpose building, and direct religious programs on campus with a firm hand. He did not seek, or much care, about any sort of official recognition from the university.[12]

Six years after he started, Hengell reflected on his appointment to serve the Catholic students at the University of Wisconsin. He noted that rather than a special parish or a college, the bishop created a special corporation called St. Paul's Chapel to serve the students. Hengell quoted Archbishop Messmer:

> St. Paul's University Chapel is a religious and educational corporation . . . to be an agent in the hands of the Church to preserve and fortify the faith in the Catholic student of the University of Wisconsin. . . . It supports a chaplain who conducts regular and special religious services, supervises the religious instruction of the students, and promotes their closer social intercourse. . . . In short, this corporation may be regarded as a Catholic "college" attached by the Church to the University of Wisconsin.[13]

In his early years as chaplain, Hengell established himself as a presence on the Madison campus through his outreach, his personal connections to many students, and his leadership in the construction of St. Paul's Chapel near the heart of the campus.

Hengell and Messmer were not alone in their enthusiasm for a Catholic campus ministry at a public university like Wisconsin. In 1905, Pope Pius X issued an encyclical, "On Christian Education," in which the Pope commanded church leaders to set up "scholae religionis" to teach the Catholic faith to students who attended "public schools from which all religious teaching" was banned. While there was some debate about the specific meaning of "scholae religionis," Hengell and Messmer defined the term to mean a command from the Pope to do what they already wanted to do: establish a Catholic center (they were happy to call the center a "college" if that fit the pope's language) at the major public university in their state.[14]

In 1907, the University of Wisconsin's distinguished—and non-Catholic—president, Charles Van Hise, issued a public letter about his concern for the lack of attention to the moral dimension of a college degree. He urged each denomination to create a position for a student pastor and provide an adequate building to strengthen the religious ties that students brought with them when they came to Madison. It is likely that Van Hise was aware of Hengell's appointment at Madison and French's at Michigan and was urging other religious bodies to follow their example (on their

Figure 3.1. Soon after the first Catholic chaplain at a state university was appointed in 1906, St. Paul's Chapel was built to serve as a base for the new Catholic chaplain and as a center for Catholic students at the University of Wisconsin, in Madison. Photo, St. Paul's 1915, Meuer Photoart Collection, courtesy of the UW-Madison Archives

budgets). The university president, like the Pope, was now telling Hengell and Messmer what they wanted to hear.[15]

Finally, lay Catholics, many of them alumni of the university, enthusiastically backed the idea of St. Paul's Chapel and raised the funds to build an impressive building that was dedicated in 1910. Some thirty alumni agreed to sit on the board of the corporation, and many more contributed the sums that were needed to finance the enterprise.

Hengell stayed at his post in Madison for thirty years. He was cautious about engaging with the Protestant chaplains who soon arrived and was ever ready to critique faculty who he thought were anti-Catholic. Hengell created what he called "truth squads" of students who showed him their lecture notes, which he would then quote in well-publicized sermons the following week—sermons that attacked some well-respected faculty like Max Otto and E. A. Ross by name. He saw his role as preaching to "warn against philosophical errors" and to "instruct in the faith."

The Wisconsin chaplain was warmer with students than with ministerial colleagues or faculty, enjoying one-on-one conversations with many. Hengell described the students as mostly "fair, decent, and straightforward (outside of fraternity rush) . . . inclined to help their fellows who are in trouble . . . earnest workers to whom the making of a life is more than the making of a living." He was consistently disappointed that so few faculty seemed "able and willing to help students to cultivate these previous moral and spiritual instincts." The priest's sister, Margaret Hengell, supported him as both housekeeper at St. Paul's, sacristan in the chapel, and counselor to many students who called her their "den mother," from 1907 until 1929.[16]

By the 1920s, Hengell moderated some of his tendency to battle with faculty, writing that "the great majority of instructors are competently teaching what they are hired to teach." Nevertheless, when Hengell died in 1937, Messmer's successor, Archbishop Samuel Stritch, said at his funeral that the long-time chaplain "defended the Church on every possible occasion, sometimes in very strong words," while his faith was "so bright that he could not actually understand the position of others." It was an interesting way to sum up a thirty-year ministry.[17]

The appointment of the first Protestant and first Catholic chaplain in such close proximity in time and location was not the result of the kind of generous ecumenical cooperation that appeared later in chaplaincy. On the contrary, the rivalry was on full display. References in the publications that appeared at the time, as well as private correspondence, make it clear that each was keeping a wary eye on the other and acting accordingly. In advocating the appointment of Presbyterian college chaplains, a 1903 committee of the Presbyterians warned that the church would fall behind since "the Roman Catholic Church is using this plan with considerable success."[18] The president of the University of Iowa, who was an active Protestant, wrote to Joseph Cochran, of the Presbyterian Board of Education, insisting that, "It would be well for our church not to delay in these matters, for even the Roman Catholics are preceding us, and wisely, in the care for the students."[19] On the other hand, a Jesuit priest who was vice president of the Catholic St. Ignatius College proposed creating Catholic chapels with assigned priests at secular campuses to ensure that Catholic "students in state schools [did not] drift away from the practice of their religion."[20]

In spite of the theological differences, French and Hengell seem to have represented some quite similar concerns and patterns in their life work. Both assumed that students at non-religiously connected state universities needed spiritual attention at a time when many church leaders—Catholic and Protestant—urged all faithful adherents to attend only religiously affiliated schools. They understood, as some of their co-religionists did not, that no matter what the urging, many young people were bound for state schools. Both men, and their sponsors, also assumed that a full-time ordained clergyman was essential to college ministry, and that student-led or lay-led organizations had run their course and were in danger of running counter to an effort to build orthodox thinking and life-long loyalty to their faith community. These first chaplains, and the colleagues who soon joined them, were appointed to strengthen institutional churches and the loyalty of college graduates to specific churches. Concern for the spiritual welfare of students existed but seemed a bit secondary.

As was the norm in 1905–1906, the early chaplains and those who hired them—Protestant as much as Catholic—assumed that clergy meant men. Both Hengell and French had the unpaid assistance of a woman—French's wife, Edna, who taught classes and helped host the student dinners, and Hengell's sister, Margaret, who served as the warm "den mother" to students at Wisconsin. On the other hand, some of the critique of the YMCA and YWCA seems to have been a not-very-subtle complaint that too many Y campus secretaries were women. Too often the chaplains and their supports in national religious organizations assumed that only men were qualified for the work of sustaining religious interest among college students.

College Chaplaincy Grows—Quickly

Soon after French and Hengell began their work, they found themselves with many compatriots and rivals. There were soon Catholic chaplains at Michigan, Protestant chaplains at Wisconsin, and several chaplains at other state schools. The University of Michigan was often the model of this early work. College chaplaincy blossomed there. As early as 1907, there were four chaplains representing different religious bodies on the campus. Looking back in 1930, Leslie French remembered:

> The writer was called as the first Presbyterian student pastor in the denomination in the spring of 1905. There are now [1930] about fifty men of this church alone with the title of "university pastor." From 1905 to 1910 the university-pastor idea swept all of the major denominations. In the fall of 1905 University of Kansas had two men in the field. Before the close of 1909 Illinois, Wisconsin, Colo-

rado, Nebraska, Minnesota, and practically all of the great western state univer-sities had groups of three to five men working on the student problem.

The Protestant clergymen French described were joined by a lone lay woman, L. A. Davis, who was appointed at the University of Arkansas.[21]

In his major 1938 work on college chaplaincy, *The Church Follows Its Students*, Clarence Shedd offered more detail on the emergence of university chaplaincy. In his opening chapter, "Exploring a New Trail," Shedd called chaplaincy—by what-ever name it was known on different campuses—the new trail, one that was slowly replacing the nineteenth century's Y and guild movements. Leading up to French's appointment, the Presbyterian General Assembly—the national governing body of the denomination—adopted resolutions in 1904 and 1905 in support of "special ministers who shall reside in and care for Presbyterian students in the state univer-sities, very much after the pattern of army and navy chaplains."

Shedd noted that after French, a Presbyterian chaplain, Reverend Martin E. An-derson, was appointed at the University of Illinois in 1908. (Anderson once referred to two predecessors though their names and dates of service are not recorded.) In any case, Anderson stayed at Illinois for thirteen years. Reverend Dean Richmond Leland, who was appointed at the University of Nebraska, stayed until 1934. A num-ber of other Presbyterian ministers began serving other campuses.[22]

The Congregational Christian Churches (now the United Church of Christ) began discussion about how to support their estimated 500 students at the Univer-sity of Michigan in 1902 but were slow to act. The first recorded full-time Congre-gational college chaplain, Richard H. Edwards, was appointed at the University of Wisconsin in 1906, fresh from his service as a YMCA secretary at Yale. He stayed at Wisconsin until 1912 and later moved to a similar role at Cornell. The Michigan and Wisconsin Baptists were no less active in supporting college chaplains, with Allen Hoben briefly in charge of Baptist ministry at Michigan in 1904, even before French's formal appointment, and Warren P. Behan following him in 1905. Hoben and Behan were succeeded by a number of other Baptist ministers in Madison, and Baptists were also appointed at Wisconsin, beginning with C. J. Galpin in 1905. Other Protestant bodies quickly followed suit.[23]

While Hengell was the first full-time Roman Catholic chaplain at a non-Catholic institution of higher education, he soon had several Catholic colleagues. In 1914, the Paulist priest Father John Elliot Ross was appointed full-time chaplain at the University of Texas, where he served until 1923 before moving on to New York's Columbia University from 1923 to 1929. A year after Ross's appointment, in 1915

John W. Keogh was appointed chaplain at the University of Pennsylvania and served until 1938 while also serving as "Chaplain General" to the Federation of College Catholic Clubs from 1917 to 1938. In 1918, John A. O'Brien became the Catholic chaplain at the University of Illinois, serving until 1939. There had been earlier part-time Catholic clergy on private, secular college campuses, including John J. Farrell, appointed by Archbishop John J. Williams of Boston to serve the Harvard Catholic Club in 1899, but Farrell kept a low profile to avoid offending the leadership of nearby Jesuit Boston College and Harvard was not his primary appointment.

The new full-time priests were an important presence on campus. Some like Hengell at Wisconsin and Keogh at Pennsylvania avoided ecumenical activities and focused on maintaining the orthodoxy and loyalty of Catholic students in what they saw as a hostile atmosphere. Indeed, Keogh's successor in Philadelphia wrote that Keogh "had a chip on his shoulder every time he went on campus."

On the other hand, Ross and O'Brien were much more welcoming of diversity in their ministries at Texas and Illinois. Ross loved the University of Texas and saw himself as priest to the "future legislators and lawyers and bankers and governors and congressmen" of Texas even if the Catholic colleges prepared future priests and bishops. He also worked with non-Catholics to help end their prejudice toward his faith. Ross joined an association of religion teachers at Texas and taught classes in ethics, Bible, and psychology of religion, leading a friend to write that because of Ross some faculty who had been anti-Catholic decided that "there were Catholic scholars in the scientific world who must be consulted." O'Brien also took his academic role seriously. Like Ross, he worked with Protestant chaplains at Illinois to set up courses approved for credit while arguing that "an open minded quest for truth, such as the university promotes, is ideal for sowing the seeds of Christianity."[24]

Chaplaincy Has Its Critics and Defenders

The creation of the profession of college chaplain was not met with universal praise— far from it. Opposition to the appointment of chaplains at state schools was most widespread among denominational college presidents. For religiously affiliated colleges, sending clergy to support the spiritual life of students in secular schools was a huge threat. If religious schools recruited students based on their promise that they offered a college education in a safely supportive religious atmosphere, what would happen to their recruiting efforts if students and their parents saw a similar atmosphere developing at larger secular schools that could generally offer more academic options and a lower price? Religious colleges also generally received financial support from their parent religious bodies. If those parent bodies started supporting college chaplains at secular schools, where would this money come from if not the same budgets?

As we will see, many Catholic college leaders feared "the alarming number of Catholic youth going to non-Catholic colleges," and perhaps even more the "encouragement lent that movement by the hierarchy by the appointment of chaplains." In the earliest years, the stand-off could be tense. (For a detailed case study of Catholic opposition to the appointment of chaplains at non-Catholic schools, see discussion of Georgetown below.)[25]

The hostility to chaplains at secular institutions was also strong in Protestant colleges. In 1904, the national moderator of the Presbyterian church noted that while "looking after students in extra denomination institutions" was important, "it was also "a way to take the edge off the argument in behalf of our denominational colleges." Joseph W. Cochran, perhaps the most vocal Presbyterian leader to support college chaplains, acknowledged that "it must be admitted that whatever antagonism to this work is being encountered finds its home in the denominational college." But Cochran, as much as he wanted to see a Presbyterian chaplain in every secular college in the land, expressed some sympathy with the denominational college opponents: "It is scarcely to be wondered at when distinguished educators boldly prophesy that the university has rung the death knell of the Church college. . . . One can hardly blame the underpaid and struggling but consecrated teachers of our Church colleges for uttering protests against threats of extermination."[26] But such sympathy did not dissuade Cochran from his whole-hearted advocacy of appointing ministers to work at state universities. Leslie French remembered his experience around the same time, writing that "when the writer began as a university pastor he was roundly denounced over the state by the college executives." By 1930, French thought the opposition from the church colleges had abated but not all his colleagues agreed with that happy assessment.[27]

Another challenge to the appointment of denominational clergy to work on campuses came from the lay-led and pan-Protestant Ys. In February 1910, John R. Mott, the revered YMCA leader and general secretary of the World Student Christian Federation, spoke to a conference of college chaplains held in Madison, Wisconsin. Mott named two players he thought were essential to meeting the religious needs of students. First, he argued, there was his YMCA and YWCA, which Mott called "the one great comprehensive voluntary, Christian society in the university" that was in the best position of any "to carry forward this work of coordination." Since the Y made no claim to be a church, it could coordinate religious life on campus especially well, owing to "the voluntary principle of student initiative." Secondly,

Mott saw a key role for the local churches in a university town. Local churches needed "the ablest ministers of the different communions [who] should be stationed in the state university towns." With such ministers, churches could combat the danger that "students will lose their moorings with reference to the church." Mott also briefly noted the important work of student-led denominational guilds, attention from denominational leaders and agencies, and the "unofficial influence of professors."[28] Pointedly, Mott did not mention a role for college chaplains.

When R. H. Edwards, the Congregational chaplain at Madison, asked Mott directly if he thought university pastors should reside in or close to guild houses, Mott responded bluntly, "Oh no: I am not an enthusiast on that point." Mott's chaplain-dominated audience seems to have responded politely but with equal bluntness. Cochran, long a critic of the YMCA, reminded the audience that "it isn't necessary for us to be so ashamed of it as to hide our denominational service, under an interdenominational work." I. C. Batman from the University of Indiana added that while the YMCA and YWCA "have done much efficient work," the Y was not the church and therefore could not "bind the young men and young women close to the church, not to some separate organization away from the church." Michigan's Leslie French added that "if it is the function of the association to feed the churches," he knew of no single example where the Y had actually led a student to join a church in Michigan.

Mott stood his ground, insisting that in the past year over 4,000 Y member students had joined local churches. (It is unclear where either French or Mott got their statistics.) Mott also restated his main point. "It is clear," he insisted, "that there is a need of a comprehensive interdenominational exponent of our varied Christianity in each state university," and that the Y was the perfect institution to do that. On the other hand, he agreed that there "is likewise a work denominational," but he was adamant "that should be related to the church in its organized local expression." For Mott, if the campus Y did its job and the local parish churches near a campus did their jobs, chaplains or university pastors were unnecessary and unhelpful. Nevertheless, even in these early years, the representatives of the budding chaplaincy movement were ready to stand their ground against perhaps the most respected Protestant religious leader in the United States.[29]

Mott was not alone in believing that rather than create the new kind of position of college chaplain, the major religious bodies should strengthen the local churches in college towns to take the lead in student work. The Episcopal church structure meant that in reality each bishop was free to proceed as he wanted with the colleges in his—always *his* for most of the next century—diocese. Episcopal chaplains did appear at state universities in Michigan, Minnesota, and Texas. But fairly soon, the bishops, and thus the denomination, coalesced around a different policy—one aimed at keeping the Episcopal parish churches near college campuses at the center of the work.

Evan Alexander Edwards, rector (senior minister) of Trinity (Episcopal) Church in, Lawrence, Kansas, home of the University of Kansas, described the Episcopal policy:

> Let the rector, then, take the place of the student-pastor. Give him an assistant if necessary, to relieve him from the details that take his time and strength. . . . Find a priest whose scholarship commands the respect of the faculty and whose humanity commands the friendship of the students.[30]

Edwards argued that the senior minister of the Episcopal church nearest the campus was to take the lead, rather than having a special assistant for college work. If the rector was not someone whose scholarly side would be respected by faculty or did not have the personality to work with students, then the church needed to find another rector rather than let the incumbent delegate the college work. As the church's official organ, *The Churchman*, editorialized in 1906, the "Church will see to it that the incumbency of the local parish is not left to chance, but that a policy of prudent subsidizing the denomination shall provide these pulpits with strong men who know the truth and are made free thereby, and who understand the needs and aspirations and perplexities of youth."[31]

Some other Protestant bodies also moved slowly in appointing chaplains. Lutherans, who were divided into several different groups, partly by language or nationality and partly by theology, went in different directions among themselves. For some, the Episcopal approach was the right one and they favored strengthening the Lutheran parishes near public colleges. The Disciples of Christ continued creating Bible chairs for ministers who could be part of the teaching staff of state schools. For the Disciples, the key to serving college students well was a teaching position, even if over time those holding Bible chairs took on more and more of the chaplain-like duties of nurturing the college students of their denomination.[32]

At the same meeting of chaplains at which John R. Mott was so roundly criticized, Wisconsin's president, Charles R. Van Hise, received a much warmer response. To Van Hise, the appointment of denominationally funded chaplains to work on his campus and those of similar state universities was a perfect solution to a problem that deeply worried him. He did not want to see the university he led spoken of "as a Godless—as an unreligious institution." This mattered to Van Hise not only because of public perception of his school, but because he felt that the moral and, indeed, spiritual development of students was as important as any other part of their education. On the other hand, Wisconsin law was clear and far stricter than the federal constitution. There could be no religious or partisan instruction, including Bible reading, in the public schools and universities of the state. For Van Hise, the solution was obvious. Let the different churches appoint whom they wanted to be pastors to students at the university, therefore "having each church look out for its own, each group of students . . . being looked out for by those who are in sympathy with their ideas, usages, faith, and hope." The result was that in addition to its Catholic chaplain, by 1910 Wisconsin had Baptist, Congregational, Methodist, and Presbyterian chaplains.[33]

Many public college presidents agreed with Van Hise, yet some went further. In 1909, Cyrus Northrup, president of the University of Minnesota, wrote that state schools "cannot teach the superiority of Catholicism or Protestantism," and needed to respect the beliefs of Jews. He also added, "But how about the agnostic or the Atheist. They are so few and so at variance with the universal religious sense of mankind that they may properly be ignored in this matter and may be treated as a negligible quantity." There were limits, it seemed, to Northrup's definition of diversity. At the same time, George E. McLean, president of the University of Iowa, defended not only chaplains but courses in religion and even required chapel— though he preferred to see it be voluntary. But he dismissed the constitutional concerns, "though sometimes challenged by extreme secularists," and insisted that colleges "are Christian in the common law sense of the term." McLean believed that the core values of American higher education were Christian.[34] Faculty, like the general public in most states, were still overwhelmingly Protestant, even if by the twentieth century more than a few of the professors were only vaguely attached to their faith. Policies that clearly would not be acceptable in American higher education a century on, and may have been in violation of the state constitutions then, were nevertheless easily accepted by the vast majority of legislators at the time even if others wanted a stricter wall of separation.

In spite of this criticism and sometimes outright hostility, the movement toward ordained Christian clergy appointed as full-time ministers on college campuses grew quickly after its start in 1905–1906. While the new college chaplains were very much denomination specific, with a few exceptions they were usually quick to begin to work together, as they were all inventing a new profession and wanted to learn from how each other was doing it. As Leslie French remembered, "As soon as two or three church workers arrived on the campus, they began to plan together to do the things that could best be done in common. In 1908 there was a University Pastors Association of five men at Wisconsin. At Michigan in 1907 four men were grouped together, and so it was everywhere."[35]

Chaplaincy Gains Momentum

As early as 1908, the Protestant chaplains from different campuses—mostly state universities in the Midwest—began meeting along with others who were concerned with religious life on campus to share ideas and encouragement. At their third meeting in 1910, there were seven recognizable chaplains among the sixty-two people in attendance representing the universities of Wisconsin, Illinois, Michigan, Nebraska, and Kansas. There were also representatives of the YMCA and YWCA, local pastors in college towns, university faculty members, seminary faculty, and state and national denominational leaders. While all those in attendance seem to have been Protestant, Father Hengell, the University of Wisconsin's Catholic chaplain, was said to be a member of the planning committee. As far as names can indicate, sixty of the sixty-two attendees were men who were joined by two women— Mary Rolfe and Theresa Wilbur—both YWCA field secretaries. A decade and a half later, in 1923, the organization of "Church Workers in State Universities," changed its name to "Conference of Church Workers in Universities and Colleges" to include clergy at private but secular schools. Also in the 1920s, Catholic and by then also Jewish religious leaders began to be part of campus-based and national planning organizations. By 1930, the redoubtable Leslie French was praising, "The development of close relations between Catholic, Jewish, and Protestant groups on the campus [as having] spiritual values, making possible larger plans for religious education." French also noted—briefly—that the "work among university women is receiving increased attention."[36]

By 1913, Joseph Cochran described the success of the movement to appoint college chaplains that he had long championed. Cochran insisted that "the results speak for themselves. . . . Wherever a vital man of God, who understands student life and makes allowance for youthful effervescence of spirits is at work among them, he will harvest rich fruitage for his labor."[37]

By the middle of the 1920s, the denominational-based and usually ordained campus ministers had successfully challenged, and in most places superseded, the YMCA/YWCA chapters as the primary leader of student religious life. Ordained ministers serving on college campuses had become the center of campus religious life in most places and, with surges and dips, would retain that position for at least the next half century.[38]

A Changing Academic Study of Religion

A quite different engagement with religion was found on many campuses in the academic study of religion. Prior to his untimely death in 1906, the University of Chicago's indefatigable president William Rainey Harper had been a leader in advocating religious studies courses. For Harper, these courses were explicitly devotional and undertaken "with a single thought in mind, to enable students to know God in his dealings with man." (See the case study of the University of Chicago in chapter 2.) But other religious studies advocates insisted on an iron curtain separating the study of religion from the practice of religion.

Harper, a devout Baptist and an academic with the most rigorous standards, was also the driving force behind the creation of the Religious Education Association (REA) in 1903. For Harper and most of the REA's early leaders, religious education was not expected to take place only in church-based Sunday schools for children—as important as they were to Harper. Religion was also to take its place as an essential part of the undergraduate curriculum in research universities. Many of those who taught religious studies courses disagreed with Harper from the beginning, however, and wanted their work to be seen as academic and disinterested. To accomplish this goal, these scholars believed, religious studies had to be as free of doctrinal or devotional content as possible.

A 1915 article in the journal *Religious Education* Laura H. Wild, a professor of biblical literature and history at Lake Erie College in Ohio, argued that "the very fact of curriculum courses being coupled up with religious agencies" undermined the academic standing of a religious studies program.[39] This clearly meant keeping a strict distance from chaplains, among others. By 1915 this view among those teaching in the field represented the dominant view and has led to distance and wariness between religious studies faculty and chaplains (and others who represent religious life on campuses) that has persisted for a century. If religious studies were to take its place among other academic disciplines, the thinking went, it had to be on the same terms as other research-oriented disciplines and not with any inspirational note.

Others, especially among the college presidents who led the REA, wanted something a bit more inspirational if still free of the doctrines of individual denominations. Thus, at the 1904 meeting of the REA, Richard Jesse, president of the University of Missouri, argued that encouraging chapel attendance, prohibiting drinking and smoking, and offering courses in religion were all parts of a university's responsibility to the religious and moral education of its students. As Jesse said, all of these rules and courses were "to lift students to higher life socially and religiously."

If the old moral philosophy course taught by the president had disappeared from the twentieth-century university, people like Jesse believed that higher education institutions, including public state universities, should still make "ample provision" for the moral development of their students in religion courses, as well as extracurricular programs.

In 1922, Yale professor Charles Foster Kent, who had been a student of Harper's, created the National Council on Religion in Higher Education (NCRHE). A key part of NCRHE's role was ensuring that a few universities created doctoral programs in religion whose graduates could staff religious studies courses, even as the organization advocated for more and more such courses. The University of Michigan and the University of Iowa went so far as to create schools of religion that would offer a series of connected courses, some for college credit, that would foster a much greater understanding of religion for college students.

What few advocates of the study of religion noticed at the time was how deeply Protestant their approach to the academic study of religion was. Just at a moment when the United States was becoming much more diverse, with many more Catholics, Jews, and assorted adherents of other traditions or also those adhering to none, they were harkening back to a nineteenth-century uniformity that had in fact disappeared. While the 1920s schools of religion were short lived, attention to religion continued even as its presence grew and ebbed through the late 1920s and the 1930s. It was only after World War II that a new clarity emerged in the field of religious studies even as new debates appeared at the same time.[40]

However celebratory Cochran and many of the chaplains, Catholic and Protestant—or those sponsoring religious studies courses—might have been about their work, it cannot be argued that either chaplaincies or the academic study of religion were central to the life of the nation's growing colleges and universities by the 1920s. An alternative view of the place of chaplains and religion professors after World War I would place them, like the grand new chapels appearing on some college campuses in the 1920s, as a nod to faith in an institution increasingly uninterested in faith. A student of religious life in American higher education might see religion scholars, like chaplains, at the center of the story of the early decades of the twentieth century. Many a student or professor of the time probably would not have said the same thing. The future pointed much more to new life on the margins.

The so-called Roaring Twenties were not an auspicious decade for any religious activity on American campuses. Many in the post–World War I student generation challenged old moral codes. Religion and religious commitments were not welcome in much of what considered itself sophisticated society, on campus or off, in the

1920s. While there were many serious students—religious or not—on college campuses in the first decades of the twentieth century, there were also many, then and later, who saw college as a four-year party of football games, booze, and sex. F. Scott Fitzgerald's 1920 novel, *This Side of Paradise*, portrays a fictional Amory Blaine, a Princeton student whose college experiences mirrored that of the real-life Fitzgerald. While snobbery and hedonism were part of college life for them, religion or much of any kind of idealism was not. At the end of Fitzgerald's novel, the fictional Amory Blaine looks back on what his college and World War I experiences had taught him, saying that his was "a new generation dedicated more than the last to the fear of poverty and the worship of success; grown up to find all Gods dead, all wars fought, all faiths in man shaken." It was a long way from the optimism of the century's first decades when evangelism was still alive among many students, participation in student religious life was strong, and working to build a better society gave them a sense of purpose.[41]

Not every student of the early 1920s shared Fitzgerald's cynicism. Chaplains continued their work. College chapels were far from empty, religious studies classes had modest enrollments, and the hope for a better tomorrow in this world still captured the imagination of many in church and college. But the earlier breadth of consensus was missing.

There were also many from working-class and immigrant worlds who were now attending colleges as the first generation of their families to do so, and their world was not the often upper-middle-class hedonistic image of a 1920s described by Fitzgerald. These students were more often found at state universities and state normal schools than at Princeton or its compatriot colleges. They often worked part-time or full-time to support their college expenses. Between jobs, studies, and often families, they had little time left for parties or cynicism. But if decades, and student generations, have names and themes, religion would not be considered a significant theme for the generation that attended college during or immediately after World War I. As we will see in the next chapters, it was two decades later after another world war that religion made a dramatic comeback in the lives of large numbers of Americans, including many college students.

Religious Life at a Public Research University: The University of Michigan

The University of Michigan traces its roots to a preparatory school founded in Detroit, Michigan Territory, in 1817. When Michigan was admitted as a state in 1837, the struggling school moved to a much larger campus and was reorganized in 1850.

The new board of regents selected Henry P. Tappan as its first president. Tappan, who served from 1852 to 1863, was an early adopter of some of the elements that later became the core of the research university ideal. He embraced student choice and believed the university should "make it possible for every student to study what he pleases and to any extent he pleases." He believed that the University of Michigan could become as great and as distinguished an institution as those he had observed in Europe. For Tappan, the European universities were the models that he wanted to recreate on the prairies of the Midwest. Tappan answered his own question about what made a university: It was an "association of eminent scholars in every department of human knowledge; together with books . . . all the means of advancing and illustrating knowledge." The books would help pass on the knowledge of the past, but the research of the scholars would create the new knowledge that was at the heart of the university's true mission.[42]

Tappan saw a significant place of religion in a state university. He opposed denominational influence and sought a broadly shared Christian culture without any institutional influence from churches. Tappan broadened the university's religion to include Catholics, Unitarians, and Universalists. But he also believed, "We are all Christians, we are all American citizens. Whatever may be our differences, we have a common agreement." For Tappan, that common agreement meant maintaining a Christian culture at the university while insisting on freedom from any specific ecclesiastical or denominational control. He also thought that it was appropriate for the university to enforce a Christian moral code, to lend support to the YMCA, and to encourage daily attendance at prayers (often led by Tappan) and church attendance on Sunday at an Ann Arbor church of the student's choice.

On the other hand, Tappan drew the line at anything that smacked of direct church influence on the university. When Tappan arrived, he discovered that there was an informal agreement that certain denominations "owned" certain professorial appointments in the school. He quickly ended that practice and insisted the only true criterion for hiring a professor was expertise in their field of study. He insisted on total academic freedom for his faculty, with no religious or political test. "Knowledge," Tappan said, "can flourish only in the air of freedom." Protecting that freedom was the highest good for Tappan even if that freedom led faculty to clash with Tappan's personal religious views. In spite of—or on some issues because of—his grand hopes for what the University of Michigan could become, Tappan was fired by the regents when his personality led to clashes with the board, but most of his policies survived him.[43]

One policy that did not long survive Tappan was Michigan's status as a single-sex school. Throughout his tenure Tappan argued that since only men voted and exercised that "sovereign power," the University of Michigan should only educate men. A few African American men had attended Michigan from Tappan's earliest years, but no women. Just after Tappan left, the university engaged in a tense debate about admitting women to its student body; in 1870 the faculty, perhaps reluctantly, voted to admit women. A year later James B. Angell became president and fully implemented the new policy.[44]

Angell was Tappan's most prominent successor. He led Michigan for thirty-eight years, from 1871 to 1909. Angell's presidency was a time of challenge for the generic Christianity that Tappan espoused. The "Baby Blaine" amendments, with their strict definition of the separation of church and state, were adopted by more than two-thirds of the states—including Michigan—in the 1870s and 1880s. Darwin's views of evolution became prominent in intellectual circles in the United States during the 1890s. Thus, Angell inherited a very different cultural context than the one Tappan experienced only a few years earlier. Michigan now included men and women, and students of different races and religions; and no religion. The genial and generalized Christianity of an earlier era could not continue. Yet Angell, more than many turn-of-the-twentieth-century college presidents, was unapologetic about his own Christian piety.

In April 1890, midway through his long and successful tenure as Michigan's president, Angell published an article in the *Andover Review*, then the leading journal of liberal Protestantism, titled "Religious Life in Our State Universities." Angell wrote that he was responding to a concern from leaders of denominational colleges and some parents, that allowing a student to attend a state university meant "exposing him to the danger of losing Christian character." Angell insisted that such fears were a "misapprehension" of the nature of the university. While he understood that since "we have so complete a separation of church and state, it was assumed by many that a college supported by a state must be devoid of the religious spirit," if not actually a "godless institution." Angell wanted to make it abundantly clear with statistics and examples that this was not at all the case.[45]

Angell explained the reasons for his assertion. Nationally, he noted, that of twenty-four state schools, twenty-two held daily chapel services and attendance was required at twelve of them, even though in his opinion voluntary attendance was preferable to compulsion. He also noted by his own best guess that 71 percent of the faculty of these institutions were church members in good standing.

Turning to the University of Michigan, the place he knew best, Angell reviewed the many religious opportunities open to students. Michigan was one of the first universities to have an active YMCA branch that held Bible study and lectures, including a recent series of lectures by the Protestant revivalist Dwight L. Moody. There were student associations for future ministers and missionaries and many alumni who were active in both fields, especially missionaries to China. There were also denominational organizations based in local churches or on campus. He reminded potential critics:

> These are guilds, provided each with a fine building, which may be called a sort of religious home or club-house, if that term is understood in an elevated sense. The Episcopalians and the Presbyterians have each such a building. The Methodists, who have a guild will probably soon have another. The Roman Catholics also have a guild. The Unitarians have their Unity Club with its library in a convenient room in their church.[46]

While "compulsion is never used," Angell was confident that religious life at Michigan was as robust as at any denominational school.

Finally, Angell concluded his argument that the current campus religious life was just what Michigan's students wanted and needed. It was not "pious platitudes, cant, mere appeal to denominational zeal," which would not work. It was—in the popular Protestant religious language of the day—"manly," broad, with a "reasonable interpretation of Scripture" and "the application of the principles of the gospels to social problems." So it was, Angell argued, the religious life of the University of Michigan was the liberal Protestantism of 1890 and the Christian citizens of Michigan should be pleased to see that.

Fifteen years later, President Angell welcomed the appointment of Leslie French as the first full-time chaplain. Other religious groups including Baptists, Episcopalians, Catholics, Congregationalists, and Unitarians also appointed chaplains or supported their local pastors in devoting time to serving students. Angell welcomed them all—the more religious groups the better.[47]

In addition to the active roles of chaplains on the Michigan campus, a School of Religion began offering close to forty courses in 1908, a few of which were taught by regular faculty and carried university credit while others were more informal. The School of Religion was disbanded on the eve of World War I, though the idea of religion courses reappeared in later decades.[48]

Soon after Angell retired, in the next decades of the twentieth century, there were two major clashes within the cooperative religious life movement at Michigan. The first signaled to many that the day of the YMCA/YWCA campus leadership was passing. In the late fall of 1911, some ministers and faculty complained that the Y's broadly Christian theology conflicted with specific denominational beliefs and more practically that the Y scheduled conflicting events with church programs. The scheduling issue was easily resolved, but there were deeper issues. In an era before state universities took much interest in student services or student unions, the Y also provided a place for students to gather, supported student social life, and offered student housing. By 1911, universities—and the University of Michigan in particular—were increasingly taking that work on themselves, and students saw the Y as both exclusive and competitive. Many not connected with the Y began to question why the Christian association had a privileged status to offer social space on campus to its members and friends when its services duplicated those offered through the student union. The Y's response that its services were "religious" rang hollow when so few programs actually looked religious and were, in fact, much more in the realm of general social activities. The issue passed, but it should have been clear to observers that by 1911 the Y's days were numbered on an increasingly diverse and often quite secular campus.[49]

By 1917, denominational leaders raised more concern about the nondenominational nature of the Y movement and the power of the Y's student leaders, who often displayed little denominational loyalty. The leaders argued for more and more adult—usually clergy—management of campus religious life. Soon another step was made in this direction, though not without resistance. Thomas St. Clair Evans, who had been YMCA field secretary at the University of Pennsylvania, was hired at Michigan as executive of a new effort to bring all student religious life under unified control. Among Evans's moves was to change the name of the local Y branch from the Student's Christian Association to the Student Christian Association. Removing an apostrophe seemed a trivial change, but students recognized it for what it was: a move to change the association from one led by and belonging to the students to one managed by religious bodies for students. By early 1920, Michigan students were in full rebellion, but Evans hung on to his belief that the association, like other religious activity on the Michigan campus, was to be managed by church-based adults, not the students. Evans won but it was a pyric victory as students drifted away from the Y to new and different interests. Between 1920 and 1930, two new University of Michigan presidents tried to reverse course and give more authority over religious life activities back to the students, but it was too little, too late and those students who took the authority found themselves presiding over a smaller and smaller slice of campus life. The 1920s were destined to be a very different decade in the religious life at Michigan, as in the nation. Religious activities that had been central to the college life of many students prior to World

War I were now marginalized. Students at the University of Michigan, as elsewhere, came to have many more options. Religion was becoming more obviously one option among many, and often not the most popular one.[50]

Maintaining Catholic Jesuit Identity at Georgetown University

At the beginning of the twentieth century, Georgetown was a small Jesuit college with a long history. John Carroll was already working to create a Catholic college in the United States when he was elected as the nation's first Catholic bishop, in 1789. Carroll acquired land in Georgetown, then in a part of Maryland later ceded to the new national government for the District of Columbia. Seeking to avoid political struggles with the Maryland legislature, Bishop Carroll did not seek a charter for his school but by 1791 a small band of faculty and six students had gathered in a not-quite-finished building in Georgetown and instruction began. As a DC institution, Georgetown University was eventually chartered by Congress in 1815.[51]

From six students when the school opened, Georgetown grew quickly and by the end of the 1790s it had educated close to 300 students, all White men. Many stayed for only a year or two, and more were in the preparatory program than doing actual college work. Georgetown attracted its mostly Catholic student body from all over the new United States and also from prosperous elite (White) families in the West Indies. The purpose of Georgetown was to ensure a well-educated supply of Catholic clergy and also influential lay leaders. Tuition was higher than at many schools, but payment was accepted in money, rum, food, or labor, and fatefully in enslaved African Americans.[52]

The Jesuit *Ratio Studiorum* defined the curriculum at Georgetown, as it did for all Jesuit colleges from the late 1500s onward. In many ways the *Ratio* resembled the antebellum classical curriculum in Protestant colleges in the United States. The ever-present Cicero was there, as well as other Latin and Greek classics, with the addition of significant reading from the Greek New Testament. But the *Ratio* was a seven-year curriculum of humanities, philosophy, and theology with little flexibility and no clear distinction between secondary and postsecondary studies. Before long, mathematics, geography, and some history, as well as both English and French language study, were added to the curriculum. But there was no science or modern literature or formal study of religion, although there was a heavy emphasis on student devotional life and the reading of Catholic devotional manuals. A century after Georgetown's founding, the *Ratio*, with minor modifications, remained the heart of the school's curriculum, long after most American non-Catholic colleges had left the old classical curriculum far behind.[53]

Unlike many colleges of the day, where students found lodging in nearby boarding houses, Georgetown preferred residential halls where students could be strictly supervised. While Bishop Carroll had directed the construction of large classroom buildings, money was a constant worry. Few generous donors could be found, and tuition, though high, was far less than the cost of operating the school in spite of the mostly clerical faculty who were paid little.

While Georgetown was Jesuit in spirit from the beginning, it could not initially be so in fact. Pope Clement XIV had disbanded the Jesuit order in 1773, feeling that the society had too much independent power. Jesuit priests continued to practice but with no link to each other. Beginning in 1801, Pope Pius VII slowly began restoring the society, believing it could be a strong force for Catholicism in the nineteenth century. Bishop Carroll himself had been a Jesuit until the society was disbanded. In 1806, as the order was being restored, he formally shifted control of the school to the American Jesuits. In doing so, Carroll ensured that not only the curriculum but the faculty and finances of the school would be Jesuit. He also set a pattern for many later Catholic colleges in the United States that were also owned by a Catholic religious order, in contrast to the elementary and secondary schools of the nation, which were nearly always under the control of the local bishop. It was to be an important difference in the twentieth century.[54]

Through the nineteenth century, Georgetown grew but often was close to bankruptcy. The few enslaved African Americans whom Georgetown had taken as payment for tuition in the 1790s grew to several hundred enslaved individuals claimed by the Georgetown Jesuits. In June 1838 the society avoided a financial crisis for the college with the sale of 314 enslaved individuals, including 272 who were sent to plantations in Louisiana. This sale—and the human cost of keeping Georgetown going—was rediscovered in the twenty-first century, and the American Ancestors project identified over 8,000 descendants of these enslaved individuals, many of whom continue to live in Houma, Louisiana. Georgetown's twenty-first-century Jesuits responded not only with a special "contrition" liturgy but by removing the names of former presidents who had approved of slavery from buildings. More importantly, the Jesuits and the university provided $1 million to create a Descendants Truth & Reconciliation Foundation, and the university pledged $400,000 per year for ongoing work by the foundation. It is a model of redress that other American colleges and religious communities might learn from.[55]

For the rest of the nineteenth century, Georgetown continued to have ups and downs in enrollment and finances. In the 1850s, it was one of the larger American colleges, with over 300 students, but the Civil War was hard on the school and it was slow to grow afterwards. Ironically, given the school's past, the most effective post–Civil War president, Patrick Healy, SJ, was the son of an enslaved African American mother and a free White father. Healy was president from 1873–1882. He sought to model at least some elements of Georgetown's life on the growing research university ideal, but he faced resistance and financial troubles. Meanwhile, the *Ratio Studiorum,* which allowed room for little beyond the humanities, remained at the core of the undergraduate curriculum.[56]

With the coming of the twentieth century, Jesuit Georgetown faced a series of interconnected challenges. Its original constituency had changed dramatically. When Georgetown was founded, there were about 50,000 Catholics in the new United States, 1 percent of the population, mostly English Catholics, many of whom were comfortable if not well to do. By 1900, there were 12 million Catholics, comprising about 15 percent of the US population. The growth of the country with the Louisiana Purchase and the conquest of northern Mexico, mostly Catholic territories, combined with the massive immigration of Irish, German, and later Italian and Polish Catholics, had changed the Catholic population from a quiet but comfortable tiny minority to a large, restive, mostly poor and working-class community that was anxious for upward mobility and acceptance in the American mainstream. By 1900, there were a good number of families of poor immigrant background who were rising to middle-class economic status and who wanted the social and educational status, including a college education for their children, to go with it.[57]

Despite a new influx of students, Georgetown felt besieged in 1900. Anti-Catholicism was far stronger in the United States in 1900 than it had been in 1800 when Catholics were a tiny minority. Georgetown's *Ratio* curriculum, taught mainly by Jesuit priests, also seemed out of step with other institutions in the fast-changing landscape of American higher education.[58]

Another threat to Georgetown, and all Jesuit schools, came from intra-Catholic battles. A new generation of Catholics were attending non-Catholic schools, especially state universities. These students established Catholic clubs, and Catholic bishops seemed to endorse this move, as had happened in Wisconsin. But many of the priests in the Catholic colleges felt that Catholic clubs and chaplains at non-Catholic universities were a threat to their very existence. The great advantage of Catholic colleges, they could tell Catholic parents, was that their children's faith was safe at a Catholic school. But for the Jesuit faculty at a school like Georgetown, too many American bishops seemed out to undermine their institutions by supporting Catholic students at non-Catholic schools.[59]

A preliminary skirmish about the challenges facing Georgetown surfaced in 1893. In an effort to raise admission standards, the Harvard University Law School began listing the schools whose graduates could be automatically admitted without an exam. None of the forty-four colleges listed were Catholic. When challenged, Harvard President Charles Eliot insisted that Catholic colleges—perhaps especially those with the *Ratio* curriculum—were so different that they could not be compared to other schools. In response, Georgetown's president, Father Joseph Richards, sent Eliot copies of the Georgetown catalogue and exam questions. Eliot recanted, agreeing that "Georgetown College should be included in the list of colleges whose degrees would admit young men without examination to our Law School."

Harvard's decision was an important boost, but five years later, in 1898, Harvard changed the policy and eliminated two Jesuit schools, Boston College and Holy Cross, and soon Georgetown from the automatic admission list. Georgetown president Richards wrote to Boston College president Timothy Brosnahan that he was "inclined to believe that there is a systematic and deliberate intention on the part of these gentlemen to discredit Catholic education and drive us from the field." Richards had good reasons for his complaint, though there was debate about why—whether the new policy was due to a far outdated classical curriculum, worry about instruction by mostly clergy faculty who may or may not be academic specialists, or just plain anti-Catholic prejudice was a judgment call on which people would have reasons to differ.[60]

In the 1890s, President Richards reinstated required attendance at Mass just as other schools were dropping required chapel attendance. While justifying the Jesuit curriculum to the American educational mainstream, he also faced challenges from his own Jesuit authorities. In 1893, the American Jesuit Provincial (the highest authority in the society in the United States) ordered Georgetown to curtail classes in calculus and chemistry. Other Jesuit schools in the United States were doing just that, as conservative leaders sought to reassert the primacy of the *Ratio Studiorum* in the face of an increasingly dominant Protestant educational establishment. Instead, Richards had wanted to expand them. He had recently abandoned a plan to create a scientific degree parallel to the classical one, and cutting these courses was too much. He appealed to the head of the Jesuit order in Rome that a "reduction of our course by eliminating modern branches will make it harder for us to compete" with other American colleges. In this case he won. But it was a tightrope.[61]

After Richards retired in 1898, a new crisis emerged for Jesuit Georgetown. This time the issue was between a more-or-less united Jesuit Order and the bishops of the same faith. But once again, it involved competition with non-Catholic colleges.

Nearly all Catholic elementary and high schools were under the control of the bishop where they were located. Most Catholic colleges in the United States, on the other hand, were not under the control of a local bishop but rather an independent religious order, especially the Jesuits. Many suspected that the bishops, who were so devoted to their own parochial elementary and secondary schools, were somewhere between indifferent and hostile to the colleges over which they had far less control. Yet the leaders of the Catholic colleges knew that the support of the bishops was essential to their future.

The issue came to a head when the bishops began to appoint Catholic priests to serve as chaplains at non-Catholic colleges. Soon after the creation of the Catholic Education Association (CEA) in 1904, long-time Georgetown faculty member John A. Conway, SJ, became the chair of the college department of the CEA. In that role the Georgetown professor became a prime defender of Catholic, especially Jesuit, colleges and a critic of the appointment of chaplains at non-Catholic schools whom, he believed, gave these schools inappropriate legitimacy in the eyes of Catholic students. While Conway desperately wanted the support of bishops, he was also not afraid of a fight with them. When Conway died in 1915, one of his obituary writers noted that there "was a militant spirit in Father Conway." Conway's showdown with the bishops and their representatives illustrated how deep that militant spirit went.[62]

The issue of the bishops' support for college chaplains came to a head at the 1907 CEA meeting when Conway and his committee directly challenged the bishops to stop supporting chaplains or clubs for Catholic students at state or other non-Catholic colleges, and instead bend all of their efforts to convincing Catholic students and their parents that every good Catholic who attended college should do so only at a Catholic school like Georgetown. This position brought Conway and his supporters into direct conflict with several of the bishops, especially Sebastian Messmer of Milwaukee, who had recently appointed Henry Hengell as chaplain at the University of Wisconsin, as well as Father John J. Farrell, whom Boston's Archbishop John Williams had appointed as the part-time Catholic chaplain at Harvard. Neither side meant to back down.

Father Conway was clear on what he thought the stakes were for the Catholic colleges if the secular universities had chaplains authorized by the bishops. He wrote:

The only reason—valid reason—we had to urge for parents to send their children to Catholic colleges was the religious one. In everything else the great colleges of the country are better equipped than ours are: state universities appeal to local pride, charge less, give greater liberty, have greater social advantages; how are we to cope with all of this, if the impression goes abroad that faith too is sufficiently safeguarded? It looks to me as a serious blow to Catholic education and to Catholic colleges.

Conway knew the struggles to keep students interested at Georgetown. He also deeply believed that a Catholic college led by priests was the only safe place for Catholic young people to go to school.[63]

Messmer and his allies also stood their ground. A new generation of Catholics were attending Harvard, Wisconsin, and many other schools in far greater numbers than were attending the struggling Catholic schools. At most of the secular schools, men and women also attended together, not segregated by sex as they were in the Catholic ones.

One 1907 survey of Catholic college students showed that of 14,000 Catholics enrolled in higher education, two-thirds were in non-Catholic schools—for all the reasons Conway himself had given. The choice was to abandon these students or support them. For bishops, the choice was clear. They had to reach the Catholic students wherever they were found. When Boston College's Father Timothy Brosnahan, SJ, sided with Conway and suggested that Catholic students in secular schools "should be left to their own fate," Timothy Harrington, a Wisconsin alumni and supporter of Messmer's chaplain plan, asked if the Brosnahan plan could be called Christian, and added that "a body of students backed by a chaplain who holds them together" could be an important influence on all the other students and faculty of a secular university—a much wider reach than any small Catholic college could have.[64]

Not all Jesuits agreed with Conway. In 1906 Francis B. Cassilly, SJ, the vice president of St. Ignatius College in Chicago, wrote an article in which he insisted that like it or not there were more young Catholics at the Universities of California, Michigan, Minnesota, or Wisconsin than at virtually any Catholic college. Cassilly might wish that more young Catholics attended schools like his own or Georgetown, but he knew they would not do so. Given that reality, he argued that "when a pastor establishes special instruction classes for children who attend the public school, he does not thereby sanction public-school education." In the same way, priests and bishops could sponsor Catholic clubs and appoint college chaplains at secular universities while also urging Catholic youth to attend Catholic schools. It was, he thought, the only way to respond "to a new phase of educational conditions."[65]

As early as 1908 there were twenty-eight Newman Clubs, sixteen chaplains, and eleven Catholic buildings or chapels proposed or under construction at non-Catholic colleges in the United States. It was an impressive development in just a few years. The goal of all of this activity, as the constitution of the University of Michigan Foley Guild—soon to be a Newman Club—said, was to "bring into closer relations the Catholic students . . . to promote among them feelings of friendship and good will to foster a deep interest and love for the sacred doctrines of our holy religion." As a younger generation of American Catholics ventured beyond the bounds of home parish and parochial school, it seemed important to many—bishops, priests, and active laypeople—for the church to follow them.[66]

In a 1912 statement that was almost parallel to Conway's complaint, Henry Hengell, the Catholic chaplain at Madison, said:

> To argue that the Catholic student should be induced to leave the secular college and universities and to enter Catholic institutions, is to advocate something that is impracticable to the point of being morally impossible. The same reasons that have brought Catholic students to the secular institutions will keep them there, and these reasons are to be found in the splendid equipment, the giving of courses that no Catholic college has the means to offer, the prestige of State university degrees, the free tuition, the proximity to home, and the other material advantages of secular institutions.[67]

For Hengell, the choice was clear: meet the students where they were or lose them.

Conway did not agree. Supported by most of the Jesuits teaching in Catholic colleges, Conway tried hard to convince the bishops to give a blanket condemnation of attendance at a non-Catholic college as they had done for attendance at a non-Catholic public school, but they were not to be swayed. At one point the bishops asked if the Jesuits and the other orders would place all of their colleges under the control of the local bishop as the parochial schools were, but this, of course, Conway could not arrange and did not want to see happen. In the end, the bishops concluded with some rather vague remarks of support for Catholic colleges and continued on their way supporting chaplains and otherwise providing services to Catholic students wherever they may be found, which was more and more in non-Catholic schools.[68]

Contrary to Conway's dire predictions, the appointment of college chaplains did not mean the end for Georgetown, though the school did struggle in the early 1900s, and some other Jesuit schools had to close or resign themselves to becoming secondary schools. In the longer run, Georgetown prospered. In 1919 Georgetown was able to separate itself from the preparatory division, and in 1940, with World War II looming and the draft draining male students, Georgetown admitted women to programs other than nursing. In the 1960s, like many Jesuit colleges, Georgetown established an independent board of trustees and the Jesuit community separated itself from control of the institution. In the late 1960s and going forward, Georgetown diversified its faculty, curriculum, and research focus, becoming one of the nation's leading research universities. Though Jesuit influence remained, the school was a very different institution in the early twenty-first century than anything that could be dreamed—or feared—by the small struggling community of committed Jesuits who led it a century before.[69]

Denomination, Region, College: Northwest Nazarene College, Nampa, Idaho

Georgetown was well over a century old when Northwest Nazarene College was founded in 1913 by a new Protestant denomination that only traced its formal existence to 1908. Northwest Nazarene College was born within the ferment that created the Church of the Nazarene, and the early history of the college and the denomination are closely intertwined. The school began as an elementary school for Nazarene families who were clustering in the Snake River Valley in southern Idaho in 1913, but under the leadership of its first president, H. Orton Wiley, it quickly expanded to admit its first college students in 1915 and award its first baccalaureate degree in 1917.[70]

The formal organization of the Church of the Nazarene happened at a small gathering of religious dissidents in the tiny town of Pilot Point, Texas, in 1908. But the religious dissent that brought them to Pilot Point had been going on for decades. From the beginning of the Methodist movement within the Church of England, John Wesley spoke of "going on to perfection." The Methodist itinerant preachers who built Methodism in the United States after the revolution always preached holiness or Christian perfectionism as did other Protestants in several denominations. The holiness movement had a significant influence on the Great Revival of 1858, played a central role in the creation of the YMCA and YWCA, and was an important influence on the later-nineteenth-century revivalist, Dwight L. Moody.[71]

Most strands of the eighteenth- and nineteenth-century holiness movements included opposition to the sin of slavery, and they were one important stream of the abolitionist movement. In the later nineteenth century, the holiness movement appealed especially to middle-class and poorer Whites who found inspiration, meaning, and purpose in "sanctification," even as the society seemed to them to grow more sinful. There was a strong holiness movement among Methodists, but also among Baptists, Presbyterians, and Congregationalists, and among some Adventists and evangelical Quakers. Followers of the holiness tradition often met across denominational lines and held enthusiastic revivals to celebrate sanctification, but most remained loyal to their home denominations, even as they debated among themselves about the best course of action. The problem for believers in the holiness way was that no Protestant denomination was willing to fully embrace them, and they remained a minority, if a large one, scattered across many faith communities. By 1900, some individual holiness churches and scattered ministers began to give up on the denominations that would not recognize their core beliefs. In response, some simply withdrew from their churches, a few ministers were expelled or marginalized, and those trying to remain loyal to their traditions found it harder to do so.[72]

In 1895, Methodist minister Phineas Bresee and a prosperous medical doctor, J. P. Widney, gave up trying to find a place within the Methodist church and created a new congregation in Los Angeles, which they called the Church of the Nazarene, comprised of eighty-two charter members drawn from several denominations or even some with no denominational affiliation. Bresee and Widney knew each other well from their time serving on the board of directors of the then Methodist University of Southern California. Together they had tried, and failed, to move the university in a holiness direction. Similar breaks and fresh starts were happening in many different places, and it was the leaders of several quite independent holiness movements who came together in Pilot Point in 1908 to create a new national denomination. Soon, other independent groups and churches heard of the new Church of the Nazarene and also joined. It was that newly formed denomination that, six years later, supported the creation and growth of Northwest Nazarene College. That college, and especially its committed first president, H. Orton Wiley, in turn saved the infant denomination from shattering before it really began.[73]

Northwest Nazarene College, originally Idaho Holiness School, was founded in 1913 by Eugene Emerson, a lumber entrepreneur in Nampa, Idaho. Emerson had spent the winter of 1912–1913 in Pasadena, California, where he was converted to the holiness movement and returned to Nampa committed to starting a school for children in which the Bible and the Nazarene faith would be central. From the beginning, Emerson also dreamed of a college. The *Nampa Leader-Herald* of August

5, 1913, reported that "Nampa is to be the home of a new college founded by the Idaho District. . . . Such is the announcement made by Eugene Emerson." Like almost every other denominational college, the announcement added, "The college, although under the direction of the Nazarene Church, will be open to all denominations." Indeed, once the college was in full operation it always included non-Nazarene students. Like virtually every other college of the previous century, it could not afford to turn away prospective tuition-paying students. The article announcing the birth of the school added that while the college would begin with "practical subjects" later "it will develop into college work with a view toward enlarging into a college of recognized standing." The school fit the profile of a nineteenth-century "booster college" for Nampa, but it succeeded far more than many such schools.[74]

Nampa itself was a very new town. In the mid-1880s, a railroad junction and a station were built there on the Oregon Short Line Railroad because geography made nearby Boise too expensive for a mainline stop. When the station opened, real estate developer Alexander Duffe created the Nampa Land and Improvement Company and began selling house lots near the station in one of the last territories of the United States opened to White settlement. The land had traditionally been part of the Northern Shoshone territory and, after a series of treaties were forced on the Shoshone in the 1860s and 1870s, the land was now seen as "empty." Nampa was a traditional booster town. Duffe made money selling house lots, Emerson made money selling lumber to build on the lots, and, devout as he was, Emerson also understood that a college would attract more people to move to Nampa and buy his lumber. That it did.[75]

The Nampa school grew quickly, buildings were rented or built, and well over 100 students were enrolled within a year. More advanced students were welcomed including soon the first college-level students. The trustees of the new school changed the name to Northwest Nazarene College and then convinced Orton Wiley, who had just resigned from the presidency of a Nazarene college in Pasadena, to become the president. Though lower-level programs continued at the college until into the 1950s, once Wiley arrived the college-level work became central.

The new Church of the Nazarene was made up of dissidents from many different Protestant denominations, and the founders of the new body did not stop being dissidents when they came together. The early records of the church reflect bitter clashes and many threatened splits. Among the clashes was an explosive disagreement in Pasadena between Wiley, who was then dean of the college there; Seth Rees, pastor of the University Nazarene church on the college campus; and A. O. Hendricks, who was pastor of the downtown Nazarene Church in Pasadena and a college trustee. The arguments among them might seem to an outsider as somewhat obscure theological debates about what it meant to truly embrace holiness beliefs, but also very practical questions of the role of college trustees and who owned church property—the local congregation or the denomination. The arguments were harder to resolve because some of those involved were long used to being dissidents and found unity difficult. Mostly because Rees kept the arguments alive and spread word of them throughout the Nazarene world, they threatened to tear the new denomination apart. It was in this context that Wiley resigned from the Pasadena school and was happy to come to Nampa if the trustees would give him a five-year contract and a free hand, both of which they were happy to do.[76]

Once Wiley was settled in Nampa in 1917, he spent a significant amount of time holding the Church of the Nazarene together. When Rees was invited to preach at summer events in Nampa in 1917, Wiley welcomed him but also invited speakers from other perspectives and clearly informed all of them that the college's loyalty to the Nazarene tradition was not open to debate. Using his position as a college president—and the promised free hand—he moved forward with a plan to place the growing number of small Nazarene colleges under the control of a central General Board of Education rather than separate, and quarreling, boards of trustees. The new board insisted that there could be only one Nazarene college for each region of the country, and so Northwest Nazarene became the official Nazarene school for Idaho, Washington, Oregon, and the Dakotas. While centralizing the control of Nazarene colleges, Wiley convinced the denomination's general assembly to avoid too much centralization and maintain great freedom to differ among individual congregations. Both moves helped the Nazarenes avoid many departures.

In addition to his denominational work, Wiley focused on leading the new college. By 1919, the school had over 300 students and was raising money from local churches. He announced a plan to make Northwest Nazarene "a missionary school," and soon the college was sending graduates as missionaries to Peru, China, and parts of Africa, while also attracting missionaries on furlough to Nampa, which in turn increased prospective student interest. Wiley and his colleagues insisted that both faith and service to those in need were the twin parts of their religion and they included a "Missionary Sanitarium and Institute," which provided some medical training for women desiring to be missionaries and nurses.[77]

As the school grew, the faculty included a larger number of women than at many similar schools, including graduates of the University of California, Harvard/Radcliffe, Glasgow, and the universities of Southern California, Chicago, and Michigan. In appealing to parents throughout the northwest to send their children—daughters as well as sons—to Northwest Nazarene, Wiley wrote that the school "seeks to awaken the students to a knowledge of his own powers . . . [and] . . . the knowledge and love of God and the service to man." Again and again, the dual purposes of a strong education and the strengthening of a revival spirit was alive and well in Idaho ninety years after the same themes had been central to schools like the early Oberlin.[78]

As had many antebellum colleges, Northwest Nazarene often experienced religious revivals that led everything else—including classroom instruction—to be suspended. The *Nazarene Messenger*, a college publication, reported that in January 1919, "On every corner of the campus students were praying, days and nights were spent in prayer and the Spirit worked with great grace and power." The college regulations were also designed to ensure a moral atmosphere, including a requirement for "strict observance of the Sabbath" and a rule that "card-playing, the use of tobacco, profanity, obscene language, the reading of trashy literature and such things are positively forbidden." Other rules excluded "rugby foot-ball nor any other brutal or demoralizing games" that might "permit the students' minds to become distracted from their school work." Men's and women's glee clubs, outdoor exercises as long as they were not "brutal," and regular college classes were permitted. Students followed a classical, literary, or scientific curriculum to a four-year college degree taught by a growing faculty.[79]

Wiley resigned in 1926 to return for a brief stint at the college in Pasadena. In his decade as the first president of Northwest Nazarene, Wiley had put the college on what he considered a stable basis in terms of its academic standing, and a deeply religious bastion for the Nazarene community. Though far from solvent, the school did not face the disastrous financial issues of some other colleges. Wiley had also played an essential role in calming the waters of the Nazarene movement. As the hopes of some early founders to one day return to their old denominations waned, it was replaced by zeal to ensure the success of their new venture, including the new venture's colleges. Both the Church of the Nazarene and Northwest Nazarene College thrived even through the Great Depression and the challenges of a second world war, and they are thriving still in the twenty-first century.[80]

Evangelical Protestantism, Women, and Mount Holyoke College

In October 1912, a year before the founding of Northwest Nazarene College, Mount Holyoke College held a two-day gala celebration of its seventy-fifth anniversary as

Figure 3.2. During its first century of existence, religion pervaded the culture of Mount Holyoke College, as these young women leaving the chapel in 1908 illustrate. From Library of Congress

the first women's college in the nation. Mary Preston, who had graduated from Mount Holyoke in 1910, spoke of the religious activity on campus at the 1912 event. She asked her distinguished audience to

> consider the Young Women's Christian Association with its student membership of six hundred eighteen out of seven hundred sixty-six college members this past year, with its enrollment of four hundred and twenty-three girls in Bible classes and two hundred and five in mission study classes, with more than a fifth of the students engaged in active work upon its committees with is influence reaching out beyond the college into the social and religious life of the village.

Preston also listed the active involvement of Holyoke students in Vacation Bible Schools in Boston and Brooklyn for "street children," and the impact of Mount Holyoke graduates in social service and religious activities over the previous decades. It was no wonder, she insisted, that there was increasing demand for Mount

Holyoke women as "secretaries of Young Women's Christian Associations, for pastors' assistants, for workers in the institutional centers connected with our churches," and for services for immigrants and the poor. Mount Holyoke women were leaders in religious activity across the nation, even if there was little chance of their becoming ordained clergy, and the college had made them ready for these roles.[81]

Mary Preston's description of the religious life and religious influence of Mount Holyoke sounds surprisingly like the language that Mary Lyon would have used to describe the Mount Holyoke she was founding seventy-five years earlier, though in fact she envisioned a very different school than the one Mount Holyoke had become in 1912. As the cornerstone for the first Mount Holyoke building was laid, Lyon said, "in laying the foundation for this new seminary I will probably do more for the cause of Christ . . . than all I have done with my life before." Though she did not come from money, Mary Lyon was a prodigious fundraiser with a deep commitment to the causes of women's education, opportunity for poor girls (who were the majority of the early students), and her evangelical Christian faith. Mount Holyoke was never a denominational school, but in its early years every aspect of the college was imbued with evangelical Christianity.

Lyon's religious convictions dominated all else in the early Mount Holyoke. Lyon gathered all of the students three days a week for religious instruction, Bible study, and the singing of hymns in a way that centered the school in an atmosphere of evangelical Christianity.[82]

The school focused on preparing teachers and missionaries who could carry learning and faith to all parts of the United States and the rest of the world. As Fidellia Fisk, an early Mount Holyoke student and later a missionary to Persia (Iran), said of Lyon, "she did love to dwell on the great work God had given woman to do; and she was convinced that to do that work well she must be educated. . . . She longed to see woman's mind better trained."

Like Oberlin, Mount Holyoke required all students to work to help maintain the school. Lyon believed that students cooking, cleaning, and doing other domestic work was as important in an education for equality and service. There were no pampered students in Lyon's world. In part because women's education had been so neglected, Lyon always also stressed a top-quality education in which Mount Holyoke offered women the same curriculum as the best of the all-male colleges like Harvard and Yale offered their brothers. For the several thousand students who studied with Lyon, the high academic standards and the deeply evangelical atmosphere and stress on service shaped their lives.[83]

The early Mount Holyoke produced very good teachers. In 1846, less than a decade after the forced removal of the Cherokees from their ancestral homes in Georgia to the Indian Territory in Oklahoma, the National Council of the Cherokee Nation voted to create seminaries to train teachers. The council had no federal or missionary support but was determined to build up the Cherokee Nation. As the *Cherokee Advocate* noted, the seminaries were especially important because "there are no inducements for female teachers to come to this country," so it was essential to provide a strong education to Cherokee women to teach the next generation in their own schools. As the new female seminary was being developed, the Cherokee Nation turned to Mount Holyoke for teachers, believing that in the 1840s Mount Holyoke could be counted on to send top-quality teachers to the distant Indian Territory. And it did.[84]

As historian Andrea Turpin has shown, the evangelical Christian commitment to prepare women who were as well educated as any man and who also were committed to using that education for social uplift as mothers, teachers, and missionaries continued more or less intact for half a century. By 1912, however, Mount Holyoke had moved religious faith to a much more marginal place at the school than when Lyon led it from 1836 to 1849.[85]

As early as the school's half-century mark in the 1880s, there were new strains on Mary Lyon's vision. Mount Holyoke still held to the twin ideals of evangelical Christianity faith and top-flight education. But while the first students were mostly of modest circumstances if not poor, the Mount Holyoke of 1880 catered much more to upper-middle-class if not rich girls.

In 1888 Mount Holyoke changed its name to Mount Holyoke Seminary and College, and it added a new collegiate curriculum with more freedom and deeper disciplinary focus. In 1902 it dropped the seminary name and the last remnants of the prescribed curriculum. Even more important for the school, the evangelical Christianity with which it had been founded morphed into the liberal Christianity of the turn of the twentieth century, with a greater emphasis on improving society and a weakened emphasis on personal salvation. Indeed, talking of personal salvation, essential in the early years, might be quite embarrassing later. In line with much of the rest of American higher education, by the end of the nineteenth century doing good for society had also morphed into doing well personally and using a Mount Holyoke education for a kind of upward mobility that Mary Lyon would have found abhorrent.[86]

By the time Mount Holyoke celebrated its seventy-fifth anniversary in 1912, the tradition of evangelism and missionary and teaching service that had been at the core of its founding had been moved to the margins, celebrated more in nostalgic rhetoric than in modern practice. Mary Preston might still celebrate the YWCA and the Bible study at the college, but although still important, they were hardly at the center as similar matters had been in Lyon's day. Helen Barnetson Calder, an 1898 graduate, celebrated the 250 graduates who had worked as missionaries in North and South America, Europe, Asia, Africa, and the Pacific islands. But by the time of the 1912 celebration, only one woman in the most recent graduating class had entered the missionary field and no one spoke, as Lyon did, of "bringing souls to Christ," though they did quote Lyon—selectively—as often as possible.[87]

After 1912, the secularization and the movement toward both the main currents of American higher education and the service of a much more upper-middle-class clientele than the poor girls of its first generation only accelerated. By its centennial in 1937, Mount Holyoke graduate Louise Porter Thomas wrote that at the Mount Holyoke she attended there was no "need fear a revival of the revivals, or any other outdated custom," but rather it was possible to attend a school that was "predominantly interested in its relationship with the world." Evangelical Christianity had morphed into "a relationship with the world."

If one looks at the Mount Holyoke of the twenty-first century, the legacy of Mary Lyon seems everywhere, but it is a highly edited legacy. The religious faith that was at the very center of everything else Lyon did is now mostly absent from the standard quotations. The history of the college on the website begins with a quote from Mary Lyon, "Go where no one else will go, do what no one else will do," and an affirmation that from the beginning Mount Holyoke was committed to "brilliant teaching and academic excellence." There are also eight religious groups, several with chaplains on campus, including Lisa Luzovaya, the Muslim chaplain; Amelia Ender, the Jewish chaplain; and Leslie Fraser, the Protestant chaplain. All students are invited to "Engage with, participate in and explore our vibrant and diverse spiritual community." The invitation is clear even if a huge part of what Mary Lyon wanted Mount Holyoke to stand for—saving students' souls—has moved fairly far from a central place in the college to become one of many voluntary options available to Mount Holyoke students if they are inclined to pursue such concerns.

Mount Holyoke's trajectory seems to be the same as that of many if not most other schools in the United States. Religious life and religious commitments may well be alive and well at twenty-first-century Mount Holyoke as elsewhere, but they exist mostly at the margins, carefully separated from the core values that the school aims to share with the world. Some would argue that voluntary engagement and living on the margins is a better, more vibrant place for religion than at the center. Certainly, there is no going back, and discussion and debate about the place of religion is likely to be alive and well for some years to come at Mount Holyoke and across the country.[88]

CHAPTER FOUR

Campus Religion and the Fracturing of American Religion, 1925–1945

In the fall of 1923, newly ordained Rabbi Benjamin M. Frankel began his rabbinical charge as minister to the Jewish students at the University of Illinois Urbana-Champaign. As part of his new ministry, Frankel also began an organization "to establish for the Jewish students of the University of Illinois a religious, moral, social and recreation center, to teach the principles of the Jewish faith, and to cooperate with other similar agencies in the cultivation of a moral and spiritual life." Frankel named his new organization Hillel, after the Jewish scholar and teacher of ancient times, Rabbi Hillel. Frankel was the first Jewish chaplain and the first leader of a Hillel student center in the United States.[1]

Chaplaincy Diversified: Rabbis Join Priests and Ministers as College Chaplains

The story of Frankel's appointment as the Jewish chaplain at Illinois bears remarkable resemblance to that of Henry Hengell's appointment as Catholic chaplain at the University of Wisconsin two decades earlier. In both cases, their work was sponsored by a small number of dedicated people concerned about the religious marginalization of Jewish or Catholic students, respectively, in a culturally Protestant university world. If there was any doubt about the Protestant nature of the University of Illinois's cultural norms in the 1920s, the dean of students, Thomas Arkle Clark, made it clear in 1920, when a Jewish student asked to use its athletic facilities, then closed on Sundays. Clark rejected the request, saying that the United States was "a Christian country established upon Christian traditions and Christian principles, and this is an Institution backed very largely by Christian communities who believe in these things . . . even when they may be opposed by foreigners or by those who would like to wipe out all our Christian traditions."[2]

Neither Hengell in his time nor Frankel in his were newcomers to their campuses, nor were they surprised by the sometimes-hostile reception their faith received. Although ordained in 1923, Frankel had been serving since 1921 as a student officiant and teacher at a religious school at Sinai Temple in Champaign-Urbana while a student at Cincinnati's Hebrew Union College. He had come to love both his Jewish faith and the opportunity to help capture the hearts and minds of Jewish students whom he found aimless, without leadership, and all-too-willing to assimilate to the point of hiding their Jewish identity. Frankel's 1923 appointment as a chaplain of his faith was the next logical step for him.[3]

As early as 1896, the Central Conference of American Rabbis had been concerned about the fate of the growing numbers of Jewish students at American universities. In 1906 a committee of the conference even recommended assistance to support Jewish student organizations. But although there was much discussion of the issue, little actual assistance was forthcoming.[4]

Well before the post–World War I boom in Jewish college enrollment, there had been Jewish students at different schools and some of these students created their own organizations. At the turn of the twentieth century—and well after—most campus fraternities and sororities excluded Jews either by national charter or local practice. In 1898, Jewish college men in New York City created their own fraternity, Zeta Beta Thu, and women soon followed with Iota Alpha Pi sorority. Separate Jewish fraternities and sororities continued to blossom before and alongside Hillel for some time. Early in the twentieth century, there were also Jewish literary societies paralleling college literary societies that had been so popular in the nineteenth century. Beginning at Harvard in 1906, some Jewish students started what were known as Menorah societies for the study of the Jewish faith and the Menorah society movement spread to several campuses, including the University of Colorado, Ohio State, Cornell, Pennsylvania State, Rutgers, Missouri, Wisconsin, and beyond. Yet other Jewish students began creating their own Zionist societies as early as 1902. In time, nearly all of the Menorah societies and many Zionist societies chose to affiliate with Hillel. Hillel added social and cultural elements to Menorah's heavily academic focus, and it welcomed both Zionist and anti-Zionist students for whom the affiliation with the growing Hillel movement made sense.[5]

Frankel's ministry and Hillel began in Illinois when local community leaders wanted something more than what they found available for Jewish students in the early 1920s. Isaac Kuhn, who operated a successful clothing store in Champaign, worried about the fate of Jewish students at the university and encouraged others in the small Jewish community of Champaign-Urbana to help. Another Champaign resident, Nathan H. Cohen, and his wife, Addie Bernstein, began inviting Jewish students to their homes for Seders and then for regular Sunday evening discussions. In one such meeting at either the Kuhn or Cohen-Bernstein home (the record is unclear) students created a group they named Ivrim (Hebrew for "Hebrew people") in the fall of 1907 to hear talks on Jewish subjects. Of the few Jewish faculty at Illinois, Simon Litman, an instructor in English, enthusiastically supported Ivrim. In 1912, the Illinois-based Ivrim became the local chapter of the national Menorah Society. While the Menorah Society promoted "the study of Jewish history, culture, and problems, and the advancement of Jewish ideal," it also kept the focus rigorously intellectual, which limited the appeal. Kuhn, the Cohens, and Litman were joined in their support of Jewish students by Edward Chauncey Baldwin, an instructor in English at Illinois and a staunch Congregationalist, who taught Old Testament in the English department. As a liberal Protestant, Baldwin was also concerned for and supportive of American Jews.[6]

University of Illinois president Edmund J. James (in office 1904–1920) was, like Wisconsin's Van Hise, among the state university presidents committed to encouraging religious activity sponsored—and funded—by the various religious bodies. Protestant churches in Champaign-Urbana sponsored cultural, literary, and ethnic clubs; arranged for religion courses for credit; and in the case of the Methodists, established a Wesley Foundation to offer programs for Methodist students. At the same time, a Catholic guild formed in 1905 at Illinois and became a Newman Center. By the 1920s, it was logical to ask, "why not Jews?"[7] All of these developments, and the regularly prodding to do more by Baldwin and the Jewish families of Champaign-Urbana, laid the foundation for Frankel's chaplaincy in 1923.

In addition to developments at Illinois, there was another reason for Jewish chaplains to be joining their Protestant and Catholic colleagues in the 1920s. World War I had seen the appointment of Jewish military chaplains. For the first time in American history, they joined their Protestant and Catholic counterparts in the wartime Army and Navy. When Rabbi Lee J. Levinger described his experience as an army chaplain during the war as including responsibility for "burying four Christian boys" because there was no other chaplain available where he was stationed, Levinger spoke of the kind of solidarity that wartime chaplaincy produced and a new vision of a so-called tri-faith America that flowered during the war. After such chaplaincy efforts, it seemed logical to Jewish leaders to look seriously at another chaplaincy—college chaplaincy. In spite of the fact that the 1920s and 1930s were hardly a time of easy comity between the faiths—witness immigration laws specifically targeting southern European Catholics and Eastern European Jews or Al Smith's failed presidential campaign of 1928 and the anti-Catholic, anti-Semitic role of the KKK, which included a cross burning in Champaign-Urbana—leaders of the major Western faiths did have new experiences working together in 1917–1918 that carried into the next decade, on campus and elsewhere. The three-faith view of American religious life limited attention to other less familiar faiths until very late in the twentieth century, even though small numbers of Muslim and Hindu students could be found at some schools in the 1920s, but it did foster dialogue among those included.[8]

As these conversations continued to percolate at the national level, the young Rabbi Frankel bent all his considerable skills to building up the Hillel Foundation at the University of Illinois. Frankel saw himself foremost as a spiritual leader. As others remembered him, Frankel "radiated Jewishness in all directions." He did not ignore the intellectual and cultural issues that had been at the heart of Ivrim and the Menorah Society but sought something broader. His was a focus on the religious nature of Judaism, and he wanted to ensure that Jewish students participated actively in synagogue services. He worried that many Jewish students came to campus with little knowledge of their faith and were only passively Jewish. He wanted to be sure that affiliation with Hillel meant a student declaring, "I am a Jew." He insisted that the Hillel Foundation's approach was "distinctly a religious one." He took special pride in the growth, from 60 students to over 200, in attendance at regular services.

Frankel welcomed a wide range of Jewish students, Orthodox and Reform, Zionists and anti-Zionists to Hillel. As he organized it, Hillel was student governed through a number of committees that encouraged the active engagement of students so that "responsibility is placed on the shoulders of the student." Frankel also worked closely with the YMCA, the Wesley Foundation, and the Catholic chaplain, at one time writing an ecumenical prayer with a Methodist minister and a Catholic priest. When the university allowed registered religious groups to offer courses for credit, Hillel did so, along with several Christian groups, offering courses History of Judaism and Social Ideals of Judaism.[9]

Hillel Becomes the Face of Jewish College Student Religious Life in the United States

In 1924, Norman DeNosaquo, a Jewish student at the University of Wisconsin, learned what was happening at Illinois and wrote an appeal to create the same kind of community for Jewish men and women at Wisconsin that Hillel was providing at Illinois, insisting that they, too, "must be given the opportunity to cultivate those aspects of their life which are now neglected, which the school by its very nature cannot, and which the social environment does not give adequate facilities." Frankel agreed enthusiastically and helped launch a second chapter of Hillel for Wisconsin. The national—eventually international—growth of the organization had begun.[10]

Initially, Frankel persuaded a small group of prosperous Chicago leaders to underwrite the Hillel Foundation. Then in 1924–1925, Frankel convinced the large Jewish organization B'nai B'rith to sponsor the Hillel Foundation, with long-term consequences for both organizations. In their general convention in April 1925, the Independent Order of B'nai B'rith voted to confirm the support of what was now the B'nai B'rith Hillel Foundation at Illinois, Wisconsin, and beyond. The convention's minutes noted:

> When a Jewish student enters either of the institutions above mentioned, he is immediately brought into contact with an organization that represents him on the campus. He openly makes the declaration, "I am a Jew," by affiliating himself with the organization, and as time goes on, if he makes a name for himself on the campus, the respect that he receives is reflected on all of his co-religionists and on the Foundation.

At a time when many Jewish college students were seeking to assimilate as quickly as possible and bring little attention, if any, to their Jewishness, helping some students say, "I am a Jew," was very important.[11]

Hillel provided an inclusive social life for Jewish students. Hillel chapters often offered college-level courses, some for college credit, and ensured there was a comfortable "safe space" for Jewish students. As early as 1927, Hillel Foundations were established at Illinois, Wisconsin, Ohio State, Michigan, California, Cornell, West Virginia, and Texas.[12]

Sadly, in December 1927, the young Rabbi Frankel died of a rare heart disease. He was only thirty and widely mourned. But Frankel had created an essential structure and Abram L. Sachar soon became the new director of Hillel at Illinois. Sachar was already a faculty member at Illinois and an adviser to Hillel. Although not a rabbi, he was given permission to lead services at Sinai Temple and to direct Hillel, and in 1928 resigned his faculty position to continue his work with the Illinois chapter. In 1932 Sachar became the national director of the Hillel Foundation while continuing with the Illinois chapter. He continued as the national leader of the growing Hillel movement quite successfully until his retirement in 1947. Sachar was a popular teacher of religion courses, worked carefully in support of interfaith efforts on campus, and helped strengthen Hillel as a national organization. He inherited a strong foundation and built well on it. Sachar developed such a strong reputation that shortly after his retirement he was invited to assume the presidency of the new Jewish Brandeis University.[13]

In 1937 Hillel commissioned a national study of the growing number of Jewish students in the United States. By the best estimates of this study, led by Lee Levinger—the World War I Jewish Army chaplain—there were "close to 104,906" Jewish students out of a total college student population of 1,148,393, which meant that 9.13 percent of all college students were Jewish. Levinger's are probably the most accurate numbers among many estimates. Those numbers also meant that as wide as Hillel's reach was, the reality was starkly clear that "the religious and cultural needs of the Jewish student bodies are by no means adequately served," especially at the many colleges that had smaller numbers of Jewish students.[14]

In response to the Levinger report, the war clouds gathering in Europe, and the terrible attack on Jews being fomented by fascist and Nazi forces in Europe, there was a strong sense that more needed to be done. The result for Hillel was a decision to expand dramatically, from the existing twelve campuses to thirty. The expansion meant moving from campuses like Illinois with 1,200 Jewish students and the University of California, Berkeley with 1,000 or Ohio State with 1,100, to a greater diversity of schools, including the University of Chicago with 1,200 Jewish students but also the University of Missouri with 40, Michigan State Normal and Bucknell each also with 40, or Alabama Polytechnic with 30. It also meant compromising some other policies. Campus directors, who had all been full-time, might now be part-time, might serve more than one campus, and might not be rabbis. The budgets and meeting spaces might be smaller, but many more Jewish students in more places would be reached, and in one case at least, a Mrs. J. J. Tabuenhaus became

Figure 4.1. After its founding at the University of Illinois in 1923, Hillel grew to serve a wide range of Jewish students and spread rapidly to other universities, as shown by this illustration of the Hillel Center at the University of Pittsburgh. From Library of Congress

the first woman to direct any Hillel program when she took a position at Texas A&M College.[15]

During the years of World War II, Hillel continued to serve those Jewish students remaining on campus, dealing with the increasingly terrible news emerging from Nazi-occupied territory, and by 1944 it was deeply engaged in planning efforts for a postwar world in which the needs of Jewish students, including sometimes traumatized veterans, the nature of anti-Semitism, the newly forming state of Is-rael, and the nature of college life would be different. In the 1990s, Hillel split from its long affiliation with B'nai B'rith and continued to grow with solid student and foundation support to include 120 campus foundations and affiliates on 400 more campuses. In the twenty-first century, Hillel continues to be a major campus orga-nization across the United States and expands internationally.[16]

Yeshiva Offers an Alternative for Orthodox Jews While Other Jews Seek Assimilation

As important and welcoming as Hillel was for many Jewish students of different beliefs and practices within Judaism, there were also other Jews who preferred to keep free of—or felt more unwelcome in—the still culturally Christian colleges and universities of the United States. The more strictly observant in terms of holidays and keeping kosher they were, the less Jewish students fit in. Eastern European Jewish immigrants entering the United States between 1880 and 1914 included many different Jews. Gilbert Klaperman wisely said of them:

> The immigrant group was by no means homogeneous. They were socialist in-tellectuals, fervent Zionists, tired peasants, bearded shoemakers, skilled artisans and craftsmen, enlightened atheists, dignified rabbis, pale yeshiva students.

For the most orthodox among these newer immigrants, the level of assimilation required for them or their children to attend most American colleges, even those that welcomed Jews, was simply unacceptable.[17]

Some among the Orthodox responded by starting their own small schools, often initially to train rabbis in their old-world tradition, including Yeshivat Etz Chaim in 1886 and the Rabbi Isaac Elchanan Theological Seminary, incorporated in 1897. Conversations about a merger between the two seminaries began early in the twen-tieth century and were finalized in 1915 when a new school, originally named the Talmudical Academy, but often referred to simply as the Yeshiva, began. (Yeshiva, a term meaning "school," was used for many secondary and college-level academic institutions in Europe and North America while "the Yeshiva" soon came to mean one specific school based in New York City and serving the orthodox community.)

The school's second president, Bernard Revel, was determined to add an under-graduate college to the Talmudic work for rabbis. He saw a college as a way to improve the education of future rabbis and to educate many young men who were not destined for the clergy but who wanted a college education in an orthodox set-ting. His plan for a college was made easier by the fact that many Jewish academics were already anxious to leave Europe in the 1920s and found it hard to get placements in American colleges and universities. Not everyone agreed with Revel's plan. Some secular Jews did not want to see Jewish college students segregated from their non-Jewish peers and preferred that they attend a state university, perhaps one with a Hillel chapter. Some among the most orthodox did not want the secular subjects of a degree-granting college to contaminate the preparation of rabbis. Revel ignored both. He received permission from the New York Board of Regents for Yeshiva College to award the bachelor's degree, and in the fall of 1928, thirty-five young men began their studies at the college; in the spring of 1932, the first graduating class received their BA degrees. A new institution at which Judaism was central to a standard American academic curriculum, not on the margins or perhaps a distraction, was born and continues to thrive.[18]

Yet other Jews had little interest in matters religious. For some Jewish immigrants, the key to success in the United States, and especially in American universities, was to leave their faith far behind. One young immigrant, arriving in New York in 1885, recalled hearing:

> Young man, you have just landed in the great city of New York, where all the opportunities are opened to you, but if you want to succeed, you must forget about God and your religion and especially about the Sabbath and the dietary laws. You must work every day including the Sabbath and eat what you can get, for God has been left on the other side of the ocean.

Or as the Jewish immigrant in the 1975 award-winning film *Hester Street* said on leaving Russia, "Goodbye God, I'm going to America."[19]

For many American Jewish college professors, especially the grandchildren or great-grandchildren of earlier generations of Jewish immigrants, the key to success in the academy had been to take the 1885 immigrant's lesson seriously, if perhaps in a more sophisticated way. Many a Jewish college student found Jewish professors on whom religious observance, rested lightly. Indeed, it sometimes happened that the more observant Jewish college students complained that it was Jewish professors who were least sympathetic to their practices. Such a wide range should not be surprising. A 1918–1919 survey found that Jews made up about 3.5 percent of the population of the United States, but in spite of some barriers, Jewish college students made up about 10 percent of the total college student body of the nation. Differences among Jews, even intense arguments about those differences, would be normal in any similar group and it was out of those arguments that so much variety in practice evolved.[20]

Catholics and Protestants, Women and Men, Liberals and Fundamentalists, Blacks and Whites, and Those Who Just Wanted to Party and Enjoy Themselves

Where once there had been fierce debates among Catholics about whether the church should follow the students or simply demand that all good Catholics attend a Catholic college, by the 1920s and 1930s the reality was that many good Catholics followed every possible route to college. On the East Coast, especially in New York and Boston, Catholic students were likely to stay segregated in Catholic colleges. Thus, it was a normal path from Catholic parochial elementary and high schools in New York to Fordham in New York City or in Boston to Boston College or Holy Cross in Worcester, Massachusetts—all three proudly Jesuit schools. Although there were also strong Catholic colleges in the Midwest and West, perhaps most of all Notre Dame in Indiana, many more Catholics there opted to attend non-Catholic schools, especially the booming state universities; with that move, the Newman Clubs at those schools also boomed.

The interwar years were a time of greatly expanding opportunity for Catholic women, whereas many of the earlier Catholic colleges had been for men only. In the Philadelphia area alone three Catholic colleges for women opened in the early 1920s: Immaculata College (1920), Rosemont College (1921), and Chestnut Hill College (1924). Just as different Protestant denominations founded their separate and competing colleges, different Catholic orders, in this case orders of women religious or nuns, each started their own school. The long-serving Catholic archbishop of Philadelphia, Dennis Dougherty (archbishop from 1918 until 1951), did not support Newman Clubs at secular schools. In 1927 Dougherty wrote, "If a parish school be necessary in the lower grades, it is still more necessary in the higher; because it is in the higher grades that history, literature, and the experimental sciences are taught . . . that are dangerous to Religion." The archbishop also condemned co-education. With such leadership, it is not surprising that many good Catholic families in the Philadelphia area sought out Immaculata and the other colleges for their daughters. The three colleges were quite similar, although the Sisters of Saint Joseph who administered Chestnut Hill saw themselves as having a special mission to the poor and Chestnut Hill had a more economically diverse student body than its sisters/rivals. Especially in the early years between 1920 and 1940, all three schools were deeply religious in atmosphere and curriculum, with all academic subjects taught from a religious perspective and everything else, from college catalogs and regular chapel services to special Masses for feast days and special retreats, reflecting their faith. As the Immaculata handbook for 1931 said, the school offered a "thoroughly Christian education . . . which . . . should find its ultimate expression in the clear-minded, right-principled actions of the Christian Catholic women" who attended Immaculata.[21]

The nation's growing religious and ethnic diversity frightened many older Protestant Americans, including sometimes students and professors. Opposition to the new diversity—including to African Americans moving beyond sharecropping, or at best historically segregated Black colleges, but also increased numbers of Catholics and Jews—was found in the rise of a reborn Ku Klux Klan in the early 1920s. Most Klan violence was directed at small-business owners and at local activities they deemed immoral or un-American (given the Klan's rigid definition of America as a White Protestant country). But the Klan was present on college campuses too. The Klan gave $1,568 (the equivalent of $22,000 today) to help Bob Jones Senior create the White-only Bob Jones University, and Jones returned the favor by campaigning for Klan-backed candidates for political office. A group of men at the University of Wisconsin organized a fraternity, Kappa Beta Lambda (Klansmen Be Loyal), to "make the university a center for the Promotion of Christianity, Americanism, and Klansmenship," they said. The 1921 college yearbook, the *Badger*, showed twenty-nine members of the Klan fraternity.

The Klan attacked Catholic schools, burning crosses and setting off bombs at the Catholic University of Dayton. Football players at Dayton and the larger Notre Dame retaliated by disrupting Klan rallies, pulling off Klansmen's robes (thus exposing individual members' identities), and generally fighting back. While opposition to the Klan was strong especially in the African American community, in the Catholic Church led by the Knights of Columbus, and among liberal Protestant clergy, the strength of the Klan was a powerful reminder of what a contested and angry place the United States, including the nation's college campuses, could be in the 1920s. Although the Klan declined rapidly in the later 1920s due especially to a Knights of Columbus–led campaign to expose financial chicanery at the Klan's national office and to the exposure of individual Klan members to their neighbors locally, the Klan's focus on "100% (white Protestant) Americanism" persisted in American society and on college campuses longer than the Klan itself.[22]

The 1920s and 1930s were decades of not only a declining Protestant presence in the United States but also a time of deep division among American Protestants. In the nineteenth century, it was possible to speak of a generalized Protestant culture that pervaded most of American higher education—both denominational schools and state universities. By the 1920s, however, it was necessary to ask "which Protestant culture?" There was one group rallying as liberal Protestants who were comfortable with their understanding of evolution, who believed that the deeper understanding that emerged from biblical criticism only strengthened real faith, and who were comfortable rubbing shoulders with non-Protestant citizens of an increasing secular and diverse nation. There were others, rallying under the banner of fundamentalism, who rejected evolution and biblical criticism as an attack on the Bible as God's Word. In the 1920s, neither side was in any mood to compromise.[23]

Well before the end of the decade, many in the anti-evolution camp were giving up on most existing colleges, however strong their religious roots. For religious conservatives, these schools were drifting into a liberal camp and beyond redemption. In response, as Adam Laats has noted, "In the 1920s, American fundamentalists became the latest . . . religious leaders to create a new network of colleges that resolutely refused to go along with the secularizing and pluralistic trappings of the modern academic revolution."[24] Indeed the modern academic world, whatever its remaining Protestant trappings, was becoming anathema to the fundamentalists.

Between 1900 and 1930, college enrollment grew from 2 percent to 7 percent of the age cohort. This growth reflected the exponential increases in the number, and also the diversity, of college students. For the 1925–1926 academic year, a total of 97,263 Americans earned a bachelor's degree. For 1939–1940, the peak before World War II, the number was 186,500, essentially double the number who received degrees fifteen years earlier. Nearly all of these students were still White, but many more White women had joined the men as many universities beyond the Atlantic coast became coeducational and as women's colleges thrived, especially where women were not welcome in men's schools.[25]

By the late 1920s, Protestant students—once an overwhelming majority of the student body but now deeply divided along modernist/fundamentalist lines—had themselves become one of several groups, including growing numbers of Catholics, Jews, a sprinkling of people of other faiths, and students on whom all matters religious rested lightly. The cultural norms in many colleges also made many unwelcome—especially Jews who were often excluded by formal quotas but nevertheless made up close to 10 percent of the nation's college students in 1918–1919, even though Jews were less than 4 percent of the total population of the country.

The United States, and the nation's colleges, remained mostly segregated by race though World War II. Although a handful of African Americans did manage to study at northern universities—public and private—other than at a few places, like Oberlin and Antioch, they were a tiny minority up to the 1960s. Most African Americans who did attend college attended historically Black colleges and universities in the South, which ran their own parallel range of religious activities from segregated branches of the YMCA to regular chapel services, to a growing number of designated chaplains.[26]

But in addition to the exponential growth in the number of Catholics and Jews attending college, there was another force at work that was especially strong in the 1920s: rejection or sheer disinterest in all things religious. Perhaps, some of these students—and faculty members—said the fundamentalists were right and religious faith and faith in science were incompatible, but unlike the fundamentalists, they opted for science. While most liberal Christians had made their peace with Darwinian evolution, many other people on campuses and in the wider society thought about the implications of evolution and concluded, as did Darwin himself, that the world described by modern science was simply incompatible with Christianity, even in its most liberal forms.

While the battles between religion and science were significant, the generalized post–World War I cynicism of society (especially the young) may have mattered even more to campus culture. In a particularly insightful 1977 book, *The Damned and the Beautiful: American Youth in the 1920's*, Paula Fass describes how American young people, especially college students, "suddenly became a social problem in the 1920s," as "the journals of the twenties were filled with an image of youth out of control, of energy released from social restraints and of raw forces unleashed." Fass notes how religion—or the lack of interest in it—became one of several among the social forces bringing about a new youth culture, increasingly separate from adult norms or supervision.[27] She quotes a 1921 *Century Magazine* article that states, "there is no more momentous social fact than the cool and decisive turning away of the young people from those forms of religious association which to the liberals of the last age seemed to be the natural and satisfying embodiment of an emancipated faith."[28]

The year before the *Century Magazine* article appeared, Katharine Fullerton Gerould, writing in *The Atlantic*, bemoaned the loose morals of college undergraduates for whom former moral dictates against drinking and sex no longer held any sway. Gerould was clear that the problem she saw was due to "the abandonment of religion." She added, that if one were looking for somewhere to lay blame, "I thought the lack of religion more responsible than war or movies or motorcars for the vulgarity of our manners and the laxity of our morals." It seems clear that for some significant number of 1920s college students, the warnings of people like Gerould held as little interest as did her plea that, "for better or worse, our Western civilization has been built up on the Christian religion." They were more interested in the next dance and the next date and the good time they might be able to have in the too brief years they were in college. The fate of Western civilization could wait.[29]

All these generalizations, like the "flapper image" of young women of the decade, describe only a portion of young people. There were many pious or simply cautious college students attending religious gatherings of different sorts, and there were other college students who were too busy with jobs needed to support their lives to enjoy all the fun. But Fass, like the journalists of the day, points to a reality that well described a significant number of students of the era and set them apart from those who came before. Religion simply did not have the hold on them that it did on previous generations.

College Chaplaincy Thrives

In spite of all the problems facing religion, the interwar years were a bit of a boom time for college chaplains. In one of the few studies focused specifically on the college chaplain, Seymour Smith's 1954 *The American College Chaplaincy* described the number of chaplains and deans of religious life as growing "at a startling rate" in the 1920s and 1930s. Protestant, Catholic, and Jewish student organizations were now appearing on campus, often with their own chaplains. The years after 1925 were important ones for the growth of Hillel Foundation. From its start at the University of Illinois in 1923, Hillel grew quickly, and by 1938 over 10,000 students were affiliated with Hillel across the country.

In the 1920s, Catholics also expanded services to their students in state and secular private colleges, most coalescing around the Catholic Newman Foundations. Earlier concerns about protecting Catholic colleges were renewed in the 1920s when Father John O'Brien, the Catholic chaplain at the University of Illinois, launched a major fundraising campaign for a much-enlarged Catholic center. O'Brien noted that there were more Catholics at the state university than all the Catholic colleges in Illinois. But the backlash was fierce, and O'Brien's ambitious plans for the Catholic center building never came to fruition, though O'Brien continued in his work on the campus. Nevertheless, by 1926, there were 134 Newman Centers on American campuses and that number grew to 262 by 1938.[30]

On some campuses, chaplains found ways to work together across denominational lines. Chaplains and students explored diverse responses to the Great Depression, including some who were attracted to the left-leaning Methodist Federation for Social Service and the writing of Union Seminary's radical Harry F. Ward. More conservative Christian students on mainline campuses were not necessarily comfortable with the liberalism of what was becoming known as mainline Protestantism or its Catholic or Jewish counterparts. Their discomfort was reflected in the establishment of the first American chapter of the InterVarsity Christian Fellowship at the University of Michigan in 1941, created to reflect a more "evangelical outlook" on college campuses. This new organization would only grow in the decades after 1945 (see chapter 5).

In the midst of so much growth, the era was devastating for the student-led YMCA and YWCA. Between 1920 and 1940, the YMCA dropped from some 94,000 members to 51,350, and the related Student Volunteer Movement dropped from 2,783 volunteers in 1920 to just 25 in 1938. Before America became directly engaged in World War II, chaplains had emerged as the dominant reflection of religious life on the nation's campuses, a notable shift from the prewar period of student-led religious activity.

A Clearer Focus in Academic Religious Studies

Increasingly separating themselves from chaplains or religious life professionals, faculty committed to the academic study of religion found a new focus in the 1920s and 1930s. The burst of patriotism during the relatively brief US engagement in World War I led some, like Wellesley College's Laura H. Wild, to focus on the importance of a religious studies professor "who makes his class a vital center for spreading the great biblical messages of democracy and brotherhood." But that focus did not last.

After World War I, those engaged in studying religion were increasingly focused on proving their place in the academic side of the college curriculum. After about 1930, efforts began to make the academic study of religion a strong part of the humanities or general education curriculum of many colleges. Insisting the study of Christianity was essential to understanding Western civilization was an easy plea to make especially as "Western civ" (as they were usually called) courses grew in many places. Insisting to those who taught other subjects and among themselves that religious studies professors were as serious, as scientific, and as scholarly as their academic peers was a crucial part of the effort.

A few in the field of religious studies balked at the kind of disinterested objectivity that was building a wall between religious studies and those concerned with matters of faith. Chester Warren Quimby, at Dickinson College, complained that religious scholars "had bowed and scraped at the door of science, asking for a certificate of intellectual decency" when there were matters of religious faith at stake.[31]

In the interwar years, religious studies was still dominated by Protestants and

Protestantism. Such a cultural core also accounted for the discomfort others felt with the work, however much the claims of objectivity were made. Catholic universities, both elite ones like Georgetown and those far down the pecking order, pretty much kept to themselves ensuring that the—usually required—religion courses were taught following the dictates of pre–Vatican II Catholic scholasticism.

For Jews, who had long struggled for greater integration into the mainline of higher education, religious studies was a fraught arena. Semitic scholarship—the study of ancient Judaism and of the Hebrew language—had been a part of the college core in many places as early as the 1600s and was certainly central to many nineteenth-century schools' versions of the classical curriculum. By the late 1800s, it was also a field that a few Jewish scholars managed to enter and to which they brought considerable expertise. One such scholar was Richard Gottheil, who was appointed to a chair in Semitic studies at Columbia University in 1886, during the last years of Frederick A. P. Barnard's presidency (in office 1864–1889). Gottheil was also active in Jewish social, educational, and political activities, but he kept his outside activism and his Columbia scholarship rigidly separate. His critics, however, noted both and wondered how compatible the different parts of his intellectual life really were. Columbia's next president, Seth Low (in office 1890–1901), had tried hard to reign in the critics and anti-Semitism when he saw it, but his long-serving successor Nicholas Murray Butler (in office 1902–1945) did not follow that path. As a result, Gottheil found himself often marginalized within Columbia despite noteworthy scholarly achievements, such as publication of the *Jewish Encyclopedia* in 1901–1905. When Gottheil died after forty-nine years at Columbia, in 1936, Butler moved quickly to appoint a non-Jew to the position. Some Jewish scholars at other institutions escaped the marginalization that Gottheil experienced under Butler, but many—out of conviction or caution—stuck with safer and much more secular fields.[32]

The American Religious Depression

In spite of the growth of college chaplaincy and religious studies, the 1920s can be seen as the decade in which American Protestantism fractured, never to recover, and in which the nation's Protestant cultural dominance began to wither under the assault of diverse but decidedly non-Protestant groups asserting their right to help define the nation's culture. Religious historian Robert T. Handy called the period from 1925 to 1935 "the American Religious Depression." Predating the economic depression, Handy saw a significant depression among traditional American Protestants as their evangelical energy to reach the world through a global missionary enterprise or transform the culture of the United States seemed to evaporate in the face of the challenge from fundamentalism within, competition from Catholics and Jews without, and most of all, the rapid growth of religious indifference in the larger society. If this was true of what later came to be called mainline Protestantism across the country, it was also true among Protestant college students. The result, Handy argued, was that:

> During the period of religious and economic depression, then, the "Protestant era" in America was brought to a close. Protestantism emerged no longer as the "national religion."

Summarizing the change that took place in the two decades up to the end of World War II, Handy, citing Will Herberg's 1955 book, *Protestant-Catholic-Jew*, argued:

> In net effect, Protestantism today no longer regards itself either as a religious movement sweeping the continent or as a national church representing the religious life of the people; Protestantism understands itself today primarily as one of the three religious communities in which twentieth century America has come to be divided.

The depression that overtook American Protestantism in the 1920s dramatically eroded what had long been the dominant religious expression on college campuses among students, faculty, and in institutional structure. After the 1920s, that cultural norm was gone for good, even if a surprising number of symbols remained on many campuses well into the 1960s.

Historian Joel Carpenter has rightly critiqued Handy for failing to note that fundamentalist colleges and Bible Institutes flourished during what Handy called a "religious depression." That is true. But they flourished by choice at the margins of both higher education and society in general. Handy is also correct that by the end of the time period he studied, Protestantism had surrendered the central place it had held in American cultural and intellectual life since the Revolution. Protestantism itself was split as never before and by the 1930s and 1940s, too many Americans were just not interested, if for a wide variety of reasons.[33]

World War II disrupted every aspect of campus life. The number of male students dropped by half as most young men went off to fight, and often the chaplains went with them to become military chaplains. Only with the end of hostilities in 1945 did campus life rebound, though rebound it did. But it did so in a form few observers of American higher education before 1945 could have imagined. And that transformation is the subject of chapter 5.[34]

Defending Liberalism, Tolerance, and Evolution— The College of Wooster

In May 1923, the Presbyterian Church's General Assembly—the highest governing body in the denomination—held its annual meeting in Indianapolis, Indiana. For the assembly, the first act of business was electing a moderator to serve for a one-year term as the top official of the denomination. Unlike some years, the choice turned out to be a momentous one that involved higher education directly. There were two serious candidates for the position. The nominees were Charles Wishart, an ordained Presbyterian minister and president of the College of Wooster in Ohio, and William Jennings Bryan, three-time Democratic nominee for president of the United States and a long-time member and elder (lay leader) in the Presbyterian Church. Wishart was a well-known advocate of academic freedom in higher education and the president of a school where evolution has been taught as a key scientific concept for decades. By the 1920s, Bryan had become a more or less full-time campaigner against the teaching of evolution in high school or college. A *New York Times* reporter covering the meeting (a century ago the *Times* covered such meetings regularly) wrote that "the Presbyterian Church is being divided into evolutionists and anti-evolutionists." Bryan lost the election for moderator by a close vote of 427 to 451. The Presbyterian Church, like most of Protestant America, was dividing into two hostile camps with an unbridgeable divide between them.[35]

For American Protestant Christians, the world had been splitting at least since the 1890s, but the split came to a head in the 1920s. By the end of that decade, the relatively unified religious world of nineteenth-century Protestantism seemed far behind, split by different views of evolution and biblical criticism. While many Protestant denominational colleges tried desperately to maintain unity between modernist and fundamentalist constituencies, such a balancing act was becoming more and more impossible. Most faculty, especially in the sciences, had lost all patience with the fundamentalists. They demanded—with greater or less success—that the institution stand behind them. The College of Wooster and its president made a clear decision to defend the proponents of evolution. For this school, it worked well.

When Charles Wishart was elected the moderator of the Presbyterian Church in 1923, he had been president of the College of Wooster for four years, following his move from being pastor of the prestigious Second Presbyterian Church of Chicago. He remained at Wooster until his retirement in 1944. His 1923 challenge to William Jennings Bryan was not an anomaly. Throughout Wishart's long tenure as a college president, he became widely known for his defense of the teaching of evolution and academic freedom in general. On evolution, Wishart wrote in his unpublished *Memoirs* that while some, like Bryan, thought that one had to choose between science or Christianity, "We felt that a truly Christian college must keep its intellectual integrity, its scientific honesty, plus its Christianity." He added that the Wooster faculty "had long held that the Genesis story was a divinely inspired poetic picture of the creative process, not a dictated scientific account."[36]

The College of Wooster opened in 1870 with thirty-four students—thirty men and four women—and with the support of the Presbyterian Church. It was coeducational at a time when many denominational colleges were not, committed to allowing women the same education as men and to "strive with him on equal terms." The college's first president, Willis Lord, in his inaugural address in 1870, imagined a botany or an astronomy student making new discoveries and asked, "Are there no sacred vibrations of his soul responsive to the grand truths which have thus beamed in on his intellect?" Lord was confident of the answer and concluded, "The God of Creation is also the God of Revelation." As early as 1870, the leader of Wooster was asserting that there could be no conflict between faith and science.[37]

Wooster's best-known advocate for the compatibility of evolution and Christianity was Horace Nelson Mateer. Mateer began teaching biology in 1886, long before Wishart's arrival. His 1939 obituary reported that when he first began teaching, Mateer thought of evolution as "of the devil," but on further research became convinced of the accuracy of evolutionary theory. He believed it was his duty to teach it as such. Mateer was a very popular teacher, so popular that Wooster's largest classrooms were too small and he taught in the college chapel. Early on Mateer's stance on evolution was challenged by some trustees, but he insisted he would resign rather than trim his teaching regarding the truth as he saw it. President Sylvester Scovel (in office 1883–1899) backed Mateer completely, and for the rest of his long career the college fully supported him until his retirement in 1926. In his class lectures and writing, Mateer defended evolution as fully consistent with Christian belief. In his best-known work, *Evolution and Christianity* (1905), Mateer began by saying that he was both a teacher of science and a Christian and thus, "I deem it my duty to exert whatever influence I may have in the direction of bringing about a better understanding within the church concerning the foremost scientific question of the day."

That better understanding that Mateer advocated began, he said, with some understanding of just what evolution meant:

> To the scientific world evolution is a universal law of nature whereby the existing order of things in the visible Universe as viewed by man, including man himself,

has come into its present state of existence through the interaction of certain forces operating in the direction of a progressive change from some unknown primitive condition of things.

While some fundamentalists were willing to accept evolution as describing "lower orders," they insisted the humans were the result of a special one-time divine creation. As both a scientist and a Christian, Mateer rejected this special creation as an insult to God because it substituted "barren coldness of the finished statue for the inspiration of the living Artist still at work." He preferred to see God still at work. Thus, "To the Christian the same thought might be expressed by saying that evolution is the divine mode of creation whereby God has wrought out the existing order of things through the continuous operation of His creative power."[38]

Even before coming to Wooster, in sermons as a pastor in Chicago, Wishart had also made it clear that the kind of evolution he believed in was also guided by the hand of God and was, indeed, God's way of continuous creation. In a sermon most likely from the early 1920s, Wishart said, "Evolution presupposes power at work . . . you must have moral and intellectual and spiritual forces at work." The idea of evolution as guided by the hand of God was, to Wishart, the best protection against the kind of "survival of the fittest" morality that justified the wealth of a few and the poverty of so many and made "social Darwinism" so reprehensible to both Bryan and to Wishart.[39]

When he arrived at Wooster in the fall of 1919, in his first speech to the college community, Wishart said he wanted the college's ideal to be "the highest academic standards of any religious center in the country, and the highest religious standards of any academic center in the country. . . . Let us have fidelity to intellectual standards, fidelity to duty." He rejected any either-or framework.

When Bryan offered to come to the college to speak to the students, Wishart, ever the free speech advocate, invited him to stay at his home and to speak freely in the chapel to all who wanted to attend. In May 1921, Bryan gave a "relentless attack, upon the theory of evolution," which seems to have gone even longer after some students laughed at him. Some remembered how Bryan seemed to be incensed by the laughter and extended his talk later and later while "Ten o'clock passed, then ten-thirty. The students were amused; the deans fidgeted with their watches."[40]

The next fall, the student Scientific Club hosted a large meeting for the student body at which some 400 students heard a geology professor, a philosophy professor, and of course biology professor Mateer discuss science and faith. Not surprisingly, the three professors agreed that there was no conflict between evolution and their faith as they understood both. For the vast majority of Wooster students and faculty, evolution it seemed was a settled matter.[41]

Not everyone agreed with the evident consensus at Wooster. Elizabeth Coyle, then a new young biology professor, recalled one woman student transferring to Wheaton College because she disagreed with what was taught by professors like Mateer. The editor of the conservative paper *The Presbyterian* attacked Mateer, saying that "his evolutionary teachings are in direct opposition to the teachings of Christ, and cannot be reconciled to them." Bryan himself was so incensed by his seeming inability to convert the Wooster students to his point of view that he immediately asked the national Presbyterian Board of General Education to cut off all funding to Wooster College, a move the school's president ably deflected.[42]

Mateer was lucky to be teaching where he was. At nearby Baptist Denison University, zoology professor S. L. Kornhauser was not so fortunate. He was fired in the spring of 1922 because of his class presentations on evolution. The college would not relent, although his students petitioned that they had "not been influenced in their religious beliefs" because of Kornhauser's lessons. The fact that Kornhauser was a Jewish professor at a Christian school added to the suspicion that Denison was not a tolerant place in 1922. As the editors of the *Daily Illini*, the University of Illinois student newspaper, wrote about Kornhauser's dismissal, "we are led to ask what is to be the future of educational tolerance." The 1920s were not a tolerant time in American education, and the College of Wooster stood on lonely ground in its strong defense of academic freedom.[43]

The debates about evolution were far from the only matters to engage the student body at Wooster. Wishart was an able fundraiser and there were new buildings to be constructed. There were also many student activities to encourage. The college hosted guest speakers on many topics, including current affairs, the sciences, music, and international affairs, especially on Palestine in the aftermath of World War I. In the early 1920s, there were returning World War I veterans who needed support to adjust to college life and ongoing student agitation for reinstating fraternities that had previously been abolished and ultimately never came back. Students had more success campaigning for ending restrictions on women and men meeting in private and the end of sex-segregated dining halls.

Well into the 1920s and 1930s, Wooster also had active YMCA and YWCA chapters which, despite "some falling off of attendance and interest," remained a force on campus. The two Ys were important in developing social activities, raising funds for the Student Volunteer Society to support missionaries and sending students as missionaries. The Ys also supported an International Club that helped launch student demonstrations for isolationism and enforced neutrality in the 1930s, as the shadow of war hung over the campus community. In a 1938 poll, 79 percent of the college's students endorsed neutrality—a view that ended quickly after December 1941.[44]

Charles Wishart retired in 1944, and its new president, Howard Lowry, announced a goal for Wooster to be "a genuine Christian college of the liberal arts and sciences." This aim led to a curriculum designed to help students write a senior essay exploring one issue in depth and to engage with the Christian religion. Finally, Wooster affirmed that it was a Christian and Presbyterian college. Students did not have to be Presbyterian or even Christian to attend, but they did have to "want an education wide and deep enough to include the quest inherent in a genuine religious faith." Religion at Wooster at that time would not be just a matter for objective study nor left to the extracurricular world of those who were interested. Exploring one's faith was at the very core of the community, at least as the new president wanted to see it develop.[45]

By the 1960s, and in the decades that followed, there seemed to be less and less emphasis on the Christian and Presbyterian nature of life at Wooster. In December 2014, the college announced a new religious safe space in the Center for Diversity and Inclusion. The campus chaplain and director of interfaith campus ministries, Linda Morgan-Clement, described the space as a response to students who felt "restricted when it comes to their spiritual or religious practice." The new space represented a big symbolic change from the time—not so long before—when an overwhelmingly Christian student body gathered for required chapel. The student diversity of the twenty-first century demanded many more options and different forms of expression for students of many different traditions including those who were "spiritual but not religious"—a term even the liberal Wishart probably never heard and probably would not have understood.[46]

The Flagship of the Fundamentalist Movement— Wheaton College, Illinois

The unnamed young woman whom Elizabeth Coyle recalled as transferring from Wooster to Wheaton in the early 1920s made a wise decision if the College of Wooster's almost unanimous embrace of the teaching of evolution was a problem for her. She no doubt found a very different atmosphere—and a very different biology course—at Wheaton.

Wheaton College was founded in 1860 on the eve of the Civil War. Its first president was Jonathan Blanchard, a Presbyterian minister and radical abolitionist. The school, known for its evangelical abolitionist radicalism, seemed a lot like its near neighbor, Oberlin College. For Blanchard, as for Oberlin's Finney, evangelical Christianity and a radical commitment to abolishing slavery fit together perfectly as a way to live out one's faith. Wheaton, unlike Oberlin, was also committed to the classical college curriculum that dominated most antebellum colleges. Wheaton made no compromises when it came to the full and equal admission of women and African American students along with White men from the opening day. Through the 1860s and 1870s, the schools could easily have operated as siblings in adjoining states. But in the 1880s, their paths started to diverge—drastically.[47]

Charles Finney retired as president of Oberlin in 1866 and died in 1875, while Jonathan Blanchard died in office in 1882. After the passing of its founding generation, Oberlin moved toward a more liberal Christianity and later secularism, and away from the political radicalism so that it more closely resembled most of the nation's leading colleges. If Finney had returned to visit Oberlin in the 1920s, his evangelical faith, even more than his radical political views, would have been seen as quaint and hugely out of place.[48]

Wheaton moved in the opposite direction. When Jonathan Blanchard died in 1882, his son Charles Blanchard succeeded him and served for forty-three years until his own death in 1926. At first, the younger Blanchard sought to preserve the college in the form in which he inherited it. But as other colleges moved to embrace modernism in theology and secularism in culture, Charles Blanchard would have none of it. By 1919, Blanchard helped organize the World's Christian Fundamentals Association and draft the association's creed, which later became the creed of Wheaton College too. By the 1920s, Wheaton had become a place that was firmly ensconced in the fundamentalist movement, which demanded adherence to fundamentalism of its faculty and trustees, and that indeed stood at the top of the fundamentalist world of higher education—a world into which many new small colleges like BIOLA in Los Angeles or the Moody Bible Institute in Chicago were born, but few older colleges, other than Wheaton, followed.[49]

Once Wheaton moved toward fundamentalism and was one of the few established colleges to do so, enrollment and national and international interest exploded. Looking at enrollment from 1916 to 1928 (that is from the middle of Charles Blanchard's term until just after his death), college enrollment grew all across the United States but very few saw the enrollment growth that Wheaton did—a total of 405 percent. The average Methodist school, by contrast, grew by 46 percent. Under Blanchard's successor, and even in the midst of the Great Depression, Wheaton just kept growing. In these same years, the school also became a national beacon for fundamentalists rather than another small regional school. In 1917, 60 percent of the students came from Illinois. By the time Blanchard died, less than half did, and by 1938, long after Blanchard was gone, it was down to 25 percent, while the majority came from across the country and internationally. While every sign indicates that the embrace of fundamentalism was a deeply felt religious commitment, it was also without question an excellent marketing move.[50]

The third president of Wheaton was the first not to come from the Blanchard family. After Charles Blanchard's death, the trustees wanted to ensure that the commitment to fundamentalism was a permanent part of the college, not just an interest of one president. Before the trustees had launched a search for Blanchard's successor, a well-known fundamentalist preacher, J. Oliver Buswell, preached a series of chapel services at the college. Students loved the sermons and petitioned to invite him back for more preaching. Instead, two weeks later, the trustees invited Buswell to be the college's next president. Buswell had several attributes that the trustees liked: He was well-known and respected in national fundamentalist circles. He was a parish minister, not an academic, and thus seemed especially suited to ensuring the college's orthodoxy. He had served as a military chaplain in World War I and was young and enthusiastic, all attributes that the college needed. Some of Buswell's flaws, which might have been uncovered in a more thorough search, remained to be seen but he served quite successfully for the next fourteen years.[51]

Buswell did not disappoint the trustees or the Wheaton students in his commitment to the fundamentalist movement. Fundamentalism was not a denomination but rather a movement across many denominations, united by a belief in the inerrancy of the Bible as written and a rejection of modernism in theology—especially, of course, biblical criticism and evolution. By the 1920s, fundamentalist views were completely unacceptable on most college campuses and in many established denominations. But fundamentalism, in spite of its minority status, included active members of many denominations, especially Presbyterians and Baptists but also Methodists, Congregationalists, and even a few Roman Catholics, as well as many independents.

While he never compromised on fundamentalism for himself or the college, Buswell's major contribution to Wheaton was to strengthen the school's academic standing. Michael Hamilton, Wheaton's historian, wrote:

> In thinking about an institution like Wheaton College, then, there is always the danger of overemphasizing its fundamentalist character. From 1919 through at least 1965 it was indeed a thoroughly fundamentalist institution—but it was also

an American liberal arts college. As a college, a good deal of its character came not from fundamentalist culture at all, but from the American culture of higher education.[52]

Fundamentalist religion was always terribly important at Wheaton, but so was being an accredited college, and most of what a student studied at Wheaton—other than evolution—looked surprisingly like what was taught in most other schools of the day.

The move toward accreditation had begun under Charles Blanchard but Buswell also cared deeply about the recognition of the college as a legitimate institution of higher education. In order to meet the standards of the North Central Association of Colleges and Secondary Schools, Wheaton separated its high school programs from the college. It created a departmental structure for the faculty, and finally surrendered the old unified classical curriculum for one of individual courses, electives, and majors. Under Buswell, it also raised the portion of faculty holding a PhD from a quarter to a half. With these changes, Wheaton became a fully accredited college by the North Central Association. In 1930, it was also added to the Association of American Universities (AAU) list of satisfactory schools. Buswell also successfully pushed for accreditation by professional societies and for recognition by honorary societies such as those in physics, journalism, social science, literature, Hebrew, and public speaking. All of this recognition seemed essential to Wheaton's leadership and a way to set it apart from the Bible colleges and institutes in the fundamentalist movement. Parents could be secure in the knowledge that Wheaton would keep their children's religious faith intact while giving them the life chances that only a recognized college degree provided.[53]

Wheaton's best-known alumni from this era or any other was Billy Graham, who transferred to the school in 1940 from the Florida Bible Institute and graduated with a degree in anthropology in 1943. Graham actually began his college education at Bob Jones College in 1936. He hated his Bob Jones experience in "an environment so rigidly regimented that it shocked me." The teaching was clear—think like Bob Jones did and don't ask questions. Even at a young age Graham disliked being told what to think and to not ask questions. Finally, Graham told "Dr. Bob" that he was leaving, only to hear that he was a failure who would also face professional failure in the future. Graham and another Bob Jones student transferred to the Florida Bible Institute, a much happier place for them, but Graham also realized its limitations. Thus in 1940 when the opportunity came to transfer to Wheaton, Graham jumped at the chance. He was lonely and miserable at first but soon came to love the place. A lifetime later, he remembered a biology professor who, quite unlike Wooster's Mateer, taught that "the human race was not up from the ape but down from the hand of God." For Graham the combination of conservative theology (and biology) and a liberal learning environment was the perfect one and "Wheaton was both a spiritual and an intellectual turning point in my life." Wheaton College was also important for Graham because there he met Ruth Bell, who became his wife for the rest of his long life.[54]

For all his success in attracting more and stronger students, and raising the academic standing of the faculty and the college far beyond anything imagined when he started in 1926, Buswell ran into trouble. By the late 1930s, he had managed to alienate a good bit of the college's constituency, including the trustees. Part of the problem was Buswell's support for the movement for fundamentalists to abandon the older denominations, just at a time when many of them had decided to stay in their home churches and fight for change. At least half of the Wheaton student body belonged to established churches, and the trustees did not want to lose them. Buswell loved the theological debates within the fundamentalist community over issues that seemed obscure to outsiders, but he loved debate perhaps too much for a college president. Many of those whom he challenged did not appreciate his efforts to set them straight. Even his own mother warned him, "You have rows enough on your hands. . . . I love you darling but don't insist on singing the piece your organist can't play, for the fun of a scrap. . . . Be peaceable." It was good advice, especially for the president of a college who needed the allegiance of many disputatious factions. But it was not Buswell's nature to take the advice. After enough complaints, and stirring rebellions within and outside the college, the trustees fired him in January 1940. For all their appreciation for his very real contributions to the college, they just could not take the self-inflicted controversy any longer.[55]

Immediately after firing Buswell, the trustees selected an internal candidate, V. Raymond Edman, chair of the political science and history departments, as his successor. Edman was as committed to the fundamentalist movement as Buswell, and he also shared his commitment to maintaining Wheaton's academic standing, though perhaps with less urgency than his predecessor. But in other ways, Edman was the opposite kind of leader from his predecessor. He was good natured, welcoming, carefully avoided as many conflicts as possible, and was seen by many as a "truly spiritual Christian leader." He was also a very successful president who led in the fundraising that supported a building boom on campus, and in the decision to become more selective and prestigious in admissions rather than to keep indiscriminately growing. Edman served through a period of considerable good will until his own retirement in 1965.

While Edman maintained Wheaton's conservative religious orthodoxy and its academic standing, the larger fundamentalist movement split further. A more sectarian group claimed the fundamentalist title, while a larger, more inclusive group of theological conservatives were content with saying they were committed to "evangelicalism." Given the breath of is reach, it was not surprising that Wheaton identified with the latter group and began calling itself an evangelical school. For the next half century, it remained solidly conservative, though not fundamentalist, and was proud of Billy Graham and its conservative evangelical heritage. It has been a lead institution in a growing network of schools, institutes, churches, and summer camps that maintain an evangelistic culture quite out of step with most of the rest of the academic world, even if exceedingly popular in a large evangelical subculture within American Christianity. In 2021, the college described itself as offering a "world class Christian education," with "world-class academics" and "Christ at the core." Perhaps that is more than enough to set the college apart from the mainstream of American higher education without any reference to fundamentalism.[56]

Defending a Public University—The University of Tennessee

By the 1920s, the University of Tennessee (UT) had a long and proud history. It had been founded by the legislature of the Tennessee Territory in 1794 when most of Tennessee (outside of a few forts or trading posts) was still beyond the lines of legal White settlement. But by the 1791 Treaty of Holston, the tribes of east Tennessee ceded a small amount of land near the North Carolina boarder to the United States and the territorial governor, William Blount, appointed by President George Washington, created his capital there at a town he named Knoxville. There the college was created. From the beginning, the school that became the University of Tennessee was a state school without religious affiliation though not very different, in fact, from the religiously affiliated schools of its day.[57]

In its early years, the college was tiny. Its president, Samuel Carrick, a Presbyterian minister, was its only professor and he taught all subjects in a four-year curriculum that reproduced, as much as one person could, the classical college curriculum: English grammar, geography, logic, astronomy, rhetoric, and natural and—of course—moral philosophy. There were no electives. Covering all of this was made easier by the fact that the school had a tiny student body. While students came and went, it was 1806 before the first one, William Parker, graduated. The legislature had stipulated that the trustees should "take effectual care that students of all denominations may and shall be admitted to the equal advantages of a liberal education . . . and that they shall receive a like fair, generous and equal treatment during their residence there." It is doubtful that the legislature imagined any non-Protestant students, but students who were affiliated with the various and often competitive Protestant bodies were all welcome.[58]

Throughout the antebellum era the college had a precarious existence. It was closed several times and as at many schools at the time, the faculty, never more than a few people, still managed to fight over revisions to the classical curriculum. The student body—all White males—remained small, under 100. A college degree seemed unimportant in the agricultural world of pre–Civil War Tennessee. In the 1850s, Methodist newspapers attacked the school as leaning too favorably toward the Presbyterians when the Methodists were the largest denomination in east Tennessee and in the university's student body. Various presidents tended toward strict disciplinary rules, but students did not always follow the rules and some were disciplined for fighting, drinking, "pistol packing," "indecently exposing their persons bathing at night in the Spring," and in one case "harboring a profligate woman in his room during a portion of the night."[59]

After the disruptions of the Civil War, the enrollment—still limited to White males—grew to several hundred students. As happened with many colleges, there were charges that the state university was a godless place and that the way to a "Devilish life" for a young man was through the college. In response, a series of presidents and professors pointed to signs of religious life on campus. The most important religious activities were through the YMCA. The YMCA was founded at what was still East Tennessee University in the mid-1870s. The official university periodical reported that the YMCA "is in a prosperous condition, and the weekly attendance is very good with prospects brightening." The school encouraged efforts by the YMCA to raise funds and build (and pay for) a large building that, like other Ys, served students' social as well as spiritual needs, with a gymnasium, reading room, and dormitory space. The Y also offered regular Bible study in addition to the university's official chapel services. University officials also expected students to attend church on Sunday. For some students, the Y and chapel created a strongly religious atmosphere in college even if others managed to ignore the piety.[60]

The school officially changed its name to the University of Tennessee in 1879, at a time when the faculty was convulsed by two major debates, one about Reconstruction and the other about the classical curriculum. Thomas Humes, who had served as president since 1865, was like many in east Tennessee a staunch supporter of the Union and an opponent of the Confederacy's secession. After the war, he prohibited a celebration of Robert E. Lee's birthday on campus. An increasingly anti-Reconstruction legislature began a continued attack on the president until he was forced out in 1883. While the Reconstruction legislature of Tennessee had mandated the admission of students regardless of race, the new Constitution of 1870 prohibited the education of Blacks and Whites in the same school. The faculty, ever cautious, resolved the issue, timidly, by having the university admit a few African American students and then pay their tuition to attend Fisk University in Nashville rather than come to campus.

Humes was not only a champion of Reconstruction in Tennessee but also the traditional classical curriculum. It cost him his job. After Humes's removal in 1883, the trustees emphasized agricultural work and the new president, Charles Dabney, enthusiastically embraced the agricultural focus as well as racial segregation. In 1893 he also convinced the faculty and trustees that for no other reason than needed enrollment, the university should admit women as equal students with men and large numbers quickly arrived. By the time Dabney left in 1904, the University of Tennessee had close to 800 students and a faculty just under 100—still small enough for faculty to have regular face-to-face contact with each other and the president, but huge compared to its antebellum incarnation.[61]

World War I changed the campus. A new president, the former dean of agriculture, Harcourt Morgan, took office in 1919 and worked closely with his dean of liberal arts, James Hoskins, who succeeded him in 1934. Between the two they led the university through the Roaring Twenties, the Great Depression, and World War II. Enrollment, still small by twenty-first-century standards, grew dramatically in the 1920s, from 1,194 in 1919 to 2,433 in 1929. The 1920s were a time when many college students were concerned with simply having a good time. Sports, fraternities, and sororities dominated the scene, as did student dances, shows, and a fair amount of student drinking, even during prohibition. (One student who entered in 1919 was said to be the college bootlegger, serving the school well in his own way.) Symbolic of its fate nationally, when the YMCA building burned down during these years, the university claimed the land back and built its own student center unaffiliated with religious life. As Paula Fass wrote of students in the era, "By the twenties the young had transferred their allegiance from the churches, broad or narrow, to a different sort of God, as they invested a kind of religious devotion to their leisure pursuits to sports, dating, and song."[62]

In the 1920s, the faculty, deans, and president were forced to confront a religious debate they were trying desperately to avoid. President Morgan, a biologist and former agriculture dean, had taught evolution for years in his own courses, but did so quietly. As president, he knew that pressure was building in the legislature to follow other states and enact a law banning the teaching of evolution. His solution was to keep his head down and to urge his faculty to do the same. J. W. Sprowles, a young professor of secondary education, did not share the caution of his elders (not unusual in the academic world) and in the summer of 1922 he ordered a textbook for an education course he was scheduled to teach that fall, *Mind in the Making*, which included a section on evolution. When Sprowles refused to change texts, President Morgan convinced him to simply teach another course instead. The bookstore returned the copies of *Mind in the Making* when they arrived. The issue might have ended there, except that Dean Hoskins did not like any challenges from faculty and decided to press the issue. For all his scholarly credentials, Sprowles had been criticized for lack of attention to the school visits, which were part of his job. Either as a pretext or based on real concern, Hoskin told Sprowles that his appointment was not being renewed for fall 1923. When Sprowles protested the decision—loudly—several faculty supported him, including A. A. Schaeffer in zoology, R. S. Radford in Latin and Roman archaeology, and R. S. Ellis in psychology and philosophy. Still not taking criticism well, Hoskins convinced the deans to fire all of the protesting professors and a few others for good measure, a total of seven professors. Officially they were simply told that their contracts were not being renewed for the 1923–1924 academic year, but it meant the same thing. If the firings were an attempt to keep the issue quiet, it failed.[63]

Even in the days when many institutions were yet to award tenure, the non-reappointment of seven long-serving professors got national attention. Even before his own job was on the line, A. A. Schaffer, the zoologist, had requested that the American Association of University Professors (AAUP) look into the Sprowles matter. Once it became clear that not one but seven professors, some of whom had taught at UT for many years, including Schaffer himself, were being fired, the AAUP moved quickly to investigate. In the case of Sprowles, the investigating committee found conflicting evidence. They were convinced that he was not good at a part of his duties—visiting schools. On the other hand, his decision to order a controversial textbook that discussed evolution had led President Morgan to ask him to "soft peddle the issue," which he did but not sufficiently to avoid the ire of Dean Hoskins. In the end, the AAUP committee decided that although the professor's competence at his job was a real question, the school visit problem also had the feel of being "merely pretext" for the non-renewal decision.[64]

The AAUP committee looked especially closely at the case of their chapter president, A. A. Schaffer, and found that he was perhaps "the most distinguished scholar on the Faculty," but also that he had a reputation for not cooperating with the administration, which had led Dean Hoskins to write to him:

> We have been considering an investigation of the recent disturbances here in the University and have been convinced by evidence of your activities that you are not in accord with the administration of the institution. You had not, before the recent disturbances came, manifested a willingness to cooperate. We have, therefore concluded not to recommend you for reappointment.

Such was the state of academic freedom in Tennessee in 1923.

In the end, the AAUP committee, while regretting the fact that the decisions were made during the summer break when faculty had already dispersed—Schaffer was in the distant Cayman Islands and very hard to reach—concluded that "The University authorities, it is readily admitted, acted within their legal rights and their procedures involved no violation of the contract rights of any professor." This conclusion came despite the fact that "there are considerations of equity, of abstract justice of tolerance, and of fair and honorable treatment which cannot be justly ignored." Nevertheless, the AAUP committee did not recommend any action. It was not the kind of stance that the AAUP came to be known for in later decades, but it was far from burnishing the reputation of the university in the eyes of the national academic community. Schaffer was able to move to a faculty position at Clark University in Massachusetts, though it is not clear that all of the others were so fortunate.

By the time of the AAUP report, Morgan's fears of state legislation were coming to pass. As he had been at the College of Wooster, William Jennings Bryan was again at the center of the action.[65] Thinking perhaps of his experience at the College of Wooster, Bryan said he was horrified that many college students were being taught "that the Bible was a collection of myths." In an article called "The Menace of Darwinism," he said, "To destroy the faith of Christians and [in reference to what he had seen of German militarism as Secretary of State] lay the foundations for the bloodiest war in history would seem enough to condemn Darwinism." Darwinism, he said, "is not science at all; it is guesses strung together."

Late in 1921, the Kentucky Baptist State Board of Missions called for a state law against the teaching of evolution in the public schools. Bryan, still at heart a politician, wrote to the board congratulating them on the resolution, saying, "The movement [to ban the teaching of evolution] will sweep the country, and *we* will drive Darwinism from *our* schools."

Bryan did not object to teaching evolution as a theory but felt that if taught the schools needed to balance information on "the theory" with equal time for religious interpretations. Bryan told the Florida legislature "that the objection is not to teaching the evolutionary hypothesis as a hypothesis, but to teaching of it as true or as a proven fact." A political campaign, however, demanded focus, not nuance, and soon Bryan's goal became banning the teaching of evolution outright. Bryan defended the anti-evolution laws on majoritarian grounds. If the majority of people in a state were opposed to the teaching of evolution, Bryan said, then they ought to rule. "Teachers in public schools," he said, "must teach what the taxpayers desire taught. The hand that writes the pay check rules the school." And for Bryan, this included a university that received taxpayer funds.[66]

Legislation was proposed in a number of states, including New York, to ban the teaching of evolution. It passed mostly in the South and the West; in Oklahoma, Kentucky, and Florida. As Morgan feared, the Tennessee legislature was also a perfect target. Anti-evolution bills had died in committee in the Tennessee legislature in 1923. In the next legislative session Bryan and his allies made certain that bills did not meet the same fate. Bryan toured the state giving major speeches on the issue. So did Minneapolis minister William B. Riley and the nation's best-known evangelist, Billy Sunday. There were opponents of the bills, such as the writer to the *Nashville Banner* who said, "Let us not blow out the lights as long as the student desires to learn." Nevertheless, in a state where 1 million of its 1.2 million citizens were church members, the momentum was hard to resist and what became known as the Butler Bill passed in early 1925. It then became

> unlawful for any teacher in any of the Universities, Normal and all other public schools of the State which are supported in whole or in part by the public school funds of the State, to teach any theory that denies the story of the Divine Creation of man as taught in the Bible, and to teach instead that man has descended from a lower order of animals.

When Governor Austin Peay signed the legislation on March 21, 1925, reluctantly he said, he saw it as a symbolic act. "Nobody believes that it is going to be an active statute." How wrong he was.[67]

The next steps in the evolution saga are well known. The American Civil Liberties Union (ACLU) was determined to fight the anti-evolution law as an attack on the free speech of teachers. They found a biology teacher, young John T. Scopes of Dayton, Tennessee, willing to test the law. The state, aided by the ever-ready Bryan, prosecuted Scopes. The ACLU, aided by the nationally famous Clarence Darrow,

defended him assisted by John R. Neal, one of the seven Tennessee professors who
had been purged in 1923. Scopes was convicted but not before Darrow thoroughly
embarrassed Bryan. Scopes's conviction was later dismissed on a technicality. After
that, Peay's hopes came true. The issue was never tested again.[68]

The Scopes Trial has been studied often but nearly always as a high school issue.
But the Butler Bill specifically included all state educational institutions, including
the University of Tennessee. Certainly in the case of the state's flagship university,
the law had a chilling effect, if not on what actually was said—quietly—in the classroom, but on what was said in the larger society. President Morgan believed the law
was unconstitutional, but the Tennessee Supreme Court threw out the Scopes conviction on a technicality so there was no appeal on the constitutional issues. Some
faculty and outside critics said they expected more from the university in terms of
resistance to the anti-evolution law, but the majority of the faculty had other concerns and little interest in further controversy once the storm of the Scopes Trial
had passed. As the university historians summarized the campus mood in the 1920s,
"It could be said that, on the whole, UT was peaceful but it was not in those days a
place distinguished by untrammeled freedom of inquiry. Circumspection was the
general rule."[69]

The Great Depression of the 1930s was also a depressed time in much of American higher education, but perhaps less so in eastern Tennessee because of the New
Deal's Tennessee Valley Authority (TVA) spending, which often included funding
for the university. President Morgan left the university for a leadership role in the
TVA itself in 1934, and the more cautious Dean Hoskins succeed him, serving as
president until 1946. Enrollment reached almost 6,000 students in 1939 but then
declined drastically during World War II. It rebounded to new heights with the
enrollment of GI Bill–funded students after 1945. Starting in 1950, civil rights activity, not seen since the ending of Reconstruction in the 1880s, led to new pressures to integrate the campus that were initially resisted by the administration.
Nevertheless, the professional schools began to admit African Americans in 1952,
and the undergraduate programs were integrated in 1961. Once admitted, the few
African American students and some White students at UT, the local campus ministers, and the National Conference of Christians and Jews pushed local businesses,
especially hotels and restaurants, to serve African Americans, with some success.
Knoxville's segregated ways were ebbing if not ending. Finally in 1967, with important efforts by zoology professor Arthur Jones at UT, the Butler Act was repealed
even before the US Supreme Court, in an Arkansas case, declared the law unconstitutional (as Morgan had predicted it should be in the 1920s).

As of 2021, UT had approximately 30,000 students and 1,500 faculty—a very different place from the 1,000–2,000 students and 100 faculty in the 1920s. In the twenty-first century, the university saw a diversity undreamed of in the nineteenth century. Religious life was served by some twenty campus ministry programs representing most Christian denominations and Hillel and a Muslim Student Association. These programs describe themselves as creating a close sense of community for students in a large school.[70]

Diversity's Home—City College and Hunter College in New York

In 1919, nearly 80 percent of City College of New York's male students were Eastern European Jews and close to 40 percent of the women at cross-town Hunter College were also Jews. As Mike Wallace said in his history of New York City, "CCNY, it was said, had become the Jewish University of America." This had not always been true, and it would not always remain true, but between World War I and World War II, to attend either City College or Hunter was to be immersed in a deeply Jewish student community (if not a faculty one) and to cross paths regularly with both the deeply pious and the totally assimilated within that community.[71]

Neither City College nor Hunter was founded to serve Jewish students. The New York Free Academy that became CCNY opened its doors in 1847 only to men at a time when there were still relatively few Jews in New York. By the 1890s, a small number of Eastern European Jewish boys followed where a few German Jews had gone a decade earlier and began attending city college. The school was free and relatively open to them. Academic standards were hardly rigorous. It was, however, far from a welcoming place for Jews. The faculty were steeped in a Protestant ethos. Chapel attendance was required. Fraternities associated with the school specifically excluded Jews, and anti-Semitic remarks by faculty and fellow students were relatively common.[72]

Hunter emerged later. There had been several proposals, none successful, to admit women to CCNY. But New York needed women as teachers, and so—perhaps ironically with the strong backing of William "Boss" Tweed—the Female Normal and High School opened in 1871, led by legendary New York principals Thomas Hunter and Lydia Wadleigh. From the beginning, the new school had much higher standards than many normal schools. It emphasized student teaching and education courses but also included a well-rounded curriculum based on Hunter and Wadleigh's belief that for teachers, "the chief reliance must be placed upon the resources of cultivated minds." Only a year later, the school was renamed the Normal

College of the City of New York. By the end of World War I, the school was a full-scale degree-granting college for working-class New York women, based as much on Vassar, Wellesley, and Smith as on the nation's many normal schools. It had a diverse student body from the beginning. As early as 1890, the *American Hebrew* journal praised the school for admitting students "irrespective of religious affiliation," when other schools had or would soon develop quotas for Jews. In 1914 the name was changed to Hunter College of the City of New York after its then former president.[73]

While CCNY had only offered a lukewarm welcome to Jewish students in the nineteenth century, there were drastic changes early in the twentieth. A new group of trustees managed to wrest control of the school from its old board, raised the academic and admission standards, and in 1903 hired John H. Finley as president. Finley reformed the curriculum, abolished required daily chapel attendance, and enthusiastically welcomed all students, even visiting tenement apartments to make sure their residents felt welcome. Enrollment—especially among recent immigrant Eastern European Jews and their American-born children—boomed. Hunter needed no such reforms. Young women of many backgrounds were always welcome at Hunter, a fact that mattered to Eastern European Jewish women in the early twentieth century.[74]

New York's public colleges were not the only ones in which large numbers of recent immigrants made themselves felt, although in different ways. Under the leadership of President Nicholas Murray Butler, New York's prestigious Columbia University transformed itself into a modern research university and an increasingly selective one. Its selection process intentionally limited the numbers of Jewish students. Up until World War I, Columbia had something close to an open admission policy but after enrollment grew, Butler sought to cap it and ensure that the past policy of accepting "any one as student who is not shown to be unfit or unprepared," be ended. Partly this was done through raising academic standards, but Butler wanted more, as he once wrote to the academic dean of the undergraduate college: "it would be highly judicious if . . . some way could be found to see that individuals of the undesirable type did not get into Columbia College, no matter what their record." An eight-page application that asked a range of questions about a student's background and ambitions did the trick. Columbia still admitted Jewish students, but Jewish enrollment was capped at around 10 percent while it had sometimes ranged as high as 25 percent of the student body prior to Butler's intervention.[75]

New York University (The University of the City of New York until 1896) had a bifurcated approach. On NYU's then-rural Bronx undergraduate campus, the school's chancellor, Henry Mitchell MacCracken (1891–1910), insisted on maintaining a strong Protestant ethos. MacCracken said, "It is hardly to be expected that the intellectual activity of either the Catholic or Jewish population would ever find its expression in Columbia or New York University." NYU's dean of the College of Arts and Pure Science used psychological tests and a loyalty oath as part of his effort to "check the growth within the college of masses of students of foreign origin and essentially foreign in their sympathies." The professional schools and undergraduate college located around Washington Square in Manhattan had no such policy and welcomed everyone, including Jewish students who probably equaled half of the 9,300 downtown students.[76]

Nevertheless, the center of Jewish student life in New York in the interwar years was CCNY. In the student council, in informal gatherings, and in classes, heated political and philosophical discussions were the order of the day. CCNY students from those years became some of the post–World War II intellectual leaders of the United States. Though classroom discussions were lively at CCNY, as often as not, the fiercest student discussions were outside of class. Student life at both CCNY and Hunter stretched all over the city, connected by subway and tenement neighborhood rather than by dorm hallways since neither school had dorms or a residential student population.

Neither college chaplains—Jewish or otherwise—or an organization like Hillel took root at CCNY or Hunter. Some students were, no doubt, deeply observant in their religious practices, but they did so at home more than at school. Others were religious skeptics and most others somewhere in between. As Hasia Diner, historian of the American Jewish experience, notes, "Observance as a category would have been all over the place. Attending a Seder or high holiday services: does that make one observant or not? Going to a synagogue every once and a while?" In any case, a Seder at a home or services at the neighborhood synagogue were not campus events. For commuter students, quite unlike residential ones, the campus was a subway ride away from religious life and, as Diner added, "Most of those students would have been commuters, living at home so even if observant (and to whatever degree) they had no need for an on campus chaplain. As such whatever their level of observance is kind of moot."[77]

The Jewish, Catholic, and Protestant students of the 1920s and 1930s all represented a small minority of their respective populations in New York City. Between 1918 and 1941, the percentage of students attending college rose from 2 percent to 7 percent of the total of the nation's eighteen- to twenty-four-year-olds, with White Protestants still dominating the nation's student body and immigrants and students of color left far behind. But well over 90 percent of the nation's young people did not attend college at all. For all the energy around Jewish culture at CCNY, one number stands out: In 1913, the entire graduating class at CCNY, with its high Jewish population, included 209 men compared to the nearly 1 million Jews living in New York City. College, and the chance to participate in college life, was a rare privilege, not available to the majority of any group.[78]

CCNY and Hunter remained mostly single-sex institutions throughout the pre-war era. Although CCNY admitted women to some graduate programs in 1930, it was 1951 before women were admitted to the undergraduate college, while Hunter only admitted men to the main campus in 1964. In 1926, the two schools were joined under a new Board of Higher Education, which added campuses in Brooklyn and Queens, and later the Bronx and Staten Island and several community colleges. In 1961, the many campuses were united in a new City University of New York (CUNY). After 1970, the admission process was revised—under massive student pressure—to make the colleges more available to more New Yorkers, and with these growing numbers, the percentage of Jews at the school declined. CUNY is today one of the largest university systems in the country, with a range of campuses, special programs, and students of many religious faiths and none.[79]

CHAPTER FIVE

A Postwar Boom in Religion and Higher Education, 1945–1960

About 11:30 p.m. on December 1, 1955, Jo Ann Gibson Robinson received a telephone call at her home in Montgomery, Alabama, that Rosa Parks had been arrested that afternoon for refusing to give up her seat on one of Montgomery's rigidly racially segregated buses. Robinson was a member of the English department of the segregated Alabama State College, chair of the local African American Women's Political Council, and a member of the political affairs committee at Dexter Avenue Baptist Church. A Black woman, she had also once been kicked off a Montgomery bus herself for sitting in the wrong seat. With that telephone call, Robinson's Baptist faith, her political instincts, and her academic connections all kicked into overdrive. She called her Alabama State colleague, John Cannon, and they and two of their students met in her office at the college around midnight, ostensibly to grade papers (something many professors do late at night) but in fact to plan direct political action in response to Parks's arrest. The four "paper graders" drafted a leaflet that said, "Another Negro woman has been arrested and thrown into jail because she refused to get up out of her seat on a bus and give it to a white person. . . . This woman's case will come up on Monday. We are therefore asking every Negro to stay off the buses on Monday in protest of the arrest and trial."

They then used the college mimeograph machines to make 50,000 copies of the leaflets, a political activity that was strictly prohibited, but seemed so necessary to them. They began distributing the leaflets across Montgomery's African American community early in the morning on December 2. One of the drop-off points was an AME Zion Church, where many of the city's Black ministers were meeting. Most of the Montgomery African American clergy thus learned of the call for a boycott from Robinson's leaflets. As she recalled, "One minister read the circular, inquired about the announcements, and found that all the city's black congregations were . . . planning to support the one-day boycott with or without their ministers' leadership. It was then that the ministers decided that it was time for them, the leaders, to catch up with the masses." With this action by Robinson and her three co-conspirators, the Montgomery protest turned into the Montgomery Bus Boycott, which would last a year and change the face of the South and the nation.[1]

The boycott that began on Monday, December 5, was much more successful than any of the organizers dreamed it might be, and as a result, clergy and non-clergy leaders became determined to continue it as long as it took to end segregation on the city buses. They formed the Montgomery Improvement Association to coordinate the boycott. Robinson declined an official position in the association so as not to jeopardize her position at Alabama State, but she did accept Martin Luther King Jr.'s invitation to unofficially join the executive board and edit their newsletter. She was arrested multiple times for driving people to work to help them avoid taking a bus, even as she tried to keep as low a profile as possible. Reflecting on the boycott, King remembered of Robinson, "Apparently indefatigable, she, perhaps more than any other person, was active on every level of the protest."[2]

Separate and Uninterested: Postwar Religion and Postwar Higher Education

Robinson's story has been told many times because of the essential part she played in the Montgomery Bus Boycott. But the facts that Robinson was both a college professor and an active church member, as well as deeply committed to civil rights is often overlooked. Her choices in December 1955 illustrate the interplay of religion, politics, and higher education. The decade and a half after World War II was a time of extraordinary developments in all three arenas, but they were seldom seen as connected. There was a huge expansion of higher education in the nation.[3] The era was one of an extraordinary religious energy. Finally, the 1940s and 1950s saw a new vibrancy in civil rights activity and also early stirrings of much additional political activity. But examination of an overlap between the academy, politics, and religion is rare. It is as if Jo Ann Gibson Robinson's determination to keep her campus colleagues (and especially superiors) at Alabama State in the dark about her role as leader in the bus boycott, or the Baptist roots of that activity, represented a paradigm for how the nation at large remembered this period.[4]

A New Kind of College and University: Growth and Change Beyond Imagination

Across the United States, college and university campuses looked very different after 1945 than ever before in their history. After the terrible war ended in August 1945, many faculty and administrators dreamed of a return to "normal," whatever normal meant to them. It did not happen. Instead, their world turned upside down. As John Thelin wrote, the architectural symbol of the postwar campus was not the massive construction of the 1920s, but rather the cheap and lightweight Quonset hut. These ugly temporary but very quickly constructed buildings were put up, or kept up after war-time programs, in significant numbers on many campuses and continued in use through the 1960s because it made it easy for colleges to expand rapidly. By the late 1940s, Quonset huts, and even the older more stately campus buildings, were all busting at the seams, hosting the huge expansion at a scale never seen before on college campuses. As Thelin also remarked, the next decades were marked by the "three Ps," of "prosperity, prestige, and popularity," such as most colleges had never known before and which many would remember with a kind of sad nostalgia in the future.[5]

Government policy was a driving force in the changes to higher education in the middle of the twentieth century, but these policies were only successful because colleges themselves, state governments, and the culture of the country were in close alignment. The GI Bill of 1944—officially the Servicemen's Readjustment Act— added educational benefits as a bit of an afterthought to a plan for a year of salary support for returning soldiers and sailors, designed mostly to avoid the depression-era discontent of World War I veterans. Few in government or higher education expected the college assistance benefit to be used very often. Returning veterans, however, had different ideas and many colleges, from the Ivy League to community colleges, actively recruited former military personnel to enroll. The men, mostly White, and the few eligible women (those who had served in uniform), responded more enthusiastically than anyone expected. Between 1945 and 1950, 2 million veterans went to college on the GI Bill, about 30 percent of female veterans and 16 percent of male veterans, although this translated into only 60,000 women out of the 2 million GIs in college.

The GI Bill made no adjustment for the segregation, and often exclusion, of Black Americans in the World War II military. Beyond the segregated nature of the services, some draft boards, especially in the South, had been reluctant to draft African Americans and teach them to fight during the war. Nevertheless, a few African Americans did attend college because of the bill, enough to raise the African American college graduation rates from around 1 percent to above 3 percent of their cohort. In 1939–1940, college enrollment had been at an all-time high of just under 1.5 million students, but it had dropped dramatically while so many were off on the war effort between 1941 and 1945. However, by 1949–1950, there were 2.7 million college students, 3.6 million in 1960, and 7.9 million in 1970. This was a huge and continuing expansion far beyond anything funded by the GI Bill itself.

Because of the GI Bill, college student bodies were more male, marginally more racially diverse, older and more experienced, and much more serious. The massive infusion of people who had spent years at war and now found themselves in classrooms that were not always prepared for them changed college life. Assumptions about who would attend college were permanently changed by the GI Bill.[6]

In July 1946, President Harry Truman appointed a Commission on Higher Education, afterwards known as the Truman Commission, to study the future role of colleges in the country and specifically to explore whether some of the benefits of the GI Bill should become a permanent federal responsibility, which the commission ultimately did recommend. While a divided Congress stalled federal action, many state governments, private foundations, and individual colleges began implementing some of the commission's other recommendations.[7]

During World War II and the long Cold War that followed, the federal government engaged in a massive increase in federal spending on research, especially in the sciences—often with military links—and in medicine. MIT's Vannevar Bush, who had led the Office of Scientific Research and Development during World War II, recommended far more research after the war, a recommendation that led to the creation of the National Science Foundation (1950), which offered competitive grant programs in which most funding went to major research universities. Where the GI Bill fostered a high increase in the percentage of college attendance across the country, the research initiatives fostered very focused growth—six universities received over half of the hundred-fold increase in postwar federal research dollars. Nevertheless, many universities—and many individual faculty—focused on federal grants, a pattern that University of California president Clark Kerr termed the "federal grant university." In many schools, the search for ever more students was replaced with a search for ever more research dollars.[8]

The changes in higher education after 1945 left church-related colleges in a precarious position. In 1947, looking at what was coming in the postwar era, Merrimon Cuninggim, usually optimistic about the place of religion in twentieth-century colleges, wrote that "the actual situation with respect to church-related colleges today is not a happy one."[9] There were moments in the next decade when many observers reevaluated their initial pessimism. The GI Bill did allow students to use their benefits at church-related colleges, and many religious schools grew as a result. Some hoped that if church-related colleges, most of them Protestant Christian colleges, could embrace the unique role of being a kind of theological center that linked faith and learning, they might play an outsize role in the future of American higher education. Others asked what would it mean for a school to treat all learning from a Christian perspective, while at the same time uphold the highest academic standards and freedoms?

Mixing faith and learning was harder to do than some thought. Colleges needed students, and most students wanted to be part of the mainstream. Faculty wanted prestige, and prestigious careers in higher education involved grants and high-status institutions more than theological reflection. While the GI Bill helped church-related colleges, many other federal and state programs did not include religiously affiliated schools. Some dedicated individuals continued to labor in the marginalized world of the denominational college. With so many students and dollars at play, some denominational colleges did thrive on the margins of a larger enterprise that was increasingly secular in spite of the religious renaissance happening all around it.[10]

All the growth in higher education, including the rising number of students, the size and influence of federal research grants, and the emerging assumption that one "should" attend college, led to a rapid expansion in the size of the professorate too. Jo Ann Robinson's hiring at Alabama State College in 1949 put her among thousands of newly minted college professors. Many, like Robinson, were the first in their families to even graduate from a college, much less teach at one. For many, probably most, in the academic world of the era, it was a quiet time. Professors wanted prestige and grants. Students were serious about their work, getting on with their lives, and with finding well-paying jobs, often in large corporations, after graduation. There were dissidents, like the handful of faculty at the University of California and elsewhere who resigned rather than sign anti-communist loyalty oaths, but they were the exception. Hodding Carter III, who graduated from Princeton in 1957, wrote of his generation of college students, "Silent or not, we weren't inclined to rattle a lot of cages." Carter, himself, went on to rattle many cages as a journalist and civil rights activist in Mississippi in the 1960s, but that was in a different era.[11]

The rapid growth of higher education also marginalized religion on campus. Religious studies, though flourishing, was not one of the popular majors among a generation who wanted to focus on careers after college, even if their religious lives may have been important to them at the personal level. The prized research dollars very seldom included dollars for research in religion, even though a few private foundations tried to counter the trend. During the century before 1945, college presidents regularly had to contend with the charge that college was anti-religious. The complaint did not go away completely in the 1950s, but it seemed to decline. Colleges were neither against or for religion or religious faith. The faculty, students, and administrators, like many funders, simply had other priorities. As we will see in the cases of Pepperdine and Brandeis, there were exceptions. But they were exceptions to a new normal that appeared in the post–World War II era.

The Unexpected Religious Revival of the 1950s

The 1949 Los Angeles crusade that launched Billy Graham's career did not get off to an auspicious start. As Graham remembered it, "If the amount of press coverage was any indication, the Los Angeles Campaign was going to be a failure. . . . As far as the media were concerned, the Los Angeles Campaign—by far our most ambitious evangelistic effort to date—was going to be a nonevent." In fact, the opposite happened. In the early days of the revival, in September 1949, 3,000 to 4,000 people arrived each evening at the Graham campaign tent—not a bad number for a "nonevent." The numbers kept growing, and by the end date of November 20, 11,000 people packed the tent, while many more waited outside for a chance to hear Graham. A new personality and a new movement had burst on the American scene. Graham's popularity was not unique. He was perhaps the brightest star in a very large constellation of popular religious voices that emerged in the late 1940s and the 1950s, although almost all operated fairly far from the world of higher education.[12]

Large-scale religious revivals were not new to the American scene. The English revivalist George Whitefield drew the largest crowds in British North America before the American Revolution, and nineteenth-century revivalists played a large role in founding colleges in their day. But by the midpoint of the twentieth century, such revivalists seemed like ancient history. Yet the Graham revivals—he preferred to call them crusades—were something new. Graham reached out across the divi-

sions of Protestantism to include both evangelistic and mainline churches. He refused to hold racially segregated campaigns when strict segregation was still the
rule of the day in many places. Something new was emerging in postwar America—
a religious revival—but the time was right and in Graham there was a revivalist to
match the moment.[13]

Graham was not alone. In 1940, 49 percent of adult Americans belonged to
a religious congregation, nearly always Protestant, Catholic, or Jewish, and about
average for the previous half century. By 1960, it was 69 percent of the nation's growing population who did so, a twenty-point jump and an all-time high. On many a
Sunday (plus a few who attended on Saturday) close to half of the American people
were in church or synagogue. New church construction rose from a valuation of
$26 million in 1945 to $409 million in 1950 and kept increasing for another decade.
The 1950s, remembered by many as the definition of normal for religious engagement, was in fact a very unique decade for religious institutions—dramatically
greater in prosperity and population, if not necessarily prestige, than anything seen
at other eras in American history.[14]

In a particularly insightful (and underappreciated) book on American religion
in the 1950s, Robert Ellwood calls the decade the era of a spiritual marketplace.
Churches competed for members and influence in ways that they had not in previous generations—where once being of English origin meant being Episcopal
or maybe Congregational, German had meant being Lutheran or Catholic, Greek
meant Orthodox, and African American meant Baptist or maybe Methodist. In the
1950s, however, many people (perhaps especially but not only those moving from
small towns or cramped urban centers to the new suburbs) felt free to try different
kinds of churches.

With the Great Migration of American Blacks, which had begun earlier but
accelerated during and after World War II, many who had attended a Baptist or
Methodist church in the South found a Pentecostal church more to their liking in
the new Black urban neighborhoods of the North. Many Jews, perhaps especially
Jews who were the children or grandchildren of very secular forebearers, flocked
to new Reform and Conservative synagogues, taking their own place in the era
of religious revival. As Ellwood noted, a small community in Europe would most
likely have one central church and perhaps, if the area was tolerant, a Jewish synagogue and two or three, small dissenting congregations. In an American town of the
same size there could easily be a dozen churches representing most of the nation's
major denominations, one or two synagogues, plus a few lively fundamentalist and
Pentecostal gatherings. Religious freedom and the new religious interest, plus the

longstanding American love of commerce, meant that in the 1950s, denominations and faiths felt free to compete for higher numbers and larger buildings, and all the signs seemed to point to a religious capitalism in which everyone was winning.[15]

Religious popularizers gained significant public notice in the 1950s. Among Protestants there was Graham, but also Norman Vincent Peale, New York City pastor and author of the best-selling *The Power of Positive Thinking* (1952); Catherine Marshall, author of *A Man Called Peter* (1951); and Dale Evans Rogers, TV personality and author of several books. There were also prominent Catholics, the most famous of whom, Bishop Fulton Sheen, wrote *Peace of Soul* (1949) and also became a major TV personality, not just among Catholics, with his weekly program that began, "Thank you for inviting me into your home." For Jews there were personalities like Rabbi Joshua Liebman, whose book *Peace of Mind* (1946) offered comfort in a world just recovering from war. In the 1950s, the older American denominations—Methodist, Baptist, Presbyterian, and others—and the Roman Catholic Church all grew much faster than the newer evangelical bodies (a trend that would be reversed later in the century), even though evangelicals, like Graham, were often the greatest single force driving the revival.[16]

In a different world—a surprisingly different world—the serious study of theology blossomed in the 1950s. Most famous of the new American theologians was Reinhold Niebuhr, author of *Moral Man and Immoral Society* and a dozen other works, who was joined at New York's Union Theological Seminary, the hub of neo-orthodoxy theology, by Paul Tillich and at Yale by his brother H. Richard Niebuhr. If these three were the best known and most widely read, there were a significant number of other so-called highbrow theologians who made the era one of extraordinary intellectual as well as emotional religious vitality. Reinhold Niebuhr and Paul Tillich were both on the cover of *Time* in the 1950s, a sign that the magazine's editors took them seriously and expected their readership to do the same. Niebuhr got there first, published on the cover of the March 8, 1948, issue celebrating the Christian season of Lent, but a decade later Tillich's cover of March 16, 1959, was even more laudatory, carrying a banner that said, "A Theology for America's Protestants."[17]

Sadly, for all of the energy exhibited in religious crusades and the serious intellectual work in religion, there was surprisingly little conversation among the various factions. As both Robert Ellwood and William Lee Miller noted, "One remarkable thing about the interest in religion among intellectuals is how separate it is from the revival in popular culture. . . . One is struck by the lack of interest in the popular revival among the theologians, and the lack of intellectual leadership in the popular revival." If this divide existed among Protestants, there were also deep divisions between Protestants and Catholics, and little interest in reaching out on either side in the years before John XXIII's election as Pope in 1958 began a significant thaw between the Catholic and the Protestant world that came to fruition with the Vatican Council of 1962–1965. Beyond Protestant–Catholic tensions, for all the surface goodwill in the postwar era there was also little Christian–Jewish dialogue either. It seems as if all the major religious groups in the United States were growing at once but talking to each other relatively little, although much could have been learned from a few conversations.[18] Americans as a whole were growing more religious—much more religious—in the late 1940s and 1950s. As the aging American president Dwight Eisenhower said, "Our form of government makes no sense unless it is founded in a deeply felt religious faith and I don't care what it is." Religion was in the air.[19]

Postwar Politics

Perhaps the deepest political and social current in the era, at least in the White and straight community, was an overwhelming desire to put the war, and also the Great Depression, with all of their terrors, privation, and shortages, as far behind as possible. People "settled down," often in new—and racially segregated—suburbs; sought their own homes; bought appliances, new automobiles, and the new invention—televisions—in quantity; and had babies at an astounding rate, launching the "baby boom" of the 1950s. Many, especially in the growing middle class, also attended church on Sunday and saved to send their children to college even if they themselves had not been positioned to do so. They did not want to hear about inequality, injustice, or post-traumatic stress disorder in the returning soldiers. Yet there were also huge undercurrents of tension in these same years that went well beyond the dynamics of the mass-market postwar consumer culture.[20]

The atomic bomb, and the far more powerful hydrogen bomb that both the United States and its now enemy the USSR developed in 1952 and 1953, meant that "mutually assured destruction" was not just a phrase but a reality hanging over everyone's life. A number of politicians, notably Senators Joseph McCarthy and the young Richard M. Nixon, rose to fame by seeking to prove that Soviet agents in and around the US government had given atomic secrets to the Russians and had "lost China" to the Soviet sphere. Anti-communism was a powerful political issue—in politics, in churches, and on campus.[21]

Politicians also invoked religion regularly, especially in the context of the Cold War. Leaders in the United States thought it important to show the world that the nation stood for something different than communist atheism. In 1954, the US Congress added the words "under God" to the Pledge of Allegiance so that every morning school children, and adults attending public meetings, would promise their loyalty to "one nation under God, indivisible, with liberty and justice for all." While some worried about the conscription of God as a defender of the "American way of life," many basked in the notion that the two were not really separable.[22]

At the same time, African American resistance to the segregation and inequality that had been part of African American life since the defeat of post–Civil War Reconstruction grew dramatically. Spurred in part by a generation of Blacks who had served in the military and had a hard time reconciling fighting for democracy abroad and not finding it at home, resistance to segregation, while it had never stopped in the Black community, blossomed in these years as national organizations like the National Association for the Advancement of Colored People (NAACP) ramped up their fight in the courts to challenge segregation, especially in schools and colleges and separate grassroots campaigns, like the one to integrate buses in Montgomery, grew. Black Christian churches, a crucial part of the core of Southern Black communities, became key supporters of the drive for civil rights. The sermons of Martin Luther King Jr. rang with the cadences of Black preaching along with the demand for justice in the current moment. Black college students sat in at lunch counters, rode buses, and marched for freedom. The Nation of Islam, as both a religious and political organization, also grew especially in urban centers in the North. A rapid push for greater equality unfolded in far more diverse ways— including on campus—in the 1960s than anything seen in the 1940s or 1950s or any time since the end of Reconstruction, but many of the seeds were planted in the 1950s. Campus life was never the same as a result.[23]

Bridges across the Chasm: Finding Places for Religion on the Campus of the 1950s

Faculty—more or less personally religious—along with campus-based clergy serving as college chaplains and deans of college chapels, and finally students in their own organizations all sought a place for religion in the colleges and universities of the 1950s. Whoever led them, most of these efforts involved finding a place for religions on the margins of the university. But in the 1950s, it was a robust margin.

The Failure of the Faculty Christian Fellowship

In October 1952, a group of Christian college professors, with support from the interdenominational National Council of Churches, organized a new group, the Faculty Christian Fellowship; by the following year, the fellowship was holding national conferences and publishing its own journal, *The Christian Scholar*. An important new movement seemed to be on the horizon that would link the world of faith to the world of the university. The fellowship aimed to bring the highest intellectual standards to the examination of faith, and at the same time engage in a fundamental critique of the university's tendency to limit its mode of knowing to what could be empirically provable and the so-called cult of objectivity, and to examine the tendency among academics to downgrade other forms of knowledge including experience, inspiration, and ethics—and therefore faith. As one of the early members of the group, Kenneth Irving Brown, put it, "The time is ripe in American education for a reorganization of our program that shall take larger concern for values, purposes, and ideals, and an even larger concern for the presentation of a world view which shall include a recognition of God and His expectation of man."

The Faculty Christian Fellowship did not depend only on the enthusiasm of a few committed college professors of faith, important as that was. It had significant financial support from the National Council of Churches and the Edward W. Hazen Foundation. The Hazen Foundation had begun promoting similar efforts since the 1920s through sponsored conferences and papers. By the 1950s, the Danforth Foundation joined the effort, and its role would only grow for the next two decades. With such a base providing funding and logistics support for conferences, papers, and new research, success seemed assured. Along with the theological renaissance associated with the Niebuhr brothers and Paul Tillich, something of a game changer seemed afoot across all American higher education and not confined to theological seminaries.[24]

The game change was not to be, however, although it would take well over a decade before the Faculty Christian Fellowship sputtered out of existence in the midst of the campus upheavals of the 1960s. In the intervening years, the fellowship never had the impact that its founders hoped for.[25] For all its seeming promise, the Faculty Christian Fellowship ran into several insurmountable problems. From the beginning, the group was plagued by a sense that perhaps these religious professors did not really want to interrogate the university so much as resume a place when people of faith, especially in its Protestant form, ruled the university. Their insistence on proving what good traditional scholars they were certainly undermined any sense that they represented radical critics of the university as opposed to a group that wanted to be "taken back into the fold," perhaps closer to the head of the table. When much more far-reaching critiques of the American university emerged in the 1960s, initially led by students and then by a new generation of faculty with their own scholarly perspective, the fellowship simply could not survive.

Equally problematic, from the beginning, the Faculty Christian Fellowship suffered from an utter lack of interest by most faculty colleagues. As Bernard Iddings Bell had warned in 1949, even before the fellowship was launched, "The American university does not in reality care a button about religion. . . . It looks on religion as one of the minor amusements like china painting or playing the flute, pleasant for those who enjoy that sort of thing, but not an intellectual or a practical necessity." In the 1950s, flute playing stood a much better chance of withstanding that sort of condescension than a lively faith that sought to engage, and also critique, the core of the modern university.[26]

In a series of studies of faculty attitudes toward religion conducted in the immediate postwar years by the Hazen Foundation, the conclusion was clear and almost unanimous: Most faculty simply did not care about the topic of religion in almost any form. Even a study of faculty at church-related colleges found the same attitude. As Edwin Espy, author of the one study reported, "There is little evidence of profound intellectual wrestling with the problems of relationship between faith and fact, 'revealed' truth and 'scientific truth.'" Despite the zealous work of some religion scholars, the vast majority of college professors seemed to be utterly uninterested in religious faith, at least as it related to their professional lives as academics.[27]

Do the Humanities Include Religion?

The number of undergraduate programs in religious studies increased nationally, from twenty to thirty-eight in the postwar era—double the number but hardly a dent on many of the hundreds of campuses across the United States. But far beyond official programs, many more colleges began offering courses in religious studies based in a variety of other departments. A renewed national interest in the humanities after World War II allowed advocates for religion courses to find a home there. Out of the many words written on the subject, the most influential was Harvard University's *General Education in a Free Society* (1945). The report made the case that the evils that had led the world to war could not be cured only by scientific research or a specialized disciplinary focus alone, but rather that all students needed the "values, attitudes, knowledge and skills . . . to live rightly and well in a free society." The Harvard report, and most other publications advocating renewed attention to the humanities, did not specifically mention religion courses. It was, however, easy enough for advocates of such courses and programs to ask who better than a religious studies professor to raise questions about ethics and social responsibility?[28]

Just where religion fit in the humanities was never completely clear. Could or should matters of ultimate meaning be taught consistent with the demands of twentieth-century scholarship? If not, might attention to religion be better lodged in the history, anthropology, sociology, or philosophy department? On the other hand, Frederick Houk Borsch, then an undergraduate at Princeton in the mid-1950s, remembered a problem with most humanities courses:

> Liberal arts courses engaged in historical overviews, surveys of knowledge and ideas, and then some closer reading of texts . . . I shall always be grateful to Princeton faculty for helping me learn how to read carefully and critically, while I also learned that questions about meaning or purpose in life had to be posed indirectly if they were to be heard at all. We could have some discussion of values and virtues in life as long as one did not press too hard.

One of the major professors in Princeton's religion department while Borsch was a student was George F. Thomas, one of the founders of the Faculty Christian Fellowship. Thomas argued that religion itself could in fact allow students to press harder and be the integrating place for values and virtues, along with critical reading and questioning. But Borsch remembered, "Professor Thomas and other faculty—in a department that wanted to be seen as having a place in a research university—were aware of the need to defend their teaching as properly academic and critical."[29]

Another question cut to the core of questions about religion as a humanities discipline, however. As A. Roy Eckardt, chair of the religion department at Lehigh University and president of the National Association of Biblical Instructors, told his colleagues in a 1957 speech, "the strangeness of religion is inevitable." Religion made ultimate claims for faith in a way that could never make it fully compatible with the disinterested work of other disciplines or the university as a whole. "Religion remains in the world yet not of the world, in the university, yet not of the university." It was a tension that always led to questions about the place of religious studies in the research university. It meant tensions with other faculty, even in the humanities, in spite of the fact that students were voting with their feet and taking more and more courses in the area.[30]

College Chaplains and Deans of University Chapels

At a national conference of college chaplains held at Yale Divinity School in 1948, the Methodist theologian Albert C. Outler described the many Hazen reports and others that he had reviewed as pointing to the work that was cut out for college chaplains in the coming decade. Calling the moment "a strategic opportunity and an awful responsibility" for college and university chaplains, Outler said:

> Education is revealed as being largely secularist, positivist, and incompatible with an adequate world view. The curriculum is dangerously departmentalized. The administration is polite but indifferent . . . as for the faculty, they are indifferent or hostile—more regularly the former. . . . In some colleges religion plays a real part, but generally it is conventional and not profoundly vital.[31]

Perhaps, Outler thought, the chaplains, operating at one remove from the academy, could succeed in making religion vital in universities and colleges where others had not.

Other voices in the late 1940s and early 1950s were more positive about new developments in religion on campus. Clarence Shedd, since the 1930s one of the best-known scholars in the country focusing on the place of religion in higher education, wrote, "Never in this century has there been so much serious and creative discussion of the problems of religion in higher education as during the past decade." The ever-optimistic Merrimon Cuninggim insisted that secularism had real strength on campuses, especially before World War II, but "since then the colleges have recaptured much of their lost concern for the religious development of their students." There was, indeed, evidence to which Shedd and Cuninggim could point in terms of new books published, conferences held, and chaplains and religious studies professors at work. The problem was, as Outler had observed, the vast majority of the faculty were more likely to be "indifferent or hostile" and the institutions structured to marginalize religion.[32]

Two decades later, in a short essay published in the massive Danforth Study of Campus Ministry, Robert W. Lynn, then a professor at Union Theological Seminary but soon to be a major force in the field of campus religion as vice president of the Lilly Endowment, echoed Outler when he said, "Like the Protestant, the Roman Catholic educator today is threatened by a crisis, the meaning of which is marginality." But much more strongly than Outler, Lynn argued for those who truly cared about the place of religion in the twentieth-century university to embrace their marginality, noting, "I am arguing not just for modesty, but rather for the freedom that comes from being on the margin—the freedom now to be selective, the freedom to be partial. At last we can forgo cultural imperialism and begin to take and select that which most needs to be done at this moment."[33]

Certainly, campus ministry (as it was usually called among Protestants) or college chaplaincy was a thriving world in thse 1945–1960 era, even if thriving on the margins. According to the Danforth Study, there were some 1,300 Protestant clergy working full-time as ministers on college campuses at the end of the 1950s. Most of them were employed by the ten mainline Protestant denominations that seemed most invested and had the most money to invest. By the end of the 1950s, there were also over 500 Catholic chaplains, 150 of whom were full-time, and close to 500 Newman Clubs, of which about 100 were full-fledged Catholic centers. Finally, Hillel—which had grown dramatically just before World War II and would grow again later in the twentieth century—mostly held steady in the 1950s with around 200 campus chapters. Most Hillel centers were staffed by full-time or part-time adult leadership; the majority were rabbis. Very few, if any, chaplains of other traditions were to be found on the mid-century landscape.[34]

What is clear from the above picture is that in the 1950s there were more chaplains on college campuses than ever before. When Seymour Smith conducted a study of college chaplains in the early 1950s, he included a survey of current chaplains asking them to account for the growth of their field. The top answers were "Need for more adequate leadership of, or stimulation of, religious activities" and "concern of administration for religion or church-related heritage." College presidents gave basically the same answers but added, "assignment to one person of responsibility for total campus programs." What was also clear in the presidents' answers was that the one person would not be themselves.

Chaplains were people (mostly men) on the margin—on the margin in multiple ways—and most of them felt that way. As John Schmalzbauer and Kathleen Mahoney described "the general twentieth-century pattern," it was one "wherein the campus minister or chaplain operated near the margins and rarely took center stage except during convocations, commencements, or times of tragedy." Chaplains might be on the margins of college life, but perhaps Robert Lynn was right: religion, and its professional representatives, seemed to be thriving quite well in that marginal role.[35]

Douglas Sloan has also described the second tension in college chaplaincy in the 1940s and 1950s: "From the beginning there were built-in tensions between the new campus ministry and the congregations that supported them," Sloan argued. The religious revival of the 1950s "was an important source of the money necessary for the churches to expand their campus ministry," but many in the churches—pastors and members—did not quite understand, or if they did understand, did not always embrace the kinds of ministries that chaplains engaged in. Most chaplains conducted fewer formal worship services than churches saw as their core mission, were far more open to cross-denominational work to the point of ignoring denominational identity, and most significant, chaplains were far to the left of parish clergy and congregations on many matters.

Phillip Hammond's survey of chaplains and parish ministers in the early 1960s—well before the campus upheavals of the 1960s began—reported startling differences in attitude on many core issues. While 53 percent of these 1950s-era chaplains thought their own denominations were too conservative in the arena of social action, only 17 percent of parish clergy did, and while 68 percent of parish clergy attended to news of their own denomination, only 35 percent of chaplains cared. The United Student Christian Council (USCC) was created in 1946 to coordinate college chaplaincy across denominations, and in 1959 the USCC merged with other groups supporting campus ministries to create the National Student Christian Federation (NSCF). For college chaplains and many students, the creation of NSCF, and the vitality of its predecessor organizations, meant that interdenominational work was still central, and in some ways reminiscent of the nineteenth-century Y. Like what happened to the Y, such an attitude sometimes stirred resentment among those for whom individual denominational loyalty was important.[36]

There were other issues that sometimes divided chaplains from parish churches of their own denomination. For decades, Protestant ministry had included, if not been centered on, evangelism, which was defined as bringing individual souls to accept Christ. By the 1940s and 1950s, leading theologians and most denominational leaders had moved to a wider definition of evangelism that more often meant saving the larger society from unfair practices and inequality. Yet just how the two definitions of the same word meshed was sometimes confusing. Chaplains were far from alone in embracing the wider, less individualized definition of evangelism. Ever since the days of the Social Gospel before World War I, most seminary theologians and many parish clergy were in agreement that the gospel had to be social and not limited to individual salvation. But chaplains were often more enthusiastic in their embrace of the newer understanding of evangelism than some clergy working in other spheres, especially in more conservative churches and denominations, and from many of those sitting in the pews—and contributing to the offerings—in the parish. While denominational leaders and defenders of chaplains made the case that "Christian witness, must be made by persons who are at home in the university community," some who paid the bills wondered about the nature of the witness. And they would wonder even more in the next decade.[37]

If chaplains were not engaged in evangelism in any traditional way, and if they did not routinely conduct worship services in a traditional form, just what did chaplains do? Chaplains resisted the notion that they were some kind of missionary sent from the churches to the college students. As Phillip Hammond described the work at the close of the 1950s, "a program of Ping-pong tables and peanut-butter sandwiches coupled with Sunday-evening worship followed by fellowship hours" was still the norm on some campuses, but it was fading. In the late 1950s, there were visiting lecturers on a range of topics, experimental theater programs, and outreach programs for communities in need off campus (all things that chaplains had long reported doing). Political and theological speakers who might otherwise be too radical for a campus faculty department were often hosted by campus ministers. In the 1950s, the kind of radical political activity that would characterize chaplaincy a decade later was already visible among those who became college chaplains. While Hammond's description focused on Protestant chaplains, observers of Catholic chaplains described many Newman houses as "a place and provision for Catholic ping-pong." Clearly, there was not only a range of kinds of ministry taking place on campus, but there was uncertainty about what that ministry should be. But looking at that range of activities—many of which had been conducted by chaplains at the religious foundations which most directed for decades—led Hammond to comment "though much of what it does is experimental, the campus ministry itself is no longer experimental." But what kind of ministry was it?[38]

The marginalization of chaplains by their academic colleagues and the divisions between chaplains and the supporting churches and denominations was only part of a larger uncertainty about role and purpose of all ministers that was characteristic of the post–World War II era. In 1956, H. Richard Niebuhr wrote that "the contemporary Church is confused about the nature of the ministry. Neither ministers nor the schools that nurture them are guided today by a clear-cut, generally accepted conception of the office of the ministry." If the problem was true of ministry in the era of some of its greatest success in the United States, it was especially true of the relatively new form of ministry that was college chaplaincy, and the clarity for which Niebuhr hoped did not emerge in the next decades of the twentieth century. Despite this uncertainty, through the 1950s and into the early 1960s, both sending churches and denominations were able to overcome or simply ignore most of the tension with chaplains. But as we will see in the following chapter, these tensions could not be papered over forever, and a much more troubled relationship was brewing.[39]

Finally, college chapels—the buildings and the staff who administered them—were often caught in some of the same uncertainty about the nature of their role as chaplains. While most chaplains were supported by their home denominations and worked on the edges of college campuses, deans of chapels were normally paid by the university—sometimes out of a special chapel endowment—but they were much more clearly at the center of the campus life, certainly in the placement of their offices and sometimes even in their work.

Howard Thurman, born in the deeply segregated Florida of 1899, became dean of the chapel at Howard University in the 1930s, and then from 1953 to 1965 served as dean of the chapel at Boston University, one of the first African Americans to do so outside of an HBCU. Thurman faced continued criticism as being both too inclusive and too cautious on civil rights, even as he preached the need for a more inclusive America that faced squarely the legacy of racism. Yet he was happy with his role. It was a tension that many other campus religious leaders would face in the next decades.[40]

Other chapel deans faced similar issues though not always with the directness of Thurman. Deans of college chapels, sometimes also called chaplains to confuse the nomenclature, were active at many schools, especially schools with denominational roots if no longer connected to any church organization. Venerable Princeton—founded by Presbyterians in 1746—created the position of dean of the chapel in the 1920s to go with the new and far grander chapel. Through the 1950s, there were two active chapel deans. The first was former Episcopal bishop Donald Aldrich, a World War II veteran, who seems to have served effectively to the many veterans attending the still all-male Princeton in the late 1940s and early 1950s, but who was much less effective, perhaps even boring, for younger students. The second dean, Presbyterian Ernest Gordon, arrived following Aldrich's retirement, in 1955. Gordon preached with a strong Scottish burr and tried his best to facilitate the individual conversion of as many students as possible. Princeton also had many denominational chaplains, and Gordon had previously been the Presbyterian chaplain before his elevation to dean. There were denominational chaplains of several Protestant denominations, a Catholic chaplain based at the Aquinas Foundation (as it was called at Princeton), and a Hillel rabbi. Chapel attendance was required on a nominal basis for undergraduates, but it does not seem to have been taken too seriously. As Frederick Borsch remembered his college years, he and his classmates mostly said that chapel and other religious ceremonies seemed "'official' and not insincere, but mostly on the periphery." Matters of religious faith at Princeton, if they mattered at all, "came across to many of us as mostly secondary and not at the heart of what the university was about." Borsch's views seem not uncommon for many college students in the 1950s.[41]

The Birth of New Evangelical Student Organizations: InterVarsity and Cru

Evangelical student organizations like InterVarsity Christian Fellowship also grew in the 1950s, though often under the radar and without the energy that many would see later in the century. Far more student-led than chaplaincy programs or formal religion courses, InterVarsity added campus chapters and national retreat centers quickly, though they generally paid more attention to the preaching of Billy Graham than theological work of Reinhold Niebuhr. Although student-led evangelical activity had been a powerful force on college campuses in the early days of the YMCA and YWCA, by the 1940s and 1950s evangelical efforts by the Ys seemed a thing of the distant past.

In 1938, the Canadian InterVarsity Christian Fellowship started a mission to the United States and by 1940, the American branch had twenty-two campus chapters and became independent. There seemed to be students on many campuses who felt a hunger for a more traditional Christianity, such as the 1940 Radcliffe College student who said, "I had gotten the idea that I was alone as a Christian on my campus, and it is strengthening to know that others are faced with similar problems." InterVarsity continued to grow, albeit slowly, during World War II. The limited number of staff available, and the limited number of students on college campuses, made the early 1940s a challenging time. After 1945 it was a new day.[42]

InterVarsity's leaders found the post–GI Bill students conformist and hard to motivate, but a "year of evangelism" campaign in which students, in spite of the hesitation of some professional staff, invited Billy Graham to campuses, beginning with the University of Minnesota, had an energizing impact. Like the Y before it, InterVarsity continued its commitment to fostering student leadership. Early in its development, the organization started building a network of training centers that encouraged deeper student engagement and new leadership skills.

InterVarsity was, by design, more restrictive than many broadly welcoming religious groups on campus. Believing that many campus religious organizations had fallen into a "liberal morass," InterVarsity in 1940 drew up a nonnegotiable creedal statement that it has held to ever since. InterVarsity was also one of the more racially integrated religious organizations on many campuses, including a diversity of students not found in many other groups. Still, as late as 1960, InterVarsity had only sixty campus ministers and went unnoticed by most campus observers. One person who did notice was Harvey Cox who, though he disagreed with the organization's theology, nevertheless found it "a remarkable organization" that was "lay-led, highly visible, and extremely mobile." Later decades would show the kind of huge impact that a deeply committed and highly mobile organization could make.[43]

Alongside InterVarsity in the evangelical student orbit was the Campus Crusade for Christ (now known simply as Cru). Campus Crusade was founded in 1951 with a single chapter at UCLA, but by 1960 it had forty chapters on campuses across the country. Consciously adopting the model of the early YMCA (and like the early YMCA, deeply focused on individual conversion), Campus Crusade was a product of the 1950s but its greatest growth would come with the evangelical resurgence of the 1980s and 1990s, continuing strongly into the twenty-first century. In addition to InterVarsity and Campus Crusade, the 1950s were the gestation period for many other groups, including the Fellowship of Christian Athletes, the Navigators, and Young Life, as well as new student initiatives by conservative denominations, including the Lutheran Church–Missouri Synod and the evangelical Baptist Collegiate Ministries. In all these cases, the fermentation of the decade would bear fruit later.[44]

For all the religious activity of the immediate postwar years, it remained the case that the separation between the academic and the religious that Jo Ann Robinson embodied was true in much of the culture. Religion was booming in the 1950s. Colleges were booming. But most efforts to bring the two together did not seem to get off the ground. In 1944, Reinhold Niebuhr wrote, "If the academic work of the college is basically hostile or indifferent to religion . . . the extracurricular religious activities can serve to maintain the religious loyalty of the minority but will accomplish little to give our whole culture a more positive religious content." With occasional exceptions, mostly in church-based colleges, religious life in American higher education was just where Niebuhr feared: in extracurricular activities, often led by college chaplains, although wide ranging, seldom got close to the heart of the 1950s university.[45]

There was, however, a religious and values-focused energy in the air at many 1950s colleges that would explode after 1960 with both positive and negative results for campus-based religious life. When the values-focused energy made its greatest impact in the 1960s, it also often took forms unrecognizable as religious, however deep the religious roots. But to that complicated decade we turn in the next chapter.

Building a Jewish University: Brandeis University, Waltham, Massachusetts

The idea of an American Jewish university, beyond orthodox Yeshiva, had been floating around in some circles since at least the interwar decades. In the early 1940s, B'nai B'rith, the nation's largest Jewish organization, convened a committee to look at the question of founding a Jewish college. But the terror of the Holocaust and the need to do everything possible to support Jewish refugees during and after the war, as well as the needs of other struggling Jewish institutions in the United States, continued to divert supporters and funds from serious attention to the college-founding idea. Suddenly in 1946, a new opportunity appeared quite unexpectedly. The small Middlesex University in Waltham, Massachusetts, was collapsing, and the campus became available. Middlesex was in trouble in large part because accreditors did not trust a school with a majority of Jewish students. The school's founders were not Jewish, but on principle they would have nothing to do with quotas and Jews gravitated to the school. At the same time, a committee in New York, based mostly in the Conservative Jewish community, was seeking a campus for a potential university and their interest appealed to the founders of Middlesex. An agreement was easily struck to turn over the campus, worth probably $1.5 million, to the New York committee. In addition, and probably even more valuable, Middlesex had a charter for a college and was willing to turn that over too. However, for the next year failed fundraising campaigns, struggles between strong personalities, and conflicts between the New York committee and a new group in Boston left the idea of a new Jewish college in jeopardy, in spite of the fact that a campus and charter now existed.

Finally, in the spring of 1948 the trustees of what was now Brandeis University—named after Louis D. Brandeis, the first Jew to serve on the US Supreme Court—was ready to begin a serious search for a president. Their first, and really only, candidate was Abram Sachar, who had retired in 1947 after twenty years leading the national Hillel Foundation and a prior position on the faculty of the University of Illinois. Sachar was honored but far from sure that he wanted to take on a new venture, or that there was much prospect of success for the college. At least one major Jewish figure, New York rabbi Stephen Wise, warned Sacher that taking on the project would lead only to "pain, hurt, and shame" given the contentions between different groups of founders and the lack of funds available. But David Niles, the administrative assistant to both President Roosevelt and President Truman, who was widely respected in Jewish leadership circles, told Sachar "that the issue was not whether there should be a Jewish-founded university, for that issue had been settled . . . [but the question was] . . . whether the university would be a pedestrian undertaking shaming the American Jewish community, or a high-quality institution that would meet the hopes of generations." Niles insisted that Sachar could make the latter future a reality. In truth, Sachar probably had the self-confidence to believe that too.

Before taking the job, Sachar insisted on a high level of autonomy for the president and a commitment to serious fundraising by the trustees. The trustees agreed to both conditions, and in May Sacher moved to Boston to begin some very fast planning to open Brandeis University as a liberal arts college in only a few months. A new player in the American religious and educational scene had arrived.[46]

While some of the tensions among the founders of Brandeis University were simply personality conflicts, some were between groups centered in New York City and those in Boston, and some were between those who leaned toward the Conservative movement and those who leaned Reform (there were few of the Orthodox involved). But there were also underlying differences about just what a Jewish university should mean.

Only a week after he arrived in Boston, Sachar set out to clarify how he, as the school's new president, defined what it meant for Brandeis to be both Jewish and a university. In a speech to about a thousand people from the Boston Jewish community, he set out to make a "distinction between a Jewish-founded university and a Jewish university." He noted that some of the earliest supporters of Brandeis had hoped it would be "the inculcator of uniquely Jewish values, an intellectual and cultural center of Jewish import, and the training ground for American Jewish leaders of tomorrow." But Sachar wanted something broader. He described his vision: "I pledged, of course, that Brandeis would be vitally concerned with Jewish studies, that there would be a close relationship to the educational institutions of Israel, and that there would be a proper respect for the Jewish tradition." Yet Sachar added a very important caveat: "there was no expectation that the University would become a parochial school on the university level." Without apology, he said, "the model was to be not the Yeshiva or Catholic University of America or [Baptist] Baylor, but Harvard, or Princeton, or Columbia." The school would offer a full liberal arts curriculum and the broadest level of engagement and freedom for students and faculty. Finally, Sachar added that the goal was not a refuge for Jewish students or faculty who were excluded elsewhere, but a great university, free of discrimination or indoctrination. The audience loved it, and enough supporters were enthusiastic about Sachar's vision to make a start to the new venture. And start it did.[47]

In the fall of 1948, 107 brave souls enrolled for what was a freshman-only curriculum that would grow with them into a four-year baccalaureate program, as courses were added, faculty hired, and the neglected grounds of Middlesex University transformed into the kind of campus of which the whole community could be proud. By starting only with freshmen and no transfer students, Sachar and the trustees were able to avoid having some students making negative comparisons to their college experiences at other schools. Equally important, the Brandeis leaders bought time—a full four years—to recruit more faculty, improve the campus, and seek more money—a lot more money but also to do so for a school already in operation. It was also their good fortune to be starting a new school just when demand for college placements was booming as never before, and when the GI Bill was providing badly needed funds that would support more than a few promising students.[48]

In the early years, Sachar used a multipronged strategy to recruit faculty (and he did all the recruiting personally). On one hand, he sought young beginning scholars of high promise, especially if they held a PhD from Harvard. On the other hand, he sought distinguished retirees who could add balance to the group he was assembling. It helped his efforts that in the 1940s most colleges and universities still had mandatory retirement ages, and so scholars of international reputation like Herbert Marcuse and Abraham Maslow were prepared to start a second career, especially when Sacher promised high salaries and a university that would soon enough reach the highest levels of academic prestige. Finally, in the immediate postwar years, there were European scholars, especially Jewish refugee intellectuals, who were more than happy to come to the United States and restart their careers.[49]

Sachar would eventually serve Brandeis for twenty years before his retirement in 1968. He excelled in never-ending fundraising—building a campus, a faculty, and a student body for a brand-new school. He also had to bob and weave through many pitfalls and challenges to his authority. In the 1950s, the challenges came from faculty who wanted more autonomy in academic matters, especially some of the senior faculty of whom Sachar was so proud, and from students, mostly those who challenged what they saw as overly strict rules and ever-increasing tuition charges. Sharper challenges would come in the very different decade of the 1960s, for which Sachar was less prepared; but for the first decade plus, he successfully resisted most challenges to his authority.

Sachar held firm in the vision for what Brandeis needed to be: a first-rate undergraduate school with appropriate graduate programs and faculty research that would enhance its prestige. Most importantly, he wanted Brandeis to be a religious school only in the way Brown was Baptist or Harvard Congregationalist. He wrote, "If [Jews] are going to create a symbol, it better be a symbol of excellence. We had to have a Harvard/Yale/Princeton/Columbia/Dartmouth kind of school . . . a university with the very best undergraduate and graduate programs that could be devised." He wanted Brandeis to be proud of its Jewish founders but, like the colleges he saw as models, to have moved beyond any sectarian emphasis. He wanted to attract the most able students and faculty in the country to this Jewish-inspired academic mecca.

Sachar was very proud that with Brandeis's growing reputation and prestige, Jews could take their place alongside of Protestants and Catholics as university founders, and indeed serve as hosts to non-Jewish students as many other schools had hosted Jewish students for the last century. He noted, "I raised millions of dollars on just four words: 'a host at last.'" With Brandeis, Jews would no longer be only guests in someone else's university but could, indeed, host people of other faiths to join them as they pursued the best there was in American higher education.[50]

Defining the Structure and Purpose of Postwar Public Higher Education—The University of California

Clark Kerr (1911–2003) received his PhD from the University of California at Berkeley in 1939 and spent almost his whole career there, until he was fired as president by members of the university's board of regents linked to the newly elected California governor Ronald Reagan in 1967. Kerr was first hired as an associate professor at Berkeley in 1944, became chancellor of the Berkeley campus in 1952, and was president of the university system from 1958 until 1967. Far more than any other individual, he was the person most identified with the University of California during those years, perhaps most of all for the work he did to create the California Master Plan for Higher Education, as well as his famous 1964 description of the "multiversity." Kerr used his position as a bully pulpit to advocate for—and in California, to implement—what he saw as a new kind of American research university after World War II. Faculty research had changed drastically during and after the war, and the university needed a new structure to accommodate the new research. Postwar society also needed to provide for far more prospective students according to their interests, ability, and budgets than ever before. Kerr believed that leaders in the different states, starting with himself in California, needed to make all of this happen.[51]

The California Master Plan that was adopted in 1960 after two years of intense work was an extraordinarily comprehensive blueprint for a new day in higher education. The plan made Kerr nationally famous—he was on the cover of *Time* that fall—and also created pressure on other states to develop similar plans. The California Master Plan did not emerge as a wholly new development. The University of California, originally with one campus, in Berkeley, was created by the legislature of the then new state in 1868, opened to men in 1869, and admitted women in 1870. The University established a "Southern Branch" in 1919, which was renamed the University of California at Los Angeles in 1927. Before long, the legislature had also created the teacher preparation Normal Schools that became the regional state colleges. California was also an early adopter of two-year junior colleges, where a student could begin college work at or near their home high school. The university was given a degree of autonomy under its own appointed board of regents that kept it at least somewhat free from political interference (though not enough ultimately to protect Kerr's job).

But as had been true of most of higher education, especially public higher education since at least the Civil War, there was great confusion, mission creep, and overlap among the different types of schools, which a recent historian christened as a "nonsystem" and "a perfect mess." The Master Plan was Kerr's effort to turn this "perfect mess" into a well-organized system in California. For the next decades he seemed to have succeeded.[52]

Within all these different higher education institutions, the potential student body was bursting at the seams. Ever since World War II, California had been growing at lightning speed, as many former soldiers who had shipped out to the Pacific remembered their short California stays as a beautiful moment and sought to return with their families. Additionally, the GI Bill, though most of the funds were spent by the time the Master Plan was written, had created a new normal in which far more of the eighteen-to-twenty-two-year-old cohort expected to go to college than ever before.[53] And the children of the World War II veterans, the baby boom generation, were preparing to go to college in the early 1960s.

The Master Plan described in detail the role of each kind of school in California. It specified the percentage of students who could be welcomed at each level (the top 12.5 percent of high school graduates for the university, the top one-third for the state colleges, and all high school graduates for the junior colleges). Awarding the doctorate was reserved for the University of California. The state colleges were to be primarily undergraduate with a few master's degree programs. The then junior colleges were confined to the first two years of college plus vocational

Figure 5.1. The University of California at Santa Barbara was one of several new campuses of the rapidly expanding University of California system that became the model for the postwar research university. UCSB was also the home to one of the nation's growing religious studies departments. From Library of Congress

programs. The report also named a number of professions—law, medicine, veterinary medicine, as well as public school teaching—that needed to be specifically accommodated.

The Master Plan did not mention molding thoughtful and moral citizens as did some reports on higher education in the 1940s. For a plan of such detail regarding standardization in higher education, the silence is striking. The words religion, morality, values, meaning, or purpose do not appear anywhere in the California Master Plan. Values may have been an unspoken assumption of a plan to provide a college education to more young people than had ever been able to attend college before. But religion was certainly not there.

Three years later, in 1963, Kerr gave a prestigious series of lectures published the next year as *The Uses of the University*, in which he reflected on what he and others were creating with the postwar "multiversity," as he called it. He argued that the old university had been a single community that "may even [be] said to have had a soul in the sense of a central animating principle." But that university was gone forever. The change from an older model to the newer was "regretted by some . . . [but] gloried in, as yet, by few."

In the most famous lines from the book, Kerr said, "I have sometimes thought of it [the university] as a series of individual faculty entrepreneurs held together by a common grievance over parking." It was a long way from the vision of moral purpose at heart of Henry Tappan's Michigan or Charles Van Hise's Wisconsin, or even Harvard's 1945 *General Education in a Free Society*, but it was probably an accurate assessment of what higher education had become by 1960. It was also one that would be challenged significantly in the next decade; but those challenges, as daunting as they were, were hard to anticipate in the heady moments of the successes of the Master Plan.[54] While soul, spirit, religion, or virtue seem to play no role in the Master Plan, and while Kerr insisted that the university could no longer be considered to have a soul, he also insisted that the new postwar university that he was building at California would be a place of great entrepreneurship and creativity. He once even called it a place of anarchy.[55]

Taking advantage of the flexibility or anarchy, a few entrepreneurs managed to find a place for religion in spite of the plan's silence. At California's Santa Barbara campus (UCSB), D. Mackenzie Brown, a political science professor, assembled a committee to consider courses in religion at UCSB. Four years later—academic innovation moves slowly—a course, Religious Institutions, was first offered in the political science department. Additional courses were added in 1959 and 1960.

The Religious Institutions course moved out of the political science department to be part of an independent program led by faculty from several departments and chaired by Brown. A year later, the faculty proposed a major for students interested in theology. The university faculty did not like the word "theology," but once it was removed in 1962, a new major "designed for students desiring a general education with emphasis upon this aspect of Western civilization and comparative cultures," was approved. Religious Studies as a new undergraduate collection of courses and a major, later expanded to include the MA and PhD, became part of the academic curriculum—at Santa Barbara and soon enough at other campuses of the UC system. Today programs ebb and flow but UCSB remains a leader in the field in the twenty-first century.[56]

Most campuses of the California system also had several active chaplains—clergy and non-clergy. At Cal Berkeley the venerable Westminster House, the Berkeley Presbyterian Student Center, had been built by the Synod of California as a residence for the newly appointed campus minister in 1911, only six years after the appointment of the first-ever Presbyterian chaplain in 1905. Westminster House also began offering student housing in 1915. John Hadsell became the new chaplain at Berkeley in 1959 after serving in a similar role at San Francisco State College.

Joan Nash Eakin handled programming in the Westminster House dorm. There were also other similar houses for other Protestants, while a Hillel and Newman Center also operated at Berkeley.

The YMCA was still active at Berkeley in the 1950s, and Harry L. Kingman, who served as the Y's field secretary at Berkeley for an amazing forty years, from 1916 to 1957, made the YMCA building, Stiles Hall, a haven for free speech at Berkeley long before the 1964 Free Speech Movement there. Chaplains' faith-based spaces were a part of the student and faculty culture at Berkeley, respected even in that most secular of settings.

Berkeley was the oldest campus and had the oldest chaplaincy program, but by the 1950s all of the then UC campuses had active chaplains. The Los Angeles and Davis campuses had active ecumenical programs—the University Religious Conference (URC) at UCLA and the University Religious Council at Davis. Both included several Protestant groups, along with Hillel and a Newman Center. The UCLA religious life program, which had started along with the then "Southern Branch" in the 1920s, became an official program of the campus, designed to "promote cooperation among various religious groups." By the 1950s, under the leadership of its then director, Adaline Guenther, the UCLA URC sponsored programs that "made it a point to promote provocative activities and entice student leaders to be involved." It also ran its own summer camp for low-income children in Los Angeles. The first Campus Crusade for Christ chapter was founded at UCLA in 1951. In 1952 the UCLA URC created a "Project India" in which UCLA students of different faiths made an often life-changing summer trip to India to experience the rich diversity of cultures and religions found there while talking about the United States to their often-wary counterparts in India. Even though the California Master Plan made no mention of religion, religion seemed to be thriving on the margins of the university—both as a subject of academic study and of deep student engagement for some.[57]

Academic Excellence and Christian Mission, an Uneasy Mix—Pepperdine University

In early 1937, Western Auto Supply Store's millionaire founder George Pepperdine decided that starting a new Christian college in Southern California should be his philanthropic priority. He announced his decision in the spring of 1937, personally purchasing land in south central Los Angeles, beginning a building program, and hiring a president, Batsell Baxter, all in the next few months. In September 1937, not that long after his initial announcement, 162 students, both men and women, showed up to begin classes at the George Pepperdine College campus. Pepperdine planned the school to be racially integrated, and the first African Americans arrived in the second year, unusual for the mostly White and mostly southern Church of Christ. Housing, however, was racially segregated until World War II. At an opening ceremony on September 21, California Governor Frank Merriam gave the main address and George Pepperdine dedicated the college to "higher learning under the influence of fundamental Christian leadership." He added, "The great difference between this college and other colleges is that we are endeavoring to place adequate emphasis and greater stress upon teaching and Christian character." If much of American higher education was well on the road to a more secular future, Pepperdine's college would be an important exception.[58]

From childhood, Pepperdine was a devout member of the conservative Church of Christ. The Church of Christ was born out of the religious awakening of the early nineteenth century. Several leading revivalists and their followers came to believe that all the existing denominations of Christians were being led astray. They wanted none of it and rallied under the banner of "no creed but the Bible," founding independent and loosely affiliated churches across the United States. By the late nineteenth and early twentieth centuries, however, this hundred-year-old movement around "no creed but the Bible" was splitting in its understanding of what the Bible did and did not allow. The larger group saw matters not mentioned in the Bible as fair game for their own ideas and coalesced into a new denomination known as the Disciples of Christ, with fairly liberal views on most matters. A smaller group, however, believed that only behavior and beliefs specifically allowed in the Bible were allowed for good Christians. Discussion of a split began in 1889, and in 1906 the two bodies formally separated. The split was not difficult since the movement had always been a loose confederation of independent congregations. In 1906 a new and loosely organized but proud body called the Church of Christ had emerged on the American religious scene.[59]

George Pepperdine began his career as a bookkeeper for an automobile repair business in Kansas City in 1907, just as the Church of Christ was being formally organized. To generate more income for his family, he also started selling auto parts by mail on the side. At the time, the automobile was new, and people needed parts. Before long the side business prospered and Pepperdine moved to Los Angeles, expanding his new company, Western Auto Supply, from one store in downtown Los Angeles to 150 stores across the American West. He had long been generous to the Church of Christ but wanted to do more. The Church of Christ did not own any colleges, but its leaders had founded colleges, and congregations often rallied around and supported them. Founding a college for the Church of Christ on the West Coast became Pepperdine's way to do more for his church.[60]

An article that appeared in the *Los Angeles Times* three years after the college opened began, "George Pepperdine College has had a phenomenal growth since its founding in 1937." It was accredited, buildings were rising on the new campus, and by the 1940–1941 school year, enrollment had doubled from the school's original enrollment. The war caused strains for every college, especially Pepperdine. The Church of Christ valued defending democracy but tended toward pacifism, since most members did not think the New Testament authorized any wars. Students and faculty had many debates about just what to do. But wartime prosperity, obvious especially in Southern California, and the backing of the Pepperdine fortune meant that faculty salaries rose and morale was high. The fact that the school had an independent board and was not controlled by the Church of Christ made faculty eligible for the Carnegie-inspired TIAA pensions. Faculty governance also grew stronger. Finally, the end of the war brought more growth. By 1948–1949, there were 1,839 students on the campus, a tenfold expansion from the first year and almost half were funded by the GI Bill, which also resulted in two out of three students being male. The student body also became more racially diverse and by the 1950s was 10 percent African American and 8 percent Asian American.[61]

Despite the seeming good fortune of the early years, the 1950s were difficult years for Pepperdine personally and for the college. On February 15, 1951, the *Los Angeles Times* carried a devastating headline, "Pepperdine Says He's Penniless Now." The article noted that "Pepperdine also testified that after retiring from active business in 1930 he devoted all his time to the George Pepperdine Foundation, an educational and charitable venture." Though the *Times* did not explore the issue, the reality was that Pepperdine had made a series of risky investments with the foundation and in twenty years had lost his entire fortune. While Pepperdine College was not liable for Pepperdine's debts, the Pepperdine Foundation, not the college, had managed the college endowment. After 1951, the college had a campus and tuition revenue but no endowment. It would be a decade before it again had a balanced budget.[62]

The disappearance of the endowment, just when enrollment began to dip because of fewer World War II veterans, was a double setback to the college budget. To make matters worse, the California education department and the Western College Association accreditation visits were scheduled just after news broke about

George Pepperdine's insolvency. The Western College Association team believed that faculty salaries were failing to keep up, lab facilities were inadequate, and too many courses were being canceled. They recommend that continuing accreditation be denied. It was a huge blow, even though accreditation was reinstated on a temporary basis in 1952 and made permanent in 1954. But important as they were, neither budget nor accreditation issues were the most serious issues the college faced.[63]

Pepperdine sought to be both a high-quality academic school and a deeply conservative Christian one. By the 1950s, very few American colleges still tried to be both, and it was a difficult balancing act for Pepperdine. The balance was made more challenging by vagueness about what Pepperdine meant by being a religious school. Was it a generic Christian school or was it specifically a Church of Christ school? George Pepperdine had been very clear in his early gifts to the college that though he was a devout member of the Church of Christ, he wanted the school to be free of denominational control. On the other hand, the endorsement of the Church of Christ was essential to the school in attracting both students and donors. For the first decade, the school's leaders managed to straddle the difference. Many of the new veterans who attended in the late 1940s were happy to be at a Christian school with its daily chapel services, even though they often did not show up for the services. The president and dean later shortened chapel services but did require attendance at least one day a week. Students rebelled against any required attendance, but external leaders of the Church of Christ began speaking and writing about what they saw as Pepperdine's apostasy in chapel attendance, campus rules and dress codes, and the actual percentage of Church of Christ members among the student body (low and shrinking) and faculty (high but never total).

Tensions also arose over the teaching in the Pepperdine religion department. The school had sought to attract serious religion scholars who were deeply steeped in the Church of Christ. But in 1947, a former student claimed that the department taught modernism, rather than the fundamentalist faith of the Church of Christ. Some religion professors, it seemed, said that many miracles could be explained and that the Church of Christ was one denomination among others. For conservatives in a conservative denomination, many of whom believed all other denominations were heretics, it was all too much. The *Bible Banner*, a conservative religious journal, attacked. No effort at rebuttal seemed successful. Ralph Wilburn, perhaps the best-known professor in the religion department, resigned (possibly under pressure) in 1951. Paraphrasing his 1937 dedication of the college, George Pepperdine, still highly respected within the Church of Christ, wrote that his idea of a Christian college was "that it shall be a private institution giving students standardized work in the liberal arts in a Christian environment." But since the Bible did not mention the word college, there could be no such institution as a completely Christian college. So, despite the respect in which Pepperdine himself was held, the attacks continued.

In March 1951, another conservative journal, the *Gospel Guardian*, said that Pepperdine College was a hotbed of modernist scholars like Karl Barth and Emil Bruner, and no longer taught what it called "New Testament Christianity." According to the *Gospel Guardian*, the college had become "a thorn in the flesh and a constant reproach and embarrassment to the faithful Christians [read conservative Church of Christ members] in California who know of her liberalism and her compromises with sectarianism." But there were few truly liberal students or professors who were ever attracted to the school.[64]

By the mid-1950s, the college was at a clear crossroads. The school could not continue trying and failing to please key constituencies. Many on the faculty, including the dean and president, seemed ready to give up on their conservative critics who could not be appeased and embrace a broader Christianity in which the Church of Christ would be one among many denominations represented; none would be singularly dominant. Instead, the trustees, eventually including George and Helen Pepperdine, decided on a different course. In early 1957, they sadly confronted the dean and president with whom they had worked closely for over a decade and requested their resignations.

The trustees turned to one of the best-known ministers in the Church of Christ, Norvel Young, who was an author and pastor of a church in Lubbock, Texas, as well as an active supporter of Church of Christ colleges, and invited him to take on the presidency. Young accepted the challenge, which clearly meant rebuilding the links to the Church of Christ. While Young talked of balancing the budget by increasing enrollment to 2,000 students, his primary goal was to rebuild the college's close connection to the Church of Christ, to end the running criticism, recruit many more Church of Christ students, and to increase donations from prosperous members of the church. He insisted that new hires to faculty and staff must be Church of Christ members, including a new chair of the religion department, and that all students be required to take multiple courses in religion as part of the college's new focus on the spiritual lives of its students. Conservative critics of the college were delighted by this change in direction. The current faculty, not so much.

In announcing this new direction, the new administration reassured the faculty that no current faculty member would lose their jobs, even if new hires were expected to be Church of Christ members. The faculty were not satisfied. They saw the new plan as an assault on academic freedom and on the very nature of a school committed to a broad Christian community. Several senior professors sent a petition to the board, asking that the outgoing dean be retained and by 1958, had appealed to the American Association of University Professors (AAUP) for help. But the direction was set. Finally, in frustration, seventeen members of the faculty resigned in April 1958. The college managed the crisis carefully and the *Los Angeles Times* article announcing the unusual number of resignations at the same time included a sub-headline that said, "Resignations Attributed to Better Pay Offers; Vacancies in Staff Already Filled." The article quoted the new president at length, including a statement that "each one will leave with a handshake," and no one was leaving under duress. The truth was more complicated.

Among those leaving were some of the most senior and long-standing members of the Pepperdine faculty and staff. Most seem to have had a very different sense of the direction for the college than the new president. Robert Young, the director of public relations, was one of the first to leave. For several months Young had been arguing that the Church of Christ was "nothing more than another denomination," created and led by fallible humans and not a "divine institution" with a lock on the truth. He wanted Pepperdine to be a welcoming Christian community even if still very different from most increasingly secular colleges in the country. He did not want to go the secularization route, but neither did he want the school to become simply a denominational college.

Woodrow Whitten, a longtime member of the faculty and president of the college's AAUP chapter, wrote to the *Times* two days after the newspaper had stated that each one was leaving with a handshake, saying that the claim was not true. He also wrote a detailed report to the AAUP, which he shared with the board of trustees and the college's accrediting agencies. The AAUP report eventually required President Young and his team to spend many hours on a detailed rebuttal of the charges. It was a difficult moment for the college, caught as it was between two significantly different visions of the institution's future.[65]

The outside observer is left to wonder what would have happened to Pepperdine if it had followed the road that was advocated by Robert Young, Woodrow Whitten, former president Hugh Tiner, and outgoing dean E. V. Pullas, instead of the direction advocated by the new president Norvel Young and eventually by George and Helen Pepperdine and the trustees. Pepperdine would have remained an unusual place as both a deeply committed interdenominational Christian community and a solidly academic one. But it did not happen.

By the late 1950s and early 1960s, the dissidents had departed, with a handshake or not. Based on the improved finances and new programs, reaccreditation was won, in spite of the AAUP complaints. The new policies, including much stronger links to the Church of Christ, less openness to other branches of Christianity, and a dominant administration, were all in place.

After 1958, the college also developed equally tight links to the conservative politics of southern California (even though from an outside perspective it is less clear how a literal reading of Scripture demanded that). From the beginning, Pepperdine himself and the board had been dominated by pro-business, free enterprise Republicans, but these links got much stronger and more conservative after the events of 1957–1958. President Young had once rejected a donor's offer for a $1 million gift because it was contingent on giving an honorary doctorate to Dan Smoot, a popular but extremist anti-communist radio personality. Nevertheless, the links to conservative politics were strong enough to lead politicians like Barry Goldwater and Ronald Reagan to love the school, while some less conservative voices started to nickname Pepperdine the "John Birch Academy" after the superconservative John Birch Society.[66]

The 1960s were tense times for the college, not for the reasons they were tough at other colleges, but for some reasons unique to Pepperdine. The college's location, which had once been on the outskirts of Los Angeles, was now in the heart of the primarily African American Watts neighborhood, and the Watts riots of August 1965 led the college to rethink its location and its connection to the Black community in Los Angeles. Four years later, a Pepperdine security guard shot and killed an African American teen, Larry Kimmons, who had sometimes played basketball in the college gym. Around the same time, Pepperdine was given new property on the Pacific coast in Malibu. After a few years of trying to operate on two campuses and maintain at least a limited program in Watts, the college gave up, and in 1971 consolidated all of its programs at the Malibu site. In 2023, based in Malibu entirely, Pepperdine describes itself as "a Christian university," committed to "academic excellence and Christian values," with somewhat less specific focus on the Church of Christ but a clear emphasis on blending faith and learning. Almost a century after its founding, Pepperdine remains a unique and unusual model of the place of religion at American universities even as it continues its operations on a far more successful course than ever seemed possible in the troubled 1950s.[67]

From Alabama State College to Pepperdine University, the fifteen years after World War II were generally years of prosperity, prestige, and popularity, as some had said of those years, but also with significant exceptions here and there. Also with some significant exceptions, they were also years of growing marginalization of religion and a time of major questions of self-definition among college chaplains and religious studies faculty. All of the issues, positive and negative, grew dramatically in significance in the next fifteen years and it is that story that we explore in chapter 6.

CHAPTER SIX

The Long Sixties

Charismatic Chaplains and Radical Students, 1960–1980

In 1958, thirty-four-year-old William Sloane Coffin became chaplain of Yale University. Coffin served until 1975, through almost two decades of significant change in the role of college chaplains and institutional changes at Yale itself. His preaching, political activism, and indeed even his depiction in the cartoons of Garry Trudeau (who made a Coffin look-alike a major figure of his Doonesbury cartoons) made Coffin a nationally recognized exemplar of the college chaplain of the 1960s. While it was a decade of social turmoil, it was a golden age for college chaplains.

It is almost impossible for the twenty-first-century observer to understand the prestige of universities in the United States in 1960. The university, especially the elite Ivy League and comprehensive state university, produced "the best and the brightest" of the Kennedy administration. Universities absorbed more students than anyone previously imagined possible. The number of American baccalaureate degrees grew from a low in the World War II era of 125,863, or 10 percent of high school graduates, to 392,440, or 27 percent of those graduating from high school in 1960. It would expand to 839,730 degrees, or for 31 percent of high school graduates by 1970. As University of California president Clark Kerr said, the university was the key producer of that "invisible product, knowledge" that would be the key in the future. College chaplains—like Coffin—were the ministers in this world, reflecting its prestige in a way that an ordinary parish minister never could.[1]

Bill Coffin—Iconic College Chaplain of the 1960s

In retrospect, Coffin's move to Yale seemed the perfect meeting of the right person and the right place. At the time, however, Coffin was the fourth choice for the position, which had previously been offered to older ministers of higher status. (Considering a woman for the position seems never to have occurred to anyone in the machismo male world of Yale and mainline Protestant ministry as it existed in 1958.)

Coffin brought a range of experiences to Yale. Drafted at nineteen in 1943, he was in uniform through the end of World War II and the early Cold War. He then completed an undergraduate degree at Yale and was seriously considering returning to his Cold War role with the new Central Intelligence Agency (CIA) when a weekend conference at New York's Union Theological Seminary—from which his uncle Henry Sloane Coffin had just retired as president—changed his life. The conference was for select young men (Union Seminary still admitted few women) considered to be the cream of the crop to hear "the elite of the academic world" talk about studying religion. Most of the elite were Union professors, including Coffin's idol, Reinhold Niebuhr, who Coffin called "as eloquent a man as I had ever heard."[2] Niebuhr's speech and Union professor Bill Webber's assurance that ministers "had greater freedom to say and do what they wanted than good people in any other vocation," convinced Coffin to change his career plans. Much to the surprise of many, he applied to Union.

Coffin loved Union, but the Korean War led him back to the CIA, which he described as not so different from seminary at the time. Coffin's move from seminary to the CIA and later back to seminary was not as odd then as it would seem only a few years later. His idol, Niebuhr, was himself a committed anti-communist, serving on the US State Department's policy planning staff in the late 1940s. After his second CIA stint, Coffin moved to the Divinity School at Yale to finish his theology degree. Coffin graduated from divinity school in 1956, was ordained as a Presbyterian minister that summer, and accepted a job as chaplain to the prestigious Phillips Academy, Andover, where the elite sent their children to get ready for college.

After a year at Phillips, Coffin moved to Williams College in Massachusetts. In both schools he created quite a stir, making the chaplaincy come alive and sometimes making enemies for his brashness. He also settled in his own mind that college chaplaincy was the job for him. Years later he remembered, "I found such satisfaction in the teaching, preaching, and counseling that went into being a chaplain that I gave up my original plan of working in the urban slums." As his biographer, Warren Goldstein, commented, "He may even have sensed the corollary truth: that given his upbringing, education, and personality, he would have been neither happy nor particularly effective working in the slums." When in March 1958 Yale president A. Whitney Griswold called to offer him the Yale position, Coffin remembered, "I told him yes with indecent haste." The Yale chaplaincy was his dream job. All of his life experiences had created the Bill Coffin—confident, effective, charismatic, and from the military, "a man's man," but also one filled with Niebuhrian doubts about the human race—who arrived in New Haven in the fall of 1958.[3]

In his first two years at Yale, Coffin brought new urgency to the job of university chaplain, but for the most part it was the same work many chaplains of the 1950s did. According to his own recollections, he spent many hours in pastoral counseling with students. He explained, "I found that any time anybody wanted to talk to me on a deep personal level I was very interested," and it was "a great privilege to be invited into the sanctuary of somebody's soul." He embraced ecumenical conversations, having little concern with denominational distinctions. Coffin was *the* university chaplain at Yale, hired and paid by the university and presiding over the university chapel, but there were also many denominational ministers at Yale. Coffin urged them to be sure that students learned from other traditions and were not just sitting comfortably in their own.

When a new Hillel director, Rabbi Richard Israel, arrived at Yale in 1959, Israel and Coffin worked together to make sure that the last vestiges of the quota system in admissions was abolished and Jews were equally welcome with others at Yale. He also supported a drive to ensure Kosher food in the Yale meal plan. Most of all Coffin preached—on Sunday morning and as many other occasions as he could—to push students to break from their upper-middle-class complacency. In one sermon he said, "Not education of the mind but a total transformation of one's whole being is what we need. Enough of these less than halfway measures!" But in the first years, just what this meant by rejecting "halfway measures" was less than clear.[4]

The year 1960 was a turning point for Coffin and the nation. The election of John F. Kennedy as the new US president brought Coffin's style—youth, vigor, talk of new beginnings, and upper-class confidence—to the White House. Kennedy recognized the affinity, appointing Coffin to the newly formed Peace Corps's Advisory Committee, and Coffin seems to have reveled in the masculine-can-do similarities.

At the same time, the civil rights movement was taking on new urgency in the aftermath of the Montgomery Bus Boycott. In 1960, a series of lunch-counter sit-ins initiated by Black college students spread demands for integration. In the spring of 1961, the Congress of Racial Equality (CORE) organized Freedom Rides across the South to challenge segregated transportation. On May 13, 1961, in Anniston, Alabama, the first Freedom Riders were savagely beaten by a White mob. Coffin, along with John Maguire, who taught religion at Wesleyan, and a few others decided that a high-profile White northern group joining the Freedom Rides would help bring national attention to the rides. Martin Luther King Jr.'s encouragement sealed the deal. They never considered the danger, either from the White mobs or from the Kennedy administration, which was furious at the Freedom Riders for highlighting the ugly nature of US racism at a moment when the new and untested president was about the meet with Soviet leader Nikita Khrushchev. Coffin was threatened by the mob and arrested in Montgomery.

The decision to become a Freedom Rider ended his access to the Kennedy administration and made Yale president Kingman Brewster Jr. uncomfortable, but the majority of faculty and students supported him. The Freedom Rides also made Coffin a national celebrity. The *New York Times* called him the bus-riding chaplain. Coffin seemed to have found his true calling and could live with the discomfort and anger. He loved the celebrity part.[5]

After the Freedom Rides, Coffin was nationally known. Nevertheless, his primary impact at Yale was in the lives of students. Jesse Lemisch, who later became an important historian, was a doctoral student at Yale in the 1960s. When Lemisch died in 2018, a literary executor discovered in his files a yellowing article from the *Yale Daily News* from 1962, describing in detail a talk Coffin gave at Yale:

> Racal prejudice is a product of man's ignoring his God-ordained duty to his fellow men—to love them as brothers. . . . The Church must help God get to the heart of men and to do this, the Church must have a voice. God must afflict the comfortable in order to comfort the afflicted.

Well over half a century after this speech, with its Christian and male language, the article was among the treasured papers of an atheist Jew who had gone on to be one of the founders of Students for a Democratic Society and who had helped to bring greater diversity of focus to historical studies.[6] Coffin's reach was undeniable.

In the years after 1961, the bus-riding chaplain became a new standard for college chaplaincy. The media loved him and he spoke in person, on the radio, and increasingly on television, for which his rugged good looks and voice seemed ready-made.

At a time when most American college students were still at least nominally Christian, Coffin's heartfelt and theologically grounded Christianity made faith come alive. Christians, Coffin said, "are called upon to love, with the same type of love that God has shown." This was not a soft love. So Coffin said that Jesus, "challenged the unjust people who were governing the society in which He lived." Students loved it. Some alumni and administrators at Yale thought he was taking on a role far beyond what was appropriate to a college chaplain, but the two Yale presidents for whom he worked, A. Whitney Griswold and Kingman Brewster, defended him even when he made their lives difficult. As Brewster said, "If in order to be a Chaplain at Yale one had to agree to refrain from any public demonstration of conscientious conviction, then I do not see how we could expect to find a Chaplain worthy of Yale." Coffin repaid this support with continued affirmations of the presidents and equally careful avoidance of any criticism of Yale. Coffin was both a prophet and a wily politician.[7]

Coffin came to his opposition to the US war in Vietnam slowly, much more slowly than some others. Breaking from his CIA past was hard for Coffin. In early 1965 more than 150 members of the Yale faculty signed a petition calling on US president Lyndon Johnson, "to negotiate the immediate withdrawal of U.S. forces from South Vietnam." Coffin did not sign. He was torn, believing that, unlike civil rights, good Christians differed on the issue of Vietnam and as a former soldier and CIA agent he had a patriotic streak that went deep.

By late in 1965, with the war dragging on, Coffin changed his mind and helped organize a new group, Clergy Concerned About Vietnam (later Clergy and Laity Concerned About Vietnam), that brought together some of the best-known Protestant and Jewish leaders, and many Catholic priests and faculty, though no Catholic bishops, to take a religious-based stand against the escalating war in Vietnam. Coffin was not only a key organizer of the group but its primary spokesman and preacher. As with civil rights, Coffin got pushback, but that only toughened his resolve to critique the war that he had come to believe was both unjust and unwinnable.[8]

Nevertheless, the war kept expanding, as did the draft of young men (not women) to fight and sometimes die in Vietnam. In response, the draft became a target of much anti-war activity. On college campuses, young men turned in their draft cards and refused to serve. Some went to jail for their convictions. Coffin, along with a

Figure 6.1. Yale Chaplain William Sloane Coffin, shown near the bus looking directly at the soldier, along with his friend John Maguire of Wesleyan University, were early and enthusiastic participants in the Congress of Racial Equality (CORE) organized Freedom Rides meant to challenge the segregation of public transit in the South. As a result, Coffin was forever after known as the "bus riding chaplain." AP Photo/Perry Aycock

few other older anti-war voices, supported them. Taking a cue from his civil rights days, Coffin talked about organizing "massive civil disobedience in opposition to the war." He did so loudly and often. In an anti-war rally in New Haven in November 1968, Coffin gave an impassioned speech about the importance of civil disobedience to the draft. A number of students turned in their draft cards. One said, "My name is Gordon Coburn and I'm a sophomore at the University of Hartford and I'm doing this because I'm a Christian." Three Hartford friends joined him as well as other students from elsewhere.

While many students were engaged in resistance to the draft, others, especially sometimes parents, were furious with Coffin. Letters poured into Yale complaining about him, leading Kingman Brewster to say he disagreed with Coffin and "in this instance deplore his style." But Brewster insisted that if Yale stood for anything it was opposition to "conformity in the name of patriotism" and "timidity in the name of public or alumni relations." He would not discipline Coffin.

The US government took a sterner position. In January 1968, Coffin, along with Benjamin Spock (famous for advice to a generation of parents about child care), Mitchell Goodman, Marcus Raskin, and Michael Ferber were charged with conspiracy to violate the federal draft laws. After two trials in July 1969, a federal appeals court threw out the charges. The Justice Department, not anxious for more bad publicity, quietly dropped the case. The threat of jail was gone. Coffin had garnered more fame on the most prominent moral issue of the late 1960s. If anything could build on the image of the bus-riding chaplain and great preacher, it was as a martyr to the government prosecuting an unjust war. Coffin made the most of it.[9]

After 1968, Coffin continued as the Yale chaplain for most of the next decade. He spoke constantly at Yale, on college campuses all over the country, at anti-war rallies, and beyond. He also continued counseling students and blessing events, from opening ceremonies to graduation, throughout Yale's academic year.

In the fall of 1969, Yale admitted women to the undergraduate college (as they had long been admitted to many of the graduate schools) and the women quickly made themselves felt, demanding that Yale—and its chaplain—attend to them individually and to issues of feminism more broadly. In response, Coffin preached about the need for Yale to be a more inclusive community and about the problem of the "sexist presuppositions that have infected Biblical and English language so secretly and forcefully." He began to see many military encounters, not only in Vietnam but things like the Cuban missile crisis, as fueled by too much testosterone. He said that if "High Noon encounters with nuclear weapons represent manliness, then we simply have to reinvent manhood." Still, the issues of the women's movement never fully engaged him.[10]

By 1970, Coffin was the best-known college chaplain and probably the best-known minister in the nation. Union Seminary's president John Bennett wrote of Coffin, "There is no more persuasive spokesman for those who seek to make the Christian message meaningful for the issues of our time." Coffin's biographer said of him:

> What made him a leader, in Saul Alinsky's famous phrase, was the fact that he had a following. And that following made up of draft-age young men, college students, Yale faculty and alumni, liberal clergy and laypeople—Jews and Catholics as well as Protestants—consisted of millions of Americans.[11]

By 1970 Coffin certainly qualified as a leader.

As the early 1970s continued, Coffin's job at Yale began to seem mundane to him. He found many Yale students to be too career-oriented and too narrow in their concerns. Problems with roommates, boyfriends, girlfriends, and parents seemed to him to have replaced concerns with civil rights and the draft. He became bored.

Coffin may also have tired of his role as the defender of Kingman Brewster and the Yale establishment. Coffin began to feel alienated from the faculty that seemed to place a higher premium on being objective and disinterested than on commitment. He saw many academics engaged in what he called peevish debates rather than engagement with the world. In 1974 he announced that the 1974–1975 academic year would be his last. After many well-wishes at the 1975 graduation, he was on his own for the first time since he had graduated from seminary.

Coffin's time in the wilderness did not last long. In 1977 he received a call to be the pastor of New York City's Riverside Church, perhaps the most prestigious church in American Protestantism. He served for a decade, bringing both his dynamic preaching and his political skills to a new situation. He retired from Riverside in 1987 and died in 2006. Coffin is still widely remembered as the model of college chaplaincy by many who came to it after him, even though the Yale of the 1960s and 1970s was a very different place than higher education is in the twenty-first century.[12]

In the 1960s, Bill Coffin made college chaplaincy important, charismatic, and frankly sexy. It should be no surprise that, in large part because of his example, many young ministers wanted to follow the same path. In retirement in 2004, Coffin told an interviewer, "What this country needs, what I think God wants us to do, is not practice piecemeal charity but engage in wholesale justice. . . . When we see Christ empowering the poor, scorning the powerful, healing the world's hurts, we are seeing transparently the power of God at work."[13] At eighty years of age, his passion for justice had not ebbed. Neither had his enthusiasm to preach to any audience.

Changing College Chaplaincy

William Sloane Coffin was the most famous but far from the only college chaplain in the United States in the 1960s and 1970s. While the media focused on Coffin, many other college chaplains went about their business during those years, counseling students, preaching, and participating in the nation's larger political questions to a greater or lesser degree.

Though the numbers are imprecise because there were so many differing definitions of the work, there were some 1,300 full-time Protestant chaplains, 500 full-time Catholic chaplains, most at Newman Centers, and about twice that number of part-time priests on campuses. Hillel experienced some slippage from the 400 staff people it had in the 1950s, due primarily to problems in its B'nai B'rith parent, before rebounding significantly in later decades. The number of chaplaincy positions grew because there were just so many more college students, and because of the "religion boom of the 1950s" (see chapter 5), churches had so much more money than ever before to support college work. In his 1954 study of chaplaincy, Seymour Smith wrote, "Probably no other religious development in higher education has had a longer incubation in its infancy or a more rapid growth in its adolescence than the college chaplaincy. . . . Up until 1920 fewer than a score of chaplains were functioning on college campuses. Since the end of World War II, however, new appointments have been made at a startling rate." From the 1950s and well into the 1960s, the money and the commitment was there, young ministers were interested, and the students seemed interested in the programs. Why not expand?[14]

There were small numbers of Muslim and Hindu college students, sometimes recognized and sometimes not, throughout the twentieth century, and volunteer spiritual leaders came and went in both groups. The first Muslin Student Association (MSA) organized in 1963 at the University of Illinois Urbana-Champaign, and then a few other MSAs were begun elsewhere. The MSAs represented a search among some Muslim students, in keeping with the campus tone of the era, to be Muslim "out loud." But in the early years they mostly served immigrant Muslim students who did not mean to stay in the United States, offering a "comfort zone during their years in the United States." Only in the 1980s, after the impact of the 1965 Immigration and Nationality Act on colleges, did more Muslim and Hindu students intend to stay in the country. Hindu students first organized Hindu Student Councils (HSC) at some schools, starting with Northeastern University in Boston, in the late 1980s and a national HSC in 1990. It was even later, at the turn of the new century, that the first full-time Muslim chaplain, Yahya Hendi, was appointed at Georgetown. The first full-time Hindu chaplain on a college campus, Vineet Chander, was not appointed until 2008. We will discuss all of those developments in chapters 7 and 8.[15]

In the 1960s and 1970s, more women entered college chaplaincy, but the vast majority were still men. Most chaplains were ordained clergy and very few women were as yet ordained, though by the 1970s that began to change. Some called themselves chaplains, some campus ministers, some deans of religious life, and some directors of centers like Hillel or Newman clubs, or Westminster foundations. Throughout this volume I have used chaplain to include all campus-based religious life professionals, though some of them would not be comfortable with the term. Some chaplains were paid by host private universities but most by sending religious organizations.[16]

Howard L. Daughenbaugh was the United Methodist chaplain at Tulane University from 1958 to 1969 and at the University of Illinois Urbana-Champaign from 1969 to 1973. Though he received none of the national recognition that Coffin did, Daughenbaugh's career overlapped with Coffin's. Daughenbaugh graduated from Methodist Perkins School of Theology in Dallas, Texas, in 1958. He had been wondering for some time what form his ministry would take, and the Perkins dean, Merrimon Cuninggim, who became a nationally recognized scholar of chaplaincy, urged him to consider a college-based role. He followed that advice and accepted the Tulane position fresh from graduation and ordination.

Daughenbaugh described the joy of being on a college campus at a time when "the sixties dawned with a great sense of hope and with the eager expectation of exploring new horizons in space and elsewhere." Student culture was changing, and as Daughenbaugh noted, after 1960 many students concluded that "house mothers were anachronisms and dorm hours incredulous." The civil rights activity brought a sense of purpose and a reason for commitment broader than that which had been present in the 1950s. It "wasn't long before the economic and civil rights revolutions were joined by the sexual and educational revolutions." He described the prophets of the early 1960s as Jack Kerouac, Bob Dylan, and Martin Luther King Jr. Hope was in the air and the early 1960s were a boom time for religion on college campuses. Students wanted "an educational experience designed to create a purposeful and meaningful life." Chaplains were in the middle of all of this, respected by both the church and the college community, and full of high hopes themselves.

It was not to last, however. As students demanded greater changes in their education, many faculty and administrators turned against the most militant students and their supporters, including chaplains. As it became evident that the civil rights struggle would be longer, more divisive, and less complete in its victories—and perhaps most of all as the war in Vietnam dragged on and on, sucking up the lives of some of the best of their generation—college students and their ministers lost their optimism. Daughenbaugh remembered, "A decade that began with hope, commitment to the ideals of our nation, and a concentration on the needs of our less fortunate neighbors, ended in despair, anger, and self-centeredness." The shift from hope to despair in a decade happened across American society—in politics, entertainment, and churches—but in few places more than on college campuses.

The churches that had supported college chaplaincies with such enthusiasm changed their collective mind. Many in the pews and the pulpits came to see the student generation as unpatriotic, sexually irresponsible, sometimes violent, and generally disrespectful of all institutions. As a result, "Campus ministers found themselves separated from the denominations that supported them, and those who didn't experience such separation were, quite often, criticized by their colleagues." Looking back, Daughenbaugh remembered, "My life changed. My vocation changed. My faith changed. I believe all three matured." Nevertheless, like many other chaplains, Daughenbaugh ended the campus-based phase of his ministry by the mid-1970s, though he remained a United Methodist minister until his retirement decades later.[17]

Religion Professors and Religious Studies

While college chaplains were the best-known public representatives of religion in American higher education in the 1960s and 1970s, they were not the only ones talking about religion at American universities. While they received less public notice, professors in religious studies were closer to the center of the academic action in the era than often-marginalized chaplains. In many places, religious studies programs grew dramatically. Sometimes the very lack of recognition shielded those in academic studies of religion from the storms that buffeted chaplains.

Since at least the 1930s, religious studies academics had drawn a clear line between the study of religion and the practice of it, and while they left the practice of religion to the chaplains, the religious studies faculty were confident that they alone were the masters of the study of religion. As James M. Gustafson, one of the most prominent among them, said, they approached religion with a "posture of analytical rigor, of disinterested objectivity, and sometimes of disinterested irreverence." At the same time, students, desperate for courses where they could talk about things like meaning and purpose and their own religious quests in these stormy decades, flocked to religious studies programs.[18]

At the University of California Santa Barbara (UCSB), one of the earliest and largest programs in the study of religion at a public university (see chapter 5 for the origins of the UCSB program), a program that had begun in the 1950s expanded significantly in the 1960s. In the spring of 1963, the internationally known theologian Paul Tillich spent a semester teaching at UCSB. In 1964, Tillich returned along with two new full-time hires, W. Richard Comstock and Walter Capps, and religious studies became a full-fledged department at UCSB, with its own major and its own graduate programs. The Institute in Religious Studies was established in 1966. Both the size of the faculty and the reputation of the department continued to grow through the 1970s as new faculty were hired, including long-time student of the sociology of campus ministry, Phillip Hammond, in 1978. The curriculum was revised and expanded, and national conferences were hosted. It was a long way from the experience of UCSB chaplains who, far more than any faculty, were caught up in the campus turmoil, especially about the war in Vietnam. When a protest at UCSB turned violent in 1970—the local branch of the Bank of America was burned down by angry students and a student was later shot and killed by police—the issues raised were ones that chaplains had to address far more than professors in religion.[19]

In 1963, the US Supreme Court gave a significant if inadvertent boost to religious studies, especially for those who worried that even the academic study of religion might violate the separation of church and state, an issue that had plagued the field in public universities since the early 1900s. In 1962 and 1963 rulings, the Court prohibited the opening of the school day in public schools (and presumably public colleges) with any devotional activity, including prayer and Bible reading. But the Court also ruled, in the words of Justice Tom C. Clark, that "a good education was not complete without the study of religion, either comparatively, historically, or in its relationship to the advancement of civilization." If any had worried about the constitutionality of religious studies at public universities, the Court had spoken, and an enterprise that so clearly separated itself from the practice of religion to focus exclusively on the study of religion had the Court's blessing.[20]

For all the success in enrollment and faculty hiring in religious studies in this era, there was a problem at the heart of the field: just what did academics in religious studies study? The field was clearer on what it did not do—practice religion—than on what it did do. In 1965, Princeton University's distinguished professor of religion, Paul Ramsey, published a volume simply titled *Religion* in a multivolume study of humanities scholarship sponsored by the Princeton Council of the Humanities. For Ramsey, religious studies included the subfields of history of religions, New Testament, Old Testament, church history, theology, ethics, and philosophy of religion. Except for the history of religions, which often meant comparative religion, Ramsey's list was a virtual replication of what every major Protestant theological seminary in the United States taught. Catholics, Jews, Mormons, and representatives of the world's many other religions felt that the study of their faith, and indeed a truly "disinterested" look at religions beyond mainline Protestantism, was missing.

To some, it seemed that the descendants of the nineteenth-century Protestant hegemony that had once controlled the university had now snuck in the back door, and at least had a department of their own. But that was not a tenable curriculum in the university of the era. Even Paul Ramsey seems to have recognized the problem. Five years later Ramsey and his coeditor, John F. Wilson, published another volume, *The Study of Religion in Colleges and Universities*, sponsored by the newly reorganized American Academy of Religion. They expanded the fields significantly to include specifically Catholic studies and Jewish studies, but also sociology of religion, comparative religious ethics, religion and literature, and religion and the arts. But the problems with the field remained. At a 1986 conference at UCSB to assess the field, the University of Chicago's Jonathan Z. Smith argued that religious studies was not "a coherent disciplinary matrix in and of itself." Absent "some principle of intellectual autonomy," the field was at best a "would-be discipline." There might be recognition, student interest, and faculty positions, but an intellectual core for the work was yet to be found.[21]

The Student-Led University Christian Movement

Among students there was significant engagement with religion in the 1960s and 1970s. A new ecumenism blossomed on campus not seen since the heyday of the YMCA's interfaith Student Volunteer Movement of the early twentieth century. The 1959 creation of the National Student Christian Federation (NSCF) merged part of what was left of the Student Volunteer Movement with the newer United Student Christian Council. Students led the merger. Denominations followed.

In 1964, four major Protestant denominations pooled their budgets for campus work to create the United Ministries in Higher Education. A looser federation that was launched in 1966, the University Christian Movement, included programs for Catholic and Eastern Orthodox college students—a sign of the times when separate denominational efforts were replaced by a more unified focus, at least among Christians. College chaplains themselves, in some cases with the endorsement of their sponsoring denominations, founded the National Campus Ministry Association in St. Louis in 1964. The flurry of new ecumenical meetings, shared budgets, and shared buildings reflected an expanded ecumenical spirit on college campuses.[22]

Postwar students read and discussed the work of theologians like Reinhold Niebuhr and Paul Tillich, along with those of the Jewish mystic Martin Buber and Catholic scientist and mystic Pierre Teilhard de Chardin. They also committed themselves to reform and especially to civil rights. Niebuhr and Tillich gave a level of scholarly credibility to the conversations while civil rights gave them passion. Martin Luther King Jr. and Fannie Lou Hamer were regular campus speakers.[23]

Student-led religious organizations also followed a similar arc in the 1960s to what Daughenbaugh described so well for chaplains. The early days of the National Student Christian Federation (NSCF) reflected a new level of interdenominational engagement and student enthusiasm. But it was not to last, and the estrangement from much institutionalized religion began early. A major study of faith and learning that was launched by the NSCF and finished in 1962 received virtually no audience as civil rights, and then Vietnam, took center stage. Faith and learning just did not have the same interest.[24]

Organized religion, especially the life and worship of White Protestant churches, enjoyed none of the prestige and self-confidence of universities in the early 1960s. In spite of—or maybe because of—the religious boom of the 1950s, more and more people inside and outside the church were raising major questions about the church. Most of all, college students asked questions. Two major best sellers of the 1960s, sociologist Peter Berger's *The Noise of Solemn Assemblies* (1961) and theologian Harvey Cox's *The Secular City* (1965), were both first written as study documents for the National Student Christian Federation. Berger was clear that "we are suggesting that Christians may freely choose *not* to become members of local congregations, *not* to identify themselves with a denomination, *not* to join the weekly traffic jam of the religious rush hour on Sunday morning." It was a sentiment that made sense to many still deeply devout students and chaplains at the time, as they felt called by their faith to focus on the world beyond church walls. It was less well received in the churches themselves.[25]

In 1966, the new University Christian Movement (UCM) described its focus as "issue-oriented ecumenicity." UCM president Charlotte Bunch Weeks (who later as Charlotte Bunch became an outspoken lesbian and leader of the campaign for women's rights) sent a "fraternal letter" to Students for a Democratic Society (SDS) saying, "We share with you the desire to build a movement on the campuses of this nation responsive to the moral imperatives for equality and justice now confronting us." Some in SDS wondered if the commitment was real or if the UCM was simply fearful of "losing its flock on leftward moving campuses." In any case, both organizations moved further left in the next years. UCM's focus on the imperatives of equality and justice led to a growing alienation from all organized authority—within universities and in the institutionalized churches. Looking back at the 1960s at the end of the decade, Myron Bloy, an Episcopal chaplain, said, "Tenured department heads and SDS leaders used to share an assumption that however great their ostensible differences, if they dug deep enough they would eventually come to the common ground on which they could join to build the new academic Jerusalem. Those halcyon days of easy hope are now over."

UCM's leaders said that institutional structures should be "kept as minimal and as flexible as possible in order that it may be free to serve as an enabling instrument of creative responsible movement." Many within the UCM were angry that the churches seemed to spend much more time and money on institutional maintenance than on the pressing issues of the day. They were determined not to replicate the model. There were fierce internal UCM debates about just how to be most responsive and engaged in the many forms of increasingly divergent political activity. Finally, at a February 1969 general meeting of the UCM, the group argued over a report that suggested they become "a community of organizers committed to a sense of total alienation from the present society." They then received a demand from the UCM's Black caucus that they should turn over $50,000 received from the Danforth Foundation, to the caucus. After thinking the issues over, the UCM met the next day and simply disbanded to be in the larger movement unhindered by institutional ties to church or university.

Robert Rankin, one of the staff behind the Danforth Foundation grant to UCM, remarked that he had "furnished the UCM with sufficient funds to purchase a fifty-thousand-dollar gun with which they committed suicide." In fact, holding any organization as diverse as the UCM together by 1969 was probably beyond the capacity of anyone, student or elder.[26]

The end of the UCM may have left many students free to enter even more fully into the radical movements of the next decade. However, severing ties to a larger religious network ended something that had sustained many students for a long time, and would not be there to sustain those who came later. For many chaplains, the virtual evaporation of student involvement in their work, combined at the anger in many churches towards colleges left them shaken, isolated and often without budgets.[27]

Not every religiously oriented student was part of the UCM or missed it after its disappearance. At the height of the war in Vietnam, there is evidence that the majority of all college students participated in at least one demonstration against the war. But radical political activity was not the only focus of campus-based religion in the 1960s. The evangelical InterVarsity Christian Fellowship, which had been growing steadily throughout the religious boom of the 1950s, had thirty-five staff engaged with more conservative student work on college campuses across the country. The 1960s—in which student protest dominated the headlines—was also a boom time for InterVarsity's "sharing the love of Jesus" on a one-to-one basis while limiting engagement in larger movements of the day. By the early 1970s, the InterVarsity campus-based staff grew to more than 200. John Alexander, the national leader of InterVarsity, described the core of the work in 1966: "We want IVCF people to become 'men of the Word,' strong in Bible study and love for Scripture. And we must be men and women of prayer, for unless IVCF kneels down, it will not go forward." Nevertheless, on some issues, especially racial justice, InterVarsity was considerably more liberal than some other groups. But it was really only in the 1980s and 1990s that the way forward opened broadly for organizations like Inter-Varsity and the parallel conservative evangelical ministries, in part because so much of the more liberal religious infrastructure had disappeared.[28]

The Movement

As students shifted their engagement from faith-based organizations to direct involvement in civil rights, free speech, and women's rights activity, they often experienced a moment of new freedom from constraints even if the source of their passion was to be found in older communities of faith. The abandonment of old organizations, however, often left an impoverished foundation for future generations.

Religion and Civil Rights

College students, often through their religious organizations, became some of the youngest and most militant leaders of the civil rights movement. After the mostly minister-led Montgomery Bus Boycott, a new student-led phase began, when on February 1, 1960, four students from Black colleges in Greensboro, North Carolina, sat down at the segregated White-only lunch counter at Woolworth's demanding that it be integrated. The students at that first sit-in had not done any planning, but within days the sit-ins caught the nation's attention, especially that of many college students, Black and White. The sit-ins expanded dramatically in numbers and locations, and the students moved between college campuses, church basements (where they planned strategy), and the lunch counters themselves.

James Lawson, himself an African American seminary student at Vanderbilt University, had a deep commitment to nonviolence and became a primary mentor to the sit-in students. He taught nonviolent tactics even as he shared the student's passion for the integration they sought. The student sit-ins, fueled by the religious fervor, energized the civil rights movement in early 1960.[29]

James Lawson was never a college chaplain, but he served as chaplain-like counselor and teacher to a generation of students willing to take nonviolence seriously, even as they militantly demanded an end to segregation. Lawson was ordained as a Methodist minister during his senior year in high school, well before Methodists required seminary degrees for ordination. While in college, Lawson joined the Fellowship for Reconciliation, a pacifist organization originally founded in 1915 in opposition to World War I. He served thirteen months in prison for refusing to fight in the Korean War because of his pacifist beliefs. Lawson then spent three years in India as a Methodist missionary and also as a student of Gandhi's non-violent resistance. On his return to the United States from India, he entered theology school at Oberlin; but in 1956, Martin Luther King Jr. recruited Lawson to help with the expanding civil rights activity in the South. The Fellowship of Reconciliation appointed him as their southern field agent, and he was able to transfer to Vanderbilt's Divinity School in Nashville to finish his graduate studies.

Based in Nashville, Lawson was both a theology student and the leader of workshops on nonviolence for area students. Within a week of the first four-student Greensboro "sit-down," as it was first called, sit-ins at lunch counters were spreading across the South. Lawson presided over a meeting of 500 students in Nashville, urging a delay for the kind of painstaking training in nonviolence that he thought was essential, as well as for time to raise funds for bail if students were arrested. But the students would have none of it. Lawson sensed the tone and determination at the meeting. Instead of pushing for a delay, Lawson gave a crash course on nonviolence, right on the spot, that lasted until late in the evening. The next morning, 500 African American students from Fisk University, Tennessee State, Meharry Medical School, and the Black Baptist Seminary sat in at lunch counters across Nashville, which soon became the center of the sit-in action.

From the beginning of the sit-ins, the students faced torment and beatings, with everything from ketchup to lit cigarettes poured on them by large crowds of White onlookers. After two weeks of sit-ins, and the often-violent local White response, the Nashville police chief announced that he was going to start arresting the students if the sit-ins continued. In response, after a night of preparation in the dos and don'ts of nonviolent responses to arrest, the students returned to the lunch counters and seventy-seven Blacks, including the intrepid Diane Nash, and five Whites, were arrested. In jail over the weekend, some of the students planned a new form of protest. On Monday, as their fines were announced, Diane Nash said: "We feel that if we pay these fines we would be contributing to and supporting the injustice and immoral practices that have been performed in the arrest and conviction of the defendants." Originally only sixteen students refused to pay the fines, but seeing their courage, others joined them, and the Nashville authorities found themselves holding some of the city's best college students. On the Black college campuses, the arrests simply emboldened others who had held back and new groups of students volunteered to sit in and be arrested.

With lunch counters unable to function normally and the city jails filling, Nashville's mayor offered to release the jailed students and appoint a biracial committee to make recommendations about accommodations in the city if the students would stop their protest. Since a civil rights commission had been one of the movement's original demands, the students agreed and were greeted as heroes. When a group of them later sat in at the Greyhound bus terminal (outside of the area of the agreement with the mayor) the management simply served them without comment. Segregated lunch counters were gone in Nashville. The college student–led sit-ins were successful, and the commitment to religiously based nonviolence had worked. It was, however, some time before the same strategies worked in the deeper south of Alabama and Mississippi.

"Graduates" of Lawson's workshops soon joined the Freedom Rides on buses and brought their disciplined nonviolence to even more volatile settings. Back in Nashville, one of the city's major newspapers kept up a campaign against Lawson, and against Vanderbilt for having him as a student. The university was not as brave as the students, and the trustees expelled Lawson. After the school was threatened with a loss of accreditation because of the action, the dean and several of the Divinity School faculty resigned. Lawson himself completed his divinity degree at Boston University School of Theology (King's old school) and served as pastor of Methodist churches, first in Memphis and then Los Angeles. In 2005, when Lawson was seventy-seven years old, Vanderbilt attempted to make amends by giving Lawson its Distinguished Alumnus award, and he continued to be a militant advocate for nonviolent civil rights in the United States until his death in June 2024.[30]

Faith and Campus Protest

Some students who had been part of the sit-ins and Freedom Rides, and later voting rights efforts, never returned to college but became full-time civil rights organizers for the next decade. Many more did return to campus to continue their education. After an arrest or two while living with death threats from the KKK and other White vigilante groups, they were not the same students, however. The civil rights efforts, and the courage that it took to face that danger, stayed with them. Back on campus, many civil rights veterans found college itself had grown intolerable. It was not just minor limitations but the sense that they were being treated like small cogs in a large machine that stirred their anger. Campus rules made for administrative convenience—from filling out endless punch cards, which were then essential to the new computers on campus, to limits on where on campus they could gather—galled in ways that had not done so before.

Mario Savio was one of the dissatisfied college students. As a twenty-one-year-old junior at the University of California at Berkeley in the fall semester of 1964, he was suddenly catapulted to fame as the voice of student dissatisfaction and the early Berkeley Free Speech Movement. Berkeley students, conservative as well as liberal, had long been used to sitting at tables on Sproul Plaza in the heart of campus to share literature and conversations and to advocate for their different views. When the university administration decided to shut down the Sproul Plaza tables, the students—from SDS radicals to Goldwater conservatives—saw it as a significant attack on their free speech. Many kept on sitting at tables in protest of the policy. On October 1, a police car arrived to arrest one of the protesters and before it left, hundreds of students surrounded the car and sat down so that it could not move. After taking his shoes off to avoid damaging the car, Savio climbed on top of the car and began a speech that changed his life and the university. The police car did not move that day or most of the next. Students formed the Berkeley Free Speech Movement to demand the right to say what they wanted and to end what they saw as a kind of assembly line education.

In December of 1964, Savio made his most memorable speech saying:

> There is a time when the operation of the machine becomes so odious, makes you so sick at heart, that you can't take part. You can't even passively take part. And you've got to put your bodies upon the gears and upon the wheels, upon the levers, upon all the apparatus, and you've got to make it stop.

The energy that Savio and the hundreds of students who were part of the Free Speech Movement released brought about a new, more student-centered, more just university. And Savio just kept speaking.

Many, friends and foes, saw Savio as coming out of nowhere, but in fact he came most directly out of his experience in the civil rights movement. Just weeks before he became famous in Berkeley, Savio had been among the hundreds of White volunteers who answered the call to participate in the Freedom Summer of 1964 by doing voter registration in some of the most dangerous counties of Mississippi. Savio remembered the orientation when they first arrived in Mississippi when Bob Moses, the organizer of Freedom Summer, said to them, "People have been killed. You can decide to go back home, and no one will look down on you for doing it." Moses's own courage and honesty, his unflappable calm, so impressed Savio that he knew he wanted to be like Bob Moses. Challenging the Berkeley administration was nothing compared to challenging the Klan in Mississippi. But Savio and many of his Berkeley colleagues were, in their own ways, students of Bob Moses.

Before civil rights and Bob Moses, part of what made Savio a leader, and made others recognize him as a leader, or what one observer called a spiritual leader, was his own deep Catholic roots. By 1964, Savio had left the Catholic church far behind, but he knew how important growing up Catholic in Queens, New York, had been. Years later when he reflected on what had brought him to the civil rights movement and the Berkeley Free Speech Movement, Savio talked about the Catholic faith of his childhood. Savio had stopped attending Mass a decade earlier, but he said of the Black freedom struggle that it had "a quality of, for me—and it's hard for me to say this—sort of like God acting in history . . . Like God was going to trouble the water. It had a very deep meaning." He saw all civil rights activity through a lens he called "secularized liberation theology" and the divine mission he had learned to liberate the poor.

Savio's biographer, Robert Cohen, said of him:

> Savio considered that mission divine long after he had broken with the Church. Secular as he was, then, his political life was part of Catholic intellectual and political history—that is, if there is a place in that history for an agnostic whose politics were influenced by the egalitarian strand in Catholicism, with its critique of materialism and greed.

The radical ideals of chaplains and professors were not the only source of student passion. Sometimes it was quiet urging from a half-forgotten parish priest, a minister, or rabbi who had planted the seeds of that passion many years before, only to have it sprout when the time was right.[31]

Faith and Women's Rights

By the late 1960s and early 1970s, civil rights and anti-Vietnam war activity expanded as many others challenged systems of oppression that constricted their lives and communities. Most of all, women challenged sexism in society, universities, churches, and indeed within the movement. Susan Brownmiller wrote of the late 1960s with the civil rights, anti-war, and counter-culture movements:

> Women on the left, affected by all these phenomena and more, were gathering in small, informal "rap" groups, study groups, and workshops to simply talk with one another.[32]

Brownmiller was describing something many more women experienced by the early 1970s. She also wrote, "of the thousand or so white volunteers who joined the southern civil rights struggle during the mid-sixties, at least half, including myself, were women." As a result, "After fighting alongside men in a radical movement to correct a grievous wrong, the women involved then woke up and wondered, 'What about us?' " So did many other women across the United States.

While the women's movement of the 1960s and 1970s has been seen as a very secular development, many women, like many men, were inspired by deep religious convictions, even if those convictions were mostly left behind. Casey Hayden—Student Nonviolent Coordinating Committee (SNCC) activist, one of the founders of SDS, and in 1964 coauthor of one of the earliest position papers for the women's movement that compared easy and unexamined assumptions of White supremacy to equally unexamined assumptions of male superiority—had entered student politics through the University Christian Movement. Shulamith Firestone, to be one of the most militant of the early feminist leaders, had first thought of a women's movement as she dealt with some of the male egos in a Jewish youth group. They were not alone in either their earlier religious commitments or the degree to which they left institutional religion behind in the 1970s, even as they continued to carry the core of religious teachings into the new political movements of which they were a part.[33]

For a few activists who tried to stay connected to an earlier religious faith, it was not an easy link to maintain. Carol Christ describes starting a graduate program in religious studies at Yale at the end of the 1960s as one of two women out of 100 students where, "My colleagues and professors saw me as charming, and though they were delighted to have a young woman around, few seemed to expect I would complete my studies." She remembered:

> Gradually I began to wonder whether I had a different perspective on theology because I was a woman. When I talked about the spiritual experiences that gave rise to my interest in theology—my connection to nature, the oneness with the universe I had experienced while swimming in the ocean or hiking in the woods— I was told that such experiences were "aesthetic," "poetic," and "emotional," or "confused" and not worthy of theological consideration.

Christ fought back, and in 1971 she helped organize a working group on Women and Religion at the American Academy of Religion that eventually became a permanent feature of the AAR. Still, it was a lonely fight.[34]

Up to the 1970s, very few women were college chaplains or ministers of any kind. In the 1970s, however, as more Protestant denominations and Jewish groups began ordaining women, women began attending seminaries in larger numbers and some started to think about college chaplaincy positions and asking, "why not me?" By the end of the decade, a trend started as women moved into chaplaincy positions. It would continue to expand later in the century. For some of the first women in college chaplaincy, the move was almost accidental. For others, it was well considered but also full of landmines. Susan Yarrow Morris recalled joining the ecumenical ministry staff at the University of Washington in Seattle in 1972 in a part-time position. Her background in social work and religion led to an invitation to start a marriage preparation program at the campus ministry center. She liked the team and was attracted to the energy she found there. As she remembered it, "This invitation to envision and develop such a program ministry lit a vocational and spiritual spark for me. . . . And so I began backing into ministry." In time, her work expanded, and she stayed on the Campus Christian Ministry staff for sixteen years. She was licensed as a minister in 1982 and subsequently served on the ministry staffs of two Seattle-area churches until her retirement.[35]

For Diane Kenney, college chaplaincy was a vocational choice. Kenney graduated from Pacific School of Religion in 1969 and almost immediately took a job as assistant to the dean of the chapel at Stanford University. Assistant positions were often the first openings for women in college chaplaincy, just as assistant minister positions were in many parish churches where a woman might never have been considered for the senior position. Fortunately for Kenney, she was assistant to Davie Napier, the dean of Stanford's chapel who supported her work, which included worship planning for the Stanford Chapel (known as Memorial Church) and "hanging out" with students. She learned a lot in this position, including how to support demonstrating students and what to say, especially after an African studies professor whom she called "generous" quietly suggested that she never mention that tragedy at Kent State without also mentioning Jackson State. She also met people who had "never met a woman clergy before," or "weren't certain women could be clergy." An important early mentor, Beverly Harrison, a professor at New York's Union Seminary, suggested that Kenney expand her skills with a Danforth Foundation grant that allowed her a year of study. Harrison then made sure she received the grant.

After her study leave, Kenney became interim chaplain at Mills College in Oakland, California, serving while the male chaplain was away. She loved the work at Mills but some of the male faculty were not comfortable with a woman in such a position. When the permanent position opened at Mills, students petitioned to keep Kenny in the role, but it was not to be. She was, however, appointed to direct the campus ministry at Youngstown State University in Ohio—a new experience both because it was an affiliated ministry with a public university and because of the breadth of the ecumenical work that included many different Protestants but also Catholic, Jewish, and Greek Orthodox ministers. She felt welcome at Youngstown as she had not at Mills, and she learned a lot in a very public arena. However, in 1982, Beverly Harrison again urged her to move on and she did, this time to be the ecumenical campus minister at the University of Southern California. She stayed at USC for thirty years, through many kinds of ministry and growing ecumenical engagement until, sadly, in 2011, the United Methodist conference withdrew its financial support and ended access to the space they had previously provided. It was a disappointing end to a long ministry, but college chaplains had been facing similar cuts for some time. One retired Disciple of Christ chaplain said, "Diane, all of this happened to everyone else twenty years ago. How did you manage for so long?" The question was a complement to Kenney, even as it reflected a reality that many in chaplaincy had been facing from the late 1970s onward.[36]

A Crisis in College Chaplaincy

While more and more women, ordained or not, became college chaplains, the women and men who entered chaplaincy throughout the last decades of the twentieth century faced some of the same isolation and drastic budget cuts. Donald G. Shockley was Methodist campus chaplain at Birmingham-Southern College in Alabama starting in 1964, then at the University of Redlands in Southern California from 1972 to 1979, and then was the long-time chaplain at Emory University in Atlanta, Georgia, before a stint on the general staff for campus ministries of the United Methodist church. When he retired after thirty-five years as a college chaplain, he reflected that "I never had a job that did not involve stress." He loved being a college chaplain, although "I have frequently been on the other side of issues that some powerful people (e.g. college trustees, District Superintendents, et al) were agitated about. I think I stood my ground without doing too many things that were stupid." In spite of that, Shockley never really considered any other form of ministry. He began as minister to the first wave of baby boomers who were swelling campuses in the early 1960s and fully experienced the work of chaplaincy in the 1960s but also long after; long enough to reflect on the field.[37]

In his book *Campus Ministry: The Church Beyond Itself*, Shockley attempted to write a theology of campus ministry that reflected major tensions that virtually every college chaplain faced in the 1960s and 1970s. The first tension was the general confusion about just what a chaplain was supposed to do. The second tension had to do with drastically declining funds for any kind of ministry on campus. While balancing those competing stressors, chaplains also faced a never-ending tension between expectations from faith communities and expectations from universities—neither of which particularly liked, respected, or cared to understand the other by the 1970s.[38]

Shockley himself was impatient with chaplains who complained about having a vague job, since he was so clear on what needed to be done by ministers on college campuses, though in his own case, the job was made slightly easier by being a Methodist minister at three different Methodist schools. But many other surveys of chaplains showed that the confusion that was so widespread in the 1950s continued well into the next decades and, if anything, grew stronger. How could one carry on with a ministry of counseling and program development when the world seemed to be exploding? But how could a chaplain explain a lack of traditional religious programs to students who wanted them, or to sponsoring religious bodies that saw offering such church-like activities as *the* work of college chaplains? By the late 1960s and early 1970s, many chaplains found themselves reinventing the nature of their work and therefore had little interest in traditions from the past that might have helped them.

David Duncombe, the author of one of the many position papers prepared for the massive 1969 Danforth study of campus ministries, offered his own definition of the confusion chaplains faced: "The word 'experimental' is in vogue today among campus ministers. The genuine experimental approach may entail 'doing something new.' But it also requires a clear hypothesis. . . . Most 'experiments' in campus ministry carry the implied hypothesis that *something* of religious significance will result from the new approach . . . but since the nature of this expected change is hardly ever specified, the hypothesis is often assumed to be supported, without recourse to normal procedure of verification."[39] The result is that many different kinds of campus-based work were proposed, implemented, and often declared a success with little evidence, and in the end with little to convince those paying the bills, whether in religious or university organizations, that it mattered.

A similar problem of focus can be found in documents of the University Christian Foundation at New York University. A September 1966 newsletter invited students to a series of fall gatherings. One fall program invited students to "look at the international and social issues which affect modern man as we seek to build a better world." Another invitation noted:

The UCF is concerned with all aspects of life, of what is essential to make and keep human life human. The search for social and international understanding, encounter with music, the arts, science, business, industry, service professions, expanding cities, urban universities, and other pertinent concerns receive the attention, study, and action of the persons who identify with UCF.

With such a broad mandate, it is not surprising that some thoughtful observers wondered if with virtually nothing left out, meaningful focus could be found. An external review of the NYU UCF from the same time asked, "Is the UCF doing a valid work? Is the UCF doing a valid Christian work?" The review concluded, "The answer to the first is probably yes—the answer to the second is not clear in the questioner's mind." It was hardly the kind of ringing endorsement of the work that would make those outside the UCF believe it to be essential to support.[40]

Finally, a case study of religious life at the University of Wisconsin saw a similar confusion of purpose. Looking at fifteen different religious groups on campus and their leaders for the Danforth study, N. J. Demerath III and Kenneth J. Lutterman concluded:

Most of the "new breed" of campus ministers on the Wisconsin campus have sought to initiate new activities and participate in nonreligious activities precisely in the interests of innovation and fresh religious air. A number walked in the Selma to Montgomery civil rights march; many have been active in the campus discussion surrounding Vietnam. One started a theatrical group with an invitation extended to nonaffiliated actors and directors; another began a series of open lecture-study programs built around religious and even some nonreligious issues of the day . . . another decided to abandon the organizational structure that has been traditional skeleton for his denomination's religious activities on campuses across the country.

This list included many good and important activities, but coherence and a goal seemed to be missing. Was this engagement with the major movements of the 1960s, civil rights and anti-war activity, in a way that brought something special that only faith could bring, or was it a desperate attempt at relevance? Sometimes it was hard for outside observers and chaplains themselves to tell. An unnamed chaplain told Phillip Hammond, "Here on this campus our nebulous position, both in ecclesiastical relationships as well as our peripheral relationship to the university because of state regulations leaves us men without a country." It was a painful place to be.[41]

The second painful reality facing many chaplains as the 1960s wore into the 1970s was related to the first. As Shockley said, "The most immediate danger for campus ministry now is the withdrawal of support by funding sources, most of which are church related, whether they be concerned individuals, local churches, or the budgets of various campus ministry boards and agencies." Looking at the era from an historical perspective, Dorothy C. Bass echoed Hammond. Chaplains, she said, "received little acknowledgment from, either church or university," which for some chaplains made the situation untenable. Bass added, "paradoxically, it seemed that they were caught in a spiral that must only make their isolation more severe. The more cosmopolitan (that is, the less religious) their university; and the more innovative their style became, the less acknowledgment they were likely to receive from the church."

The lack of acknowledgment was not only a matter of recognition of college chaplaincy by churches; it came in the form of budget cuts for chaplaincy programs. The cuts were drastic. Catholic student participation in the national Newman Club effort dropped from 47,000 in 1963 to 18,000 a year later, and of a national budget of $41,000 that was covered by student dues, only about $4,000 was actually available in 1964. In the Bay Area of California, the Protestant United Ministries in Higher Education supported seven campus ministers with a budget of $176,365 in 1966, but it was trimmed to five ministers with a budget of $87,776 in 1972. Between 1970 and 1981, the number of people on the national staff of the United Ministries supported by the ten member denominations fell from thirty-one to fourteen and a half. Campus religious offices closed. Far fewer campuses had a chaplain, and on larger campuses with several chaplains, there were fewer to be found. By the end of the 1970s, college chaplaincy was in for a hard, slow slog but there seemed to be fewer and fewer chaplains doing the slogging.[42]

By 1978 or 1979, the picture of religion and religious engagement on college campuses was grim. The academic study of religion was thriving but at its core confused about meaning, purpose, and what constituted the field. College chaplains were suffering a confusion of purpose and a hugely significant loss of funds that made much of the future of this form of ministry problematic, perhaps most severely among Protestants but also among Jews and Catholics. And the student religious organizations, from the University Christian Movement to smaller gatherings on many campuses, had simply disappeared as many of the students had migrated into larger political movements and left the religious organizations behind. In many cases, students like Savio, Firestone, and Christ found their courage and commitment fueled by earlier religious roots. But the disappearance of any organizational structure and the decline in the level of available support meant that the next student generation would be left with less—much less. The bridge role between faith and engagement that organizations like UCM had provided and that many chaplains and religious life centers had once offered simply was not there for future student generations. The story of how all of this played out—in the 1980s and 1990s and into the twenty-first century, is the focus of the next two chapters.

The Sixties and Then Some—Traditions Shattered at Santa Clara University and Other Jesuit Colleges

Catholic colleges, perhaps especially those associated with the Jesuit order, experienced all of the transformations that most other colleges and university faced in the 1960s and 1970s, and some important—indeed, earth shattering—additional ones. Santa Clara students, like their counterparts across most of American higher education, challenged college authorities over issues of civil rights, the response to the war in Vietnam, issues of gender and sexuality, and the authority of college leader to control their lives. In addition, students, faculty, and administrators at Santa Clara also experienced the impact of secularism and growing demands for vastly expanded academic and intellectual freedom unleashed in the Catholic Church in the 1960s. Changes that had been emerging slowly in Protestant, formerly Protestant, and state universities over the previous century came to many Catholic colleges, Santa Clara included, all at once in the decade of the 1960s.

Santa Clara University was founded in gold-rush era California. In December 1849, two Jesuits, Michael Accolta and John Nobili, moved from Oregon to San Francisco to develop a ministry to the gold rush inspired booming population of Northern California. In less than two years, they had defined their work, as Jesuits so often did, as college founding. The local bishop gave them the old Santa Clara Mission. The Jesuits put up a sign, "Santa Clara College," and quickly admitted 12 students, a number that grew to over 100 in less than five years, while the Italian Jesuit province in Turin, Italy, adopted the college as its mission and sent a steady stream of faculty.[43]

The founders knew exactly what they wanted to teach: the Jesuit *Ratio Studiorum* curriculum—based in scholastic philosophy and expected at all Jesuit colleges. The Santa Clara Jesuits also knew who they wanted to teach. Catholic schools were rigidly single sex and Santa Clara only taught men, though like many Catholic colleges in the United States they admitted Protestant, as well as Catholic, men. The men came in surprisingly large numbers—both new immigrants from the East Coast and longtime Californians from the Mexican era. Few stayed for the full course, however, and in the early years only a tiny percentage received their degrees.

It is hard to imagine 100 young men in gold-rush California poring over ancient philosophy, much of it in Latin. But that is what the college taught and what the faculty believed was essential. In time, the Jesuits started to offer some nondegree commercial courses. But any further curricular reform was stopped in the 1890s when a visitor general sent from Rome ordered that the *Ratio* was to be the only curriculum from which "no one should be allowed to wander in the future." And even though some of the Jesuits on the faculty decried what that called a frozen curriculum, little wandering did happen well in to the twentieth century.[44]

As late as the late 1950s, Santa Clara was still a small, somewhat cloistered men's college that taught a version of the *Ratio* curriculum to fewer and less satisfied students. Santa Clara might easily have gone the way of many other colleges and simply disappeared. Instead, under the leadership of Patrick Donohoe, who was installed as the new Jesuit college president and rector of the Jesuit community on campus in 1958, the faculty started questioning every aspect of the college's life. Donohoe, the first Santa Clara president to hold a PhD, decided that the 1960s needed to be the decade in which the school needed to change, and change quickly. By the time Donohoe left the college in 1968 (to become head of all the Jesuits in California), it was a very different place, although more changes were implemented under his successor, Thomas Terry, SJ, who was president from 1968 to 1976.

Donohoe knew that the school had no future without more students paying tuition. "While size is in itself not an objective," Donohoe wrote, there was a minimum size that the college needed to "stay alive financially." As others before him had discovered, Donohoe thought that if the college wanted to grow quickly, there was one easy way to do that: admit women. The fact that Santa Clara was a Catholic and Jesuit school complicated matters, however. Pius XI, pope from 1922 to 1939, described coeducation as false and harmful to Christian education, because it ignored "divinely established differences." Previous popes had prohibited it outright, though by the 1950s the Vatican position was softening.

The leaders of the Jesuit order also worried about offending the nuns who had established the many Catholic women's colleges in the United States by threatening to drain badly needed students. And so, in a college still under the tight control of the Jesuit order, the president had to abide by a ruling from his Jesuit superiors in Rome that the school could only admit women with the permission of the local bishop. Donohoe sent his petition to Archbishop John J. Mitty of San Francisco asking for the needed permission. Mitty was slow to act, even though he was prodded by the president's brother, Auxiliary Bishop Hugh Donohoe. Happily, after months of waiting, the needed permission came and in March 1961, Santa Clara's president announced the significant news that starting with the 1961–1962 school year, Santa Clara would admit women on an equal basis with men to all of the academic programs of the college.

Some twenty Jesuit colleges in the United States did the same thing in the 1960s and 1970s. There was surprisingly little resistance at Santa Clara, though a few students and graduates grumbled. When asked how he felt about the change, the head of the alumni association said, "I have four daughters." The move to coeducation meant a different Santa Clara and a different kind of more open, less fearful, Catholic college education.[45]

The next change in the college cut even more closely to what it meant for Santa Clara to be a Jesuit school. In 1958, the Santa Clara curriculum still reflected a slightly—very slightly—modified version of the old *Ratio* curriculum. Undergraduates took 24 semester units of scholastic philosophy and 16 units of theology. There were only 21 units of electives in a 128-unit, four-year curriculum. By 1960, something drastic needed to change. As with the move to coeducation, part of the impetus was simple economic calculations. The rigid curriculum severely limited the number of interested students. In addition, outside accrediting agencies, whose decisions mattered more and more to Catholic colleges, were not happy. And the current students were not happy either. As one philosophy professor said, "Students were beginning to feel spoon fed and indoctrinated," and the philosophy and theology professors were tired of facing classrooms full of hostile and obviously bored students. They were among the strongest advocates for change, and it came quickly.

Between 1960 and 1970, the philosophy and theology requirements were slowly reduced, until in 1970 there were no required philosophy courses and only three in a field now called religious studies, with a wide range of electives. The students were much happier and the faculty in the previously required fields felt that they now taught students who wanted to be in their classes. Austin Fagothey, a long-time philosophy professor, said the revised curriculum had a "broader, less confined look," and Santa Clara was "a far, far better school educationally than before."[46]

As it would with other changes, the question emerged about what it meant to call Santa Clara a Jesuit school when it had abandoned the 400-year-old Jesuit college curriculum. Gerald Campbell, SJ, president of Washington, DC's venerable Jesuit Georgetown University, which was also going through the same transition in the 1960s, spoke for Georgetown, Santa Clara, and other schools facing a new world in 1967 when he wrote:

> Tradition, however glorious, is useless, even detrimental, if it serves as an anchor; it is of inestimable value as a rudder. . . . For if we are heirs of the past, we are no less trustees and brokers of the future.

Across the country, a new generation of Jesuits were convinced that only these changes could preserve what was truly at the heart of a Jesuit education. If some, inside and outside the order, were unconvinced, they never had the numbers or the bully pulpits to stop the changes.[47]

In October 1962, Pope John XXIII convened an Ecumenical Council of the Catholic Church, known as Vatican II, in order to "open the windows and let in some fresh air." The decrees of the council changed most aspects of Catholic life around the world. They especially changed Catholic higher education, nowhere more than in the United States. For the leaders of Santa Clara, Vatican II gave permission to keep moving in the direction they had already embraced and, in fact, added new urgency to the effort. No longer would the college be a safe, protected enclave that enforced Catholic teaching and Catholic morality. It would "open the windows" to new ideas, new influences, and new directions.

Vatican II also called for lay participation in decision-making, and Santa Clara made two significant moves: The college added lay people to the previously all-Jesuit board of trustees, and by 1970 the lay members constituted a majority of the board, though the bylaws specified that the president had to be a Jesuit. President Donohoe also formally separated the college from the Jesuit order and separated the job of college president from the rector of the local Jesuits. No longer was the order responsible for the college budget shortfalls. But the college was freer to seek federal funds and support and never again would it need to ask for hierarchical approval of moves like coeducation. The moves were not without criticism, but they followed what the college insisted was the spirit of Vatican II.[48]

The spirit of the 1960s also led Santa Clara to an embrace of a level of free speech that was new to it and unheard of at Catholic schools before 1960. When he became president, Thomas Terry described the new openness:

> The Santa Clara polity on speakers opens the campus to the world in which we live. This indicates no weakening of our commitment to fundamental Christian values but rather a confidence that this commitment will be strengthened by facing important problems of our times.

Santa Clara's leaders held to this position through Christian-Marxist dialogues and a campus speech by Eldridge Cleaver of the Black Panther Party, as well as on-campus protests by the school's own Black Student Union, Mexican-American Student Committee, and Students for Democratic Action. All of these groups would have been unheard of in any earlier era of Santa Clara's history.

In the spring of 1970, students and faculty protested the place of the Reserve Officers Training Corps (ROTC) on campus and some students laid down in the middle of the ROTC parade ground, forcing the student corps to march (carefully) around them. At the same time, the strict rules in dress and dorm hours that the college had adopted with coeducation brought their own protests, as issues of personal and sexual freedom swept all of higher education and Santa Clara was no exception.[49]

The school did not respond with complete openness to every encounter—ROTC continued and a request from 923 out of 1,092 students who wanted a coed dorm was rejected by the Jesuits. Nevertheless, the old paternalism was gone for good and the new day had come. At his inauguration as the new president in 1977, William Rewak, said, "A university must also be a place where freedom of inquiry is paramount." By the late 1970s, the promise of freedom of inquiry was part of Santa Clara's new culture. It was a far cry from what the school had been only two decades earlier.[50]

With so many radical changes taking place in a single decade producing a school that looked a lot more like non-Catholic colleges and universities, the question that a series of Santa Clara presidents had to answer after each new development was: Is Santa Clara still Catholic? By implication, this question also meant, in what ways, if any, did Santa Clara reflect its Catholic identity and not just Catholic history? Clearly the school was prospering. It had grown from 1,100 male students in 1958 to 7,000 students, one-third women, in 1977. The curriculum was completely different, the governance was different, the outside world was welcomed as it once had been excluded.

Most saw all of these things as progress, but the question remained: was the school still Catholic? President Thomas Terry had to answer this question often. At times he did apologize, but only for insufficient inclusion of alumni, saying, "We have changed our policy and have not sufficiently informed our alumni and friends of that change." But he would not waiver from a commitment to the new openness at the school. Where the university once invited only speakers it endorsed, it now invited a wide range of views, though "alumni of that era understandably find it difficult to comprehend how Santa Clara could give a platform" to some of those who spoke. But that was the role of a modern university and, the president insisted, the "university must and will live up to the responsibility in spite of any pressure." Terry spoke regularly of leading a university "informed by Catholic principles." He was confident, he said, that for most students, open discussion only strengthened their faith and "Catholic universities like other universities, stand for the discussion of ideas, not the suppression of ideas."

Terry always insisted, "We are still a Catholic university but we are very different today than we were 15 years ago." His defense and his assertion of the school's ongoing Catholic identity did not convince everyone, but it was all he could offer and it convinced enough people so that the school prospered. Half a century later, in 2023, Santa Clara's website affirms both its welcome of diversity and its Catholic commitments saying, "One of the greatest things about Santa Clara University is its robust religious, spiritual, and worldview diversity. Religious and spiritual diversity is such an important value here at SCU not in spite of our Jesuit, Catholic tradition, but because of it." The website also notes that the university has many chaplains, Catholic, Protestant, and representing several other traditions, while also noting that "the resident and visiting Jesuits who serve SCU are an important influence in shaping the kind of university Santa Clara is and aspires to be." It was a religious blend that left the university on a fine line, but Santa Clara seems to thrive on that line.[51]

Symbols of Tragedy, Places of Hope: Kent State University and Jackson State University

In May 1970, Kent State University in Ohio and Jackson State College in Mississippi, two state schools that previously had little to do with each other, became inextricably linked as symbols of all that was tragically wrong in the United States. As the war in Vietnam dragged on, its violence impacted domestic life. In April 1970, President Richard Nixon, who had promised to end the war, instead expanded the war to include previously neutral Cambodia. College campuses, filled with draft-age young men, and women who supported them, erupted in the angriest demonstrations in generations. On May 4, unprepared National Guard troops fired on Kent State students demonstrating against the war, killing four and seriously wounding others. Then on May 15, police officers from the all-White Jackson City Police and Mississippi Highway Patrol fired on demonstrating Black students in front of a women's dormitory at Jackson State, an historically Black college, killing two and wounding twelve more. Instantly, the two schools became internationally known for the damage of which US governments were capable, not just the federal government perpetuating war in Vietnam but also state and local governments reacting violently on college campuses.

Kent State University, not far from Cleveland, Ohio, was founded in the fall of 1910 when the Ohio legislature authorized new teacher-training normal schools in Kent and Bowling Green. By 1925, Teachers College Columbia University added Kent to a relatively short list of schools from which it automatically accepted graduates for the master's degree. Like many other schools, Kent prospered in the late 1940s and early 1950s when the GI Bill directly funded many students and indirectly made college the thing-to-do for a growing middle class.[52]

Kent was a working-class school that kept its working-class status even as it grew. There may be a stereotype of working-class students as keeping their heads down and wanting to get ahead, but Kent's students represented a working class that was a far from unified. There were conservatives and liberals, religious and very secular students. Along with a majority of White working-class students, there were also a number of African American students, many from Cleveland's small Black middle class and by the 1960s more Blacks from poor and working-class backgrounds.[53]

Among the students coming to Kent in the 1950s, there were some interested in religion, or at least finding ways to talk about meaning and purpose. When philosophy professor Joseph Politella offered four courses in religious studies, students flocked to them. Ronald Lewton remembered a Politella course that taught him "the great secret," which was "how to live my life." Many denominations sponsored work on the Kent State campus with or without full-time college chaplains. The local United Church of Christ, Methodist, and Presbyterian churches all moved to new buildings closer to the Kent campus to reach students. The school's then president, George Bowman (president since 1944), sponsored a Religious Emphasis Week that brought a wide range of religious speakers to the campus, though the event did not survive the turmoil and distrust of the 1960s.[54]

By the late 1960s, continuing through the 1970s and beyond, interested students could find multiple ways to explore or strengthen religious faith on campus if it was important to them. They were also free to ignore it if so inclined. The 1969–1971 catalog listed an array of campus religious organizations that "provide to students of many faiths a variety of experiences through worship, study, and fellowship within their individual groups." The catalog also said that the "purpose of all these groups is to apply the faith of their heritage to the intellectual development of the student experience in the University." Thus, according to the catalog, the practice of faith at Kent was to be connected to students' intellectual development. Among the groups listed in the catalog were B'nai B'rith Hillel, the Christian Science Organization, the Orthodox Christian Fellowship, InterVarsity Christian Fellowship, the Newman Club, Student Religious Liberals (Unitarians), the Lutheran Student Fellowship, the Wesley Foundation, and the United Christian Fellowship (American Baptist, Church of the Brethren, Disciples of Christ, Episcopal, United Church of Christ, and Presbyterian churches). The same catalog included several courses in religion, though not yet a minor or major, but available as electives. In 1969, the course list included Introduction to the Bible, World Religions, Doctrines of the Christian Religion, and Mysticism and Transcendentalism. The courses, like the campus faith-based organizations, represented a fairly diverse spread of the Protestant/Catholic/Jewish world of religion at the time, with very little attention to the wider religious diversity that would be found in later decades. Nevertheless, religion did seem to have a robust presence at Kent State on the eve of the 1970s.[55]

While some students had an interest in religious matters, more students (and perhaps the same students) had a passionate interest in political matters. They were certainly not immune to the national political turmoil on campuses across the country in the 1960s. The first recorded demonstration on the Kent campus was inspired by the Greensboro lunch counter sit-ins. Kent students created their own Council on Human Affairs, whose initial action was a fall 1960 sit-in at popular student bars in the town of Kent that refused to serve Black students. After a visit from James Lawson, spiritual guide of the Southern sit-in movement, the council focused closer to the campus, demanding that the administration refuse to list off-campus housing opportunities unless the landlord signed a non-discrimination agreement. Whether Lawson's deep spirituality, which had been so essential to the Nashville sit-ins, also affected the Kent students is unclear, but his deep commitment to ending discrimination certainly did.

When President Bowman refused the council's request, some forty students picketed in front of his office, embarrassing a furious president who threatened them with expulsion after writing, ironically, that he was confident that unlike some other schools, Kent would continue to see "a stability in our student body, which will save this University from some of the grievous demonstrations" seen elsewhere. Contrary to Bowman's wishes, the demonstrations only continued and expanded. In April 1965, Kent saw perhaps its first demonstration against the war in Vietnam when nine students and seven professors held a noontime anti-war demonstration.[56]

While the 1965 demonstrators were a minority on a generally patriotic campus, the ongoing war in Vietnam led many more students and faculty to a radical polit-

Figure 6.2. By the late 1960s, the killing of students at Kent and Jackson State Colleges signified the anger—toward and by students at the end of the decade. Library of Congress

ical stance. At Kent, this radicalism was often based on a solid labor union or Black power foundation. In 1953, Carl Oglesby, later to be national president of Students for a Democratic Society (SDS), came to Kent State as an eighteen-year-old freshman from a strong union home in Akron, where his father had struggled with rubber companies and his mother had been a civil rights supporter. By 1968, there were many more students moving to the left on issues of civil rights and the war. Carole Teminsky was the daughter of a Youngstown steelworker who came to Kent as a good Catholic Democrat, supported Robert Kennedy's presidential bid, and slowly moved further left as anti-Vietnam protests expanded. Among African Americans, there were students like Dwayne White (Brother Fargo), Robert Pickett, and several others, most of whom as younger children had participated in the United Freedom Movement's school boycotts in Cleveland. They arrived at Kent State in the mid-1960s, distrustful of White student organizations and ready to form their own Black United Students (BUS). Such students were often experienced in protest, whether on or off campus.[57]

Throughout the rest of the 1960s, the demonstrations became more and more militant. They attracted many more Kent students as the war continued. The invasion of Cambodia in the spring of 1970 was the last straw for many students. On May 2, angry students burned Kent's ROTC building to the ground. Ohio governor James Rhodes, locked in a competitive Senate race, was trying to show how tough he could be. He had already brought the National Guard to Kent and now pushed them to be tougher on the students, while the lack of training, food, and sleep did not help the mood within the guard.

Around noon on May 4, after firing teargas at demonstrating students, someone in the guard—never fully identified—gave an order to fire and within seconds four students—Jeff Miller, Alison Krause, Sandy Scheuer, and Bill Schroeder—lay dead or dying while nine others were wounded, including at least one paralyzed for life. The investigation of just what happened at Kent State would continue for years, but no action was ever taken against any individual guardsmen or any officer who might have given the order, in spite of a scene that offered significant video evidence.[58]

While the Kent killings led campuses across the country to explode in anger, at Kent State the immediacy of the killings and injury led to extraordinary anger but also great sadness, mourning, and concern about what it all meant for the school's continuing students. Kent State's campus was closed for the rest of the spring semester. Half a century later, the Kent State archives recorded a number of oral histories with people who had been there on May 4, 1970. One member of the Kent faculty, Barbara Child, remembered the days after the shooting well. Child had been teaching in the English department at Kent since 1963 and remembered being on "the outside edges of SDS" in the late 1960s. She also remembered that right after May 4, the state of Ohio made it illegal to gather on the campus for any reason, with barricades all around and chains on the doors of buildings. But like a number of her colleagues, Child had many seniors in her classes and "we were just hell-bent on getting our students who were seniors to graduate." Gordon McKeeman, the minister of the Unitarian Universalist Church in Akron, welcomed the faculty who were locked out of campus for crucial meetings to plan their next moves, and especially to ensure that the Kent seniors did indeed graduate on schedule, despite the school being closed. The warm welcome of faculty to the Unitarian Church gave

Child great pride in her own Unitarian Universalist membership and eventually led her to a career change to ordained Unitarian ministry.[59]

Anne Andrews, who had been a graduate student in chemistry at the time of the shootings, also recorded an oral history remembering her grief and fear, as well-armed and seemingly ill-disciplined National Guard troops continued to occupy the campus. For Andrews, one way to deal with her grief was to sing in a Requiem Mass offered at the Kent United Church of Christ soon after the shootings. A bit later the Quaker American Friends Service Committee sponsored a series of sensitivity trainings to try to heal the deep hatreds that existed between the guardsmen and their local supporters, and most students and faculty. Andrews found them helpful. The healing meetings took place at the United Christian Ministries center, a bit off campus. For both Child and Andrews, the churches were crucial supports especially at a time when many of the local residents of the town of Kent remained deeply hostile.[60]

With the news of the Kent State killings, over 4 million high school and college students in the United States walked out of classes in protest. Not only were students now demonstrating against the terrible war in Vietnam and Cambodia but also at the government-sanctioned killing of students on an American college campus. Historically Black colleges and universities (HBCUs) responded along with the rest, including Jackson State University in Jackson, Mississippi. While Jackson State had a reputation for mostly quiet students who saw the college as their one chance at a better life and did not want to blow it, there were always activists among them who were willing to challenge the deep segregation and racism that reigned in Mississippi.

Jackson State's roots went back further than Kent State's. The school was founded as Natchez Seminary in 1877, during the last years of Reconstruction, by local Black Baptist ministers and with the support of the White northern American Baptist Home Mission Society. As the local founders of Natchez Seminary said, the school existed for "the maintenance of liberty and the elevation of our race."[61]

In the early twentieth century, the school moved to its current location in the city of Jackson. In the midst of the Great Depression in 1930, the Baptists ended their support, but the school continued on its own as a private school. In 1940, the state of Mississippi, perhaps in an attempt to convince federal courts that it was living up to the "equal" part of "separate but equal," absorbed the school to train teachers for the segregated African American schools of the state. It was renamed Mississippi Negro Training School and later Jackson State College in 1956 and finally Jackson State University in 1974.[62]

Jackson State's status as a public HBCU in the state of Mississippi limited many of the school's activities—religious and political. The all-White Mississippi state board of higher education made sure things stayed that way. Jackson State's 1960s African American president, Jacob Reddix, did all he could to tamp down civil rights activism, leading Jackson student Anne Moody, who later became a national voice of the civil rights movement, to call him "every kind of fucking Tom I could think of." But students found ways to act on their own. When students from Jackson's private HBCU, Tougaloo College, with support from that college's chaplain, John Mangram, planned a "study-in" at Jackson's downtown White library, at least one Jackson student, Dorie Ladner, joined them. She was among the group when the "Tougaloo Nine" were arrested, and she sang, prayed, and demanded freedom along with them. To the great frustration of President Reddix, more Jackson State students joined the Tougaloo students in protesting the arrest of the library study-in students.

In 1963, Tougaloo students, along with Jackson State student George Raymond, former student Walter Williams, who had been expelled for civil rights activity, and Tougaloo's new chaplain, Reverend Ed King, sat in at a lunch counter in downtown Jackson. Soon thereafter African American high school and college students across Mississippi formed a secret Mississippi Improvement Association, which included Jackson State student James Meredith, who would later integrate the University of Mississippi. The student association claimed to include the majority of Jackson State students among its members. In 1967 Benjamin Brown, a civil rights organizer supported by the Delta Ministry of the National Council of Churches, was shot and killed by Mississippi police after a police standoff with Jackson State students. After a decade of marches, boycotts, and planning, Jackson State students were hardly new to militant activity in 1970. Indeed, they had been at it far longer than their White northern counterparts and had already seen too much state-sanctioned violence to be as surprised as those in Ohio when violence was unleashed on their campus.[63]

When word reached them of the Kent State killings, 200 to 300 Jackson State students boycotted classes and held a rally "in sympathy with the Kent State University situation." In the next few days the campus was full of rage around Kent State as well as the draft, which was sending disproportionate numbers of young Black men to fight and die in Vietnam. Many students still wanted to get on with final exams, but many were also determined to take some action.[64]

On May 13, students pelted cars on Lynch Street—a major street for commuters that ran through the center of the Jackson State campus—with rocks, and the head of campus security told the president, "It looks pretty bad. . . . I've never seen the students so angry." A few of the angriest students attempted to follow the Kent State example and burn the ROTC building on campus. Two Molotov cocktails were thrown at the building, but the fire was quickly extinguished.

While May 14 was mostly a quiet day, the anger flared occasionally and by evening students were out in some numbers and the White Jackson City police, who had previously held off, now entered the campus. They were joined by White Mississippi Highway patrol officers under the command of an inspector already known to the students for his mistreatment of Black people. Even if most students were not doing much more than watching events that night, they were angry. Some students gathered in front of the Alexander Hall dorm and others were watching from the dorm windows. Early in the morning of May 15, someone threw a bottle; the police and highway patrol reacted, firing buckshot, rifles, and submachine guns. The reign of bullets killed James Earl Green, a high school student who dreamed of going to college and liked being on the campus, and Phillip Gibbs, a junior at the college. Twelve other young people were wounded in the gunfire, which shot out the windows of Alexander Hall from top to bottom. There was evidence, like the dispatch of Jackson ambulances to the college before the gunfire, that the shooting had been planned. In spite of multiple investigations, no one was ever identified or punished for what happened at Jackson State that night. College students all over the country saw the Jackson State killings as both a continuation of the Kent State killings and further evidence of the racism that was alive and well in the United States. Few campuses anywhere in the country went back to normal that semester.[65]

There was a nation-wide outpouring of grief, anger, and frustration about the killing of college students on their own campuses. A presidential commission chaired by former Pennsylvania governor William Scranton, which held hearings in August 1970, issued a blistering final report that called the shootings at both Jackson and Kent "unjustified," and noting that, contrary to some accounts, there had been no sniper fire at either school nor small arms fire at Alexander Hall in Jackson. Attorney General John Mitchell responded to the commission report with a contradictory conclusion that the shootings were "unnecessary, unwarranted, and inexcusable," but that the case was closed, and he would not call a grand jury. The National Council of Churches and the Methodist Board of Church and Society along with local supporters raised funds to support further trials. Sadly, even the liberal National Council of Churches was able to raise much more money for the

Kent State cases than for those at Jackson State. Nevertheless, grand juries were convened and court cases supported. Various court cases continued for a decade but with no conclusions.[66]

Fifty years later, Jackson State and Kent State are still known primarily for the events of a few seconds in May 1970. Of course, much has happened in the life of the schools since then. Students at Jackson State acted quickly to make sure the memory of May 15, 1970, stayed alive. Only two years after the events, influential professor Margaret Walker Alexander reminded them that "we must recall those painful hours and re-examine what happened here and know why we must never forget those martyred men." Students created a permanent memorial to Phillip Gibbs and James Green that remains as part of an expanded plaza near where they died in front of Alexander Hall.[67]

Campus religious groups at Kent joined with other student organizations to create the King-Kennedy Center to serve high-poverty communities off campus. The summer 1977 Kent bulletin carried the same list of campus religious activities as the 1960s bulletin had done, but with all campus ministries now coordinated through a university Center for Human Understanding. The bulletin also reported that the academic study of religion, now called religion studies, offered a new certificate, and advertised a somewhat wider range of courses, including courses in African and African American religious experiences and the "Problems in Philosophy of Religion," even if not yet specific courses in the world's many different religions.

In 1977, Kent students also continued the activism of an earlier student generation, setting up a Tent City on the site of the Kent shootings to demand it be protected from any future construction and serve as a place of remembrance. Although the site was eventually cleared and almost 200 Tent City residents arrested, the students won their point and the memorial, not a gym annex, was built.

Students at both schools also worked to maintain a link that was forged between them. Led by Alan Canfora and Laura Davis, who were wounded at Kent, and others, they remembered that college students on both campuses were shot by governmental authorities and that fact needed to be remembered.[68]

By the twenty-first century, religious life at both schools was flourishing. No longer did Jackson State students need to rely on a chaplain from Tougaloo. They had their own. A religious life council within the Division of Student Affairs included the college chaplain and representatives from several affiliated religious organizations, including the Baptist Student Union and the Fellowship of Christian Athletes, both usually conservative groups.

A look at the Kent website shows something similar—Luther House of the Lutheran Campus Ministry nearby, a United Church of Christ and an Orthodox community that met in homes, and a Late Night Christian Fellowship that had Room 307 in the Student Center reserved at 8:30 each evening while the university website shows a Buddhist Temple, a Hindu Temple, a Muslim center, a Hillel chapter and two other synagogues, a Catholic church, and a number of Protestant ones. From all appearances, religious life was alive and well, if mostly off campus, at both state schools in the 2020s, perhaps significantly more alive than it had been a half century earlier.[69]

A Conservative Alternative in the Radical 1960s— Dordt College, Sioux Center, Iowa

On January 23, 2016, less than two weeks before the crucial 2016 Iowa Republican presidential caucuses and more than sixty years after Dordt College was founded, then presidential candidate Donald Trump gave an impassioned speech at the very conservative Christian school. The Dordt speech made international headlines for Trump's boast that "I could stand in the middle of Fifth Avenue and shoot somebody and I wouldn't lose voters." As provocative as the taunt was, the more important part of the speech were Trump's opening words, "Christianity is under tremendous siege," and his promise in the speech, "If I'm elected . . . Christianity will have power . . . you're going to have plenty of power. You don't need anybody else."

The Trump speech on that cold Iowa evening to nearly 2,000 people, about 400 more than the entire student body of Dordt College, in a remote corner of Iowa, was not aimed at Dordt students or faculty or the local town of Sioux Center. Rather, it was the Iowa follow-up to a speech Trump had given a week earlier to 10,000 people at Liberty University, where he was introduced by Liberty's president Jerry Falwell Jr., and made a similar pledge to a much larger audience. In both cases, the author of *The Art of the Deal* was offering conservative Christians a deal: ignore my personal life, elect me, and you will have real power. The deal seemed to have worked. In both the 2016 and 2020 presidential elections, Trump carried the evangelical vote by larger percentages than almost any other demographic subset of the American people, and among other actions as president, he appointed three judges to the US Supreme Court who, though not themselves evangelicals, were very acceptable to most evangelical Christians.[70]

As Trump anticipated, the media—conservative and mainstream—carried the speech all over Iowa and the other forty-nine states. Fewer people asked the obvious question: why pick Dordt College to give such a speech? But Dordt was the perfect venue. The college had begun as the younger and more conservative sister of Calvin College in Grand Rapids, Michigan. Both schools were launched by the Christian Reformed Church, a denomination created by Dutch immigrants who came to the Midwest in the 1870s and found the larger Dutch Reformed Church to be too liberal and in Holland too beholden to the Dutch state. Some of the leaders of the church in Iowa, such as B. J. Haan, who would be the first president of Dordt, also "detected a different influence coming into the academic world of the Christian Reformed Church" at Calvin College, which they saw as a departure from the strict Calvinism of their forebearers. In Iowa, Christian Reformed ministers and congregations launched Midwest Christian Junior College as an alternative to Calvin College to prepare Christian teachers steeped in the true faith, as they understood it, for the Midwest.

By 2024, the Dordt administration had moved toward a more neutral position. They invited all candidates in both parties, to hold "educational" events on campus with time for student questions. Ultimately, they also canceled a Trump event, originally scheduled on the campus just before the January 2024 Iowa caucuses because they said, "the vision of the Trump campaign and Dordt were incongruent, and the event will not take place at the university." Like other colleges, the place of both religion and politics in the life of Dordt College is continuing to evolve.[71]

Dordt began operations in 1955 with thirty-five students and five teachers. From the beginning, its uniquely religious orientation was clear. Every student in the two-year teacher education program was required to take two semesters of Bible. At his graduation in 1957, Herm Nibbelink, who entered the school with the first class in 1955, described the college choir and added, "In a Christian college all should be done to God's glory and we felt that the music department offered excellent opportunity to praise and glorify God." Finally, if there was any doubt remaining, the *Dordt College Bulletin* of 1958 said:

> It is the aim of Dordt College to give an education in the large and broad sense whereby every expression of personality and culture will be dominated by the spirit and rule of the Word of God.

At the end of the 1950s, American higher education was not as secular as it would become in the next two decades, but words such as these were still not likely to be found at most other American colleges, whether church related or not.[72]

In 1959, while the school was still in its infancy, the board voted to expand from a two-year teacher training school to a four-year degree-granting liberal arts college, in part because Iowa began to require a four-year baccalaureate degree for a teaching license. The board also wanted a liberal arts college, independent of Calvin College, which they no longer trusted. Having claimed college status, the trustees renamed the school after the Synod of Dordt that was held in the Netherlands in 1618–1619 and that had affirmed the strictest reading of John Calvin's theology, which is exactly what the Christian Reformed Church meant to do—in its churches and in its college—in Sioux Center.[73]

In 1956, the college's board also named a local Christian Reformed pastor, B. J. Haan, as the school's first president. He served until 1982. Under Haan's leadership, the school published a long mission statement, *The Educational Task of Dordt College*, in 1961. The mission statement made it clear that Dordt was no average college and certainly not one open to any kind of secularization. The statement began by saying that the "Word of God is divinely inspired, the infallible and only rule for faith and practice." Justifying the need for the college, proposition 15 of the college's core document said that the "subject matter for education is the entire universe, nature and man." But in echoes of the nineteenth-century "unity of truth," Haan and his colleagues always insisted that for Christians studying the whole of the universe meant study it in light of the Bible, and in light of their faith, which in Dordt's case meant a very conservative interpretation of the Bible, their faith, and the universe.[74]

The nature of the conservative Christianity that animated Dordt had its impact in its political orientation. Before the 1964 presidential election, Barry Goldwater defeated Lyndon Johnson 164–74 in a student poll. A year later, with college students around the country protesting the war in Vietnam, a group of Dordt students marched to the Sioux Center park to show support "not for particular government action but for government in general . . . which has been placed over us by God almighty." Dordt professor Arnold Koekkoek told the rally, "The person who burns his draft card or, infinitely worse himself, in the name of a baseless 'morality' or because he is opposed to evils such as war, is not serving the cause of goodness." Later the student newspaper editor, Terry Jonker, added that the rally and professor's speech were a "showing of patriotism and respect for authority [that] did much to enhance the name of Dordt College as a Christian college." In 1968, while so many American students were demonstrating against the war, a poll of Dordt students showed 75 percent favoring Nixon in the presidential election. On the bombing of North Vietnam, 8 percent of Dordt student voted to stop it, 20 percent to suspend the bombing, 52 percent to intensify it and 3 percent favored the use of nuclear bombs on North Vietnam.[75]

On issues closer to themselves, Dordt students and faculty were equally conservative, perhaps the students more than the faculty. The student newspaper ran articles such as some in 1966–1967 complaining that some faculty did not do enough to bring the material of their courses "under the Kingship of Christ," and that some courses were being taught from a humanistic rather than "operate from a Christian basis." The school excluded beards, blue jeans, films, dancing, drinking, and smoking. Again, the student newspaper commended the discipline code, as one said, "Rules are necessary to keep Dordt Christian."

The one issue where there was argument was dancing—square dancing. When some students asked for permission to dance, the argument went back and forth between college officials, church bodies, and trustees, all issuing report after report. After more than twenty years, in 1989–1990, Dordt finally adopted an official dance policy that allowed dances in specific contexts, but only after the sponsors completed an application that attested to "how this event is going to be an expression of Christian growth," and received prior approval for the music. The approved music had to avoid "promiscuity, lewdness, sadism, masochism, profanity, narcissism, selfism, nihilism, substance abuse, antisocial behavior, civil disobedience, undue flippancy, sarcasm, etc." The campus pastor was the final arbiter of what was and was not permissible. To say that Dordt was not Berkeley, or virtually any other college in the United States, was an understatement.[76]

Outsiders could not figure out what to make of Dordt College, and no outsiders mattered more than the accrediting teams sent from the North Central Association, which had the responsibility for the school's accreditation and therefore continuing existence. On the one hand, Dordt was clearly solvent, students and faculty seemed happy, and of course, every college has a kind of ideology. On the other hand, Dordt's ideology was far from the norm. Team after team had severe misgivings. As one noted, "if Dordt College is not an extension of the church, then it is a church-college with heavy emphasis on the first term of that equation." The college did not contest that conclusion. In their own self-study, the school wrote that a faculty member whose views were "antagonistic to the confessions and creeds upheld by the College would be expected to resign or he will be dismissed." The school puzzled the accreditors, but they never completely revoked its accreditation, and it continued its unique educational path. Between 1960 and 1980, as so much of American higher education was engulfed in controversy, and as most schools dropped any efforts to control students' personal lives, Dordt held steady to its own way.[77]

Holding steady sparked the major crisis at the college in the 1970s. When several faculty, supported by many students, joined a new Association for the Advancement of Christian Scholarship (AACS), other faculty and students reacted strongly, seeing the AACS as heretical. President Haan steered a middle course, defending the AACS as consistent with the mission of the college and "committed to promoting a radically Christian response in all areas of life." Though he also defended the critics, Haan thought they were actually reflecting an individualistic version of American fundamentalism more than the Calvinistic Reformed faith. Although he found both sides of the debate a bit un-Christian in their vitriol, Haan steered through the debate until it subsided. That an American college would be divided in the 1970s between two camps, each of which claimed to be more Christian than the other, says much about the unique culture of Dordt College.

Though some worried that the new century would bring a move away from its heritage, there was surprisingly little evidence of that happening between Haan's retirement in 1982, when his handpicked successor John B. Hulst became president, and the 2020s. American higher education is more diverse than most realize.[78]

As Dordt, Jackson State, Kent State, and Santa Clara illustrate, American higher education is still an extraordinarily diverse enterprise—and nowhere is it more diverse than the campus-based expressions of religion. It was so in the decades between 1960 and 1980, and it is even more so today. There may be many on most campuses—if not Dordt—with no interest in matters of faith, but there are many others who want to contend with religion from the deeply personal to the key motivation of public expression, from the conservative to the liberal, and from a subject of academic study to a lively personal faith. At many colleges, religious expression may best be found on the margins, but those margins are very lively and in many different places.

CHAPTER SEVEN

A Second Religious Depression on Campus, 1980–2000

Fresh from an undergraduate degree from Rutgers University in New Brunswick, New Jersey, and an MDiv ministerial degree from Fuller Theological Seminary in Pasadena, California, Brenda Salter McNeil joined the staff of InterVarsity Christian Fellowship (IVCF) as urban project director and regional coordinator for multiethnic training, where she served from 1987 until 2000. In those years, Salter McNeil played a crucial role in ensuring that the voice of African Americans who were also conservative Christians was heard in the most important campus-based evangelical organization of the 1980s and 1990s. Under her leadership and that of others in its growing African American staff, InterVarsity sponsored a series of National Black Student Conferences that brought Black students together from different regions of the United States to help define—and expand—their role in the larger organization. The conferences helped further grow the number of Black staff and foster conversations about new ways to discuss racial issues on campuses where InterVarsity had chapters. At the same time, the conferences also helped usher InterVarsity itself to a new level of interracial diversity, if still theological uniformity, by 2000.[1]

The Great Exception: Evangelical Christianity's Growth

Brenda Salter McNeil had come to InterVarsity well before her staff appointment in 1987, but it was not always an easy or comfortable experience. She had a powerful conversion experience in 1974 while a sophomore at Rutgers, after what she described a rowdy college life that was becoming "completely devoid of any real meaning and purpose." Soon after her conversion in the Black Church, Salter McNeil found InterVarsity at Rutgers. She thought she had found a group that would welcome and support her, but she felt a bit out of place in the Bible study. Worse was to come in the prayer circle. When it was her turn to pray she closed her eyes, lifted up her arms, and prayed loudly in the style of prayer that she had learned in the Black Church. When she opened her eyes, all of the White students were staring at her. She realized they were used to short and far less emotional prayers and didn't quite know what to make of her prayer. She never went back. No one had been hostile, but she just did not fit in. She had many subsequent experiences of deep tensions between the African American religious culture and the White religious culture of her college compatriots. Nevertheless, after college, seminary, and some independent work, Salter McNeil found InterVarsity to be a place of support. It was also a challenge, as she brought two quite different evangelical Christian communities together as a staff person for a dozen years, and as a preacher and leader at national InterVarsity conferences in the 2000s after she had moved on from her staff role.[2]

The inclusion of African Americans as individuals, and as a recognized group within InterVarsity, did not always come easy—just as it took struggle to expand racial diversity in more liberal White religious bodies. Some of the earliest groups of Black students to demand a place at the InterVarsity table appeared in the aftermath of the organization's post–World War II growth. This was especially true after IVCF conducted outreach to non-elite schools, especially New York's Brooklyn College and Detroit's Wayne State University, which had many more Black students than did elite schools in the late 1940s.

There were some difficult moments when not all IVCF supporters welcomed Black students, but in June 1948 the InterVarsity board voted that it would never allow racially segregated meetings in the future. Also, in 1947–1948 Eugene Callendar, later a long-time Harlem pastor and a major figure in New York civil rights activity, became the first Black staff member for InterVarsity and Hong Sit, a veteran of the China Inland Mission, was hired to develop work with Chinese students.

Early in the 1950s, Ivery Harvey and Ruth Lewis (Bentley) were hired to create African American chapters, especially at historically Black colleges in the South.

By the late 1960s and early 1970s, the impact of the civil rights movement was being felt within InterVarsity. At a 1967 Missions Conference, 200 Black delegates from several different campuses met all night and in the morning presented the larger group with a petition demanding greater recognition in the organization. The petition was far from the disruptive one that led the liberal National Student Christian Federation to disband two years later, but it was a wakeup call to Inter-Varsity that shaped race relations in the organization in the 1980s and 1990s. Enough African American staff members were recruited to create a Black Staff Fellowship, and a new outreach effort began specifically to African American students at White colleges, not only chapters at HBCUs. In 1980, the first national director of Black campus ministries was appointed. New urban outreach projects under the leadership of Salter McNeil and her colleague Kevin Blue began, and the 1990 National Black Student Conferences followed. By the twenty-first century, the attention to Black students expanded to include parallel work with Hispanic students, a 2015 conference that included 690 students from 95 campuses, and a pilgrimage to Ferguson, Missouri, and later focused attention on the meaning of Black Lives Matter for the evangelical community.[3]

InterVarsity Christian Fellowship had long been deeply committed to student initiative and leadership. Early in its history, Charles Troutman, one of the founders of InterVarsity in the United States, said, "Student initiative is so natural and necessary in the university world that, if any organization abandons it [as many had], God will raise up another movement which will place student leadership as its operating principle." John R. Mott, who had led the YMCA to some of its greatest heights before World War I, echoed the same sentiment when in 1943 he said, "Youth have never disappointed me. . . . heroic appeal makes possible heroic action." Troutman and Mott—whatever their theological differences—both reflected sentiments often discarded in religious life on campuses that seem to emerge with new energy again and again.[4]

Unlike many other student ministries, InterVarsity continues to be a conservative evangelical organization. All leaders and staff of IVCF agree to what the organization calls "the basic Biblical truths of Christianity." While many Christians might disagree with the InterVarsity list of basic Biblical truths, the organization spelled out what it meant by the term:

a.   The unique, divine inspiration, entire trustworthiness and authority of the Bible.

b. The deity of our Lord Jesus Christ.

c. The necessity and efficacy of the substitutionary death of Jesus Christ for the redemption of the world, and the historic fact of His bodily resurrection.

d. The presence and power of the Holy Spirit in the work of regeneration.

e. The consummation of the kingdom in the "glorious appearing of the great God and our Savior Jesus Christ."

This very specific creed excluded many from InterVarsity, but it also energized those who were drawn to the community. Unlike the earlier Y movement, which welcomed a wide range of students, there is no mistaking what IVCF stands for, both for those who feel secure within it and those who simply cannot agree.[5]

Part of the genius of IVCF was not only its mostly student leadership, along with a few charismatic adult leaders, but also its ability to bring evangelical students together to create a large sense of energy. While the organization plateaued in the early 1980s, in large part because of staff tensions, the leadership stabilized in the late 1980s and more growth came in the 1990s. By the early 2000s, InterVarsity claimed some 40,000 students and 600 campus groups served by 1,000 staff. In keeping to its core mission, InterVarsity was always both marginalized and vibrant, often the location of religious energy. InterVarsity may still fly below the radar on many campuses, but by the end of the 1990s it was clearly a force to be reckoned with in the world of campus religious life.[6]

Students especially active in InterVarsity were often tapped to move into staff roles after graduation, just as the Y had done almost a century earlier. There was— intentionally—high staff turnover in InterVarsity as young staff moved on to other careers, often as ministers or in religious organizations, and new staff took their place. InterVarsity has always been focused on one-on-one evangelism, trying to convert other students to its form of Christianity, inviting students to Bible studies and campus gatherings, as well as inviting them to the national retreats and conventions that are a hallmark of InterVarsity. While InterVarsity is campus based, it also has many specialized groups including an Athletes InterVarsity, a Greek InterVarsity, and a Nurses Christian Fellowship. It also has special ministries for Asian American students, Hispanic students, and of course African American students, but also law students, art students, and a range of others.[7]

In 2016 InterVarsity was rocked by a major division. While it continues to hold to its creedal position without compromise, LGBTQ students and staff noted that the creed said nothing about sexuality, and they wanted recognition. After some debate, the national leadership took a hard line. Not only LGBTQ staff, but any staff who supported gay marriage or disagreed with the organization's stance opposing it, were asked to identify themselves for "involuntary termination . . . due to misalignment with InterVarsity ministry principles." It is unclear how widespread dissent was, but it was certainly present. Bianca Louis, the staff leader of the InterVarsity chapter at California's Mills College who had served for four years, left the organization over the issue. She said, "I don't know how InterVarsity can do ministry on campuses with integrity anymore." The response to LGBTQ staff and supporters was very different from the stance taken by Stacey Woods, InterVarsity's first general secretary, who in the late 1940s insisted that on matters of race, all were welcome, since all were equal in the sight of God, and that no racially segregated facilities could ever be used to host InterVarsity events. He then promptly hired the first staff members of color. It was a very different closed door that was experienced by LGBTQ students and staff. More battles are certain to come on the issue—within InterVarsity and across the evangelical world.[8]

The development of InterVarsity and especially its rapid growth in the 1990s is symbolic of the emerging strength of evangelical churches and student organizations in the last decades of the twentieth century. The years between 1980 and 2000 were the highpoint of evangelical growth in the United States, in terms of both church membership and campus activity. The rise of the evangelical movement was never as great as some commentators, either celebratory or terrified, described it. In part the rise of evangelicalism that started in the 1970s and expanded significantly in the 1980s and 1990s was more noticeable because it coincided with a virtual collapse within liberal Protestantism. It was also a two-pronged movement, reflecting growth in some evangelical denominations like Southern Baptists and separate growth in independent nondenominational churches and parachurch organizations—like InterVarsity. In any case, though less noticed by either supporters or critics, by the end of the 1990s the evangelical boom was over, and by 2000 evangelicalism was contracting, not expanding, even if it was contracting more slowly than some more liberal religious bodies.[9]

InterVarsity was not the only conservative Christian organization on college campuses in the 1980s and 1990s. Campus Crusade for Christ was founded in 1951 by businessman Bill Bright to end what Bright called "the present pagan condition on our campuses." Less rigidly theological than InterVarsity, Campus Crusade (a name perhaps adopted from the Billy Graham crusades that started at the same time) was also very businesslike in its strategy, keeping close track of the numbers of converts on each campus. Campus Crusade grew steadily, if a bit underground.

In the late 1960s and early 1970s, Campus Crusade also became more involved in conservative politics than InterVarsity. Campus Crusade directly challenged contemporary musicians like Bob Dylan and radical campus activity like that of SDS. They brought a conservative evangelical—and not very successful—blitz of activity to Cal Berkeley in 1967 and efforts to "convert" demonstrators at the 1968 Democratic Convention.

By the 1980s, Campus Crusade was promoting "family values," including "complementarianism," which said that men and women were equal but had very different roles in family life and church leadership (with family leadership and all senior clergy positions reserved for men). It also maintained a strongly anti-gay stance. In these same years, Campus Crusade's membership seemed to explode, involving over 20,000 students and 200 chapters in the early 1990s to an estimated 80,000 students on over 2,000 campuses in the twenty-first century. The organization also spread far beyond campus work and moved internationally into 191 countries. Later, in 2011, Campus Crusade shortened its name to Cru, in part a recognition that it was working outside of college campuses and that the word crusade created unfortunate images for a new generation more conscious of past aggressions.[10]

Yet other campus evangelical groups, including the Fellowship of Christian Athletes, the Navigators, and Young Life, had similar explosive growth in an era when many other churches and campus ministry programs were shrinking. The growth of evangelical student groups may have been especially strong in colleges that attracted more conservatively inclined students, but evangelical groups also grew on liberal campuses. Campus Crusade, for all its conservative anti-countercultural overtones, started at UCLA and grew exponentially at Ivy League colleges. Before long, it could be found at most every other institution of higher education, from elite and secular public universities to small evangelical colleges. To see the story of religion on campus as one of decline in the 1980s and even more in the 1990s is to simply look in the wrong place for counterexamples.[11]

The rapid growth of InterVarsity, Cru, and similar evangelical student-centered organizations, even while more liberal campus ministries were shrinking, should not have surprised observers of American religious life at the time. As early as 1972, Dean M. Kelley of the National Council of Churches, published *Why Conservative Churches Are Growing* (which could have been subtitled *Why Liberal*—or Kelley called them ecumenical—*Churches Are Shrinking At an Alarming Rate*). What Kelley found, and emphasized even more in a 1977 update, was that liberal churches seemed to be declining in part because in an effort to embrace many, they had lost focus and purpose. Kelley rejected the notion, advanced by some, that conservative churches were growing because their members rejected the more liberal and sometimes radical politics of mainline clergy, but because other things that were being left behind in liberal churches. Quoting one large-scale survey of American church members, Kelley found that the top priorities among members, liberal and conservative alike, were:

1.   Winning others to Christ;
2.   Providing worship for members; and
3.   Providing religious instruction.

These three were followed, however, and not contradicted, by helping the needy, serving as social conscience of the community, and specifically supporting minority groups, influencing legislation, and building low-cost housing.

While many debated the details of Kelley's argument, his warning to liberal campus ministry advocates—and indeed liberal churches in general—was clear: people in the churches, and it turned out that many among the students themselves, would support them if they maintained a religious focus at their core and would support political activism if it was based on that core. At least as Kelley described it, it was not so much the liberal political activity as the abandonment of the faith-based core that bothered many people. If political activism became the core, it was not surprising, as ironically the leaders of the University Christian Movement had argued, it was better to focus on one's political life and give up keeping one foot in a religious world of fading significance.[12]

The Great Disinvestment: Liberal College Chaplaincy and Its Discontents

The growth of evangelical churches and organizations like InterVarsity toward the end of the twentieth century was all the more impressive because these same decades saw a significant shrinkage in the liberal and mainline denominations nationally. As traditionally dominant mainline Protestant denominations shrank, they cut funds for work on college campuses. College chaplain after college chaplain, especially those who had experienced the 1960s and 1970s as a time of hope and possibility, bemoaned the changes that came in the last decades of the twentieth century. Howard Daughenbaugh, the long-time Methodist college chaplain, remembered when campus "ministers found themselves separated from the denominations that supported them." Wayne Bryan, a United Ministries in Higher Education chaplain put it more bluntly: by the 1980s, his work was hit by "death through a departure of dollars."[13]

In the late 1980s, John Worrell, Episcopal chaplain at Rice University in Texas, spoke at an Evangelism conference of the Episcopal Church and warned the Episcopalians that their disinvestment in campus ministry was like "eating the seed corn." A decade later, in a 1998 essay that was part of an otherwise upbeat discussion of campus ministry in the Episcopal Church, Timothy Hallett, at the time the Episcopal chaplain at the University of Illinois Urbana-Champaign, reminded Episcopalians of Worrell's words, telling the church that it seemed to have been "chomping away ever since." What Wayne Bryan had called the "death through a departure of dollars" for campus ministries was to Hallett something even more serious. Since the late 1960s, Hallett said, the church "deliberately turned its back on young people." Hallett saw the churches giving up on the next generation by cutting off financial support for campus ministries, and with it the ability to nurture religion in college students.

Hallett had an arrogance about other forms of ministry, dismissing "perpetually dying missions in dead-end towns," and the working-class congregations that were found there. But he made an important point about what the Episcopal Church—and virtually every other liberal Protestant denomination—was doing to campus ministry: disinvesting to the point of abandonment. The church and many of its members, Hallett said, may have been angry at college students in the 1960s, and even more angry at the chaplains who supported them, but thirty years later it was more than past the time to "get over it." Too often, Hallett reminded his audience, church agencies and most dioceses cut funding for chaplains again and again. He concluded, "We lost the baby boomers, which makes it all the easier for us to lose Generation X. If we keep it up, the church will not have to worry about losing the next generation because there will not be any of us left." Hallett's words were sobering, but for many who had been living with the cuts, they were all too accurate.[14]

Donna Schaper, who had worked with Bill Coffin and was an associate chaplain at Yale shortly after Coffin's time, echoed Hallett when she spoke of the development of chaplaincy nationally in the years after Coffin. She described denominational divestment in campus ministry. "For some reason," Schaper said, "while denominations were ringing their hands about losing youth, they also stopped assigning campus ministers to colleges and universities. . . . The loss of significant campus ministries exacerbated the flight of youth from mainline churches—and ironically the denominations paid for their own demise."[15]

The story, however, may be more complex than Hallett or Schaper imply. If chaplaincy espoused an approach to religion which, as Peter Berger had said, could include the choice "not to become members of local congregations, not to identify themselves with a denomination" then what was the return on investment for local congregations to invest in professionals who did not seem to respect them? As Dean Kelley had warned, if campus ministry was seen as so preoccupied with political issues that it lost its roots in worshipping communities, why should a member of a worshipping community, facing their own budget difficulties, care about the work, even if they agreed with the politics and even more so if they didn't?

Without his knowing it, Berger's lack of concern for traditional church bodies had mirrored the 1911 YMCA that Joseph Cochran had complained about. As Cochran advocated sidestepping the Y, after 1975 others advocated the same response to campus-based ministries. Whatever the mix of reasons, by the 1980s institutional religion was disinvesting in chaplaincy but only after chaplains, and especially the most vocal among them, had disinvested in the churches. The result was a deep crisis of faith—and of budgets—for chaplains and for numbers of college students in the last decades of the twentieth century.

The crisis was not limited to denominational funding in churches running short of funds. Yale—a private university that supported its own chaplain out of university funds—reduced the chaplain's role once Coffin departed in 1975. Symbolically, the chaplain's office was moved from a large suite at the heart of the campus to a basement office further away. Administratively, the chaplain no longer reported directly to the president but to an official several steps lower in the hierarchy. Of course, chaplains were not the only religious leaders facing bleak times as the century wound to a close. Conservative historian Thomas C. Reeves described the fate of the mainline churches saying, "these one-time pillars of the religious establishment are frequently ignored, their power to bestow social prestige has greatly dissipated, and their defining theological doctrines have been largely forgotten." While many may disagree with the remedy Reeves proposed when he argued for a return to orthodox theology, few would argue with his historical analysis of the fate of mainline churches.[16]

By the 1980s, disinvestment in college chaplaincy was all too real, but it was not the whole story. There continued to be college chaplains in the 1980s and 1990s, just not as many of them and more who were part-time. Jane Gould served as Episcopal chaplain at the Massachusetts Institute of Technology in the 1990s. For Gould, part of her ministry was to help MIT students critique the ethically neural scientism all around them and "recognize that no action is morally neutral." It was also a ministry that helped busy MIT students engage with a world beyond the university. Community service meant not only "doing good for others," but also entering a world that included poor and marginalized people who often had much to teach bright college students. It was also a ministry that involved building community among isolated students, including regular worship and community celebrations that reminded these super bright and privileged students that they needed to "affirm that people of faith do not need to check their intelligence and rational capabilities at the door when they go to church." Gould also understood her marginal role at MIT and sometimes wondered if the brick walls of the chapel were meant "to protect the rest of the campus from spiritual influences." She and the other MIT chaplains "have no illusions: God and the life of faith are not central to discourse on our campus." Perhaps, yet again, chaplains needed to find ways for themselves and their faith to thrive on the margins. Nevertheless, Gould, at least, found the work fulfilling and important.

Gould's ministry also reflected the significant increase in women chaplains in the 1980s and 1990s. Where once women had been on the margins of college chaplaincy, as more and more women became clergy (Gould's Episcopal church only began ordaining women in the mid-1970s), and as men deserted the field, many of the remaining chaplaincy positions were filled by women. As women entered the field, the image of the Protestant chaplain as a charismatic male faded quickly.[17]

Other campus ministers, male and female, also found ways to survive and sometimes thrive through the lean times at the end of the century. Thomas Philipp began campus ministry during an intern year at Union Seminary in 1960 but managed to stay in the field for forty years, including a twenty-five-year term in the Long Island United Campus Ministry from 1972 until his retirement in 2005. After 1982, however, Philipp's campus work was part-time, supplemented by a part-time Presbyterian parish pastorate. On Long Island, Philipp was able to support a Peace Education Project, programs for LGBTQ students, and a program to support single adolescent mothers—fulfilling work, but his part-time status was also symbolic of what budget cuts were doing to campus ministry in many places.

Darrell Yeaney, also a Presbyterian minister doing campus work, experienced the impact of retrenchment firsthand when he accepted a position as a campus minister in the University of California at Santa Cruz in 1972. He quickly faced a rude awakening when many other campus ministers in the region considered the UCSC appointment folly while they faced drastic budget cuts. Yeaney remembered, "I found myself unwelcomed by colleagues and had to overcome resentment of a policy decision about which I had no foreknowledge and for which I had no responsibility." In the end, Yeaney was slowly welcomed to the campus ministry fold and stayed at Santa Cruz for fourteen years, until 1986 when he became UCM pastor at the University of Iowa, where he stayed until his retirement in 1998.[18]

Catholics did not have the same losses in the 1980s and 1990s as Protestants. Many Catholic students, now including children of Hispanic immigrants who were entering college in larger numbers, continued to participate in Newman clubs and attend Mass. Indeed, as Robert Putnam and David Campbell note, only the arrival of Hispanic Catholics saved the Catholic church from a collapse at least as dramatic as that of liberal Protestantism. But as Putnam and Campbell wrote, fortunately for many parishes and Newman clubs, "In recent decades as large numbers of white ethic Catholics (the grandchildren of an earlier wave of immigrants) were slipping out one door of the church (mostly to vanish into the category of lapsed Catholics), a large number of Latino immigrants have rushed in through another door." Newman clubs, like churches offering Sunday Mass, were the beneficiaries.[19]

The long-standing hostility of some Catholic college presidents toward Newman Centers was gone before the end of the century. In 1985, the US Catholic bishops issued a pastoral letter, "Empowered by the Spirit: Campus Ministry Faces the Future," which energized Catholic priests and the students with whom they worked at secular schools. Later, drastic declines in the total number of priests in the United States, and thus priests available to staff Newman Centers, hampered the work. Diocesan budget cuts hurt and would only hurt more in the twenty-first century as diocesan spending on sexual abuse settlements increased, depleting funds for anything else. But there were countervailing developments. New programs like the Jesuit Volunteer Corps gave college students or recent graduates with a religious interest an opportunity to live out a renewed faith commitment through one or two years of service with a modest salary at modest cost to the Jesuit order. Private fundraising at some schools helped a lot. At Kansas University and at Yale, for example, the Newman clubs were able to build extensive new facilities with private donations. The absence of priests led to an increased role for lay women and women religious, as campus ministers, countering the losses of male priests.[20]

Jews faced a crisis as institutional participation, and interest in Jewish programs, seemed to decline rapidly among the increasing numbers of very secularized Jewish college students in the 1980s. Hillel funding also lagged significantly until it cut ties with B'nai B'rith in the early 1990s and struck out on its own with fundraising campaign that netted millions from individual donors and Jewish family foundations. By the late 1990s and beyond, Hillel was the beginning of a turnaround. It not only invented new forms of fundraising but found new forms of outreach, especially for Jewish students, with a focus on community life and kosher or, as the organization said, "Jews doing Jewish with other Jews." It was, however, only in the twenty-first century that Hillel was again growing significantly.[21]

Deep Tensions in the Academic Study of Religion

Lucy A. Forster-Smith, long-time chaplain at Macalester College in Saint Paul, Minnesota, recalled a sparsely attended campus gathering in 1996 at Macalester on the "Silence of Faith in the Academy," which she sponsored. The first speaker was a popular professor in the religion department, Professor Jack Hanson, who opened the conference with a robust defense of religious studies—a popular field at Macalester—which he insisted needed to be an academic discipline carefully separate from the practice of faith. Hanson said, "We have to be very careful about allowing belief or conviction into the academic discussion of religion." Hanson continued, insisting that religion was no different than any other academic subject and that it was essential to separate religious life and religious studies. Only the latter, Hanson seemed to say, belonged in the academic world.

Forster-Smith heard Hanson saying (or at least implying) that religion was best discussed by an agnostic, who could be more objective, even though she knew that Hanson was an ordained minister (though he did not mention that fact). Other speakers took a less hard line than Hanson, but his talk left Forster-Smith wondering if she, as the college chaplain who did talk about matters of faith, had any role at Macalester. Chaplains there had long since stopped crossing the line into teaching courses but, she wondered, was Hanson saying that the next step was for chaplains to leave the academic community completely, since silence on faith seemed to be what he wanted as the hallmark of religion on campus?[22]

Given the decline in support for college chaplains in the 1980s and 1990s, the religious energy of the last decades of the twentieth century seemed most robust when it shifted from the chaplain's office to the religion departments. The academic study of religion grew in the 1980s and 1990s. James M. Gustafson, an important scholar in the field, defended religious studies as a discipline and religious studies departments, as long as they produced "significant scholarly work," as expected of academics in any other field.

Gustafson raised another important issue in religious studies. He criticized the "Protestant Christian myopia," which had characterized the field for some time and continued to do so through the 1970s. As D. G. Hart noted, however, "a negative definition of religious studies—that it is not Protestant theology—did not resolve what constituted the field." Hart might have added that the same issue was true of another assertion—that religious studies did not involve the practice of faith—did not tell anyone what it did involve.[23]

The tensions in the field were well illustrated in 1985 when the American Academy of Religion (AAR), the largest scholarly society in the field, celebrated what it called its seventy-fifth anniversary. As the American Academy of Religion it was, in fact, barely twenty years old since it adopted that name in 1964, but its roots did go back to the founding of the Association of Biblical Instructors in 1909. By the 1960s, however, it had broadened its work beyond the study of the Bible alone. In any case, the major speaker at the 1985 anniversary celebration was Gustavo Gutierrez, a Catholic theologian and leader in the development of Liberation theology, who gave the official anniversary address.

The journal carrying the proceedings of the meeting included articles by two Protestant theologians, James H. Cone on "Black Theology in America" and Rosemary Radford Reuther on "The Future of Feminist Theology in the Academy." Cone and Reuther were on the cutting edge of new developments in American theology, along with well-known White male theologians including Paul Ricoeur and Langdon Gilkey, and a smattering of other voices. Some scholars better known in the secular world than the theological, including Jacques Derrida, Umberto Eco, and Michael Foucault, were also in evidence but they were not the leaders.

Ray Hart of the University of Montana, the 1984 president of the AAR, was proud that the 1985 celebration reflected "Blacks, Jews, Roman Catholics, Buddhists, Muslims, Hindus, et al," in an organization that had been founded exclusively by White Protestant Christian men. Nevertheless, anyone attending the AAR in the mid-1980s sensed that the field, for all of its commitment to "objectivity," was nevertheless basically the academic curriculum of Protestant theological seminaries transplanted to more secular settings, and that most of the leading scholars in the field were still the graduates of those same seminaries.[24]

A decade after its anniversary celebration, the AAR reflected far greater diversity than it had just a few years previously. A special 1994 issue of the association's journal on "Neglected Questions in the Study of Religion" included articles on a much wider range of religious traditions than had been visible at the earlier anniversary celebration, as well as several articles that took a hard look at the field and asked for more. There were articles in the issue about the study of Judaism, Islam, Buddhism, and Hinduism, some of which took the AAR to task for its previous lack of attention. There were also articles about just what constituted the field of religious studies, including Mark Taylor's piece on "Unsettling Issues," Mary Gerhard

Figure 7.1. By the last decades of the twentieth century, the American Academy of Religion had emerged as the major association for those interested in the academic study of religion—a diverse group of scholars, as this illustration from an annual meeting shows. Photo courtesy of the American Academy of Religion, aarweb.org.

on "Dialogical Fields in Religious Studies," and Charles Winquist's on "Theology: Unsettled and Unsettling."

An article by Susan Thistlethwaite, a Christian theologian, asked a key question: "How is religion to be studied?" It might have been titled instead, "Can the AAR's core belief in a critical examination of religion ever be compatible with how religion is understood by many people?" Some, Thistlethwaite said, will argue that there is no study of religion (or perhaps any other topic) outside of personal engagement in practice. Others might ask about the political implications of any such study. Still others might consider a critical study—or any criticism—of their own tradition or positive look at other traditions as heresy for a true believer. Citing Toni Morrison on race and theologian Dorothee Sölle on gender, she also asked what "free inquiry" without attention to those culture-pervading issues even means. Certainly, she argued, the very idea of free inquiry about religion may be strongly tinged with the Western Christian roots of the enterprise. In the end, Thistlethwaite concluded by noting that while the AAR had much to offer the world, it would be well served to do its work with a degree of humility and curiosity about what is being overlooked, even as it proceeded.[25]

There is yet at least one other tension within the field of religious studies: student interests versus faculty interest. Scholars and teachers in the field may be deeply committed to ensuring that "belief or conviction" has no place in the "academic discussion of religion." But students taking courses in religious studies may not agree. So, John Schmalzbauer, wise observer of campus religious life, warns, "Don't assume that the syllabus tells you what students are experiencing in religion courses or in the rest of the humanities. Don't assume that students have given up on the search for meaning." Instructors in the field may adamantly mean to keep faith and belief out of their courses. Students have their own way of exploring questions of faith and belief through just those courses in spite of the instructors' best efforts.[26]

All of the controversy within religious studies, some a century old and some new to the 1990s, could be seen as evidence of a field in the midst of extraordinary intellectual ferment and excitement. Other more critical observers might see the same questions as signs of a field in utter disarray with "not there, there" at its core. As religious studies sought new directions, some argued that a wide-ranging study of the history of religions would allow scholars to look at the diversity of human engagement with religion over time while others sought sociological and anthropological approaches to understand the impact of religion on culture. Scholars who asked if religion made any sense without commitment and faith were seldom heard.[27]

The lack of consensus in the field led some academic administrators to a different question: Isn't religious studies a place where we can make cuts without too much pain? If the field is uncertain about its focus, maybe it would not be missed? If religious studies departments included anthropologists, sociologists, historians, and philosophers, couldn't those people move to the appropriate disciplinary department, perhaps have lunch occasionally or call themselves a program, but spare the university the cost and administrative burden of a specific department?

In 1995 the journal *Method & Theory in the Study of Religion* ran a special issue with six case studies of North American colleges and universities where the administration had proposed abolishing the religious studies department. E. Ann Matter, a professor of religious studies at the University of Pennsylvania, described a 1993 recommendation by the dean of Arts & Sciences to abolish religious studies there. Penn had always had some courses in religion and a department of religious thought since the early 1960s, renamed religious studies in 1977. However, by the

1990s the department seemed ripe for the chopping block. As Matter saw it, part of the issue was the continuing discomfort with any discussion of religion and a dismissive attitude toward it in a secular university like Penn. She also argued that there was a general hostility to studying religion "because the deepest shared insight of all religious traditions is that there is more to existence than meets the eye," a value-based idea that ran counter to a university as professionally and success focused as Penn.

In the end, the religion faculty at Penn won, and the department stayed. They did not get dispersed into their different disciplinary departments as the dean wanted and as they feared. They won in part because of their arguments but they were also pragmatic and worked hard at organizing, lobbying, and gaining support from other faculty, especially in the humanities. Perhaps surprising, given the general wariness of the practice of religion among religious studies scholars, the faculty also reached out to and received support from the campus religious life communities, including the Christian Association, Hillel Foundation, and Newman Center. They succeeded in countering the complaint that religious studies was too amorphous a field, arguing that "this self-consciousness [in the discipline] does not imply a devaluation of the reality of religious experience," and that religion scholars "know that for better and worse, religion remains one of the fundamental components of community life even in our most secular of places and times." It was an important victory for the field. It was also not the outcome everywhere.[28]

At the relatively new University of California campus at Santa Cruz, which only opened in 1965, the first faculty member in comparative religion was appointed in 1967, and in 1975 religious studies was recognized as a full-scale, if small, department. With departmental status came dissension within the religion faculty as to what constituted religious studies at UCSC. Gary Lease, a leader of one faction, described a "deep inability on the part of the religious studies faculty to reach unanimity concerning the program's academic identity." The departmental divisions reflected national splits in the field, with some focusing on individual students' religious growth, and others saying that such a focus weakened the academic nature of their work. Such debates might be robust, even exhilarating, in professional meetings like American Academy of Religion. But on a college campus facing unusually steep budget cuts, they were suicidal. In 1980, the University of California president accepted a recommendation by the Santa Cruz chancellor and abolished the program. Many disagreed with the decision. The student newspaper lambasted it, but it was not revisited. Interested faculty in different departments might work together on joint projects and departments could offer courses, but a major or a department were gone. For the Santa Cruz department, confusion and debate in the larger field worked against all efforts to defend religious studies on a campus strapped for resources.[29]

In presenting multiple case studies of religious studies departments in crisis, the editors of *Method & Theory in the Study of Religion* hoped to be of service to other departments that might face similar issues. They understood how the debates among scholars within the study of religion caused confusion in the larger academic world. They also understood how the failure—certainly evident in the AAR at least through the 1980s—to distinguish religious studies from theology made it all too easy to "imagine a fiscally hard-pressed administrator at a public university eliminating its department of religion, not because it is considered to be an 'expendable luxury,' but because it is a relatively new field that might, in any case, be better served by more traditional and established schools of theology or church-related private colleges and universities." Most of all, the editors made a plea to religion scholars "to articulate just what distinguished the study of religion from religious involvement and to develop theoretically defensible arguments—instead of a priori assertions—concerning the place of our field within the university." The failure to do so was all too clear to any wise observer in the mid-1990s.[30]

D. G. Hart, a scholar of the history of religious studies, expressed pessimism that the needed focus could be achieved, or that the academic study of religion could really emerge from the many different directions in which interested faculty were moving. In 1999, he wrote:

> Without the older centripetal forces of providing spiritual guidance and adding humanistic depth, religious studies lacks a center. It is now little more than a collection of those academics who have inherited the older Protestant structures and rationales for religion, conceded that the old way was too exclusive, and added a mix of non-Christian religions.

It was not an encouraging analysis, but for the late 1990s it was probably accurate.[31]

Like the 1920s and the 1930s, the last two decades of the twentieth century can be seen as a time of religious depression. This was evident on Sunday (or Saturday) morning when attendance at services was a fraction of what it had been only a short time before. It was evident in local and national church budgets. Gone were the building booms and new programmatic initiatives including, perhaps especially, initiatives focused on college students. It was also evident on most college campuses. Religious studies departments, though popular with a subset of students, were often floundering, as were campus ministry programs, especially among liberal Protestants but also among Catholics and Jews. There were small rumblings of new religious traditions, but into the 1990s they were not noticed by most observers except later in retrospect.

There were exceptions. Evangelical Protestants experienced explosive growth in campus organizations just as they did elsewhere in American society. Indeed, the 1980s and 1990s were a time of a great revival for evangelical movements, just as the 1950s and earliest 1960s had been for liberal Protestants. Hillel, once it broke with B'nai B'rith, experienced a significant rebirth, but it was mostly in the twenty-first century when a newly envisioned Hillel became a significant campus institution serving growing numbers of Jewish students across the country. Nevertheless, for the most part, the religious depression analogy fit until after 2001, when there was a new, quite unexpected resilience of religion and a significantly new direction for the place of religion in the American university. It is to that story that we will turn in the next chapter. First, however, three case studies of three very different colleges shed further and perhaps clearer light on the different roles played by people with different convictions about the study and practice of religion at the end of the twentieth century.

Education in Harmony with the Natural World and Universe—Diné College

Diné College, in Tsaile, Arizona, founded and administered by the Navajo Nation, is the oldest of what are now some thirty recognized tribal colleges that are tribally led and preserve Native American culture, which inevitably means native religious practices deeply integrated with modern knowledge and professional skills.

Diné College describes its educational philosophy as "Sa'ah Naaghái Bik'eh Hózhóó," a framework that includes thinking, planning, living, and assuring. Another translation of the term by Vincent Werito, a Navajo scholar and student of Navajo philosophy, says, "we want to live our lives in beauty/harmony." It is a philosophy that reflects Navajo values associated with the natural process, including the daily cycle of day and night and the annual cycle of the seasons. To ask what the separate place of religion is in such a culture, or college based on that culture, is to ask a question that makes no sense. At the heart of the college's work is an effort to reflect a harmony to be found in the natural world and between all people and elements of the world. When disharmony arises, the goal must be to restore harmony. Understanding and living in this harmony and studying Navajo language, history, and culture are the highest priorities of the college. Preparing for further studies and employment, social responsibility, and scholarly research are all important, but they come a bit lower on the official institutional priorities, if not so for every student.[32]

Vincent Werito elaborates the philosophical principles that underlie all Navajo life—principles that the college claims as its core. Navajo philosophy is based on "hózhó," which can be translated as living "in a state of harmony and peace and/or a positive ideal environment." Whether in religious ceremonies or day-to-day life, living in harmony with the earth and all around is the Navajo version of what twentieth-century Protestant theologian Paul Tillich called "the ultimate concern" or God. Werito says that striving for this harmony is "part of our thoughts, language, prayers and songs and is integral to our inherent human quality for making sense of our lives and striving for harmony, peace, and justice." Prayers, in special ceremonies or at the morning greeting of the start of the day, say "it begins with beauty," and end "it is done in beauty." With this commitment at the core of traditional Navajo life and the goal of the college's curriculum, a separate discussion of religion, a religious studies department, or a specialized college chaplain would create an intellectual and a spiritual disconnect.[33]

It is important, of course, not to romanticize life at Diné College. As with other colleges, there are concerns with preparation for a job and exposure to a wider world. Some students are drawn to learning more about and maintaining their Navajo identity, and others want to get the skills that will land them a job or expand their personal horizons. For faculty and administrators balancing the budget, maintaining enrollment, and accommodating accreditation agencies—which may or may not have much understanding of Navajo philosophy—can quickly push the core commitments to the background.

Diné College began as the Navajo Community College in 1968, the first tribally controlled college in the United States. It changed its name to Diné College in 1997, a move that reflected its increasing focus on maintaining Diné or Navajo culture. The school was accredited by the North Central Association in 1976 and granted its first baccalaureate degree in a partnership with Arizona State University in 1998. Its independent board is made up of representatives of different regions of the huge, 27,000-square-mile Navajo Nation in Arizona, New Mexico, and Utah. While education for jobs—and especially jobs that support the economic and political development and cultural strength of the Navajo Nation—are important, the college serves equally as a center for strengthening Navajo identity and teaching others about Diné culture. After his retirement, Bob Roessel, the first president of what was then Navajo Community College, remembered Navajo "history, language, and

culture was the institutions *raisond'etre* and a non-negotiable foundation of the curriculum." This core seems have become more, not less, significant as time passed.[34]

The founding of Navajo Community College and later a dozen other similar
tribal colleges in the decade between 1968 and 1978 had both short-term and
longer-term roots. Certainly, this new kind of college was a product of the ferment
of the 1960s. While the civil rights movement of the decade began in the African
American community, civil rights activity expanded in many directions, including
a militant "Red Power" movement across Indian country, especially among young
people. In response to the pressure from Indian communities, President Lyndon
Johnson included "a policy of maximum choice for the American Indian," in the
Great Society policies—a policy that included a focus on self-determination at its
core. On the other hand, Johnson's foreign policy fueled the anger that inspired
many early leaders of the tribal college movement. Jim Shanley, who became the
long-time president of Fort Peck Community College of the Fort Peck Assiniboine
and Sioux Tribes, remembered, "I had just come from experiencing the Vietnam
war and was very disenchanted with the United States, and the war really brought
back to me what had been done to our own people." He saw the tribal college movement as a way to "move that state of hypocrisy back—to try to make the United
States of America live up to its promises and to live up to those things for all its
citizens." The hope and the anger of the 1960s, combined with the new policies
focused on self-determination, made the tribal colleges possible.[35]

In the 1950s, Raymond Nakai, a Navy veteran who fought in World War II
at Guadalcanal and Tarawa, returned home to the Navajo reservation and in off
hours from his day job started a morning radio program speaking in the Navajo
language to an audience of 50,000 to 70,000. In between airing the news, music,
and advertisements, Nakai talked about the need for an academy where Navajo
people could learn a trade but also learn to be proud of their Navajo heritage. He
spoke of the right of Navajo to practice their own religion and of the importance
of tribal control of education to maintaining their lives and culture. Nakai also met
with Bob Roessel and his wife, Ruth Roessel, and they shared their dreams for the
reservation, and as Bob Roessel remembered it, "I think the three of us came up
with the idea that we needed a college . . . controlled by Indian people." The dream
became more possible in 1963 when Nakai was elected tribal chairman.

When the Great Society made funds available for demonstration schools to
provide a different kind of education in low-income communities, Allen Yazzie,
along with Nakai and Roessel, saw an opportunity and started the Rough Rock

Demonstration School as an Indian-controlled K–12 school, the first of many such schools among many different tribes. But while Rough Rock was a K–12 school, it also provided a step into higher education.

To announce the plan for a college, Nakai convened corporate and political leaders and said, "Ladies and gentlemen, I'd like to announce that the Navajo tribe is going to start the first college controlled by and located on an Indian reservation." After the initial applause, one business leader responded, "Good God, Mr. Chairman, you don't mean to think that you Navajos can run a college?" But Nakai told opponents, "We're not asking for your permission. We're just telling you what we're going to do." And they did. In July 1968, the Navajo Tribal Council approved the establishment of Navajo Community College. Within a decade, other Indian nations were following the same path, and there were a dozen such schools and eventually some three dozen. The early years were consumed with finding federal and private funds, building a campus, hiring a faculty, and seeking accreditation. But with Navajo Community College, a new development in American higher education was established.[36]

By the 1980s, schools like Diné College were well enough established to survive the budget cuts of the Reagan years. The school had a beautiful campus designed to reflect Navajo values, two- and four-year programs graduating students with skills and knowledge they needed in the late-twentieth-century world. With stability, the college's founding purpose loomed larger: "What did it mean to be an Indian—or more specifically a Navajo—college?" Some spoke of what they called the dual mission of the schools—to teach the skills that would lead to economic advancement, and equally, and to teach traditional culture, religion, and values, and to build pride in an Indian way.

In 1987, Carty Monett of the Crow Tribe's Little Big Horn College said it was important that her college's Crow tribal culture not be a separate subject but rather something that infused the entire college. She also admitted that infusing culture in all of the programs was "easier said than done." Navajo Tribal College's Roessel recalled a battle he had with the school's accreditor, the North Central Association, about faculty qualifications, which the association said must include a master's degree. He told the accreditors that he had no argument with a master's degree for math or English instructors, but it made no sense for instructors in Navajo language or culture. He added, "we know better than universities know what constitutes knowledge in these areas and we won't attempt to become accredited if you don't recognize that right." The NCA backed down. Navajo culture and religion won, but it would be a continuing battle—between the college's core mission, and not only external accrediting agencies but often tribal expectations, that the school look like a "real college."

While Raymond Nakai was tribal chair, he always supported Navajo Community College's joint mission of culture and traditional academic work. His successor, Peter McDonald, had less interest in culture. McDonald called the school the "Harvard of the Navajo Nation," which to Roessel sounded like the new chairman wanted a school that modeled itself on a White style more than on the social and cultural values of the Navajo. The tension between a mission of economic and personal advancement for students, and a mission of sustaining Indian culture, will probably always exist at Diné College.[37]

At a 2005 national symposium in Austin, Texas, David Gipp, who had been president of the United Tribes Technical College of the Lakota and Dakota Sioux Nations since 1977, gave a talk on "The Tribal College Approach to Spirituality." Gipp said that tribal colleges had a key role in building "a system of education that directly served and corresponded to our own needs and our own goals" and "were founded to help preserve, protect, maintain and build upon the strengths of our tribes relative to our history, language, culture and spiritual beliefs."

Gipp reminded his audience that in the nineteenth and much of the twentieth centuries federal policy was to "civilize and Christianize" Indians. Among Gipp's own Standing Rock Sioux Tribe, native ceremonies were totally banned from the time Sitting Bull was killed in 1890 until the first sanctioned ceremony in 1949. Even after 1949, traditional religious ceremonies among the Sioux often had to be held in secret, away from governmental and Christian church eyes until at least the 1970s. It was in the context of that history that he insisted, "In fact, we are in a race to preserve, protect, and rebuild the languages, the history, the customs and practices and the spiritual knowledge and our values."[38]

Navajo scholar and teacher Larry Emerson asked what it meant to teach traditional Navajo culture. He insisted that the idea of "traditional" culture only came into being when the modern world began to take a sense of the sacred out of what generally constituted knowledge (as most of American higher education certainly does). Emerson argued:

> I think we should always include and integrate Dine traditional knowledge into all that we do. The most compelling reason to do this is because Dine traditional knowledge embraces a sense of harmony, beauty, peace, happiness, and balance. As scholars, we should learn how not to compromise hózhó and all the ways of knowing and being that are vital to knowing the past, the present, and the future.

To the degree that Diné College lives up to this vision, it is truly a different kind of institution from most of American higher education. Being different is never easy, as there are many pressures toward conformity. There will be times that the sacred and secular are separated again, but also people who will continue to remind the college of its core mission. So, Emerson concludes with a question: "After all, isn't it still important for all Dine people to be able to declare, in all four directions, 'in beauty it is finished?' "[39]

A Word on Religion and Spirituality at Community Colleges Beyond Tribal Colleges

While most tribal colleges are community colleges—two-year institutions often with strong partnerships with four-year baccalaureate schools—most community colleges are not tribal colleges. Community colleges (originally called junior colleges) began in 1901 when J. Stanley Brown, principal of the Joliet High School in Joliet, Illinois, and William Rainey Harper, president of the University of Chicago, began a program, housed at the high school, to allow students to begin college work there. By 1918, eighty-five junior colleges, almost all housed at the nation's growing high schools, served 4,500 students with similar programs. These schools grew rapidly in the 1920s, and by the end of the decade there were over a thousand junior colleges. In California alone, nearly 14,000 students enrolled in these "people's colleges," mostly administered by local school districts and giving students an opportunity to begin college work at low cost and in a convenient location.

Beginning in the 1930s, junior colleges began changing their name to community colleges and shifting much of their focus to vocational preparation in fields like the construction trades or biomedical technology. While doctors and nurses may go to college and graduate school, most of those who do the technical and lab work in modern medicine are community college trained. Pressure from students who wanted to start to earn a living as soon as possible and government funding for "career training" made the shift in primary emphasis almost impossible to resist, in spite of resistance from liberal arts transfer advocates. There was virtually no funding for religious studies programs or chaplains at these schools even though by the start of the twenty-first century close to half of all students in higher education were enrolled in community colleges, including the majority of African Americans and Hispanics in college.[40]

In his discussion of the history of community colleges, historian Charles Dorn rightly criticizes most others for ignoring the history of these institutions. But few community colleges, other than tribal ones, pay much attention at all to the spiritual life of their students and only a very tiny fraction of either college chaplains or religious studies professors can be found there. It is a reality that offers a sad commentary on the priorities of those who support the religious life of students at more elite schools.[41]

"If Americans Are So Religious, Why Does Our Educational System Ignore Religion?"—The University of North Carolina

Warren Nord completed his PhD at the University of North Carolina (UNC) in 1978, and from 1979 to 2004 he was the director in the program in the humanities and human values at UNC, where he was also a professor of philosophy until his retirement in 2009. In those years, the center sponsored over 700 conferences and workshops involving some 40,000 participants. Many of the programs focused on matters of religion that were close to Nord's heart, including his own seminars in topics like "Good and Evil" and "God and Suffering" that were especially popular. Through the program, the seminars, and his publications, Nord became one of the best-known authorities on matters of religion's place in education in the United States. Ironically, although he spent his whole career at the University of North Carolina, he was never formally associated with the religious studies department or the campus chaplains, though he did make his mark in the thinking of the religious studies faculty. Religion at North Carolina, as at so many other schools in the United States, was often a siloed affair—separated in different programs among those who were interested in the topic but perhaps saw their form of engagement differently from each other.[42]

Nord's basic critique of the modern university, including his own UNC, was quite specific. Nord reminded readers, especially academics, that most people in the world, including even most college faculty, in spite of the atheists among them, have some level of at least "amorphous spirituality," whether in conservative churches, liberal churches, the "bustling mix of the world's religions," or something much more generalized. But the university—in its curriculum and its structure—barely seems to take notice of any forms of religion.

While Nord was clear that there were constitutional reasons to avoid privileging or promoting a particular religion—or religion in general, especially at a public university—that was not a reason, he argued, to do nothing, which was what he saw happening on most campuses. Indeed, Nord saw doing nothing as, in fact, simply privileging hostility to religion, if only by a deafening silence. Nord argued that "the study of religion is essential to liberal education." He added, "The big question, after all, is about what it means to be well educated whatever the setting." Nord insisted that by failing to discuss religion, universities, like secondary schools, were failing to offer a liberal education, or as he concluded, "Socrates was right. The unexamined life is not worth living. An educational system that ignores the great existential questions—political, moral, spiritual, religious—is not worthy of respect, indeed, it should not count as educational at all."

Over a decade earlier, Nord had asked, "If Americans are so religious, why does our educational system ignore religion?" Religion, he said in the 1995 book, was essential to understanding the modern world. A proper constitutionally mandated neutrality, Nord insisted, should not be allowed to morph into either hostility to religion or ignorance of the subject, but rather religion "must be taken seriously in public schools and universities."[43]

Warren Nord was widely known and widely respected, indeed loved in the circles that knew his work the best. In a special issue of the journal *Religion & Education*, published just after his death in 2010, some of the leading scholars of American religion, including historian Martin Marty and also Charles Haynes, Melissa Rogers, Robert Nash, James Carper, and several other well-known names, wrote appreciative responses to Nord's work. Looking back from another decade, however, one must conclude that Nord did not make the difference he wanted to make. He may have been a prophet, but neither the University of North Carolina as a whole nor those responsible for the curriculum, budgets, or hiring at most of the great and small universities in the United States, seem to have taken his plea very seriously.

The University of North Carolina, though a secular state university, had long given some level of attention to religion, however marginalized that attention might be on the broader campus. The university at Chapel Hill was established by the state legislature in 1789, leading to its claim to be the first public university in the United States. (Harvard, William & Mary, and Yale were all semipublic when they were founded, but UNC has stayed public.) As early as the 1920s, as the university was creating a School of Education, a School of Business, and a School of Social Work, the North Carolina Baptist State Convention proposed a school of religion at UNC modeled on UNC's other schools, as well as on the Bible chairs and schools of religion at other universities (see chapter 2). The UNC faculty voted down the idea, but by the later 1920s they did vote to allow a few interdepartmental university courses in the history and literature of religion. The enterprise remained small, however important it might be to university administrators fending off charges of fostering impiety with the state's voters and legislature.[44]

In 1946, a gift from James Gray, the chair of R. J. Reynolds Tobacco, created endowed chairs in biblical literature and a department of religious studies to house the appointment. While professorships in biblical studies were popular across the United States in the middle of the twentieth century, North Carolina was ahead of most schools, especially most state universities, in creating a formal department of religious studies. Many other schools would follow in the 1950s and 1960s.[45]

The first person to serve as an endowed professor of religion was an internationally recognized Oxford scholar, Arnold Nash, who brought star power to Chapel Hill. Nash was part of a postwar trans-Atlantic movement to claim a central place for the Christian faith in higher education. Nash and fellow scholars argued that the supposed neutrality of the modern university was simply a cover for intellectual chaos. What was needed, they said, was for theology to provide the synthesis to hold the intellectual life of the university together and to organize all the disciplines, including the sciences. Nash wanted the department of religion to be the "Department of Knowledge Integration by Means of Judeo-Christian Theology." While he may not have known it, Nash seemed to be wishing for a return to the nineteenth-century moral philosophy capstone course (see chapter 1).[46]

In the following decade, Nash's view of an entire university integrated intellectually by the Christian faith was espoused by other scholars. The National Council of Churches sponsored Faculty Christian Fellowship and its journal *The Christian Scholar* sought to take religion far beyond the confines of any one department (see chapter 5). At UNC, another professor, L. O. Kattsoff, along with Nash, helped lead the charge toward this vision of the university integrated "in the service of God." Indeed, Kattsoff argued that it was a mistake to believe that any scholar in any field could continue "to believe he could be neutral." For Kattsoff and his contemporaries who sought a new Christian unity of knowledge, the scholar "who does not do God's work and does not glorify God in his life inevitably [will] be doing the work of those who alienate themselves from God and either curse or deny God." It was a harsh judgment, however well-meaning the goal of intellectual unity. It was also not a goal that could survive the diversity and division of the 1960s, just as the Faculty Christian Fellowship did not last through that decade.[47]

For most faculty at UNC or elsewhere, the idea that the university would return to a version of the nineteenth-century dominance of Protestant theology over all the other fields was anathema. One did not need to be an agnostic to find the Nash–Kattsoff–*Christian Scholar* approach oppressive as a limitation of academic freedom and an insult to those outside mainstream Protestantism. The majority of the

UNC faculty and administration responded by keeping the department of religion small—mostly just two professors—and marginalized. Any Christian imperialism would be limited to a very small empire.

While Nash and Kattsoff fought a lonely and quite unsuccessful battle to return Christianity to the central organizing place in the curriculum, a very unhappy donor kept threatening to withdraw the money on which the department was based. This was solved in 1950, when Bernard Henry Boyd was hired as the James Gray Professor of Biblical Literature and the newest member of the department. Unlike Nash, Boyd's focus was indeed the Bible, and his courses like the "Religious Background of Western Civilization" were wildly popular. His public lectures and his grasp of educational television with his "Dr. Boyd and the Bible" programs made him, and by extension the university, popular across the state.[48]

Although his star faded within the academic community over time, Bernard Boyd remained popular until his death in 1975. But by the 1970s, and even more in the 1980s and 1990s, the academic study of religion had settled back into the religious studies department, but it was also a very different department than it had been a few decades earlier. The image of religious studies as essentially the Protestant seminary transported to a secular university was long gone by the late 1980s. The department added new approaches to the study of Western religion not found in most seminaries and also added courses in Buddhism, Hinduism, and African religions. By the 1990s, it was hiring renowned scholars outside of the Christian world, including Carl W. Ernst, who specialized in Islamic Studies, especially Sufism, who came to UNC in 1992, and Yaakov Ariel, who joined the department in 1994 after a career at Haifa University and Hebrew Union College in Israel. By the twenty-first century, the department was also diversifying further, including by gender, and its 2020 chair, Barbara Ambros, was a scholar of Buddhism and gender studies.

Long focused on undergraduate programs, the department added an MA degree in 1978 and a PhD in 1985. When Carl Ernst became chair of the department in 1995, he found himself leading a very different department than the one of the Nash–Boyd years. As the fall semester got underway, Ernst called for a departmental retreat to examine the changing landscape of the study of religion, a field that he saw growing nationally but under budget pressure within his own institution. To facilitate a conversation on the general topic of religious studies at the university, Ernst asked his colleagues to read parts of Warren Nord's then recent *Religion in American Education* and then use it to talk about how the department should relate to "theology" (as the department once did), how it might think about what is or can be normative in the field, and what courses and public outreach might be needed. The use of Nord as a resource reflected an unusual cross-campus level of outreach.

By 2000, as a result of the retreat and many follow-up conversations, the department of religious studies had updated its course offerings and structure. The result was a program that in no way looked like a mini-Protestant theological seminary as had most such departments prior to the 1970s. Instead, it was organized with programs in Islamic Studies, Religions of Asia, Religion and Culture with a critical studies approach to the study of culture, Religions of the Americas with a focus on African American and Latinx cultures, and an Ancient Mediterranean Studies concentration that continued biblical and archeological research.[49]

In the twenty-first century, the department describes itself as a place "for exploring the ways in which human beings find meaning, purpose, and wonder in their lives." It is a mission all too rare in the modern research university. However small the number of students who actually study in the field, UNC offers students a place to look for "meaning, purpose, and wonder."[50]

While Warren Nord's work became a kind of bridge between philosophy and religious studies, in other ways the University of North Carolina was no exception to the siloed reality of American higher education. As at most schools, campus ministry stood on its own, sometimes supporting the same students, sometimes different ones, but doing so quite separately from any course work in the study of religion. And, indeed, religious studies courses seem seldom to have been mentioned in campus ministry gatherings. Unlike many other campuses, however, campus ministry at UNC remained robust through the lean years of the 1980s and 1990s. Two examples describe a wider experience.

When in 1975 Manuel Wortman moved to Chapel Hill to take up his duties at the school's Wesley Foundation, he entered a long line of distinguished Methodist campus ministers at UNC. The UNC Wesley Foundation had already become legendary as a home to protest and folk music. Wortman's previous experiences in campus ministry led him to understand that the job included abortion counseling for students (eighteen young women in one month) and providing a safe home for gay and lesbian students when such places were still hard to find. Wortman also supported the first African American student newspaper on the UNC campus. All these moves led one leading Southern preacher to call Wortman's ministry the "best damn thing he had heard about the church in a long time."

On the other hand, Wortman saw a shift among students, especially White students, after the end of the 1960s and the killings at Kent State and Jackson State.

There was a growing sense, as he heard students say, that "There ain't no peace without, so we will look for peace within." For some students this meant a turn toward meditation and Eastern religions, and for others a turn toward a more evangelical Christianity. "InterVarsity may have had the largest chapter in the US at Chapel Hill," he noted. Yet other students found themselves engaged in new mission trips to work in Mexico, the Caribbean, and rural poor communities in North Carolina. What he did not find was much denominational loyalty among students or any sense that the Methodist student movement, as such, or the ecumenical student movements, could be revived.

Wortman served as Methodist campus minister at UNC until 1998, when he moved to an administrative position. His successor, Jan Rivero, picked up many strands of the same ministry but got more pressure from Methodist church officials who were unhappy with the Wesley Foundation's support for gay and lesbian students and LGBTQ people in ministry. Perhaps the officials thought it might be easier to get her into line because she was younger than Wortman, perhaps because she was a woman. But Rivero was tough and knew how to defend her position. She stayed until 2010. Both Wortman and Rivero saw the same budget cuts happening that ended the careers of so many others in campus ministry, but they managed to keep going. Rivero defended her work with gay and lesbian students, insisting hers was a ministry of "holy hospitality" and she was gratified when North Carolina Bishop Charlene Kammerer told the Methodist campus ministers in the state, "As campus ministers, you have a ministry of hospitality. And in this regard your ministry should be open to all."[51]

Within the Presbyterian church, the campus ministry had long been the responsibility of state and local governance bodies in the church. But as happened across liberal Protestantism in the 1970s and 1980s, there were massive budget cuts for campus ministry (see chapter 6). By the beginning of the 1990s, the Presbyterian presence at UNC was virtually nonexistent, except for a small gathering of graduate students. The local Chapel Hill Presbyterian Church changed its name to University Presbyterian Church and made a proposal to the state Presbyterian administrators to support a three-year transition period after which University Presbyterian Church would take full responsibility for campus ministry at UNC Charlotte. Perhaps out of desperation, and perhaps with some glee at being rid of the responsibility, the administrative bodies agreed. University Presbyterian Church took over and hired Oliver Wagner as an associate minister of the church and a more-or-less full-time campus minister. Unlike many places where campus work was in decline, with Wagner's appointment, there was a new burst of energy in Presbyterian work in Chapel Hill.

Wagner arrived committed to expanding student engagement, especially among undergraduate students. He made sure that students, not the chaplain, were in the lead. Some wondered about a loss of theological and biblical rigor from the student leadership, but none could question the energy and good will that Wagner's work inspired. Wagner and other campus ministers at UNC benefitted greatly from the support of the vice chancellor for student affairs, Donald Boulton, who served in that position for twenty-six years, from 1972 to 1998. Boulton, himself theologically trained and as a former youth minister, saw campus ministry as an essential element in a well-rounded student service plan. Although he could not legally provide university (and thus state) funds, he took religion and the work of college chaplains seriously. While quite separate from the religion-focused academic initiatives (including the work of Warren Nord), campus ministers like Wagner did feel that they had a direct connection to the highest levels of the university administration with Boulton. Along with their own energy and creativity, that connection helped sustain the work greatly through the remainder of the 1990s and into the twenty-first century.[52]

Religious Diversity at the End of the Twentieth Century— Rutgers University, Newark

The Newark campus of Rutgers University (RU-N) began in 1908 when a Newark lawyer and entrepreneur, Richard D. Currier, opened a private for-profit law school in Newark. People in the bustling city had long looked across the Hudson River at the resources available to New Yorkers, especially at the new campuses of Columbia University and New York University. But Newark also had its own, potentially more democratic, way of doing things, as when the city librarian focused on branch libraries rather than an architecturally beautiful central library. On the New Jersey side of the Hudson, the goal was to get books into the hands of working Newark in all of its then mostly White immigrant neighborhoods.

The new college in Newark had a similar goal—not elite education but an education that the people of Newark could afford, starting with legal education. By the 1920s and 1930s, the Newark college had grown to offer undergraduate and several specialized programs and became the University of Newark. Nevertheless, by the end of World War II, and just in time for the GI Bill surge in student enrollment, the University of Newark and Rutgers University based in New Brunswick, New

Jersey, completed negotiations for a merger in which the Newark school became a branch campus of the state university, continuing to serve the not-so-prosperous but now increasingly diverse college students of Newark and surrounding northern New Jersey communities.[53]

In 1948, soon after the merger with Rutgers, a study of the religious affiliation of the Newark student body showed little change from the 1930s. Reflecting the ethnic diversity of the mostly working-class and poor communities in and near Newark, about 40 percent of the students were Jews, 27 percent Catholic, and almost as many, 25 percent, were Protestant. A few years later, Elizabeth Norman, who later earned her doctorate and became a professor at New York University, was one of those working-class students. Norman remembered her time at RU-N, which she attended as an undergraduate from 1969 to 1973. She described the school, as it had been since its beginning in 1908, as one primarily for the White, mostly immigrant working class and a few African Americans from northern New Jersey. Most of the students were the first in their families to go to college. They did not have the financial resources to attend private or distant colleges. Norman fondly remembered the school's Catholic chaplain, Father Eugene McCoy, who married her and her husband just before he left the priesthood himself. There was also a well-known and popular Jewish chaplain. The working class of RU-N did have their spiritual needs and interests addressed in Norman's day.[54]

By the time Norman was a student at Rutgers-Newark, the demographic mix had already begun to change as Newark itself had begun to change. In 1967, African American students staged a peaceful sit-in at the school's Conklin Hall, demanding that many more African Americans, by then the majority of the city of Newark's population, be recruited and admitted to the school. A sympathetic faculty and administration acted quickly to turn the demands into reality. Before long, RU-N had become a majority non-White campus, with not only African Americans but many different ethnic groups—some representing much more recent immigrant communities. Copies of *Encore*, the school's yearbook, reflect some of the religious changes that accompanied the racial and ethnic changes, perhaps at a slightly slower pace. The 1984 yearbook shows a Jewish Student Union and a Christian Fellowship, the latter showing a number of Black students but the majority White along with Linwood Bagby, the group's chaplain. By 1992, the yearbook added a Muslim Student Association.[55]

There were other signs of the active religious diversity at Newark. After the departure of Father Eugene McCoy, the Newman Center, one block from campus, continued to be active in the 1990s under the leadership of Brother Robert Clark, Father John Dennehy, and Mrs. Noel Wick. The center was proud to provide a "Home Away From Home" for Rutgers-Newark students through retreats, volunteer programs, club activities, and Mass four days a week, plus meals at the center. Norman Samuels, chancellor at RU-N from 1982 to 2002, remembers the Newman Club as an active force on the campus during his time in office, especially as the growing diversity of the school brought more Hispanic students, many of whom were Catholic, to campus. He also remembered the important contribution of Joel Daner, who as a representative of the Jewish Metropolitan New Jersey Federation from 1968–1978, did much to ensure a strong Jewish presence and support for Jewish students at the school.

Samuels also remembered significant growth in the number of Muslim students in the 1980s, partly as a result of the school's growing outreach to Newark residents, partly as a result of new immigration from the Middle East and parts of South Asia, and partly because of a partnership that brought graduate students from Turkey to study at RU-N. Integrating Muslim students into the school community took time. When they rightly requested a dedicated prayer room on campus, finding room was relatively easy but arranging the necessary plumbing for ritual bathing before prayers took more work. While many Muslim students found local mosques to support their spiritual journeys, the campus also needed to provide halal food, places to eat, and support for those, especially women, who faced harassment for wearing a hijab.

Finally, Samuels remembered the essential role that John Faulstich played at Rutgers-Newark, where he was dean of student affairs from 1973 to 1998. Faulstich had been a Presbyterian minister in New Jersey before coming to the student affairs position. He brought his pastoral style into the new role, listening carefully to and supporting hundreds of Newark students while also supporting the religious activities of many faith groups at the school over his twenty-five years there.[56]

Academic catalogs from the 1980s and 1990 also reflect an interest by Rutgers-Newark students in the academic study of religion. The 1986–1988 catalog gave students the option of a philosophy major with a concentration in religious studies that included courses in the philosophy of religion and an introduction to religion, as well as other courses in the Bible as literature, history of religious movements in the United States, Eastern philosophy, and sociology of religion, several based in other departments. By the 1992–1994 catalog, some of the same courses could also be grouped as a minor in religious studies administered by the philosophy department. Non-Western religions did not seem to have a significant role in the curriculum, but many faculty from several different departments were clearly involved in teaching about religion.[57]

Also reflecting the changing demographics of the student body by the 1980s, the school was hosting conferences on the "Literature of the Urban Experience" and "The Puerto Rican in Literature," and hosting a range of student groups, including a Filipino Student Association, a Haitian Association, and in the 1990s, a West Indian Student Association and the Institute for Ethnicity, Culture and the Modern Experience. Beginning in 1997, the school was ranked as the most diverse campus in the nation by *U.S. News & World Report* for many years—diverse in race, ethnicity, and religious background.

The extraordinary ethnic diversity of RU-N was reflected in a school that was host to students from many different religious communities, so that when Steven Diner became dean of Arts & Sciences in 1998 and chancellor of Rutgers-Newark in 2001 he was told that the school included 12 percent Muslim students and 10 percent Hindu students—a religious diversity not found on many campuses in the United States at the end of the 1990s. A quick visit to the Rutgers-Newark website twenty years later reflects a school still proud of and deeply committed to its extraordinary diversity while seeing its many diversities in race, ethnicity, sexual orientation, religion, and more as a key to its excellence.[58]

In three very different schools, a tribal college, a major state university, and a branch campus of a respected state school, religion is alive and well. With the exception of the tribal college, where Native spirituality is so central, religion was thriving only on the margins of most schools, not just the University of North Carolina and Rutgers-Newark. Whether in the form of lively evangelical groups like InterVarsity, the work of surviving college chaplains, or the scholarly battles at the heart of the American Academy of Religion, it is clear that in the last decades of the twentieth century religion in higher education was a lively enterprise and equally one—perhaps happily—far from the central concerns of most colleges and universities in the United States.

CHAPTER EIGHT

Resurgence and Difference after 9/11, 2001–2021

The March 3, 2008, issue of *The Daily Princetonian* newspaper announced that the dean of religious life, Alison Boden, planned a search for Princeton University's first Muslim and Hindu chaplains. Princeton's decision to hire a more diverse group of chaplains, made a few months before the announcement, reflected much that was happening on college campuses in the twenty-first century. Across the board, in elite universities and regional colleges, there was a growing student interest in religion, spirituality, and purpose in life. But the new religious upsurge was not the religious interest of the nineteenth or twentieth centuries, when a majority of Christians and a minority of Jews defined what religion meant. In the twenty-first century, religion meant Christianity and Judaism, liberal and conservative, but it also meant Islam, Hinduism, Buddhism, and none of these, along with a large measure of students who called themselves "spiritual but not religious." As one graduate student said in a seminar in 2023, "we are the children of parents who had lost all interest in religion. We are interested, and we don't have any preconceptions." In the twenty-first century, American colleges may be in the midst of a religious revival quite unlike any seen before in the United States.

A New Diversity among Students and Their Chaplains: Muslim, Hindu, Buddhist, and More

After what seemed a short search, Princeton's newspaper announced in July 2008 that Sohaib Sultan, Muslim chaplain at Trinity and Wesleyan colleges in Connecticut, and Vineet Chander, chaplain to Hindu groups at Rutgers and a consultant, would be coming to Princeton that fall in new positions as coordinators of Muslim and Hindu life, respectively. The appointments were major victories for Princeton's Muslim and Hindu students. The Muslim Student Association (MSA) had been lobbying—since September 2001—for a Muslim chaplain and, as *The Daily Princetonian* noted, Hindu students were insisting on the same opportunity. Chander served half-time on an experimental basis for a year, and then in 2009 became a full-time chaplain at Princeton. This was a historic development, making him the nation's first full-time Hindu college chaplain appointed by a university in the nation (and not a volunteer), while Sultan joined a handful of Muslim college chaplains nationwide. Sultan's and Chander's primary work was with the Muslim Student Association and the Princeton Hindu Satsangam, supporting students in what were still minority communities at Princeton. The new chaplains also had a wider mission to join with other chaplains in interfaith work. As Chander noted, "To the average non-Hindu Princeton student, much of the Hindu faith and culture remains a mystery or a patchwork of Hollywood stereotypes and exotica." He meant to ensure that interfaith outreach and dialogue changed that situation.[1]

When she announced the search, Boden, a United Church of Christ minister, had served for less than a year as Princeton's dean of religious life and chapel. She was the first woman permanently appointed to that prestigious position though she was the eighth Protestant minister to fill the deanship since it was created in 1928. The appointment of a woman as dean of the chapel in 2007 and of Hindu and Muslim chaplains in 2008 symbolized how different religious life was at Princeton in the twenty-first century than it ever had been before. In the mid-1950s, the all-male Princeton student body was more than three-fourths Protestant, with small numbers of Catholic and Jewish students (the Jewish numbers kept small by an anti-Semitic quota) and 3 percent of students who declined to state their religion. Only after William Bowen became president in 1972 and ended the quotas did the number of Jewish students grow to 18–20 percent of the entering class within a decade. As late as 1966, the entering undergraduate class was still 95 percent White, 2 percent Black, 1.4 percent Asian, and 1.5 percent listed as "Other."

Catholic and Hillel chaplains could be found alongside of the Protestant chaplains, and there was a strong scholarly—but all-Protestant if multidenominational—religion department at Princeton. As Frederick Houk Borsch, dean of Princeton's chapel from 1981 to 1988, remembered his own student days at Princeton, "many of us undergraduates would likely have said that it [religion] seemed 'official' and not insincere but mostly on the periphery. . . . God was prayed to and occasionally referred to in addresses. The figure of Jesus could, as it were, be given honorable mention. . . . Yet with regard to any vibrant religious faith at Princeton, all of this came across to many of us as mostly secondary and not at the heart of what the university was about."

Princeton's roots were deeply Presbyterian. Until the appointment of Woodrow Wilson as president of Princeton in 1902, every president of the college was a Presbyterian minister. And Wilson was the son of a Presbyterian minister and active in that church. The Presbyterian and more generic Protestant ties faded slowly as the school grew more religiously diverse and secular. Requirements for attending chapel had been reduced several times and abolished in 1964. The result was perhaps a more willing but certainly a smaller congregation in the massive university chapel on Sunday morning and at the alternative Jewish services on Friday evenings. Robert Goheen, the university president when required chapel was abolished, said he hoped that in place of required attendance, students would find religious services of their choice to attend. For many the choice was to skip the whole thing.

Enrollment in courses in the religion department held steady and even grew in the 1960s as the department added a greater range of courses. The fate of the school's Presbyterian heritage might be seen in the Presbyterian campus ministry programs, which had already shrunk to a hundred students in 1955 and stood at just twenty in the larger Princeton of 1970. Another kind of diversity came to the undergraduate student body, which had been all-male since Princeton's founding in 1746, when in 1969 women were admitted and soon became close to half of a much larger student body.

Given all these changes, it was inevitable that the official symbol of the Protestant establishment, the position of dean of Princeton's chapel, should also be in for a change. In 1978, President Bowen appointed two task forces, one of faculty and the other of trustees, to reconsider the position. The title was changed to dean of religious life and the chapel. From 1978 on, the dean did not have to be a Protestant Christian, though to date all have been. The dean's job changed from the pastor of a Protestant chapel to one focused on incorporating all the growing religious diversity at Princeton. Some alumni complained that with these changes Princeton was becoming "syncretistic" or a religious "hodge podge" they said. Nevertheless, after the 1970s, a new direction was set for religion at Princeton, probably beyond the imagining of President Bowen and the trustees and faculty who made them. The appointment of Boden as dean in 2007, and the appointments of Sultan and Chander as Muslim and Hindu chaplains in 2008, were consistent with an almost half-century trajectory in Princeton's religious life.[2]

Only a few months into his new position at Princeton, it was Chander's job, along with Princeton's Hindu students, to organize the annual Diwali celebrations in late fall. Diwali, a major Hindu religious event, celebrates the triumph of good over evil and light over darkness and is observed by Hindus, Jains, and Sikhs. There had been small Diwali celebrations for the school's Hindu community for several years, but Chander moved the event into the large university chapel and invited people of all faiths and none to participate. He said, "Interfaith happens when people of different faiths interact." By inviting a diverse crowd to the event, moving it to the university chapel, which he considered a sacred place, and making it sacred for multiple faiths, Chander was making interfaith real at the heart of Princeton's campus. At the celebration, the chapel was filled with light but also with dancing and song—kinds of music that had not been heard in that space before. In his sermon, Chander encouraged people to "destroy the darkness . . . in our hearts . . . with a string of light: knowledge." He also added that "we cannot do it on our own," but that in the shared Diwali celebration "we're not alone." It was a moving event for many, Hindu and non-Hindu, and the start of a new Princeton tradition. The fourteenth such event took place to a capacity crowd on November 6, 2021. Diwali at Princeton's gothic chapel was also a sign that the Hindu presence at the university was there to stay at the center of the campus and no longer on the margins.[3]

Sohaib Sultan's and Vineet Chander's appointments at Princeton in 2008 were not only signs of significant changes in the religious life of one university but were the result of decades of struggle for recognition by Muslim and Hindu groups on campuses around the country linked to significant growth in the number of Muslim and Hindu students present on American college campuses. This growth meant that their presence had to be recognized by the colleges and universities that hosted them. Several Muslim chaplains were appointed mostly at private colleges following the initial appointment of Imam Yayha Hendi at Georgetown at the beginning of the new century. New York University's appointment of Faiyaz Jaffer to serve as Shia Muslim chaplain alongside Imam Khalid Latif as a Sunni Muslim chaplain symbolized a new respect for the diversity within Islam on college campuses. While there are still fewer Hindu chaplains, Yale and Georgetown followed Princeton in short order with their own Hindu chaplains. All of these appointments were dramatic symbols of just how different campus religious life would be in the twenty-first century than ever before.[4]

There were small numbers of relatively isolated Muslim and Hindu students on American college campuses throughout the twentieth century, long before either faith had its own college chaplains. One early Hindu student in the United States was Satyadeva Parivrajak, who immigrated from India—in part avoid the authorities in British India who considered him seditious. He was a student at the University of Washington from 1908 to 1909. Satyadeva experienced hostility as a "Black Hindu" and difficulty keeping his religiously based vegetarian diet while in college. He was also quite alone. There were occasional Muslim immigrants at early twentieth-century colleges, but they were rare. Neither Hindus nor Muslims received much attention and were often treated as exotic when they were noticed. It was only in the 1960s that American higher education took much, often reluctant notice, of the fact that there might be students outside of the Protestant/Catholic/Jewish/non-religious categories.[5]

The 1960s were an important decade for many people to begin fighting for their civil rights in society and on campus, and the establishment of the Muslim Student Association in 1963 and the Hindu Student Council in 1990 were both results of the breadth of civil rights activity. It was really in the twenty-first century, however, that both groups grew, established chapters on many other campuses, and successfully lobbied for the appointment of Muslim and then Hindu chaplains."[6]

Though not yet inclusive of many African American Muslims who were members of the Nation of Islam, early Muslim Student Associations did welcome and include a surprising diversity of Muslims, women as well as men, and members of both Shia and Sunni communities until political and religious disputes in the Muslim world began to spill over into the United States. Some MSA chapters began to splinter, and their Shia members withdrew to separate Ahlul-Bayt Student Associations (named Ahlul Bayt in honor of the Prophet Mohamed's family household, especially important in Shia Islam).

Much more recently, students from the Nation of Islam (Black Muslims), who often felt marginalized in larger Muslim organizations, started their own separate Black Muslim student organizations. Nevertheless, both the demands of their faith and the growing Islamophobia often found not only in the larger society but also on too many campuses, have often led diverse Muslim student organizations to band together. They have focused their demands on key support for all campus-based Muslims, including dedicated prayer rooms, the availability of halal food, supportive student service staff (if not Muslim chaplains), and a place to be proud of their Muslim identity in an often-unwelcoming world.[7]

From the 1960s to the 1980s and beyond, more and more South Asian students, a majority but not all identifying as Hindu, arrived on American college campuses as permanent immigrants or later the children of immigrants. There was often confusion among these students as to whether they were identifying primarily as ethnically Indian or religiously Hindu. Sometimes neither they nor others were quite sure which. For example, Diwali celebrations (like Christmas celebrations for Christians) might be more or less cultural or spiritual. There were also experiences of subtle and not-so-subtle taunting. Little noticed outside the South Asian world was the fact that the 1984 film *Indiana Jones and the Temple of Doom*, with its villainous Hindu priest, led to a significant upsurge of anti-Indian harassment.[8]

The formation of the Hindu Students Council (HSC) in 1990 began a new era in the experience of Hindu college students. The HSC was a specifically Hindu, not just Indian, student organization. From the beginning, reactions to the HSC were split between admirers who saw it as an example of students from a minority faith tradition coming together to educate and advocate for themselves, as had the MSA and other groups, and critics who saw it as the American youth-wing of the Hindutva or Hindu nationalist party in India. Thirty years after its founding, most of those associated with the HSC acknowledge the important role that organizers from the Hindu nationalist party played in starting the organization but feel themselves quite free of any outside control. Nevertheless, as nationalist-inspired violence accelerates in India, especially anti-Muslim violence, others are not so sure, and the criticism continues.[9]

The pain that many felt in the aftermath of 9/11—the attack on the World Trade Center and Pentagon on September 11, 2001—ushered in a new moment in the history of the United States and began a radical transformation of the place of religion on college campuses. Almost immediately after 9/11, there was an upsurge of Islamophobia, and many educators sought ways to stop the blame of all Muslims for the violent radicalism of a few. At the same time, the emergence of a new generation of Americans who were the children of families who had long been discouraged from college attendance, or who had come to the United States after the changes in the immigration laws in the 1960s, brought a much broader mix to the nation's college student body. There were more African Americans and Hispanic

Figure 8.1. Muslim students at New York University share a halal meal on campus as they break a time of fasting. Courtesy Dr. Faiyaz Jaffer

students on campus in the twenty-first century, but there were also more Hindu, Muslim, and Buddhist students arriving on college campuses than ever before.

Janet Cooper Nelson, chaplain at Brown University, noted, "Admissions officers traveled broadly to increase numbers of under-represented minorities and inadvertently increased campus spiritual diversity as well."[10] While spiritual diversity did not seem to be a goal of the new outreach by admissions officials, it was a result, Nelson noted.

Finally, a new generation of students were sobered by tragedy and war, and deeply dissatisfied with traditional church-based Christianity or temple-based Judaism, and also with the secularism and religious indifference of many of their parents. As a result, they sought more opportunities in college to examine their spiritual lives. Whether in religious studies classes, discussions of religion led by college chaplains, or more informal opportunities hosted either by emergent evangelical groups like Campus Crusade or new non-Western religious communities, or simply by identifying as spiritual-but-not-religious and seeking others with the same identification, students on college campuses by the twenty-first century were actively exploring their options.

Figure 8.2. Hindu students at Princeton chose to hold an annual celebration of Diwali, the festival of light, in the historic Princeton chapel, claiming what they saw as sacred space as their own. Courtesy Dr. Vineet Chander

An Unexpected Comeback

In their 2018 book, *The Resilience of Religion in American Higher Education*, John Schmalzbauer and Kathleen A. Mahoney note that, "As the twenty-first century opened, religion staged an unexpected comeback in American higher education. . . . Most visible in church-related colleges, divinity schools, and campus ministries, the teaching and practice of religion persisted in a wide variety of institutions." The authors also note that while religion on campus is experiencing a kind of renaissance in the twenty-first century, it is not a renaissance of twentieth-century religion. So, they add:

> While some have evinced a strong propensity for traditional religious expression, "spirituality," with all its diverse meanings and forms, has made strong headway on campus and sometimes vies with religion. Today's campuses are diverse, with Baha'is, Buddhists, Muslims, and Wiccans joining Protestants, Catholic, Jews, and the religiously unaffiliated.[11]

It is a new religious diversity being born.

Many in a new generation of college students are attracted to Eastern religious traditions, or call themselves "spiritual but not religious," a category in which 32 percent of college students placed themselves in one 2013 survey. There are also neo-pagan, humanist, and agnostic groups while mindfulness meditation, sometimes with links to Buddhism but sometimes not, can be found in many places.[12]

The twenty-first century brought a number of traumatic events for Muslim students of which the terrorist attacks of September 11, 2001, were only the first. According to a 2014 FBI report, almost immediately after 9/11, and continuing for well more than a decade, there was a huge spike in anti-Muslim hate crimes. Religious-based violence against Muslims constituted some 14 percent of all hate crimes when Muslims were just half of 1 percent of the population. Women wearing a head covering or a hijab were often special targets. Ironically, although college campuses are often seen as unusually tolerant places, negative attitudes and behaviors, including harassment, threats, and violence, were actually more common on campus than among the general population. Muslim women felt they were labeled as anti-feminist, and the extent to which Muslim women and men spend more time in prayer and other religious observances was often seen as isolating them from their fellow students.[13]

It was not only the hostility or indifference of fellow students but also the seemingly constant targeted surveillance by local police and national Homeland Security officials that gave Muslims an impression that any sign of their religious faith was considered subversive by many. When the Associated Press broke a story of the extent of surveillance of Muslims, it included a confirmed report of an undercover officer joining Muslim students from City College of New York on a white-water rafting trip in upstate New York in 2008. The names of the officers of the CCNY Muslim Student Association were recorded, as was the fact that the group prayed at least four times a day and spent time discussing Islamic religious issues. Jawad Rasul, one of the rafting trip students, was "speechless" when he learned that his name was in the official files of the New York Police Department. He said, "It forces me to look around wherever I am now." He added that such surveillance "further alienates young Muslims on the fringes of society," the opposite of its goal. Newark students were also followed, along with those from New York City. Newark's then mayor, Cory Booker, responded to the surveillance based on religious belief that it "strikes against some of my fundamental ideals as an American."

The campaign and election of Donald Trump in 2016 only exacerbated these issues, followed by the Trump travel ban on several Muslim majority countries, which specifically reduced the number of international students who were Muslim on many campuses. US-born Muslim students felt a new vulnerability. For many, a turn to their religion and a stronger embrace of their religious identity as Muslims was a way to respond and protect themselves emotionally, physically, and spiritually.[14]

Given the growing numbers of Muslim students on college campuses and the painful experiences faced by many of them, it seemed that small but important steps like establishing a Muslim prayer room, making halal food available on campus, and developing policies around religious holidays—not just Christian holidays— was the least universities could do to support them.

Finding the funds to support Muslim chaplains took on new urgency in the twenty-first century in the face of both rising Islamophobia on and off campus and the simple fact of growing numbers of Muslim students. Hiring chaplains of any kind on a university budget is virtually impossible for public universities, but private ones have more freedom. Prior to 2001, only eight universities had Muslim chaplains, starting with Wellesley in 1993, but the numbers grew quickly, tripling with the advent of sixteen more chaplaincies by 2008 and continuing rapidly after that. As at Princeton, Muslim Student Associations often lobbied to hire a chaplain and then enjoyed having one as an advisor and advocate.

Adnan Zulfiqar, Muslim chaplain at the University of Pennsylvania, said his job included three primary areas: interface with the school administration and other chaplains on issues related to Muslim students, counselor to Muslim students and the Muslim Student Association (MSM), and education on Muslim issues to Muslim and non-Muslim students. Khalid Latif, Muslim chaplain at New York University, adds a fourth role: supporting external Muslim communities surrounding the campus. College chaplaincy also opens opportunities for Muslim women to become religious leaders, a rare role in religious leadership for them. In spite of some roadblocks, Marwa Aly and Heba Youssef, Muslim chaplains at Wesleyan and Fairfield universities, respectively, have found ways to be effective as women religious leaders on their campus even if they do not take on certain ceremonial roles reserved for male Imams.[15]

There is a degree to which support for Hindu, Buddhist, and other non-Western religious students, such as Sikhs, was able to build on the new strength of Muslim students and chaplains. Once the door was pried open, more and more universities came to recognize the need to support the religious interests of students far outside the old Protestant/Catholic/Jewish categories. The Muslim Student Association now has over 500 chapters in the United States and Canada, and there are some fifty chapters of the Hindu Student Council. There are Buddhist groups on many campuses serving both students from Buddhist families and other students seeking

"Eastern spirituality." Some immigrant students from Asia are Buddhist, although many Chinese and Korean students are evangelical Christians and active in groups such as Cru and InterVarsity, which have large Asian memberships.

According to student surveys in 2013 and 2016, 32 percent of students identify as "spiritual but not religious," and 31 percent say they have no religion. Other studies have also shown that students can move from one religious category to another in the course of a college career. But on more and more campuses, there are student groups for them, and sometimes chaplains for humanist students as for those of many different faiths.[16]

Even among the twentieth century's leading religious groups, there are new diversities appearing in the twenty-first century. While Hillel began to provide for the spiritual and social lives of Jewish students in the 1920s, by the twenty-first century it was experiencing sometimes friendly, sometimes not so friendly, competition from the relatively newer Jewish student organization, Chabad. Chabad is based in the traditional Orthodox community and in the smaller Jewish Chabad Lubavitch movement. It traces its roots to the 1940s and even earlier, but its major growth on US college campuses is a twenty-first-century phenomenon. Chabad's primary approach is to send a husband–wife, rabbi and rebbetzin, team to a new campus to start a family-style house, live there, and invite students for Shabbat dinners and then other programs and social events. The rabbis starting Chabad centers are all Orthodox rabbis, and as Rabbi Menachem Schmidt at the University of Pennsylvania says, "we all have black hats, we have beards. On Shabbat we wear long coats. . . . We don't pretend we're somebody else." But Chabad staff are careful not impose their style of Judaism on the students who come to their programs. A recent study of Chabad says, "People with minimal Jewish backgrounds are strongly attracted to Chabad for all kinds of reasons, not because they necessarily want to be practicing Orthodox Judaism, but because they find a very warm, inviting, fun, I would even say sort of hip and cool environment that they feel very comfortable in."[17]

Chabad has grown quickly on many campuses. Dovid and Goldie Tiechtel started Chabad at the University of Illinois early in 2003, and nineteen years later it has grown from attracting fourteen people for dinner to around 150 per week and recently moved to a larger building that houses thirty-two students, plus themselves and can accommodate 300 for a holiday dinner. In the United States, Chabad has grown from 36 centers in 2000 to 207 centers in 2022, offering a new option for Jewish students at many colleges.[18]

In August 2021, the *New York Times* reported that Harvard University's organization of chaplains had elected an atheist chaplain, Greg Epstein, as its new president. Epstein described his chaplaincy at Harvard saying, "We don't look to god for answers. We are each other's answers." He also added, "There is a rising group of people who no longer identify with religious tradition but still experience a real need for conversation and support around what it means to be a good human and to live an ethical life." Epstein's election was widely praised but also raised a firestorm of anger, especially from organizations that support some of Harvard's more traditional chaplains.

At Harvard, as at many other schools, denominational chaplains are loosely connected to but welcome at the university, though the university does not pay for these chaplains. Harvard officially sponsors and pays for a separate Memorial Church and a very separate Divinity School but welcomes the denominally selected and paid chaplains. Many news accounts conflated all these organizations and assumed that Epstein was the head of religion at Harvard, rather than the new president or moderator, a rotating position among the denominational chaplains at Harvard.

Epstein's elevation was nevertheless important, and a reminder that twenty-first-century chaplains are a diverse lot, far beyond the traditional Protestant/Catholic/Jew (in spite of the fact that Epstein's immediate predecessor was Rabbi Jonah Steinberg, head of Harvard Hillel), but also far beyond the addition of Muslim/Hindu/Buddhist chaplains. Harvard students, whatever their own faith, were ministered to by a very wide range of faith leaders of many traditions. It may be worth asking why so many religious bodies were spending scarce funds on a chaplain at Harvard while far fewer supported chaplains for the University of Massachusetts–Boston or other less prestigious colleges nearby. But the issue did not arise in the midst of the debates about Epstein's appointment.[19]

On some campuses, religious diversity is expressed in multifaith worship spaces that can be used by many faiths. Today's religious life professionals on campus represent more different traditions than ever before. While New York University hosts seventy different chaplains, the University of Southern California hosts ninety. In March 2021, historically Methodist Emory University announced that in addition to its current Christian and Muslim chaplains, it was adding Buddhist, Hindu, and Jewish chaplains to its interfaith religious life team. In this world, the college chaplain, though usually appointed as a representative of one faith tradition, needs to understand diversity with a sophistication not required of previous generations.[20]

While public universities are generally prohibited from financial support for religious professionals, some have found creative ways to support campus ministry.

California State University at Monterey Bay lists three chaplains—Lutheran, Unitarian, and Episcopal clergy—who are also ministers of, and presumably paid by, local churches but have an office on campus and can be contacted through the university. At Ball State University, a public university in Muncie, Indiana, religious advisors from multiple organizations make themselves available to new college students through a special "Spiritual Life Fair," as part of the university's Welcome Week in August, just before the start of the academic year.

The public University of Florida offers a dynamic range of religious life links, either through the University Health Services, which include services of two chaplains (presumably) a Protestant minister and a Catholic priest, and an Interfaith Chapel that is open for prayer and meditation and holds services including a Catholic Mass, Bahá'i Devotional, and Muslim Friday Prayers. Florida also has a Campus Multi-Faith Cooperative (CMC) as part of its Multicultural and Diversity Affairs program. The CMC is sixty years old. Originally home to Protestant, Catholic, and Jewish organizations, the CMC provided a way for them to come together for joint social justice programs and a day of prayer after the Kent State shootings. The founding groups remain active, but the group has expanded to include Quakers, the Metropolitan Community Church (a Protestant group focused especially on the LGBTQ community), Mennonites, Hare Krishnas, Seventh-day Adventists, Mormons (LDS church), as well as African American churches, Islamic, Bahá'i, Unitarian, and other local religious communities. While meeting space and email addresses are independent of the university, the CMC is closely connected to the university and available through institutional channels.[21]

Another aspect of today's diversity is the fact that more conservative religious groups have also continued to grow even when unnoticed by others. In 2016–2017, InterVarsity had 1,000 campus chapters and 38,404 students while Campus Crusade for Christ (the Cru) had 2,400 campus chapters and 82,000 students, with both reflecting considerable racial diversity. InterVarsity membership was 40 percent non-White.[22]

In an earlier paper, written for the Lilly Endowment, John Schmalzbauer noted another change in the nature of twenty-first-century chaplaincy. The field, Schmalzbauer wrote, "experienced the dual process of feminization and laicization," and that, "Reflecting larger shifts in American culture and religion, today's college chaplains are beginning to look a lot less like William Sloane Coffin, Jr. and a lot more like Carolyn Cruz. . . . Cruz reflects the growing presence of lay people in college chaplaincy. The daughter of immigrants, she is part of a new generation of multi-ethnic chaplains." Cruz also illustrates the change in emphasis that Schmalzbauer found to be present in most of the 335 chaplains he studied. Although it was "missing from midcentury studies of campus ministry," for Cruz and many her contemporaries, "spirituality has become a center focus of the American college chaplaincy." A chaplain, no matter what her or his own tradition, finds themselves ministering to all. In having a community that is much more homogenous in age than a traditional parish, but much more diverse in terms of religious traditions, interests, and commitments, the college chaplain's job seems more different from that of a traditional faith leader than ever before.[23]

In 2013 Lucy A. Forster-Smith, then finishing her twentieth year as chaplain at Macalester College, in Saint Paul, Minnesota, edited a book, *College & University Chaplaincy in the 21st Century*. In her book, eleven of the twenty chapter authors were women, and all of the authors reflected an extraordinary diversity that no chaplain of the 1960s could have imagined. There are the usual mix of Protestants, Catholics, and Jews, and Black and White. But they were now joined by an Asian Buddhist, a Middle Eastern Muslim, and a Latino Protestant. Most of all, the mix was joined by women—women ministers and rabbis as well as lay women Catholic chaplains.

In her foreword to Forster-Smith's book, Brown University's chaplain, Janet Nelson, noted that the twenty-first-century chaplains stood on the shoulders of now-departed giants like Boston University's Howard Thurman and Yale's William Sloane Coffin, who had changed the national conversation in the 1960s and 1970s. But now, "a new, quieter conversation became audible." She noted, "The vast new work of embracing the previously marginalized embodied much of the prophetic dream of the earlier generation." Indeed, twenty-first-century students are finding themselves marginalized by "race, sexual orientation, ethnicity, culture, gender, and socioeconomic status." It was a different day with different students and different adults working with them.

Ian Oliver, pastor of the University Church at Yale, wrote, "The very fact that a kid from El Paso, Texas—a kid from immigrant and poor southern roots—now stands in the pulpit at Yale in itself shows how places like Yale—and even chaplaincy itself—have changed." Oliver adds that while he is the successor to William Sloane Coffin as minister of the Yale chapel, the answer to the "question of whether I now occupy Coffin's pulpit is 'no.' " Services are in the same chapel, but the ornate, elevated pulpit is no longer used except in rare ceremonial occasions. Instead, a simple lectern in the middle of the congregation is preferred. As he notes, "There is still preaching in the Yale chapel but it is from a different place, to a different student body, and meeting different needs."[24]

Diversity's Difficulties

While many celebrate the growing diversity and the many different forms campus-based religious life programs are taking, diversity is not easy and indeed it sometimes causes intense, seemingly unbridgeable differences. One of the most intractable issues on many campuses centers on the support some Jewish religious life leaders and activist students in Hillel and Chabad have for the state of Israel, while others, especially Muslim but also Eastern Orthodox, secular, and occasionally Jewish students and faculty, demand greater attention to Palestinian rights. This issue exploded with heightened alienation and anger after October 2023 with the Palestinian terrorists in Hamas's attack in Israel and the state of Israel's subsequent massive attacks on civilian Palestinian people in Gaza (see afterword).

In the twentieth century, support or opposition to policies in the state of Israel seemed to have been less significant on campus. For example, a 1968 study by Irving Greenberg focused on what the author said was the fact that "college is a disaster area for Judaism, Jewish loyalty, and Jewish identity." Far from focusing internationally, Greenberg focused on courses and programs that would support Jewish students in maintaining their Jewish identity in the United States. An earlier 1956 study of Jewish college students found many Jewish culturally isolated on campus and facing anti-Semitism when they ventured out, but it was much more a domestic anti-Semitism within the campus community than anything to do with international issues. But things began changing for Jewish students around the turn of the twenty-first century.[25]

Perhaps it was the growth of the Birthright Israel program in 1999, which over time brought hundreds of thousands of Jewish college students to Israel and fostered a new kind of engagement with the Middle East for American Jewish students. Perhaps it was the birth of the pro-Palestinian Boycott, Divestment, Sanctions (BDS) movement starting in 2005, which demanded an end to all support and investment in Israel by universities and others until the occupation of Palestinian-claimed lands ended. Perhaps it was simply the seemingly unending tensions around Israel and Israeli government policies. As the *New York Times* reported in May 2015, at "dozens of college campuses across the country, student government councils are embracing resolutions calling on their administrations to divest from companies that enable what they see as Israel's mistreatment of Palestinians." Students and student groups that were often twentieth-century allies have become deeply estranged from each other, leading to fierce discussion such as the five-hour debate at a Northwestern University student government meeting in 2015 that ended with a 24-22 vote on BDS and new anger on both sides. While some see critique of Israeli policies, especially on the West Bank and Gaza, as valid and necessary political expression, others see the same debates as pure anti-Semitism. The estrangement and anger on US campuses as well as in the Middle East is not as new as some assume, but the campus-based explosions over the issues are sure to grow greater after 2023. Students, faculty, presidents, and trustees, as well as external groups and indeed the US Congress are now taking positions. It is going to be a long time before any healing of relationships might begin, even as some are already seeking some form of reconciliation.[26]

A study of Jewish life on campus in 2006 found major tensions around Israel already strong, not only among students but also among Jewish professionals, especially between chaplains and faculty. The report noted that "faculty in some universities have low regard for Hillel," while Hillel directors complain about academics whom they see as "anti-Zionist or self-hating Jews" who care more about their disciplinary work than fostering Jewish identity. It was a mix of an old tension between the academics and practitioners of religion but with new focus and intensity. Later 2014 and 2015 studies found that across fifty-five different universities more than half of the Jewish students had experienced some form of anti-Semitism, but the percentages got higher among students who were more pro-Israel than others. The 2015 research found that in spite of the tensions, there were widespread appreciative attitudes toward Jewish students but also a need for much greater engagement between Jews and non-Jews. What all these studies made clear was that religious differences can quickly escalate into multiple forms of hostility that were experienced very differently by the different religious minorities found on most twenty-first-century campuses.[27]

Tensions around Israel are far from the only ones that may be inevitable given the new levels of religious diversity in American higher education. In December 2021 the Federal District Court ordered the University of Iowa to pay almost $2 million for legal fees spent by two conservative Christian student religious groups at the university—Business Leaders for Christ and InterVarsity Christian Fellowship. Both groups, and almost forty others, had been deregistered by the university starting in 2017 because they refused to allow gay and lesbian students to hold leadership positions based on the groups' religious beliefs. The US Court of Appeals for the 8th Circuit backed the local district court in finding for the conservative religious groups because the university seems to have looked at diverse religious groups, but not secular ones, for violations of the inclusivity rules, and so the Appeals Court wrote it "targeted religious groups for different treatment" from other groups, which was clearly unconstitutional.

The issue began when LGBTQ groups on campus complained that the policies of groups like Business Leaders for Christ and InterVarsity discriminated against their legally protected civil rights. Whatever the specific merits of the case, what is clear is that huge tensions exist between LGBTQ groups, which are growing stronger and more militant, and conservative religious groups, which seem to be toughening their opposition to gay rights in response to a changing culture of acceptance, especially with the Supreme Court's decision to legalize same-sex marriage in June 2015. Deep, seemingly insurmountable divisions around core issues of what religious morality means are not likely to be resolved soon.[28]

Methodology, Money, and Diverse Voices in the Academic Study of Religion

A very different sort of tension can be found within the academic study of religion—tensions that are more methodological than moral but no less sharp for being so. In 2003 Russell T. McCutcheon, a leading scholar in the field of religious studies, published a book, *The Discipline of Religion*, in which he attempted to "write a political theory of religion" or to "understand the relationship between various sorts of group identities" of the diverse people who understand some or all their lives as religious. It was, in a sense, an attempt to define what religious studies scholars meant by the very word *religion*. For McCutcheon, serious scholars need to find real data to see what "faith as an object of study" looked like.

Another leading scholar in the field, Robert Orsi, wrote a review of the book in which he found the work "chilling," because of the author's failure to attend "to the moral requirement of obtaining the consent of those upon whom this theoretical action is to be performed." Orsi added, "Rather, the assumption appears to be that the scholar of religion by virtue of his or her normative epistemology, theoretical acuity, and political knowingness, has the authority and the right to make the lives of others the objects of his or her scrutiny." McCutcheon wrote a response to the review in which he accused Orsi of making any sort of objective or critical studies of religion or religion's role in society impossible. As one example, he accused Orsi of implying that no non-Hindu could critique the Hindu nationalist attacks on religious minorities in India.

If the heated and angry nature of the exchange made one thing clear, it was that the twentieth-century inability of some of the leading scholars in the field to agree on its focus of religion as an academic discipline continued into the twenty-first century. Indeed, in the new century arguments about what was and was not the appropriate reach of religious studies seem to be growing more contentious and certainly not moving toward consensus.[29]

While sharp arguments about the core of religious studies continue in the twenty-first century, the field's range also keeps growing, often in response to student demand or faculty interest. A much wider group of universities—public as well as private—established courses, minors, and majors in religious studies after 2000. These majors and minors were spreading far beyond the few places where one might expect to find them. In Muncie, Indiana, Ball State University, in addition to, and quite separate from its Spiritual Life Fair, the Department of Philosophy and Religious Studies now offers a major and minor in religious studies and a separate minor in ethics. At the University of North Dakota, the Department of Philosophy and Religious Studies offers a major and a minor in the department, and a number of elective courses. The University of California at Santa Barbara had been one of the first public universities to develop a department in religious studies. By 2021, the UCSB department listed twenty-six faculty, undergraduate and graduate programs, and centers or programs in Buddhist studies, Sikh and Punjab studies, Islamic studies, Catholic studies, among others.[30]

On the other hand, as universities become more cost conscious, proposals to close religious studies departments continue. Some departments that serve many students through electives still have few majors, and this does not look good on financial balance sheets. An April 2021 article in the Jesuit magazine *America* noted that Canisius College in Buffalo, New York, was eliminating nine majors including religious studies because of low enrollment and a general deficit budget. In addition, according to *America*, Elmira College (New York), Hiram College (Ohio), and Connecticut College were all in the process of eliminating religious studies programs. What makes the decision to eliminate religious studies at Canisius all the more surprising is that it is a Jesuit school where not so long ago, multiple required courses in religion were the core of the undergraduate curriculum. But what is clear is that, while religious studies departments and programs are strong at some places, they are shrinking if not disappearing at others. Financial tensions plague all of American higher education in the twenty-first century, but nowhere more than in religious studies.[31]

With the coming of the twenty-first century, some of the allergic reaction to the study of religion in other parts of the university seemed to be receding. A 2009 study by the American Historical Association reported that many more younger historians were interested in the study of religion than their more senior colleagues. If in the late twentieth century historians, and their colleagues in sociology, political science, English, and related departments ignored religion, even when it might have been important in their area of study, by the twenty-first century the needle was moving. While only 4.6 percent of historians said their work focused on religion in 1999, by 2009 the number was up to 7.7 percent—more than in any other area reported in the study. As Yale's Jon Butler commented, "I think the category has become more popular because historians realize that the world is aflame with faith, yet our traditional ways of dealing with modern history especially can't explain how or why." For faculty in religious studies departments, these developments could mean new colleagues sharing their interests although they could also mean that in the never-ending competition for resources in the modern university, they would have had new competitors. Yet others noted that 7 percent of historians indicating an interest in religion could mean that over 90 percent of historians did not have any interest. In any case, the new interests across the humanities and social sciences may be a trend well worth watching in the decades ahead.[32]

The venues for conversations and academic presentations about religion kept growing, however. At Indiana University Purdue University Indianapolis (IUPUI), a secular public university that has since split into two universities, the school established a Center for the Study of Religion and American Culture in the late twentieth century and began hosting Biennial Conferences on Religion and American Culture. At the sixth conference, in 2019, Laura Levitt from Temple University reviewed the discipline of religious studies and said, "I think that the field of North American Religions has grown significantly over the past thirty years. The kinds of papers presented at academic conferences are now more diverse in terms of content, in other words in terms of what constitutes North American religion."

Levitt continued:

> Lots of different traditions are more part of the discourse. Afro-Caribbean traditions, Border traditions, Indigenous practices and communities, Muslim, Buddhist, Sikh, Hindu, Jewish, and New Religious Movements are a part of the discourse. And there is also and importantly, a powerful and sustained engagement with a broad range of African American religious traditions and the cultures that surround them.

Levitt was happy to see a new wider range of scholars in the conversations.[33]

Two years earlier at the 2017 conference, a full panel was devoted to the religious "nones." As part of that panel, Matthew Hedstrom of the University of Virginia argued:

> In fact, if we are to take the Nones themselves seriously—and aren't we supposed to do that with our subjects?—we must dispense with the category that defines them only according to the very thing they reject. If the rapid religious disaffiliation of recent decades is to teach us anything as scholars of religion, it is that we cannot continue with business as usual, to normalize religion, or at least to normalize normal religion.

Hedstrom continued by noting that religion had not disappeared in the twenty-first century, even in its so-called normal forms of churches, mosques, synagogues, and temples, but finding a new more positive vocabulary for studying new religious forms might be important.[34]

At the 2019 IUPUI meeting, Rudy V. Busto of the University of California, Santa Barbara, made an informal comparison of the 2019 gathering with one that met half a century earlier at Yale. He found that the 2019 meeting had a greater representation of public universities than the earlier one. He also found that while eighteen of twenty-five participants were still White, twelve of twenty-three participants were women compared to the mid-twentieth-century Yale conversation at which all but one of those presenting were White and all were men. Busto, Hedstrom, and Levitt were making similar points—whatever the limitations of the field, and all three acknowledged that they were many—there were a much more diverse set of voices included in the conversation in 2019 than ever could have been imagined in the 1960s.[35]

The Overlooked Strength of Religiously Affiliated Colleges in the Twenty-First Century

One other continued reality in the twenty-first century is the enduring strength of avowedly religious colleges. For all the talk of secularism in American higher education, there are 197 degree-granting Catholic colleges that are members of the Association of Catholic Colleges and Universities (ACCU) in the United States. There are also 150 Protestant colleges, found in virtually every state of the union, that are members of the Council of Christian Colleges and Universities. There are also several Protestant colleges that have chosen not to be members of the council. Some colleges that were denominationally founded but now more independent keep informal contacts through groups like the 101-member United Methodist Higher

Education Foundation or the 54-member Association of Presbyterian Colleges and Universities. It is also important to note the rise of other non-Christian religious colleges. Brandeis University celebrates its Jewish heritage while Yeshiva is more specifically Jewish. But there are also specifically Buddhist colleges and universities, as well as Muslim ones and one Hindu college in the United States.

Many of the more conservative Protestant colleges belong to the Council for Christian Colleges & Universities (CCCU), which has a total of 185 member colleges—150 are in the United States. CCCU schools enroll half a million students and include 90,000 faculty and staff. Member schools can be found in most states, with California, Texas, and Illinois having the most. It is not a small organization and a real, if under-recognized, part of the configuration of American higher education. CCCU describes itself as having a dual mission of promoting academic excellence and Christian Mission. All of the member schools are accredited colleges, most have a strong liberal arts focus for undergraduates, and many promote faculty research. The organization describes its religious mission "to advance the cause of Christ-centered higher education and to help our institutions transform lives by faithfully relating scholarship and service to biblical truth."[36]

Many of the CCCU members are Baptist, independent, or nondenominational evangelical schools, while others are affiliated with other denominations including the Church of Christ, the Assemblies of God, and the Christian Reformed churches. Many of the schools are quite conservative, but not all. Several CCCU members are Lutheran colleges that take a strong stand on religious issues but carefully avoid those they consider political. Five of the eight Lutheran Missouri Synod colleges are CCCU members. Lutheran Concordia University in Chicago describes itself as "a place where the Gospel lives and forms our students, a place where students engage important questions and . . . discover their God-given talents and gifts and determine how best to carry them out into the world to serve others." The school has daily chapel services, but they do not seem to be required. Students are encouraged to take their Christian faith and a call for service seriously but also have a lot of freedom in seeking their own truth.[37]

The issue of what the council means by "biblical truth" came to a head in the second decade of the twenty-first century over LGBTQ issues. In the summer of 2015, Eastern Mennonite University and Goshen College, Mennonite schools in Virginia and Indiana, respectively, amended their charters so that the college could hire married gay faculty as they did straight faculty. Mennonites are a peace church with some conservative impulses but also strong social justice concerns. Loren Swartzendruber, the president of Eastern Mennonite, described his school's decision, saying, "We're attempting to follow our mission as founded by the Mennonite Church and our goal is to be faithful to our own mission." Other CCCU members saw their mission very differently. After intense discussions over the summer, the Mennonite colleges withdrew from the CCCU. The organization had no specific policy on same-sex marriage, but the Mennonite school's new policies would clearly have led to a major split in the CCCU if they had stayed. John Fea, a professor at CCCU-member Messiah College in Pennsylvania, said that "there was really no other way to move forward" but that the schools would be missed for their "educational mission rooted in peacemaking and social justice that is often sorely lacking in the council's colleges." Other school leaders were less generous to the departing members. The president of Cedarville University in Ohio said that his school would have left CCCU if the Mennonite schools had stayed, and it was time to "clarify their position on biblical marriage." The president of Oklahoma Wesleyan University, a school whose motto is "Influencing culture with the Grace & Truth of Jesus Christ," led his school to quit the council for its slowness to expel the Mennonite schools, saying, "The propensity to engage in prolonged conversation with the apparent desire to come to a creative consensus or compromise has made me feel uncomfortable." He would not consider returning.[38]

Another community of conservative Christian schools, the International Alliance for Christian Education (IACE), based in Wheaton, Illinois, home of evangelical Wheaton College, describes its mission "to unify, synergize, and strengthen collective conviction around biblical orthodoxy and orthopraxy, cultural witness, scholarship, professional excellence, and resourcing Christian education at all levels." While not limiting itself to higher education, IACE is yet another reminder that though most go unnoticed in many conversations about American higher education, there are strong and lively efforts to strengthen and define the meaning of professional excellence among the schools that share a general agreement about the meaning of "biblical orthodoxy." For a study of religion in higher education, or indeed higher education in general, to fail to reference organizations like CCCU and IACE and the colleges they serve is as egregious an error as failing to mention other better-known manifestations of religion on twenty-first-century campuses."[39]

Conservative Christian colleges came under fire again in the spring of 2021 when a survey of 3,000 students found that LGBTQ+ students at colleges with anti-LGBTQ+ policies were much more likely to feel marginalized because of their sexuality than similar students at other colleges. As the director of the Religious Exemption Accountability Project wrote of the study, "Not only are LGBTQ+ students more likely to feel that they do not belong to their campus community, they are also more likely to experience disciplinary action from their institutions them-selves." A month later, a number of students at evangelical colleges sued the US Department of Education, demanding that the federal government stop funding for schools that violated their civil rights rather than bestow what seemed to be its approval and financial support to such schools. At the same time, the CCCU filed its own lawsuit, saying their understanding of biblical marriage was protected by the First Amendment and that while they were committed to supporting and wel-coming all students, including LGBTQ students at member schools, they rejected government interference. Battles about human sexuality, theological and legal, are probably going to define the council and similar organizations and their member schools for some time to come.[40]

In addition to divisions over the meaning of biblical sexuality, quite a few Chris-tian colleges are also struggling with basic finances. While some schools like inter-denominational Wheaton, Baptist Baylor, and Catholic Jesuit colleges like George-town or Santa Clara are popular and thriving, others simply cannot maintain their operations when even a slight dip in enrollment and tuition income, along with quickly rising expenses, puts them in jeopardy.

St. Gregory's University in Shawnee, Oklahoma, a 550-student Catholic liberal arts college, was forced to close in the fall of 2017. Many small religious colleges are totally dependent on tuition, yet as part of their mission have sought to keep tuition low and financial aid high. Such tuition discounts, however, have made life precarious. In 1956, there were 300 Catholic colleges in the United States, but that number had shrunk to just under 200 by 2020. Though the total enrollment in Catholic colleges has doubled, growth has also been concentrated in the larger schools. At the time of its closing, St. Gregory's president Michael Scaperlanda said, "The transition from a mom-and-pop shop to a niche boutique has been difficult for many colleges," and today, "you need to have a niche market and very sophisticated business practices, and I think that has been difficult for many small Christian universities, including St. Gregory's." Nevertheless, Scaperlanda saw the loss of St. Gregory's, where Benedictine monks pray multiple times daily, as "just a tragic and sad loss."

Three years later in the fall of 2021, Ohio Valley University, a Church of Christ college in West Virginia, also announced it was closing because it did not have the funds to pay its bills or continue operations into the new calendar year. In be-tween these closings, Grace University, a Christian college in Omaha, Nebraska, Marygrove College in Detroit, and other schools either shut down or contracted significantly with faculty and staff lay-offs. The general atmosphere in American higher education has been cruel to small schools in the twenty-first century and the COVID-19 closings of 2020–2021 hit them especially hard. Small religious schools that have not been able to draw enough students to pay the bills have been especially impacted.[41]

While Catholics, Protestants, and to a much lesser degree Jews account for most religious colleges, newer religious traditions that have been emerging in the United States have also started their own colleges and universities. These newer schools are becoming an important part of the configuration of American higher education, even though they often go unnoticed. Buddhists have four accredited colleges plus a handful of more informal institutes. The four current universities are Naropa University in Colorado, founded in 1974 following Tibetan Buddhism; Dharma Realm Buddhist University in northern California, founded in 1976 following Chinese Buddhism; Soka University in southern California, founded in 1987 following Japanese Buddhism; and the University of the West (formerly His Lai University), also in southern California, founded in 1991 and based on Taiwanese Buddhism. Like their predecessors founded by competing Christian groups, all the Buddhist colleges started as very small organizations but have been able to reach some level of stability, often based on the generous support of donors and stabilizing enrollment. As Protestant denominations once competed with each other, the new Buddhist schools compete with each other based on their different understandings of Buddhism.

Naropa traces its roots to a summer institute that attracted 1,500 people to meetings in Boulder, Colorado. From the beginning, Naropa featured an eclectic mix of Buddhists and spiritual seekers, including in the early years Chogyam Trungpa, an exiled Tibetan religious leader who attracted attention, and criticism from more traditional Buddhists, for his secular life that included smoking, drinking alcohol, and marriage. However, the Dalai Lama said of him that he "made a powerful contribution to revealing the Tibetan approach to inner peace to the West." In the early years of Naropa, Trungpa attracted a mix of followers including Allen Ginsberg, Anne Waldman, Ram Dass, Diane di Prima, and John Cage. Today, Naropa is an accredited school that offers a diversified curriculum in what it calls a "Buddhist-inspired non-sectarian tradition."

The University of the West and Dharma Realm, though different from each other, both reflect more traditional forms of Buddhism than Naropa. Dharma Realm's founder, Hsuan Hua, came to San Francisco in 1962 after a sojourn in Hong Kong that helped him escape the Cultural Revolution in China. He began teaching at the San Francisco Zen Center and taught Zen Buddhism before being given a 448-acre campus in 1976. Dharma Realm reports that it "does not merely transmit academic knowledge. It emphasizes a foundation in virtue," and thus it "advocates a spirit of shared inquiry and free exchange of ideas." For all their differences, Buddhist universities also have much in common, including great concern for the environment and for all living things, with a general preference for vegetarianism, serious meditation practices, a lack of competition, and a key role for mindfulness in all aspects of a Buddhist education.[42]

Muslim schools, although fewer in number, are also flourishing. Zaytuna College is an accredited school in Berkeley, California, that opened in 2009, based on an earlier Islamic institute and offering Islamic studies and the Islamic scholarly tradition with efforts to both apply the tradition to the modern United States and interpret Islam to a broader American audience. It offers a BA in liberal arts and Islamic studies and an MA in Islamic theology or Islamic law. Zaytuna describes its goal to provide an education that will lead students "to think deeply and systematically about the world (creation), to ponder its ultimate source and purpose (Creator), and to live ethically in the course of our individual and collective lives (spirituality and politics)." The school's location in Berkeley allows a close relationship with the University of California and the Graduate Theological Union, a consortium of seminaries and centers for the study of religion.

Respect Graduate School in Bethlehem, Pennsylvania, opened in 2015 with an inaugural class of twenty students in a program "dedicated to furthering the scholarly study of Islam." Other Muslim schools represent different Islamic traditions and are in other parts of the country but will likely emerge as holding their own place in American education.[43]

Finally, the Hindu University of America traces its inspiration to an Indian guru, Swami Tilak, who hoped to found a school but died in 1984. Some of those attracted to the vision were able to secure authorization from the state of Florida to start a religious institution in 1993 but only in 2001 and 2002 did a series of generous donations allow the university to secure a campus and offer courses. Further interruptions have slowed progress, but the goal of a flourishing Hindu University remains.

Other religious traditions including Sikhism, Jainism, Baha'ism, Confucianism, Taoism, and Indigenous American shamans all offer informal teachings but not formal colleges or universities. The variety of religions represented in American higher education is bound to grow in the coming decades as others did before.[44]

In the middle of this, several dozen religiously affiliated colleges have joined in a network for Vocation in Undergraduate Education, which is committed to resurrecting the religious notion of "calling" among today's students. Nevertheless, in the more secular universities, public and private, the senior administrator who is willing to invest in religious activities is hard to find. Across the board, from mainline Protestant and Catholic religious bodies to newer religious groups, the resources to invest in anything are in agonizingly short supply. Far from disappearing, however, student interest and committed professionals means that religion is on campus to stay, though often in forms and represented in traditions unimaginable not long ago.

The Evangelical Christian University—Liberty University, Lynchburg, Virginia

There are several hundred evangelical Christian colleges and universities in the United States. Liberty University, however, is often the school that first comes to mind if many Americans are asked to identify an evangelical college. In 2021, Liberty celebrated its fiftieth anniversary with considerable fanfare. The anniversary marked the day in January 1971 when Jerry Falwell Sr. announced plans to open a new kind of university in connection with the church where he had been pastor since 1956, Thomas Road Baptist Church in Lynchburg, Virginia. Lynchburg Baptist College held its first graduation in 1974, became Liberty Baptist College in 1976, gained accreditation in 1980, and quickly became simply Liberty University. Its school colors of red, white, and blue probably say more about the politics of its founder than about the wide-ranging academic programs of the college. In its fifty years of life, Liberty has grown from 154 students in its first year to 15,000 students on campus and 94,000 online students, though not all of the online students are degree candidates.[45]

Jerry Falwell Sr. played many different roles in the life of Liberty University. Not only was the university his creation, but he was its guiding spirit until his death at his desk in the president's office of the university in 2007. In his early years as the pastor of the Thomas Road Baptist Church and emcee of *The Old-Time Gospel Hour* radio and television show, both of which he founded at the age of 22 in 1956, he was a staunch fundamentalist and segregationist. Prior to any dreams of a college, he started a segregated academy, originally the Lynchburg Christian Academy, in 1967 at a time when church-based private academies for White students were popular across the South as part of the resistance to the Supreme Court's *Brown v. Board of Education* decision. After founding what would become Liberty University in 1971, Falwell was drawn deeper into politics, starting the Moral Majority in 1979 "to turn the country upside down for Christ," he said. Falwell said the Moral

Majority was "pro-life," "pro-traditional family," "pro-moral," and "pro-American." Critics, on the other hand, said that the Moral Majority was neither moral nor a majority. The Moral Majority did, however, make Falwell famous and a national religious power broker within the Republican Party. Both Ronald Reagan and Jimmy Carter credited Falwell with playing a major role in Reagan's electoral victory over Carter in November 1980—Reagan with more appreciation than Carter!

As he moved deeper into politics, Falwell left much of the administration of Liberty University to others, though he never stopped being the school's presiding spirit. Critics said "he maintained absolute control but was hardly ever around." He also moderated some of his social views, welcoming African American students to Liberty where he proudly pointed to the 200 African American students, out of a then total student body of 3,000, and supported a Black Student Fellowship to offer support to these students. These changes did not mean that Liberty had become an anti-racist institution or that Falwell or his school had moved far from their fundamentalist roots. It had not. He reached a broader audience, however, and that mattered to him.

When Falwell died suddenly at the age of 73 in 2007, his son, Jerry Falwell Jr. became president of the school in his father's place. The new president assured the 2007 Commencement audience that, "We have prepared for this transition for 15 years or more. All is well at Liberty." All was very well in terms of Liberty's institutional health as it continued to grow and be a national influence. It was not so well with Jerry Falwell Jr., himself, who never had the draw of his father and who was forced out as president of Liberty in 2020 when his personal life was engulfed in scandal. By 2021, Liberty was finding new ways to honor the memory and institutional heritage of Jerry Falwell Sr., even as it was locked in court battles with Jerry Falwell Jr.[46]

The historian of American education Virginia Brereton wrote, "Whatever it was or was not, the fundamentalist movement was decidedly an educational movement and most fundamentalists were educators. . . . To understand fundamentalism, then, it is absolutely necessary to examine their educational efforts." And while there are many fundamentalist or evangelical colleges, among them Wheaton, Bob Jones, Biola, and Gordon College, to understand the conservative evangelical college in twenty-first-century American higher education, one needs to try to understand Liberty University.[47]

In October 2021, Scott Lamb, Liberty's former senior vice president for communications, had a falling out with the university and released a tape recording of Liberty's third president, Jerry Prevo, saying that Liberty needed to get better at "getting people elected." The university responded, "President Prevo knows the lines established by the IRS for political engagement." Whether or not Prevo had stepped over the line by mixing a tax-exempt educational institution in politics, he was not the first leader at Liberty to walk close to the line. Jerry Falwell Sr. had been doing similar things from the year the school was founded.[48]

In the very early years of what was then Liberty Baptist College and not long before the fall presidential election in 1980, Liberty invited Ronald Reagan to speak on the campus. The Republican presidential candidate said just what his audience wanted to hear. Echoing the words of the Moral Majority, he promised to use the Oval Office to lead a renewed moral vision for the nation and end what he called the national wrong turn when the country "expelled God from the classroom" and from public life. Pierre Guillermin, who was presiding over the college in Falwell's absence, said simply, "We believe in America," making it fairly clear that the America he believed in looked more like the one Reagan envisioned than anything Carter had led for the last four years.

A year after Reagan won the election, Ed Hindson, another senior leader at Liberty, insisted that the school was leading "the resurgent Fundamentalist Phenomenon." For leaders like Hindson, fundamentalists were now returning to their God-given role of rescuing American politics led by "a few thousand highly committed and thoroughly trained young people" who could be the vanguard of the Moral Majority. Liberty was precisely the place to train these young people.

Historian Adam Laats has noted that for all the assumption by friends and foes that Falwell was leading fundamentalists back into politics, the reality was that they had never really left. Certainly, in the 1920s fundamentalists had not done well with their political attacks on evolution, but they never really stopped campaigning against it. The Supreme Court's decisions banning devotional activities such as prayer and Bible reading in the schools in the early 1960s led many religious conservatives—fundamentalist and others—to be more politically active well before many people outside of Lynchburg, Virginia, knew about Falwell or Liberty. With Falwell and Liberty University, however, fundamentalist had a new leader for political action and a new educational institution to train the ground forces needed for their agenda.[49]

Well after Jerry Falwell Sr. and Ronald Reagan had departed the scene, the alliance between Liberty University, fundamentalism, and conservative Republican politics continued. In May 2017, newly elected president Donald Trump gave the graduation speech at Liberty. It was Trump's third speech at Liberty, and the school had certainly provided a boost to him as it had to Reagan before him in the presidential elections. Trump said that he knew that his election as president "would really require major help from God," but he also insisted "we got it." Later in the speech, the president thanked Liberty's presidents, past and present, for the vision that created "a world-class university for evangelical Christians." He also thanked them "because, boy, did you come out and vote . . . you voted, you voted." Finally, Trump concluded with the promise he had made at Liberty the year before: "As long as I am your president, no one is ever going to stop you from practicing your faith or from preaching what's in your heart." In the twenty-first century, President Trump and a new President Falwell were making it clear that they had an enduring alliance. In 2021, Liberty President Prevo was simply building on that alliance with the remarks that got him accused of crossing the line from education into politics. Liberty was born on that line.[50]

Liberty also held to its conservative views of faith as well as politics. While many evangelicals tried to work out some compromise on the divisive issue of evolution, Liberty did not. Perhaps the most popular compromise was the view that each day of creation may have lasted far longer than what we now think of as a day or that creation itself had evolved over time. Liberty's leaders would have none of it. God created the world and everything in it in six days, days as we think of a day, they insisted. God created each plant, animal, and humans just as the Bible said. God did all of that during those six actual days, not metaphorical days. Anybody who wanted to teach at Liberty needed to sign a statement that they "believe in the Genesis account of creation . . . literally and not allegorically or figuratively." The college's position clearly differentiated it from other schools that were open to a bit more diversity of views. Even as it drove some away, it made Liberty popular with many conservative parents and potential students.[51]

Fifty years later, little has changed on the evolution-creationism front at Liberty. The college's 2021 Doctrinal Statement stated, "Human beings were directly created, not evolved, in the very image of God, as either biologically male or female from the womb." And the college also houses a Center for Creation Studies "to promote the development of a consistent biblical view of the origins in our students." Liberty sees its role as molding politically nimble leaders but also Bible-believing conservative Christians.[52]

One part of the Liberty belief system that was not as prominent in the early Liberty as it is today can be found in the claim that not only were human beings created by God in the image of God, but they were created "as either biologically male or female from the womb." The founding generation at Liberty would not have disagreed with that statement, but they might not have felt the need, as the twenty-first-century leaders did, to add among the long list of sinful acts, "denial of birth sex by self-identification with a different gender," or "Sexual relations outside of marriage between one natural-born man and one natural-born woman; romantic coupling among persons of the same sex," and so on. The growing focus on seeing men and women as permanently what they were born as and hostility to any LGBTQ lives, especially transgendered lives, has grown in significance in the evangelical world. Part of this growing emphasis includes seeing men and women, separately, as half of a heterosexual couple that only in their coming together represent the fullness of the image of God. It is part of a theological development that has swept evangelical circles called "complementarianism."

Complementarianism is a response to the sexual revolution of the 1960s and the feminism of the 1970s. A meeting of the Council on Biblical Manhood and Womanhood (CBMW) in Danvers, Massachusetts, in December 1987 sought a clear definition of complementarianism. The council issued the "Danvers Statement" condemning the "widespread uncertainty and confusion in our culture regarding the complementary differences between masculinity and femininity," and the "tragic effects of this confusion in unraveling the fabric of marriage woven by God out of the beautiful and diverse strands of manhood and womanhood." The Danvers Statement also decried, "The increasing promotion given to feminist egalitarianism with the accompanying distortions or neglect of the glad harmony portrayed in Scripture between the loving, humble leadership of redeemed husbands and the intelligent, willing support of that leadership by redeemed wives."[53]

In theory, complementarianism assigned equal but very different roles to women and men and decried any effort to make one role more important than the other. But for many, assigning leadership in society, church, and home to the "humble leadership" of men while women focused on "vocational homemaking, and the many ministries historically performed by women" did not look like equality. Partly to answer critics, the CBWM issued a second statement—the Nashville Statement of 2017—which strengthened the view that while men and women had different roles, they were equal in the sight of God and should be with each other, even though the roles were quite distinct and hierarchical. Both statements condemned all forms of homosexuality, divorce, or sex outside of marriage.[54]

Complementarianism has become surprisingly popular in many evangelical circles, none larger than the Southern Baptist Convention, which officially adopted it. While no one from Liberty was among the original signers of the Danvers or Nashville statements, signs of the belief system can be found across the Liberty campus and in the doctrinal statements of the school.

Complementarianism has also had more than its share of critics, often within the same conservative circles. Perhaps the best-known critic is Beth Moore, a teacher and curriculum developer who was called "the very model of a modern Southern Baptist." But Moore could not abide the Southern Baptist embrace of Donald Trump. In a widely publicized move, Moore broke with the Southern Baptists and blamed the problem not only on Trump and the Baptist leaders who wanted to be near him but also on complementarianism, which did not justify what Trump was doing but did justify the demand that women, like Moore, who objected, needed to remain silent. Other Southern Baptists followed the same route as Moore and refused to keep silent. Indeed, some wondered if complementarianism fell into the ideas criticized by Jesus when he condemned those people "teaching as doctrines the commandment of men."[55]

Although complementarianism denies "that the divinely ordained differences between male and female renders them unequal in dignity and worth," some women—and some men—at Liberty do not experience it that way. In July 2021 twelve students and employees sued the university, saying that the school "has intentionally created a campus environment where sexual assaults and rapes are foreseeably more likely to occur in the absence of Liberty policies." The suit claims that the school's strict conduct code, "the Liberty Way," and its Community standards process, make it all too easy to blame women for inviting any sexual assaults and to privilege the voices of men over women, as well as to let men off with light punishment in the name of restorative practices.

The women making the complaint see what they call a "weaponization" of the conduct code that makes it "difficult or impossible for students to report sexual violence." Josie Young, a senior at Liberty and the spokesperson for the group bringing the suit, had some hope that the new president, Prevo, replacing the unsympathetic Jerry Falwell Jr., might make it easier to address the issue since Prevo seemed to be "taking our demands more seriously." But Young added, "we don't want to let the small victories appease us. . . . There's still no transparency—they haven't told us what they plan on doing with the information they are going to get."[56]

Sexual harassment is not limited to conservative or fundamentalist colleges. Indeed, all of American higher education has been wrestling with how institutions respond—or don't respond—to sexual violence for much of the new century, especially since the #MeToo movement. Some defenders see no link between complementarianism and sexual violence since complementarianism seems to explicitly state that sexual violence or any unwanted sexual overtures are condemned. Nevertheless, even some who defend complementarianism, insisting that it "does not offer biblical protection, legitimate or not, to abusers," also recognize that it can all too easily be twisted to sound like it does. Others see a very clear connection.

Kristin Kobes Du Mez, who teaches at Calvin College, another conservative Christian college, sees a very tight link. She insists that the ideology results in "forgiving perpetrators, shaming victims, and rationalizing sexual aggression as God-given." Complementarianism seems to justify men being "very sexually aggressive," because "that's what you need in a leader," even if it leads to protecting "the masculine leaders even if they are perpetrators."[57]

Liberty's position on complementarianism, evolution, and conservative politics seem to set the school apart—far apart—from the mainstream of American higher education and even in some cases from other evangelical schools. There are other ways, however, in which Liberty seems like just another college. Comparing the feel on public university campuses and Liberty, Adam Laats notes, "The students were dressed in identical non-uniforms: Jeans, flip-flops, and carefully slovenly T-shirts. [Perhaps a little less slovenly at Liberty given its strict dress code.] They seemed to spend their time in similar ways: skateboarding, playing guitar, and chatting. They carried the same ubiquitous coffee mugs and smartphones." When he visited Liberty, Laats noticed that:

> Things at Liberty University, too, can seem very similar to those on any other university campus, if maybe a little—or a lot—nicer . . . . It could seem just like any other booming elite university campus. After a little while, however, you start to notice a strange sound, a sound you wouldn't hear on secular campuses: everywhere on campus there is Christian contemporary music piped out to the sidewalks through a mysterious system of hidden speakers. It serves as an ever-present aural reminder that Liberty is meant to be a different type of school.[58]

Very similar but very different seems to be the definition of what Liberty University offers.

The college catalog lists a dizzying array of undergraduate majors, including many found on the most secular campus and others not dreamed of in other colleges, from accounting to business (with twenty-one sub-fields) to zoology but also from applied ministry to biblical studies to worship studies. The strict 24-page Liberty Way Student Honor Code might be the secret dream of many deans of students, but it is very detailed and very strict, including banning the possession or use of alcohol, drugs, or tobacco, and a detailed dress code that especially focuses on female modesty. The rules on sexuality say:

Sexual relations outside of a biblically-ordained marriage between a natural-born man and a natural-born woman are not permissible at Liberty University. While mental thoughts, temptations and states of mind are not regulated by The Liberty Way, statements and behaviors that are associated with LGBT states of mind are prohibited.

It is a long way from the sex and alcohol-fueled reality of many mainstream campuses. So similar and so different, Liberty is, in the end, certainly one iteration of the place of religion in the American university.[59]

Multifaith Conversation at a Public University— The University of Nevada, Reno

When Nevada was admitted to the Union in 1864 in the middle of the Civil War, the new state's constitution specifically provided for the creation of a "State University." Following the constitutional mandate, the University of Nevada opened in 1874 and moved to Reno in 1886. The same constitution prohibited any use of state funds for religious purposes whatsoever—a stricter separation of church and state than in some other states, though several other states added such provisions to their state constitutions soon after. The line of separation between state schools and religious practices is often murky, but there are religious observances that private colleges can allow—even if many do not—that a state-supported school simply cannot do.

Given its strict state constitution (Article 11, Section 10), the University of Nevada is very limited in endorsing anything that can be construed as a religious observance as opposed to teaching about religion. The university also seems to have been especially creative in supporting activities that allow the students of the university, and the community surrounding the university, to take religion seriously without implying any institutional endorsement.[60]

Baccalaureate services—special quasi-religious ceremonies for the school's graduating class—do happen at some state schools, although they are usually off campus and without official connection to the university. At the University of Nevada, Reno (UNR), members of the 2009 graduating class who wanted to participate in a baccalaureate religious service had a unique opportunity: a Hindu baccalaureate service. The event was organized off campus by the Indian Student Organization, which wanted its own event but also wanted to share it with their fellow graduates and add a bit of an ecumenical flavor to a primarily Hindu event. Graduates received a Tilak, or religious mark, when they arrived. The keynote was given by

Swami Vedananda, a Hindu monk who blessed the graduates with readings from the Hindu scriptures—the Vedas, Upanishads, and Bhagavad-Gita. In addition to Swami Vedananda's blessing, the students heard a Hebrew prayer from the Torah, a Buddhist prayer in Pali, a Muslim prayer from the Koran in Arabic, a Native American blessing in Paiute, and prayers by religious leaders from Catholic, Presbyterian, Latter-day Saints, International Community of Christ, and Baha'i religious communities. It was far from a traditional baccalaureate event where students from many traditions sit through an essentially Christian service, but it seemed right for a school that finds a variety of ways to celebrate the importance of many religious traditions while avoiding the endorsement of any.[61]

UNR also often partners with different community organizations, including religious ones, for public events that are open to all but again do not imply any official endorsement. For example, when the Temple Sinai Library Committee had an idea for a panel discussion of women's leadership in religious life, they reached out to several different programs and departments at UNR as well as the Northern Nevada Women's Leadership Initiative and created "Breaking the Stained-Glass Ceiling," a panel discussion to explore gender, leadership, and faith. They invited five exemplary leaders to serve as panelists: an Interfaith chaplain who was a member of the Reno Buddhist Center, another resident from the Buddhist Center, a woman from the Northern Nevada Islamic Center, another from the Church of Jesus Christ of Latter-day Saints, and the Rabbi of Temple Sinai. All five panelists were women.

Speaking about a photo exhibit that accompanied the "Breaking the Stained-Glass Ceiling" panel, Rabbi Sara Zober said, "Issues of gender marginalization are still alive today, both in religious spaces and our secular world. Highlighting them through this exhibit and panel puts a spotlight on the work we still must do to achieve equity." In introducing the conference, Debra Moddelmog, dean of the College of Liberal Arts at UNR, said, "Women's leadership options in religious organizations and spiritual communities have often been limited due to doctrine, tradition, practice, and bias.... This promises to be an exciting evening of conversation with amazing women leaders who have blazed paths within religious and spiritual settings." Most universities, public and private, talk of reaching out to the community. Not nearly as many are prepared to join with community religious organizations to sponsor events such as this one, which both honored and challenged religious communities while maintaining the appropriate distance from trying in any way to function as a religious community itself.[62]

UNR does not have a religious studies department as such, even though many state universities do. However, the Interdisciplinary Department of Gender, Race, and Identity offers an undergraduate minor in religious studies to be completed alongside a major in another field. The description of the minor is not very different from many similar minors and majors in religion, telling students that in the program they will "grapple with fundamental questions concerning the nature of religion and its continuing relevance to contemporary life in a rapidly globalizing world." But something else is unique at UNR. The minor includes a required introductory course in religion but also courses in a wide range of areas, including anthropology courses like "Magic, Witchcraft and Religion" or "Anthropology of Islam and Muslim Cultures"; English department courses like "The Bible as Literature"; or history courses like "Religion and Society in Latin America" or "Modern Jewish History."

The variety of courses in UNR's religious studies minor indicates that there are more than a few faculty across several department who are interested in religious topics. Interested students have many choices. In a world where religious study is too often sealed off from the rest of the university, it is refreshing to see this diversity of departments, programs, and people involved in the academic study of religion at UNR. Something interesting at UNR attracted so many members of the faculty to the university in northern Nevada, as well as fostered an attitude of unusual welcome to community groups and student organizations who care about religion in its many diverse forms.[63]

A Private Secular University with an Active Religious Life— The University of Southern California

The recent past has been good to the University of Southern California (USC). The twenty-first century opened with both *Time* magazine and the *Princeton Review* naming USC as the 2000 "College of the Year." It was a long way from USC's beginning in a much smaller city of Los Angeles, when a civic-minded group of men planned a school in the 1870s and opened it in 1880 for fifty-three students, with ten teachers. For the 2023–2024 year, USC reported a total of 47,000 students and over 4,400 full-time faculty.[64] When USC opened, the total population of Los Angeles was just under 11,000 people. In 2024 it was close to 4 million. Of the four Los Angeles civic leaders in the 1870s who created USC, most had come to California during the gold rush but eventually settled in the southern part of the state and prospered in business. They donated the land for the campus as part of the civic development they dreamed of in their city. While one of the four was a Roman Catholic and another Jewish, the school was operated by the Southern California

Conference of the Methodist Episcopal Church and all its early presidents were Methodist ministers. It was open to students of any faith, but it was a Methodist college.[65]

There were times in the 1880s and 1890s when internal Methodist debates dominated the life of USC's board of directors. Robert Widney had made a fortune in Los Angeles real estate. He not only helped found USC and chaired its board, but he kept the school solvent in its early decades by simply paying many of its bills personally. He and the school's first president, Marion Bouvard, a Methodist minister, also supported Phineas Bresee, who was vice chair of the board and a Methodist minister who left the Methodist ministry to become a missionary to the poor and eventually one of the founders of the breakaway Church of the Nazarene, which Widney also supported (see Northwest Nazarene College, chapter 3). While still hoping to reform the Methodist Church itself and avoid a rupture, Bresee and Widney pushed the USC board to adopt a resolution that said, "we enquire closely into the purity of private life and character, and soundness of Christian faith and practice . . . of each person to be a member of the faculty. That no one be elected or retained who is not only a professed Christian but sound in doctrine, consistent in personal life, and an aggressive worker." Whatever their theological views, the board wanted Widney's money and adopted the resolution.

Eventually both Widney and Bresee became convinced that the Methodist Church itself was not of sound doctrine and tried to pull the school into the Nazarene camp, but the majority of the USC board was not ready for a break. The school stayed Methodist well into the next century. A century later, it may be very hard to imagine the USC board debating doctrinal issues or making demands for soundness of faith in its faculty, but such was the state of much of American higher education far beyond the denominational colleges in the decades USC was formed. USC was never controlled by the Methodist Church, but its link was far more than nominal.[66] Only in 1928, on the eve of its fiftieth anniversary and under the leadership of its first non-ministerial president, did the board of trustees negotiate an apparently amicable separation from the Methodist Church.

USC's fate was closely linked to that of the burgeoning Los Angeles area, and it served as a key institution in the early development of the city. The establishment of the southern branch of the University of California that became UCLA in the 1920s created serious competition for USC. However, the rapid growth of Los Angeles in the 1920s because of the film industry and the good weather, followed by World War II industrial growth and the post–World War II population boom on Southern California and the huge increase in students due to the GI Bill, flooded both schools with students. The once small, formerly Methodist and very local school dealt with the competition and the growing affluence of the area by reaching for a new status as a nationally recognized research university. By the middle of the twentieth century, USC's status as a nationally, even internationally, recognized university seemed secure. Any connection to the Methodist church was long forgotten.[67]

A cursory review of how USC describes itself in the 2020s would lead to the conclusion that it is now, as its leaders envisioned in the 1920s, a very secular university. Most celebrated are the research honors won by the faculty, including a Nobel Prize in Chemistry, its hugely successful fundraising efforts, its campus expansion, and its sports victories. One needs to dig much deeper to find a university research center focused on religion's impact in society, an academic department called the School of Religion, and the vibrant Office of Religious & Spiritual Life. But if one digs, all of these can be found.[68]

The USC Center for Religion and Civic Culture was created in 1992 after the uprising in Los Angeles that followed the acquittal of the four police officers who beat Rodney King months earlier. The uprising shook Los Angeles and revealed the depth of race-based violence in the city. The center was established by USC to investigate the way civic and religious coalitions could help heal, reunite, and change the city in the aftermath of that painful episode. From the beginning, it was also expected to address the underlying political, economic, and social problems in the city that led to the uprising. In time, the center expanded to bring scholars and practitioners together to study the role of religious communities in building a more moral world and a stronger civic culture for the city and the world. As a research center, the CRC has attracted millions of dollars of research grants but focused its research on direct impact.[69]

The School of Religion is an academic department within the College of Letters, Arts and Sciences. Like most religious studies programs, the school offers students analytic tools for the study of religions around the world and religions of the past, present, and future. The school offers elective courses, an undergraduate major, a master's, and doctoral degree as well as graduate certificates. The school website says:

> A degree in Religion can take you anywhere. Journalists, policy-makers, film makers all need to know how religion affects the lives of people around the world. Business execs must understand the religious contours of foreign markets. Politicians and lawyers must maneuver among the religious rights of individuals and entire nations.

There is no mention on the website of preparing clergy or college religious life professionals. There is, indeed, little evidence of formal collaboration between the School of Religion and the many activities of the Office of Religious & Spiritual Life on the same campus. The catalog lists seventeen professors with primary appointments in the School of Religion, plus a number of affiliate faculty. Several faculty focus on various aspects of Christianity. Sherman Jackson holds an endowed chair in Islamic Thought and Culture and other faculty are studying gender and spirituality, California Native American beliefs, different aspects of Judaism and Jewish-Muslim encounters, and several people focus on Eastern religions, including the school's chair, Duncan Williams, who focuses on Japanese Buddhism and Japanese religious history.[70]

The Office of Religious & Spiritual Life (ORSL) has a different focus than the School of Religion. Where the academic department invites students to study religion, the religious life office begins with an invitation to, "Find a Religious Home on Campus," adding:

> The Trojan [USC's mascot] Family is as diverse in faith, belief and philosophy of life as it is in other regards. There are over 90 different student religious organizations on campus, representing almost every major world faith and life stance; students are invited to attend gatherings of any and all of these groups.

The website proudly claims that USC has more different religious organizations than any other university in the country, and it may well be true. Students from most of them are represented in an interfaith student council that meets regularly. Among the many different religious groups there are groups for Atheist/Secular Humanists, Baha'i, Buddhist, and fifty-five different Christian groups—Catholic and Protestant, Fundamentalist and Liberal—as well as Jain, Jewish, and Sikh groups. Indeed, if one looks at where the formerly Methodist college is in the twenty-first century, there is striking evidence of the most religiously diverse university in the country with active programs for a very wide range of faith traditions and none.

The Office of Religious Life was created in 1996 when a committee of faculty, students, and staff recommended that the university need to do more to coordinate and strengthen religious life on USC's very secular and often atomized campus, and the former Hillel director at the school, Susan Laemmle, was appointed as dean of religious life with a mandate to make that happen. By 2004 there were eighty religious groups associated with the religious life efforts at USC. Dean Laemmle, who had welcomed such a wide diversity of religious faiths to a place at USC, told the alumni magazine, "We're hoping to get a Zoroastrian group going soon." Her successor kept the expansion going.[71]

Alongside some current ninety different religious organizations, ORSL has between forty and fifty religious directors who, according to the website, "are professionals, some ordained as clergy within their respective faith traditions, who advise many of the student religious organizations on campus. They represent and are supported by their own denominations or religious movements." In addition, ORSL hosts an extended group of chaplains and other clergy (not all like to be called chaplains) who support each other, support a respectful and religiously inclusive environment, and speak up for each other when they feel under assault, as did the Muslim religious leaders several times in the last few years.

ORSL offers a wide range of programs and community service opportunities for students and faculty at USC. One of the most popular is a noon-hour series in which different people—from the president to deans and faculty in many different department and schools—talk about "What Matters to Me and Why" (WMMW). As the office describes the program, "the series encourages reflection about values, beliefs, and motivation in the lives of those who help shape our university." And:

> WMMW also represents a creative solution to an important and often unrecognized problem in the university setting: the separation of intellectual life from personal and spiritual issues. For some time, students have been asking for more informal contact with faculty. They have expressed their desire to encounter faculty and administrators as rounded human beings professional models, and mentors. The people who shape USC who teach students the ways of their particular disciplines, and who help them develop marketable skills also have a great deal to pass on in terms of worldly wisdom, moral guidance, and sources of spiritual strength.

The series sparks conversation that may be more or less religious in terms of using any religious language. But they generally reflect people for whom the questions of meaning and purpose loom large in their professional and personal lives.[72]

In the twenty-first century, the Office of Religious & Spiritual Life is led by Dean Varun Soni, who is Hindu. Soni replaced Rabbi Laemmle when she retired. Soni is supported by two associate directors, one a Protestant minister and the other a humanist chaplain. The core team reflects the religious diversity they seek to foster. In addition to his role of dean of Religious Life, Soni has been appointed USC's vice provost of Campus Wellbeing and Crisis Intervention.

Varun Soni remains the only Hindu to hold the senior religious life position in a major American university, although a few universities—very few—have rabbis in such positions. The overwhelming majority of senior chaplains or deans, where such roles exist at all, are Protestant ministers or priests in Catholic colleges. Soni's appointment also represents the extraordinary growth of religious diversity on American campuses. He was born into a Hindu family from the Punjab in northern India. He attended Catholic elementary school in California, had a Buddhist grandfather, and says his extended family around the world represents every major religious tradition. He attended Harvard Divinity School and has a law degree from the University of California.

Soni coordinates the religious life work at USC and functions as the campus religious life leader at campus-wide occasions, such as speaking to students when a well-loved professor was murdered. He leads retreats, supports an LGBTQ Bible study, and tries to bring students together in multiple settings. He says his "programming is my pulpit." Among the messages he preaches is a reminder to an older constituency that today's students are a different generation, more diverse, but also often alienated from religious institutions and any form of organized religion. He tells students how important it is to be oriented around "meaning and purpose and authenticity and identity and significance" not just status and success, social and economic. He adds:

> My concern is that as students leave traditional religious congregations, they haven't been taught how to build an intentional community of like-minded people in a way that creates empathy and compassion and a sense of belonging. That's compounded by the fact that this is a generation that was born into technology. . . . You may have 500 friends on Facebook, but what does it mean in real life?

For Soni, thinking about meaning, purpose, and building an intentional community in a way that is respectful of many different religious traditions is the key to building a new kind of religious engagement on campus and in the larger society. It is especially important at a time when so many, on campus and beyond, are terribly isolated and lonely no matter how many Facebook friends they may have.

Eboo Patel, who leads the Chicago-based Interfaith Youth Core, which brings students of different religious traditions together, described the importance he sees in people like Soni who knows how to bring diverse groups together and inspire them to take religion and community seriously. As Patel says, "You don't get interested in that unless you're influenced by somebody like Varun. Now multiply that by 25 or 50 young people a year and multiply that by 10 or 15 years and think about the number of people . . . who have a really refined sense of religious diversity." If one further thinks about the growing attention to religious diversity on many college campuses across the country, large and small, and thus multiply those number further, there is indeed reason to be optimistic about a growth of a new diverse religious spirituality as the twenty-first century unfolds.[73]

At the midway mark of the third decade of the twenty-first century, it is unclear what the future of religious life will be on American campuses. Certainly, all of the very different examples in this chapter point to a resurgence of interest in spirituality and questions of meaning in this generation of college students. Almost certainly religious offerings and religious interests will be more diverse, more robust, but also more contentious in the coming decades. While many parents—and federal education policy—view college in increasingly vocational terms, not all students and faculty agree. And within many colleges there are those who are deeply nervousness about the direction in which the nation is moving, leading some to new interests in ethics and a sustaining spirituality. Student interest in religious matters is often more in the realm of the "spiritual but not religious," or in new forms of mindfulness and spirituality than anything along traditional denominational lines, or within the older Christian and Jewish categories, but the interest is strong and likely to grow in the future.

Afterword

On December 16, 2021, the Baylor University community received the long dreamed of news that Baylor had been moved to an R1—research one—status in the Carnegie Classification system for higher education. In her announcement to the Baylor community, President Linda Livingstone noted, "Our R1 aspirations have represented an incredible opportunity—one given to us by God—to do what very few, if any, universities have achieved: maintaining our foundational Christian mission while reaching R1 status as a top-tier research university." Out of several thousand four-year colleges in the United States, only 137 universities are in the research one category. In few if any of this select group—other than Baylor—would a twenty-first-century president view the status as "given by God" or commit to "maintaining our foundational Christian mission while reaching R1 status." That is, indeed, Baylor's unique mission.[1]

Baylor was founded by Texas Baptists in 1845 and has remained resolutely Baptist through all its life. For most of its history, Baylor also remained a regional school focused on undergraduate teaching and a limited number of professional programs. Baylor faced a crisis in the 1980s when fundamentalists won control of the Southern Baptist Convention. Although the convention did not control Baylor, the leadership of the school was worried. Baylor was Christian and conservative, but not fundamentalist, and meant to stay that way. In 1990, in order to protect the school's freedom to chart its own course, the trustees made the school independent with a self-perpetuating board instead of one appointed by Baptist churches. Over the last century, such a move has often preceded the rapid secularization of a college, but Baylor resisted that direction. In fact, it moved in the opposite direction.

By 2000, Baylor still faced a crossroads: which way would it move to survive and thrive in the twenty-first century? Would it remain primarily a teaching school, or would it chart a new direction? In response, Baylor adopted a goal statement, *Baylor 2012*, that made clear it sought a unique path. The goal statement began, "It is a legacy of modernity to believe that the pathway divides between the uncompromising pursuit of intellectual excellence and intense faithfulness to the Christian tradition." The plan's authors recognized that many originally religious schools had chosen the path toward intellectual excellence and with it, secularism. They also noted that, "Accepting the same premise of the divided way, many Christian colleges have chosen insularity and self-protective intellectual mediocrity as the way to preserve their Christian vitality." But the Baylor leadership rejected the choice, saying, "Christian faith, at its best, motivates a love of all truth; and true knowledge supports and deepens our love of God in Jesus Christ."

A century earlier, the first generation of leaders at another Baptist school, the University of Chicago, said much the same thing and meant to ensure that Chicago represented deeply held Baptist beliefs and the leading edge of academic scholarship in the United States. But while a second generation of leaders at Chicago placed more and more emphasis on scholarship and less and less on the school's religious commitments, Baylor chose a different course. The result, in the years after the statement was adopted and became the core of Baylor's strategic planning, is that Baylor remains deeply Christian, as it defined Christian, in all aspects of its life, and it is also now an R1 university.[2]

As Baylor rightly celebrated its hard-won new status, the school's direction raises important questions about the place of religion in American higher education in the twenty-first century. Very few colleges have gone the route of Baylor in an uncompromising embrace of academic research and a strongly held religious faith. Even within Baylor some ask, why not let the Baptist Student Ministry handle faith and the faculty handle research? At nearly all other R1 schools an overwhelming majority of the faculty would insist on an affirmative answer to the same question. But not for most people at Baylor.

Baylor also faces questions of just how its Christian commitments will work in a more diverse world. After years of requests from LGBTQ students, in the summer of 2021 Baylor began exploring creating a recognized LGBTQ group on campus. However the issue plays out, it may well threaten Baylor's standing with other conservative Christian and specifically Baptist colleges, many of which strongly oppose such a move, and the larger research university world, which mostly expects a university to support all students and certainly LGBTQ students.

Regarding Baylor's exploration of the issue, Albert Mohler, president of Southern Baptist Theological Seminary, accused it of "trying to have its cake and eat it, too." Mohler added that Baylor still wants to present itself as, "in some sense, a Christian institution, a Baptist institution," but it was, to his mind, surrendering that role. Of course, there are many Christians in the United States who see an embrace of LGBTQ people as simply the only way to live out the command to love our neighbors, but that is not Mohler's view. It is but one example of the tensions that trying to offer both an "Unambiguously Christian Educational Environment" and "Research Scholarship Marked by Quality, Impact, and Visibility" and to do so in a world where many research scholars and a fair number of Christians think the mix is impossible.[3]

One also asks whether Baylor's requirement that faculty demonstrate personal religious commitment with membership in a Christian or Jewish congregation and embrace the "Baylor way" will hinder the recruitment of the kinds of scholars necessary for continued research excellence. Some within Baylor, and more outside it, see that as a distinct possibility. What will happen if a faculty member changes their mind about faith once at the school, and what does that imply for academic freedom? What about a Muslim or Hindu or nonreligious scholar? What about a nonreligious newly minted PhD depending on an academic career who wants a job? Will Baylor institute a sincerity test? These and other questions are going to perplex future generations at Baylor, whatever form their solutions take. Perhaps the fork in the road is more real than the *Baylor 2012* statement's authors were willing to admit.[4]

Whatever route Baylor takes in the next decades, other colleges and universities will also need to find their way. The standard solution of "let the chaplains handle religion and the faculty do their own teaching and research mostly with no attention to religion" has more critics than it once did. It may be that all of American higher education is at a crossroads, if not the same one Baylor once faced. In *The Great Upheaval: Higher Education's Past, Present, and Uncertain Future*, Arthur Levine and Scott Van Pelt remind us that the research university itself is a product of the Industrial Revolution, but the Industrial Revolution is in the past as the world has moved well into an Information Age. Might the Information Age require American higher education to return to nineteenth-century questions of meaning and purpose, values, and even spirituality in ways that are very different from the "old time college," but also different from the ways of the industrial era research university that ignored values questions more often than not?[5]

Certainly, Baylor's commitment to a both/and approach to faith and reason raises intriguing questions even if it is far too soon to begin to have answers. Nevertheless, in his book *Rescuing Socrates: How the Great Books Changed My Life and Why They Matter for a New Generation*, Roosevelt Montás argues, "Liberal education looks to the meaning of a human life beyond the requirements of subsistence—instead of asking how to make a living, liberal education asks what living is for." How to make a living versus the purpose of living may also be a false choice. Of course, students expect a college education to help them make a living. But in twenty-first-century American higher education, many students desperately also want to talk about "what living is for," and about meaning and purpose and values—in their lives and in society. They may use different language for the conversation, and it is certain that the traditional religious structures no longer are able to contain the conversation, but many of today's college students see the meaning–purpose–values–spirituality questions as pressing in a way that their immediate predecessors may not have.[6]

The fact that questions of meaning and purpose are often asked in the humanities classroom as well as the chaplain's office does not mean that the questions are free from controversy. In the fall semester of 2022, an art history professor at Hamline University in Saint Paul, Minnesota, Erika López Prater, warned students in her online global art history course that she was about to show a painting depicting the Prophet Muhammad, and since some Islamic cultures forbid showing such pictures, she also said that students were free to turn their cameras off. Nevertheless, she wanted to show the painting, she said, because:

> There is this common thinking that Islam completely forbids, outright, any figurative depictions or any depictions of holy personages. While many Islamic cultures do strongly frown on this practice, I would like to remind you there is not one, monothetic Islamic culture.

The painting she then showed was from a work of art commissioned in the 1300s by a Muslim king showing the angel Gabriel revealing the Quran to Muhammad.[7]

In spite of the warning, a student complained about the picture and the Hamline administration sent an email to all university students saying that the class had been "undeniably inconsiderate, disrespectful and Islamophobic." At the end of the term López Prater's contract was not renewed. She was an adjunct with no tenure or contractual protection, and the Hamline president, Fayneese Miller, insisted that "The decision not to offer her another class was made at the unit level and in no way reflects on her ability to adequately teach the class." Given the earlier statement that the class had been "disrespectful and Islamophobic," the president's statement was hard for some to believe.

The failure to retain López Prater evoked a storm of protest from many different people who saw it as trampling on academic freedom and making Hamline look foolish. Out of the 92 full-time members of the Hamline faculty who voted, 71 voted to fire president Miller, who had defended López Prater's firing most strongly. The trustees were also looking into the matter.

University of Pennsylvania professor Jonathan Zimmerman, a thoughtful observer of the dangers of a growing cancel culture in American higher education, argued that there might have been a better response than firing the president:

> What if Hamline used this moment to demonstrate another way? It might start by declaring—in no uncertain terms—that [President] Miller and other officials messed up, in a very big way. . . . Hamline needs to provide a full account of the episode, including all the missteps that occurred. But in the same breath, it could also announce that it is retaining Miller. She is not the sum total of her worst decisions, any more than the rest of us are. That would also strike a more effective blow for free expression than simply sacking her. . . . A chastened Miller will be a much more powerful spokesperson for academic freedom than any of the usual suspects.[8]

Other voices were less willing to forgive the Hamline administration.

The Muslim Public Affairs Council also expressed deep misgivings about what Hamline had done, criticizing the firing of López Prater in no uncertain terms:

> Given the ubiquity of Islamophobic depictions of the Prophet Muhammad, it hardly makes sense to target an art professor trying to combat narrow understandings of Islam. . . . Additionally, misusing the label "Islamophobia" has the negative effect of watering down the term and rendering it less effective in calling out actual acts of bigotry. . . . On the basis of our shared Islamic values, we affirm the need to instill a spirit of free inquiry, critical thinking, and viewpoint diversity in the university setting.

In the end, the president left Hamline. But the case certainly makes it clear that in the 2020s, with matters of religion, as in many other matters, respect for "free inquiry, critical thinking, and viewpoint diversity," is a distant goal in American higher education.

A year after the Hamline imbroglio, a much larger crisis emerged especially for Jewish and Muslim students but also for virtually all students on college campuses across the United States. The October 2023 invasion of the state of Israel by Gaza-based terrorist organization Hamas and the subsequent massive attack by Israel on Gaza—killing thousands of civilians in Gaza, including women and children and aid workers, as well as members of Hamas—led to anger, fear, and recriminations at many colleges.

Large numbers of students, Muslim but also students of many other faiths, including Jews, were horrified by the huge loss of life in Gaza and protests erupted in many places. One need not condone the loss of life in Israel or Gaza to condemn the ongoing killing happening in Gaza. Nevertheless, in American colleges many Jewish students felt threatened or marginalized by the tone of the anti-war protests, and many of those protesting against the war in Gaza were threatened with arrest and suspension from college for their actions, which only made them angrier. Some students saw any criticism of the state of Israel as anti-Semitism, while others saw it as an absolutely essential condemnation of state violence. Some saw any defense of the people of Gaza as a defense of terrorism, while others saw it as defending the lives of the many innocent Palestinians caught up in a horrific situation. Seeing a group of Jewish students celebrating a Passover seder while engaged in a pro-Palestinian protest while some evangelical Christian students enthusiastically support the state of Israel shows how confusing the religious and political lines and alliances on campus are. As this book goes to press, it is too early to know what the long-term fall-out of the hostilities—on American campuses as well as in Israel–Gaza—will be, but it is fairly certain that it will take years if not decades to repair some of the relationships between different groups of American students and their teachers and school administrators that have been fractured by the war.

Johns Hopkins University president Ronald J. Daniels provoked important conversations with his 2021 book, *What Universities Owe Democracy*. One answer that Daniels offered is that part of what higher education owes democracy, beyond additional courses, are what he calls "habits of reflection and correct action." Skills in reflection and action greatly benefit from the kind of passion that courses, especially those in the humanities, and religious life programs are able to foster. Opportunities for students to talk about values and purposes and current events can unleash new energy for further reflection and further community engagement when they are properly managed.

At the end of 2021, Jennifer Rubin wrote a column in the *Washington Post* in which she investigated the current status of religious values and the democratic dialogue in the United States and found both wanting. What does it mean when people seek a religious exemption from a vaccine that not only protects them but protects their neighbors and people they meet only casually, she asks? What does it mean for politics, but also for religion, when religious people allow politics to turn brutal and hate-filled? If Rubin had written the column two years later, she might also have asked how people of different faiths and perspectives can coexist in a place where brutality—so often fueled by retaliation—seems to run rampant. One must also ask how many of today's college students, undergraduate and graduate, earn their degrees without ever having to think about these issues, or how they might respond when they arise in the society in which they will live their lives—professional and personal.

Students may have strong opinions, and many do, but it is another matter to have done the hard ethical and yes, spiritual, reflection to be able to engage in a meaningful dialogue with those with whom one disagrees. Unless there are opportunities for students to talk about—and learn about—issues of meaning and purpose, and how to talk to students who come to very different conclusions, we can't really talk about democracy. So, Roosevelt Montas wrote "Indeed, the possibility of democracy hinges on the success or failure of liberal education." But in much of American higher education these questions and concerns—this kind of liberal education—is not near the center of the educational action. The questions are often not asked, nor is time to contemplate them often part of college life.[9]

This situation represents a profound critique of the twenty-first-century American university. As the University of North Carolina's Warren Nord reminded us a decade ago, "An educational system that ignores the great existential questions—political, moral, spiritual, religious—is not worthy of respect, indeed, it shouldn't count as educational at all" (see chapter 7).

Too often, the research university focuses only on the professional goals that Nord critiques, academic professional success for the faculty and doctoral students, and a wider range of professional success for the undergraduate students. Professional success across the board is not a bad goal for higher education, but it must not be the only goal. That is the success that recruitment programs promise to those who pay undergraduate and professional school tuition. Nevertheless, in the next decades universities must do more. For most universities in the 2020s and

2030s, the answer to what allows a college education to include "the great existential questions" will not mean a return to an older Christian model of asking and answering those questions. It will also not mean ignoring the world's trauma in favor of a sheltered college experience. The nineteenth-century Moral Philosophy course is not likely to be revived. Neither is William Rainey Harper's vision of the University of Chicago as a school spreading liberal Christianity and offering reform as well as cutting-edge research to the nation. Baylor may thrive in its sphere. But for higher education as a whole, the new answers must serve Buddhists and Baha'is as well as Baptists. They must also serve Jews and Muslims, the spiritual-but-not-religious and the nones, as well as taking seriously the beliefs of the evangelicals and the atheists. And they must create new opportunities for students to engage these all-important issues and teach students the skills to talk, teach, and learn from those with very different perspectives . . . not just to make nice but to have deeply difficult but important conversations that may not yield agreement but must yield new understanding and ways to live together, in college and beyond.[10]

Baylor's leaders may be right that one need not, indeed should not, choose one fork in the road, or another between spiritual values and academic excellence even if many places will think of spiritual values much more broadly than the Texas Baptist school. In the last century, the research university has vastly improved life in the United States and around the world, from new advances in agriculture that allow the world to feed more people than once imagined possible, to developments in psychology and education that help more children and young adults thrive than ever before, to advances in nutrition and in medical science that allow people to live lives twice as long as was normal only a few decades ago. Society would jettison the research university at its peril. Given the life-threatening crises of war, new pandemics, and climate change, a robustly inventive research university is more badly needed than ever.

On the other hand, in the twenty-first-century world, there are other equally pressing questions that need to be addressed—questions about what is living for? How do we ensure a vibrant democracy in which the voices and needs of all citizens, regardless of race, sexuality, religious belief, or no-belief matter? How do we ensure respect for deeply held religious beliefs without silencing the voices of people with other beliefs or none? How do we respond to the spiritual yearnings of so many people without letting religion become the divisive and hate-fueled force it has too often been? Beyond that, while research scientists developed a COVID-19 vaccine with amazing speed in 2020, getting people to care enough, love their neighbors enough, to get the vaccine is an ethical and spiritual matter. Getting people to make the more difficult sacrifices necessary to address the climate crisis is also more than a scientific question. Science has told us what must be done. Having the will to do it is a different order of thinking. Such a step requires the habits of reflection and ethical action that the university is not yet very good at fostering. But humanity will not survive without that new step. Perhaps the place of religion and spirituality, ethics and old-fashioned words like "virtue," "kindness," "forgiveness," and "love" are what is needed for the future of higher education. This will be a much more diverse sense of spirituality, with as many questions as answers, and in many forms and incarnations, including new ones, in the future. Religion, a different and much more inclusive religion, at the American university of the twenty-first century is a more vital matter than it has been in some time.

Notes

Preface

1. John Schmalzbauer and Kathleen A. Mahoney, *The Resilience of Religion in American Higher Education* (Waco, TX: Baylor University Press, 2018), 7.

2. See Arthur Levine and Scott Van Pelt, *The Great Upheaval: Higher Education's Past, Present, and Uncertain Future* (Baltimore: Johns Hopkins University Press, 2021).

3. D. G. Hart, *The University Gets Religion: Religious Studies in American Higher Education* (Baltimore: Johns Hopkins University Press, 1999); James Turner, *Religion Enters the Academy: The Origins of the Scholarly Study of Religion in America* (Athens: University of Georgia Press, 2011); Julie A. Reuben, *The Making of the Modern University: Intellectual Transformation and the Marginalization of Morality* (Chicago: University of Chicago Press, 1996); George M. Marsden, *The Soul of the American University: From Protestant Establishment to Established Nonbelief* (New York: Oxford University Press, 1994); and Marsden's revised work, *The Soul of the American University Revisited: From Protestant to Postsecular* (New York: Oxford University Press, 2021).

4. Schmalzbauer and Mahoney, *The Resilience of Religion*; Andrea L. Turpin, *A New Moral Vision: Gender, Religion, and the Changing Purposes of American Higher Education, 1837–1917* (Ithaca, NY: Cornell University Press, 2016); Jon H. Roberts and James Turner, *The Sacred & the Secular University* (Princeton, NJ: Princeton University Press, 2000); Adam Laats, *The Other School Reformers: Conservative Activism in American Education* (Cambridge, MA: Harvard University Press, 2015) and *Fundamentalist U: Keeping Faith in American Higher Education* (New York: Oxford University Press, 2018); Margaret M. Grubiak, *White Elephants on Campus: The Decline of the University Chapel in America, 1920–1960* (Notre Dame, IN: Notre Dame University Press, 2014); Philip Gleason, *Contending with Modernity: Catholic Higher Education in the Twentieth Century* (New York: Oxford University Press, 1995); William C. Ringenberg, *The Christian College: A History of Protestant Higher Education in America* (Grand Rapids, MI: Baker Academic, 2006).

5. Schmalzbauer and Mahoney, *The Resilience of Religion*, 7.

6. Marsden, *The Soul of the American University Revisited*, 6.

CHAPTER ONE: Religion at the "Old Time College," 1800–1870

1. James B. Reynolds, Samuel H. Fisher, and Henry B. Wright, *Two Centuries of Christian Activity at Yale* (New York: G. P. Putnam's Sons, 1901), 5, 137–42, 152–55. See also Richard J. Purcell, *Connecticut in Transition, 1775–1818* (Middletown, CT: Wesleyan University Press, 1963).

2. Reynolds, Fisher, and Wright, *Two Centuries of Christian Activity*, 145–47.

3. Timothy Dwight, "The Nature and Danger of Infidel Philosophy, Exhibited in Two Discourses, Addressed to the Candidates for the Baccalaureate, in Yale College," September 9, 1797 (New Haven, CT, 1798).

4. Lyman Beecher, *Autobiography* (New York: 1864; reprinted Cambridge: Harvard University Press, 1961), 1:45. See also Jon Butler, Grant Wacker, and Randall Balmer, *Religion in American Life: A Short History* (New York: Oxford University Press, 2003), 182–96.

5. Julie A. Reuben, *The Making of the Modern University: Intellectual Transformation and the Marginalization of Morality* (Chicago: University of Chicago Press, 1996), 3.

6. Yale History Timeline, 1800–1809, Yale University archives, https://guides.library.yale .edu/c.php?g=296074&p=1976330, downloaded February 8, 2023.

7. Julian Sturtevant, *An Autobiography* (New York, 1896), 235–37 in Richard Hofstadter and Wilson Smith, *American Higher Education: A Documentary History* 1:242.

8. Haystack Celebration Collection, MC-27. Williams College Archives & Special Collections. https://archivesspace.williams.edu/repositories/2/resources/95, accessed December 27, 2020. See also Diarmaid MacCilloch, *Christianity: The First Three Thousand Years* (New York: Penguin, 2009), 873–902.

9. Thomas C. Richards, *Samuel J. Mills, Missionary Pathfinder, Pioneer and Promoter* (Boston: Pilgrim Press, 1906, reprinted by Alpha Editions in 2019), 21–35.

10. "The History of the Haystack Prayer Meeting," Board of Global Ministries, United Church of Christ, https://globalministries.org/the_history_of_the_haystack_prayer_meeting, downloaded November 16, 2020. See also Richards, *Samuel J. Mills*, 69–74.

11. "Original Papers in Relation to a Course of Liberal Education" [almost always known simply as "The Yale Report," in Hofstadter and Smith, ed., I:275–291.

12. Reuben, *The Making of the Modern University*, 1–3.

13. For recent scholarship on the Moral Philosophy course, see most of all Reuben, *The Making of the Modern University*, 17–35. See also Bruce Kuklick, *A History of Philosophy in America, 1720–2000* (New York: Oxford University Press, 2003); Elizabeth Flower and Murray G. Murphey, *A History of Philosophy in America*, 2 volumes (New York: Hackett, 1977); Frederick Rudolph, *Curriculum: A History of the Undergraduate Course of Study Since 1636* (San Francisco: Jossey-Bass, 1977).

14. G. Stanley Hall, "Philosophy in the United States," in *Mind* 4, no. 13 (January 1879): 89–105. Downloaded from *JSTOR* on January 29, 2021.

15. Hall, "Philosophy in the United States."

16. Andrew Preston Peabody, *A Manuel of Moral Philosophy: Designed for Colleges and High Schools* (New York: A. S. Barnes, 1873), advertisement and pp. 41–60.

17. Noah Porter, *The Human Intellect with an Introduction upon Psychology and the Soul* (New York: Charles Scribner's Sons, 1883), see especially pp. 634–35, 657, 660.

18. Asa Mahan, *A System of Intellectual Philosophy* (New York: A. S. Barnes, 1854); William A. Smith, *Lectures on the Philosophy and Practice of Slavery* (Nashville, TN: Stevenson and Evans, 1856).

19. George M. Marsden, *The Soul of the American University: From Protestant Establishment to Established Nonbelief* (New York: Oxford University Press, 1994), 81–82 and 157–60. For Gilman quote, see Daniel Coit Gilman, "The Johns Hopkins University in Its Beginnings," in *University Problems in the United States* (New York, 1898), 39.

20. See, for example, Louis P. Pojman and Lewis Vaughn, *The Moral Life: An Introductory Reader in Ethics and Literature*, 4th ed. (New York: Oxford University Press, 2011) or Daniel R. DeNicola, *Moral Philosophy: A Contemporary Introduction* (Peterborough, Canada: Broadview Press, 2018).

21. Note: Much of the material on Randolph-Macon College is taken from my earlier

Schooling the Preachers: The Development of Protestant Theological Education in the United States, 1740–1875 (Lanham, MD: University Press of America, 1988). For further analysis of Randolph-Macon and similar schools, see that volume.

22. Peter Cartwright, *Autobiography* (New York: Carlton and Porter, 1857), 79.

23. "Address, To the Members and Friends of the Methodist Episcopal Church," January 13, 1825, printed copy, Walter Hines Page Library, Randolph-Macon College, Ashland, Virginia.

24. Gabriel P. Disosway to "Dear Bro. Early," Petersburg, January 17, 1835, handwritten Ms Walter Hines Page Library, Randolph-Macon College; Stephen Olin to the Rev. Mr. Landon, Leicester, September 4, 1834, in Stephen Olin, *The Life and Letters of Stephen Olin*, 2 vols. (New York: Harper & Brothers, 1853), vol. 1, 182.

25. Olin, *Life and Letters*, vol. II, 84–85.

26. W. H. Moore, "An Historical Oration on the Life and Labors of Rev. Hezekiah G. Leigh," December 8, 1896, printed pamphlet in the Walter Hines Page Library, Randolph-Macon College.

27. "History of Randolph-Macon," www.rmc.edu/about/history, downloaded November 23, 2020; advertisement for Randolph-Macon College, *The North-Carolina Standard*, Raleigh, January 1, 1845, downloaded Randolph-Macon College Library, January 10, 2021.

28. Daniel Boorstein, *The Americans: The National Experience* (New York: Vintage, 1967), 152–60.

29. George F. Pierce, "Church Colleges," an address delivered in Oxford, Georgia, February 22, 1852, on the occasion of the laying of the cornerstone of a new college building, in *Bishop Pierce's Sermons and Addresses*, ed. Atticus G. Haygood (Nashville, TN: Southern Methodist Publishing House, 1886), 41.

30. "S. Olin to G. F. Pierce, Randolph-Macon College," December 7, 1835, in George G. Smith, *The Life and Times of George Foster Pierce* (Sparta, GA: Hancock Publishing, 1888), 79.

31. Pierce, "Church Colleges."

32. Donald G. Tewksbury, *The Founding of American Colleges and Universities before the Civil War* (New York: Bureau of Publications, Teachers College, Columbia University, 1932), 102.

33. Sturtevant, *An Autobiography* (New York, 1896), 181–89 in Hofstadter and Smith, *American Higher Education: A Documentary History*, vol. I, 240–41.

34. *Journal of the General Conference of the Methodist Episcopal Church for 1840* (New York: Carlton & Phillips, 1856), 163. See Richard Hoftstadter, *Academic Freedom in the Age of the College* (New York: Columbia University Press, 1955), 209–21.

35. Advertisement for Randolph-Macon College, *The North-Carolina Standard*, Raleigh, January 1, 1845, downloaded Randolph-Macon College Library, January 10, 2021.

36. Olin, *Life and Letters*, vol. I, 49–50.

37. Fredrick A. Norwood, *The Story of American Methodism* (Nashville, TN: Abington Press, 1974), 185–209. See also Charles Elliott, *History of the Great Secession from the Methodist Episcopal Church in the Year 1845: Eventuating in the Organization of the New Church, Entitled the Methodist Episcopal Church, South* (Cincinnati, OH: Swormstadt & Poe, 1855).

38. William A. Smith, *Lectures on the Philosophy and Practice of Slavery* (Nashville, TN: Stevenson and Evans, 1856), 11–12, 231.

39. H. B. Stanton and George Whipple to Charles G. Finney, Cumminville, Ohio, January 10, 1835. Document #1151, Finney papers, Oberlin College Archives, Oberlin, Ohio; "A Statement of the Reasons Which Induced the Students of Lane Seminary to Dissolve Their Connection with That Institution," December 15, 1834 (Cincinnati, 1834).

40. *The First Annual Report of the Oberlin Collegiate Institute* (Elyria, OH, November 1834), p. 5; Robert Samuel Fletcher, *A History of Oberlin College from Its Founding through the Civil War* (Oberlin, OH: Oberlin College, 1943).

41. Geoffrey Blodgett, *Oberlin History: Essays ad Impressions* (Kent, OH: Kent State University Press, 2006), 12–13.

42. Bertram Wyatt-Brown, *Lewis Tappan and the Evangelical War Against Slavery* (Cleveland, OH: Case Western Reserve University Press, 1969), 128–29; Charles G. Finney, *Memoirs* (New York, 1876), 332–333; Gilbert H. Barnes, *The Antislavery Impulse, 1830–1844* (New York, 1933, 1964), 7–77; Fletcher, *A History of Oberlin College*; Blodgett, *Oberlin History*, 14–18.

43. www.oberlin.edu/about-oberlin/oberlin-history, downloaded January 15, 2021.

44. Fletcher, *A History of Oberlin College*, vol. II, 576, 688, and 889–93.

45. William A. Westervelt, Lecture Note, handwritten manuscript file 30/120, Oberlin College Archives, notes probably taken around 1845, p. 2.

46. Fletcher, *A History of Oberlin College*, vol. II, 893.

47. Fletcher, *A History of Oberlin College*, vol. I, 115 and 232, vol. II, 507.

48. Fletcher, *A History of Oberlin College*, vol. II, 507–11.

49. Fletcher, *A History of Oberlin College*, vol. II, 511–13.

50. Fletcher, *A History of Oberlin College*, vol. II, 532–33. See also my *By the People: A History of the United States* (New York: Pearson, 2nd ed., 2019), 373–74.

51. Fletcher, *A History of Oberlin College*, vol. II, 515–16, 525, 533.

52. Oberlin *Evangelist*, September 10, 1851, cited in Fletcher, *A History of Oberlin College*, vol. I, 208.

53. Fletcher, *A History of Oberlin College*, vol. I, 209, 212.

54. Fletcher, *A History of Oberlin College*, vol. I, 209 and vol. II, 694–700.

55. Fletcher, *A History of Oberlin College*, vol. II, 688, 700–703. See also Asa Mahan, *A System of Intellectual Philosophy* (New York: A. S. Bares, 1854) and James Fairchild, *Moral Science; or, The Philosophy of Obligation* (New York: Sheldon & Co., 1892).

56. H. Tracy Schier, "History of Higher Education for Women at Saint Mary-of-the-Woods: 1840–1980" (unpublished doctoral dissertation, Boston College, 1987), 38–46.

57. Herman Joseph Alerding, *A History of the Catholic Church in the Diocese of Vincennes* (Indianapolis, IN: Carlon & Hollenbeck, 1883), 121–22, 573–77; Schier, "History of Higher Education for Women," 38–40; Mary Theodosia Mug, ed., *Journals and Letter of Mother Theodore Guerin* (Saint Mary-of-the-Woods College, 2005, originally printed 1937), xx; "Sister Mary, Superior General to Sister Theodore June 16, 1840," in *Life and Life-Work of Mother Theodore Guerin*, ed. Mary Theodosia Mug (New York: Benziger Brothers, 1904), 102–3. Note: The seat of the diocese of Vincennes was moved in 1898 when it became the Archdiocese of Indianapolis.

58. Alerding, *A History of the Catholic Church*, 578–86; Schier, "History of Higher Education for Women," 49–62.

59. Alerding, *A History of the Catholic Church*, 585–86; Schier, "History of Higher Education for Women," 61.

60. "Mother Theodore Guerin to the Most Reverend J. B. Bouvier, Bishop of Le Mans, August 22, 1842," in Mary Theodosia Mug, ed., *Journals and Letter of Mother Theodore Guerin*, 83.

61. Mary Theodosia Mug, ed., *Journals and Letter of Mother Theodore Guerin*, 192–222.

62. Alerding, *A History of the Catholic Church*, 586.

63. "Prospectus of St. Mary's Literary Institute, Vigo County, Indiana, 1865," p. 8, from the archives of Sisters of Providence. I am deeply grateful to Sister Janet Gilligan of the Sisters of Providence Archives who took the time to copy this prospectus and other materials from St. Mary's at a time when the COVID-19 pandemic made travel to archives impossible.

64. Julie A. Reuben, *The Making of the Modern University: Intellectual Transformation and the Marginalization of Morality* (Chicago: University of Chicago Press, 1996), 1–3.

65. "Prospectus," 9.

66. Sister Mary Borromeo Brown, *History of the Sisters of Providence of Saint Mary-of-the-Woods* (Chicago: Benziger, 1949), vol. I, 518.

67. "Prospectus," 5; Brown, *History of the Sisters of Providence*, 517.

68. Brown, *History of the Sisters of Providence*, 517–518.

69. Brown, *History of the Sisters of Providence*, 521.

70. "Mother Theodore Guerin to the Right Reverend J. Bouvier, Bishop of Le Mans, July 10, 1850," in *Journals and Letter of Mother Theodore Guerin*, ed. Mary Theodosia Mug, 297–98.

71. "Guerin to Bouvier," July 10, 1850, p. 298 and "Guerin to Bouvier," December 18, 1850, pp. 302–3.

72. Robert T. Handy, *A History of the Churches in the United States and Canada* (New York: Oxford University Press, 1976), 156.

73. Daniel A. Payne, *Recollections of Seventy Years* (Nashville, TN: Publishing House of the AME Sunday School Union, 1888), 162.

74. Frederick A. McGinnis, *A History and an Interpretation of Wilberforce University* (Blanchester, OH: Brown Publishing Company, 1941), 36. (The now very dated McGinnis study appears to be a doctoral dissertation written at the University of Cincinnati. It is, however, a goldmine of information especially since McGinnis had access to the Wilberforce archives and quotes extensively from early reports and trustee minutes that are not accessible now.) Yolanda Pierce, cited in Henry Louis Gates Jr., *The Black Church: This Is Our Story, This Is Our Song* (New York: Penguin Press, 2021), 85. See also Yolanda Pierce, *Hell without Fires: Slavery, Christianity, and the Antebellum Spiritual Narrative*, Yolanda Pierce, *History of African-American Religions* (Gainesville: University Press of Florida, 2005), and Yolanda Pierce, *In My Grandmother's House: Black Women, Faith, and the Stories* (Minneapolis, MN: Broadleaf Books, 2021).

75. McGinnis, *A History and an Interpretation*, 29.

76. See Payne, *Recollections*, 112–15, 161–63; McGinnis, *A History and an Interpretation*, 29, 194–95; Gates, *The Black Church*, 85.

77. McGinnis, *A History and an Interpretation*, 22–36.

78. McGinnis, *A History and An Interpretation*, 37–41, 194; Payne, *Recollections*, 114; Horace Talbert, *The Sons of Allen* (Xenia, OH: Aldine Press, 1906), 268–69.

79. William A. Smith, *Lectures on the Philosophy and Practice of Slavery* (Nashville, TN: Stevenson and Evans, 1856), 11–12, 231.

80. "Articles of Association—Wilberforce University," in McGinnis, *A History and an Interpretation*, 210.

81. For details of Payne's life see his *Recollections* and also Nelson T. Strobert, *Daniel Alexander Payne* (Lanham, MD: University Press of America, 2012).

82. Payne, *Recollections*, 164–65.

83. Payne, *Recollections*, 152–53, 158; Strobert, *Daniel Alexander Payne*, 101.

84. Payne, *Recollections*, 113, 163–66.

85. McGinnis, *A History and an Interpretation*, 46–47; Talbert, *The Sons of Allen*, 268.

86. "Minutes of the Meeting of the General Faculty, January 19, 1888," cited in McGinnis, *A History and an Interpretation*, 164; Payne, *Recollections*, 156.

87. McGinnis, *A History and an Interpretation*, 45–47, 58–59, 164, 173, 194.

88. "Richard Harvey Cain, 1825–1887," in *Biographical Directory of the United States Congress*, https://history.house.gov/People/Detail Downloaded February 20,2021. See also Henry Louis Gates, Jr., *The Black Church: This Is Our Story, This Is Our Song* (New York: Penguin Press, 2021), pp 79, 81–82, 93–95 and also Reginald F. Hildebrand, *The Times Were Strange and Stirring: Methodist Preachers and the Crisis of Emancipation* (Durham, NC: Duke University Press, 1995), 50, 55.

89. Hallie Q. Brown, "Discussion," in *The World's Congress of Representative Women*, ed. May Wright Sewall (Chicago: Rand, McNally & Company, 1894), 726; "Hallie Quinn Brown," in *Women's Work: An Anthology of African American Women's Historical Writing from Antebellum America to the Harlem Renaissance*, ed., Laurie F. Maffly-Kipp and Kathryn Lofton (New York: Oxford University Press, 2010), 218–19; "Hallie Quinn Brown," *Encyclopedia Britannica*, downloaded from www.britannica.com/biography, February 21, 2021; "Hallie Quinn Brown," https://library.arlingtonva.us, downloaded February 21, 2021; Hazel V. Carby, *Reconstructing Womanhood: The Emergence of the Afro-American Woman Novelist* (New York: Oxford University Press, 1987), 3–4; Hallie Quinn Brown, *Homespun Heroines and Other Women of Distinction* (Xenia, OH: Aldine Publishing 1926); Payne, *Recollections*, 163.

CHAPTER TWO: From Moral Philosophy to a Research University, 1870–1905

1. Diarmaid MacCulloch, *Christianity: The First Three Thousand* Years (New York: Penguin Books, 2011), 856–57.

2. Charles Darwin to Asa Gray, May 22, 1860, cited in Edward J. Larson, *Summer for the Gods: The Scopes Trial and America's Continuing Debate over Science and Religion* (New York: Basic Books, 1997), 17.

3. Asa Gray, *The Elements of Botany for Beginners and Schools* (New York: Ivison, 1887), 177, cited in Larson, *Summer for the Gods*, 23.

4. A. Hunter Dupree, *Asa Gray: American Botanist, Friend of Darwin* (Baltimore: Johns Hopkins University Press, 1988, originally 1959); Larson, *Summer for the Gods*, 21.

5. Martin E. Marty, *Modern American Religion, Volume 1: The Irony of It All, 1893–1919* (Chicago: University of Chicago Press, 1986), 36–39; B. B. Warfield, *Biblical and Theological Studies* (New York: Scribner's, 1911), 238, cited in Larson, *Summer for the Gods*, 20.

6. See Andrew Dickson White, *History of the Warfare of Science with Theology in Christendom*, 2 vols. (London: Macmillan, 1896); Gary Ferngren, ed., *Science & Religion: A Historical Introduction* (Baltimore: Johns Hopkins University Press, 2002); Larson, *Summer for the Gods*, 21–22.

7. Larson, *Summer for the Gods*, 24; Thomas D. Snyder, ed., *120 Years of American Education: A Statistical Portrait* (Washington, DC: National Center for Education Statistics, 1993), 75.

8. MacCulloch, *Christianity*, 858–60; William R. Hutchison, *The Modernist Impulse in American Protestantism* (Durham, NC: Duke University Press, 1992), 76–77.

9. For a careful examination of the complex relationships of German and American higher education, see Emily J. Levine, *Allies and Rivals: German-American Exchange and the Rise of the Modern Research University* (Chicago: University of Chicago Press, 2021) and Arthur Levine and Scott Van Pelt, *The Great Upheaval: Higher Education's Past, Present, and Uncertain Future* (Baltimore: Johns Hopkins University Press, 2021).

10. Marty, *Modern American Religion, Volume 1*, 38.

11. Hutchison, *The Modernist Impulse*, 76–90. See also Marty, *Modern American Religion, Volume 1*, 37–40 and Jerry Wayne Brown, *The Rise of Biblical Criticism in America, 1800–1870: The New England Scholars* (Middletown, CT: Wesleyan University Press, 1969).

12. See E. Levine, *Allies & Rivals*, 12; A. Levine and Van Pelt, *The Great Upheaval*.

13. See Roger L. Geiger, *A History of American Higher Education: Learning and Culture from the Founding to World War II* (Princeton, NJ: Princeton University Press, 2015), 326–48. See also Laurence R. Veysey, *The Emergence of the American University* (Chicago: University of Chicago Press, 1965), 121–79. While Veysey outlined this story in the 1960s, more recent scholars like Roger Geiger and John Thelin have dramatically expanded it and added important complexity. Nevertheless, the scholarship of the rise of the research university continues the same basic story line.

14. George M. Marsden, "Introduction," in *The Secularization of the Academy*, ed. George M. Marsden and Bradley J. Longfield (New York: Oxford University Press, 1992), 5, 7.

15. George M. Marsden, "Introduction."

16. See, for example, John R. Thelin, *A History of American Higher Education*, 2nd ed. (Baltimore: Johns Hopkins University Press, 2011), 110–54.

17. D. G. Hart, *The University Gets Religion: Religious Studies in American Higher Education* (Baltimore: Johns Hopkins University Press, 1999), 21.

18. Vineet Chander, "Hindus in Higher Education" (EdD dissertation, New York University, 2023).

19. George M. Marsden, *The Soul of the American University: From Protestant Establishment to Established Nonbelief* (New York: Oxford University Press, 1994), 281–87; John Schmalzbauer and Kathleen A. Mahoney, *The Resilience of Religion in American Higher Education* (Waco, TX: Baylor University Press, 2018), 61–62.

20. Orrin Leslie Elliott, *Stanford University: The First Twenty-Five Years* (Stanford, CA: Stanford University Press, 1937), 137–41.

21. Clarence Prouty Shedd, *The Church Follows Its Students* (New Haven, CT: Yale University Press, 1938), 9; Julie A. Reuben, *The Making of the Modern University: Intellectual Transformation and the Marginalization of Morality* (Chicago: University of Chicago Press, 1996), 121.

22. Reuben, *The Making of the Modern University*, 209–212; See also Abram W. Harris, "The College Chapel," *Religious Education* 1:6, 228–36.

23. Merrimon Cuninggim and Luther A. Weigle, *The College Seeks Religion*, Yale Studies in Religious Education, vol. 20 (New Haven, CT: Yale University Press, 1947), 133–34; W. R. Harper to F. T Gates, October 10, 1892, Correspondence of J. D. Rockefeller and Associates; cited in Reuben, *The Making of the Modern University*, 121; Marsden, *The Soul of the American University*, 246.

24. Margaret M. Grubiak, *White Elephant on Campus: The Decline of the University Chapel in America, 1920–1960* (Notre Dame, IN: University of Notre Dame Press, 2014), specifically pp. 2 and 41. Reuben, *The Making of the Modern University*, 123–24; Marsden, *The Soul of the American University*, 246.

25. David P. Setran, *The College "Y": Student Religion in the Era of Secularization* (New York: Palgrave Macmillan, 2007), 32–34.

26. Setran, *The College "Y"*, 13–19; Mary S. Sims, *The Natural History of a Social Institution— The Y.W.C.A.* (New York: The Woman's Press, 1936). See also Amanda L. Izzo, *Liberal Christianity and Women's Global Activism: The YMCA of the USA and the Maryknoll Sisters* (New Brunswick, NJ: Rutgers University Press, 2018). While long out of date and out of print, Sims's book is a detailed history of the early development of the YWCA, including its work with women college students. Izzo's also provides significant insight but neither has a primary focus—as does Setran—on college students. Hopefully such a book will be written in the near future.

27. Sims, *The Natural History of a Social Institution*, 23–24.

28. C. Howard Hopkins, *A History of the YMCA in North America* (New York: Association Press, 1951), 273–74, cited in Setran, *The College "Y"*, 20–23.

29. Sims, *The Natural History of a Social Institution*, 60; Izzo, *Liberal Christianity and Women's Global Activism*, 103–4 and 93, citing Elizabeth Dilling, *Should Christians Support the Y's?* (Chicago: Patriotic Research Bureau, 1938), 1–3.

30. Setran, *The College "Y"*, 36–37, 138–39.

31. Peter Dobkin Hall, "The Civic Engagement Tradition," in *Taking Faith Seriously*, ed. Mary Jo Bane, Brent Coffin, and Richard Higgins (Cambridge, MA: Harvard University Press, 2005); Setran, *The College "Y"*, 3–22; Izzo, *Liberal Christianity and Women's Global Activism*, 19–20.

32. Setran, *The College "Y"*, 1–9, 62–64; Sims, *The Natural History of a Social Institution*, 48, 54.

33. Setran, *The College "Y"*, 94–95; *Two Centuries of Christian Activity at Yale*, 154–56; Sims, *The Natural History of a Social Institution*, 242.

34. Sims, *The Natural History of a Social Institution*, 37.

35. John Whitney Evans, *The Newman Movement: Roman Catholics in American Higher Education, 1883–1971* (Notre Dame, IN: University of Notre Dame Press, 1980), 10.

36. Setran, *The College "Y"*, 156–59.

37. Cuninggim and Weigle, *The College Seeks Religion*, 13. For perhaps the best overview studies of the changing place of religion in the late nineteenth- and early twentieth-century colleges, see George M. Marsden, *The Soul of the American University*, and Julie A. Reuben, *The Making of the Modern University*.

38. For more on college efforts to take on and provide more student services, see Gwendolyn Dungy and Stephanie A. Gordon, "The Development of Student Affairs," in *Student Services*, ed. John H. Schuh, Susan R. Jones, and Shaun R. Harper (San Francisco: Jossey-Bass, 2011), 63–79.

39. Setran, *The College "Y"*, 159–67.

40. Setran, *The College "Y"*, 167–76.

41. Setran, *The College "Y"*, 159–76.

42. Shedd, *The Church Follows Its Students*, 11.

43. Samuel Earp, "Hobart Hall at the University of Michigan," *The Church Review and Ecclesiastical Register*, vol. LIII (April 1889), 317–20.

44. Edna Cumming French and James Leslie French, *The Pioneer Years of the University Pastorate* (Synod of Michigan of the Presbyterian Church, U.S.A., 1959), 6–9.

45. Alexander Winchell, "The Wesleyan Guild at the University of Michigan" (Ann Arbor?, 1890?) pamphlet in the Bentley Historical Library, University of Michigan, Ann Arbor, Michigan.

46. Shedd, *The Church Follows Its Students*, 11–12.

47. John Whitney Evans, "The Newman Idea in Wisconsin, 1883–1920," *The Wisconsin Magazine of History* 54, no. 3 (Spring 1971): 204–19.

48. Edward P. Robertson, "The Affiliated College," *Religious Education* 1, no. 6: 226–27.

49. See my *Between Church and State: Religion and Public Education in a Multicultural America*, 2nd ed. (Baltimore: Johns Hopkins University Press, 2016), especially pp. 56–58. See also Steve Greene, *The Second Disestablishment: Church and State in Nineteenth Century America* (New York: Oxford University Press, 2010), 296.

50. Robertson, "The Affiliated College," 226–27. Shedd, *The Church Follows Its Students*, 21.

51. W. C. Payne, "The Opportunity of the University Pastor in a Semi-Official Bible Chair," in *Church Work in State Universities: 1909–1910 Report of the Third annual Conference of Church Workers in State Universities*, ed. Charles Josiah Galpin, held at the University of Wisconsin, Madison, February 15– 17, 1910 (Madison, WI, May 1910), 50.

52. Anna R. Atwater, "Sixth Annual Meeting Council of Church Workers," *Religious Education* 8 (1914): 171; Hart, *The University Gets Religion*, 76–77; Shedd, *The Church Follows Its Students*, 25–27, 105.

53. Wallace N. Stearns, "Report of the Committee of Six," *Religious Education* 1, no. 6, 201–25.

54. Sterns, "Report of the Committee of Six," 219.

55. Sterns, "Report of the Committee of Six," 205–8.

56. Joseph W. Cochran, *Religious Education* 5 (1910–1911), 120–21, cited in Shedd, *The Church Follows Its Students*, 10.

57. Joseph W. Cochran, "Preparation for Leadership," *Religious Education* 5 (1911), 123–24.

58. Joseph W. Cochran, "Preparation for Leadership," *Religious Education* 5:2 (1910), 116–23. See also Cochran, "State Universities and the Religious Denominations," *Religious Education* 4, no. 2 (1909), 166–178.

59. For a thorough review of the Briggs trial and its outcome, see Robert T. Handy, *A History of Union Theological Seminary in New York* (New York: Columbia University Press, 1987), 69–93, from which this account is taken. Both critical quotations are from Marty, *Modern American Religion, Volume 1*, 42.

60. Handy, *A History of Union Theological Seminary*, 69–93. Critical quotations on pp. 71–72, 75, and 91.

61. Stanley N. Gundry, *Christian History*, no. 25, 1990.

62. Handy, *A History of Union Theological Seminary*, 1, 47, 82.

63. Handy, *A History of Union Theological Seminary*, chap. 5, "Liberal Evangelicalism Faces Twentieth-Century Realities (1894–1908)," 95–120.

64. Henry Tatiyopa to Alice Mary Longfellow, December 14, 1897. Box 3, Folder 24. Della Stodghill to Alice Mary Longfellow, n.d. Box 3, Folder 26. Alice Mary Longfellow (1850–1928) Papers (LONG 16173, Longfellow House-Washington's Headquarters National Historic Site, Radcliffe College, Cambridge, MA. Alice Longfellow was the daughter of poet Henry Wadsworth Longfellow and a benefactor to many different initiatives and one of the founders of Radcliffe College; Augusta Rust to Emily Howland, February 12, 1912 [Reel 8] Emily Howland papers #2681 [Microform]. Division of Rare and Manuscript Collections, Cornell University Library, Ithica, NY. Emily Howland was a Quaker suffragist-abolitionist educator who was one of the many women who after the Civil War went South to teach newly freed African American students. Returning North in 1880, she continued to support education and advocated for women's rights until her death at the age of 101 in 1929. I am especially grateful to Troy Smith, who generously shared his rich archival collection on Hampton Institute with me.

65. David P. Setran, *The College "Y"*, 20, 36–37, 231–37, 294 footnote 36; Sims, *The Natural History of a Social Institution*, 205–6.

66. Adam Hochschild, *King Leopold's Ghost: A Story of Greed, Terror, and Heroism in Colonial Africa* (Boston: Houghton Mifflin, 1998), 259–265, quotation from the *Kassai Herald*, published by the American Presbyterian missionaries for supporters in the United States, January 1908, on p. 261.

67. Larryetta M. Schall, "William H. Sheppard: Fighter for Africa Rights," in *Stony the Road: Chapters in the History of Hampton Institute*, ed. Keith L. Schall (Charlottesville: University Press of Virginia, 1977), 119–120.

68. The above paragraphs are based primarily on the Hampton University website, "History," https://hampton.edu/about/history.cfm, downloaded March 16, 2021. For further discussions of the complex history of Hampton, see John R. Thelin, *A History of American Higher Education* (Baltimore: Johns Hopkins University Press, 2011), 102–3. For a masterful but critical look at Hampton, see James Anderson, *The Education of Blacks in the South, 1860–1935* (Chapel Hill: University of North Carolina Press, 1988). For more recent books that paint a more complex picture, see Eric Anderson and Alfred A. Moss Jr., *Dangerous Donations: Northern Philanthropy and Southern Black Education, 1902–1930* (Columbia: University of Missouri Press, 1999) and Joan Malczewski, *Building a New Educational State: Foundations, Schools, and the American South* (Chicago: University of Chicago Press, 2016).

69. William H. Robinson, "Indian Education at Hampton Institute," chap. 1 in Schall, *Stony the Road*, 1–33, quotation, p. 9. Robinson says the Indians came to Hampton from Fort Marion in Florida rather than Fort Sill, Oklahoma, but in any case, the prisoners arrived at Hampton

in 1878. Later Native Americans were recruited to the school by Armstrong or other Hampton agents, but the federal government always paid the costs.

70. Troy Smith, "Not Just the Raising of Money: Hampton Institute and Relationship Fundraising, 1893–1917," *History of Education Quarterly* 61, no. 1 (2020): 1–31; Charles D. Walters, "Projections, Projects, and Finance: The Letters of Hollis Burke Frissell," in Schall, *Stony the Road*, 51–62.

71. Harper to Rockefeller, January 8, 1891, University of Chicago Founders' Correspondence, Box 2, folder 1, Special Collections, University of Chicago Library, cited in John W. Boyer, *The University of Chicago: A History* (Chicago: University of Chicago Press, 2015), 493, footnote 241.

72. Boyer, *The University of Chicago*, 48–57.

73. These paragraphs on the early University of Chicago are based on Boyer, *The University of Chicago*, chap. 1, 5–65.

74. Boyer, *The University of Chicago*, 52–65.

75. See, for example, Grady C. Cothen and James M. Dunn, *Soul Freedom: Baptist Battle Cry* (Macon, GA: Smyth and Helwys, 2018).

76. Boyer, *The University of Chicago*, 72, 496, footnote 29.

77. Boyer, *The University of Chicago*, 67–73; "if this is your Bible" quote on p. 72 and p. 496 footnote 28 from an editorial in *Old and New Testament Student*, July 1889, 2.

78. *Chicago Tribune*, March 16, 1891, p. 2 cited in Boyer, *The University of Chicago*, 510, footnote 224.

79. William Rainey Harper, "Some Features of an Ideal University," in *Third Annual Meeting of the American Baptist Education Society, Held with the Southern Baptist Convention, Birmingham, Alabama, May 8 and 9, 1891* (Chicago, 1891), 49–60, 510, footnote 223.

80. Steven J. Diner, "Department and Discipline: The Department of Sociology at the University of Chicago, 1892–1920," *Minerva* 13, no. 4 (Winter 1975), 514–53. Most of the material in the paragraphs on sociology is taken from this article, though the conclusions are my own. I am deeply grateful to Professor Diner for extended conversations about these issues.

81. I am arguing here to some extent with a scholar whom I greatly respect, Julie Reuben. Reuben is not wrong in her focus on the marginalization of morality and its religious inspiration, but the emphasis on secularization or the marginalization misses an important role that religion itself played in the development of the new research university. See Reuben, *The Making of the Modern University*.

CHAPTER THREE: Chaplains, Professors, and Their Students, 1905–1925

1. J. Leslie French, "Historical Statement of the Conference of Church Workers in Universities and Colleges of the United States," in *Religion in Higher Education*, ed. Milton Carley Towner (Chicago: University of Chicago Press, 1931), 252; Clarence Prouty Shedd, *The Church Follows Its Students* (New Haven, CT: Yale University Press, 1938), 13–14.

2. John Whitney Evans, "The Newman Idea in Wisconsin, 1883–1920," *The Wisconsin Magazine of History* 54, no. 3 (Spring 1971): 204–219 (see p. 210). See also Evans's article, "Making the Best of a Bad Job? Newman Chaplains between the Code and the Council," *U.S. Catholic Historian* 11, no. 1 (Winter 1993): 35–50.

3. The Baptists actually beat the Presbyterians with the appointment of Rev. Allen Hoben as full-time minister to Baptist students at Michigan in the fall of 1904, but Hoben resigned after two months to lead a church in Detroit and none of his successors stayed long until a permanent Baptist chaplain arrived in 1919. See Edna Cumming French and James Leslie French, *The Pioneer Years of the University* Pastorate (Synod of Michigan of the Presbyterian Church, USA, 1959), 15–16. It is always dangerous for historians to note "firsts." There is often one just before

that. But the French story is much better recorded than that of the early Baptist ministers at Ann Arbor.

4. Charles Josiah Galpin and Richard Henry Edwards, ed., *Church Work in State Universities, 1909–1910*. Report of the Third Annual Conference of Church Workers in State Universities, Madison Wisconsin, May 1910, p. 12.

5. Happily, French left two autobiographical reflections on his call to college chaplaincy and his early work. The first, published twenty-five years after his appointment, was "Historical Statement of the Conference of Church Workers in Universities and Colleges of the United States," chap. 22 in *Religion in Higher Education*, ed. Milton Carsley Towner (Chicago: University of Chicago Press, 1931), 249–263. The second, written on the fiftieth anniversary of his appointment, was a pamphlet written with his wife, Edna Cumming French, *The Pioneer Years of the University Pastorate: With Particular Reference to the Presbyterian Student Work at the University of Michigan* (Ann Arbor: Synod of Michigan of the Presbyterian Church, USA, 1956).

6. Towner, *Religion in Higher Education*, 252.

7. French and French, *The Pioneer Years*, 20.

8. French and French, *The Pioneer Years*, 6–11, 20–22.

9. J. L. French, "Shall a Home, Commodious, But Not Institutional in Character, Be the Center of His Work?," in *Church Work in State Universities, 1909–1910: Report of the Third Annual Conference of Church Workers in State Universities*, ed. Charles Josiah Galpin and Richard Henry Edwards (Madison, WI, May 1910), 47–48.

10. French and French, *The Pioneer Years*, 44–46.

11. Evans, "The Newman Idea in Wisconsin," 204–19.

12. Evans, "The Newman Idea in Wisconsin," 209–10.

13. H. C. Hengell, "The Catholic Mission at the University of Wisconsin," *The Ecclesiastical Review*, XLVII (January 1912): 99.

14. Evans, "The Newman Idea in Wisconsin," 208.

15. Charles Van Hise, "To the Public," March 18, 1907, cited in Evans, "The Newman Idea in Wisconsin."

16. Evans, "The Newman Idea in Wisconsin," 218–219; interview with Margaret Hengell, June 22, 1964, reported in Evans, "The Newman Idea in Wisconsin," 219.

17. See John Whitney Evans, "Making the Best of a Bad Job? Newman Chaplains between the Code and the Council," *U.S. Catholic Historian* 11, no. 1 (Winter 1993): 35–50; Evans, "The Newman Idea in Wisconsin."

18. Shedd, *The Church Follows Its Students*, 14.

19. MacLean, Iowa City, to Cochran, New York, September 28, 1907, in Special Collections, Iowa State university, cited in Evans, "The Newman Idea in Wisconsin," 217.

20. Quoted in Shedd, *The Church Follows Its Students*, 14.

21. French in Towner, *Religion in Higher Education*, 252–53.

22. Shedd, *The Church Follows Its Students*, 14–17.

23. Shedd, *The Church Follows Its Students*, 17–28. It is important to note that dates, like claims to be the "first" chaplain, can be misleading. While some people and groups kept careful records, others relied on memory for surveys taken many years or decades later. What is very clear is that between 1905 and 1910 a number of chaplains representing a wide diversity of Christian faiths began their work across the United States, especially in the Midwest and far West.

24. All material in this paragraph taken from Evans, "Making the Best of a Bad Job?"

25. John Whitney Evans, *The Newman Movement: Roman Catholics in American Higher Education, 1883–1971* (Notre Dame, IN: University of Notre Dame Press, 1980), 33.

26. Joseph W. Cochran, "State Universities and the Religious Denominations," *Religious*

Education 4, no. 2 (1909): 169. Shedd quotes a part of this statement but, as he too-often does, misattributes it to a different article in *Religious Education*.

27. J. Leslie French, "Historical Statement of the Conference of Church Workers in Universities and Colleges of the United States," in Towner, *Religion in Higher Education*, 253.

28. John R. Mott, "A Policy of Co-Operation in Meeting the Religious Needs of State Universities," in *Church Work in State Universities: 1909–1910 Report of the Third Annual Conference of Church Workers in State Universities*, ed. Charles Josiah Galpin, University of Wisconsin, Madison, February 15–17, 1910 (Madison, Wisconsin, May 1910), 58–65.

29. "Discussion: On a Policy of Co-Operation," in Galpin and Edwards, *Church Work in State Universities*, 62–69.

30. Rev. Evan Alexander Edwards, *Spirit of Missions* LXXVII (1913), 692.

31. Editorial, "The Religious Life in Colleges," *The Churchman* XCIV (August 4, 1906), 171.

32. Shedd, *The Church Follows Its Students*, 24–27. See also Ronald Flowers, "The Bible Chair Movement in the Disciples of Christ Tradition: Attempts to Teach Religion in State Universities" (unpublished PhD dissertation, University of Iowa, 1967).

33. Charles R. Van Hise, "President Van Hise Gives Welcome," in Galpin and Edwards, *Church Work in State Universities*, 13–14.

34. Cyrus Northrop, "Religious Instruction in the State University," and George E. MacLean, "The State University of Iowa Plan for Religious Education," *Religious Education* 4, no. 2: 158, 159.

35. J. Leslie French, "Historical Statement of the Conference of Church Workers in Universities and Colleges of the United States," in Towner, *Religion in Higher Education*, 254.

36. J. Leslie French, "Historical Statement of the Conference of Church Workers in Universities and Colleges of the United States," chapter XXII, in Towner, *Religion in Higher Education*, 249–263. See also Gilpin, *Church Work in State Universities*.

37. Joseph Wilson Cochran, "The University Pastorate Movement," *Religious Education* 8, no. 1 (1913): 80

38. David P. Setran, *The College "Y": Student Religion in the Era of Secularization* (New York: Palgrave Macmillan, 2007), 167–183. John Schmalzbauer and Kathleen A. Mahoney, *The Resilience of Religion in American Higher Education* (Waco, TX: Baylor University Press, 2018); Phillip E. Hammond, *The Campus Clergyman* (New York: Basic Books, 1966).

39. Laura H. Wild, "The Equipment of a Department of Biblical Literature," *Religious Education*, 10 (February 1, 1915), 337–45.

40. Julie A. Reuben, *The Making of the Modern University: Intellectual Transformation and the Marginalization of Morality* (Chicago: University of Chicago Press, 1996), 101–18; D. G. Hart, *The University Gets Religion: Religious Studies in American Higher Education* (Baltimore: Johns Hopkins University Press, 1999), 69–73, 80–87.

41. F. Scott Fitzgerald, *This Side of Paradise* (New York: Scribner, 1920), see last page, 147 in my edition.

42. Catharine Stimpson, "Tappan's Truths," in *A Student's Search for Meaning: Reflections on the Intersections of College Chaplaincy, Liberal Arts and the University*, ed. Melissa Cater, James W. Fraser, Chelsea Garbell, and Amy Wilson (London: Ethics International Press, 2023), 67–80; "The University of Michigan," *Encyclopedia Britannica*, January 2021, downloaded April 30, 2021; Andrea L. Turpin, *A New Moral Vision: Gender, Religion, and the Changing Purposes of American Higher Education, 1837–1917* (Ithaca, NY: Cornell University Press, 2016), 92; Henry P. Tappan, "The University; Its Constitution, and its Relations, Political and Religious: A Discourse," speech delivered June 22, 1858 (Ann Arbor, MI: Printed by S. B McCracken, 1858), 7–13, quotation on p. 7.

43. Tappan, "The University," see especially 6, 29, and 34.

44. Harold S. Wechsler, *The Qualified Student: A History of Selective College Admission in America* (New York: Routledge, 2017, originally 1977), 15; Turpin, *A New Moral Vision*, 90–94.

45. James B. Angell, "Religious Life in Our State Universities," *The Andover Review: A Religious and Theological Monthly* XIII, no. LXXVI (April 1890): 365–372.

46. Angell, "Religious Life," 368.

47. C. Grey Austin, *A Century of Religion at the University of Michigan* (Ann Arbor: University of Michigan, 1957), 15–20.

48. Austin, *A Century of Religion*, 21–25.

49. *Michigan Daily*, November 29, 1911, through December 22, 1911, and Austin, *A Century of Religion*, 25–27.

50. Austin, *A Century of Religion*, 28–44.

51. Robert Emmett Curran, *A History of Georgetown University, Volume 1: From Academy to University, 1789–1889* (Washington, DC: Georgetown University Press, 2010), 10–38.

52. Curran, *A History of Georgetown University, Volume 1*, 38–41 and 370.

53. Curran, *A History of Georgetown University, Volume 1*, 44–46. For a detailed discussion of the *Ratio Studiorum* curriculum and the century-long debate about its place in Catholic education in the United States, see Philip Gleason, *Contending with Modernity: Catholic Higher Education in the Twentieth Century* (New York: Oxford University Press, 1995), 5–6, 51–61.

54. Curran, *A History of Georgetown University, Volume 1*, 4–9, 48–54, 61–62.

55. Adelle M. Banks, "History of Slaves Sold for Georgetown Detailed in New Genealogical Website," *National Catholic Reporter*, June 24, 2019; https://www.georgetown.edu/news/george town-continues-support-as-jesuits-descendants-of-enslaved-form-foundation/, downloaded May 31, 2021.

56. For a review of nineteenth-century Georgetown's history, see Curran, *A History of Georgetown University, Volume 1*, and also Joseph T. Durkin, *Georgetown University: The Middle Years, 1840–1900* (Washington, DC: Georgetown University Press, 1963).

57. Willian P. Leahy, *Adapting to America: Catholics, Jesuits, and Higher Education in the Twentieth Century* (Washington, DC: Georgetown University Press, 1991), 1–4.

58. See Kathleen A. Mahoney, *Catholic Higher Education in Protestant America: The Jesuits and Harvard in the Age of the University* (Baltimore: Johns Hopkins University Press, 2003). Mahoney's book is a goldmine of material on the Catholic–Protestant curricular fights that are also referenced, in less detail, in many earlier sources.

59. John Whitney Evans, *The Newman Movement: Roman Catholics in American Higher Education, 1883–1971* (Notre Dame, IN: University of Notre Dame Press, 1980), 32–36; James Howard Plough, "Catholic Colleges and the Catholic Educational Association: The Foundation and Early Years of the CEA, 1889–1919" (unpublished doctoral dissertation, Notre Dame University, 1967), 189–250.

60. The Georgetown battles with the Harvard Law School admission policies are well told often, see especially Robert Emmett Curran, *A History of Georgetown University, Volume 2: The Quest for Excellence* (Washington, DC: Georgetown University Press, 2010), 22–23; Durkin, *Georgetown University*, 191–193; and, of course, the detailed Mahoney, *Catholic Higher Education in Protestant America*.

61. Durkin, *Georgetown University*, 193–194; Curran, *A History of Georgetown University, Volume 2*, 22–23; Gleason, *Contending with Modernity*, 51–54.

62. Plough, "Catholic Colleges and the Catholic Educational Association," ii–vii, 216–223. For the Conway obituary, see Hugh J. Fegan in *Georgetown College Journal* (November 1915), 82. For an overview of the issues discussed in this paper, see Plough, "Catholic Colleges and the Catholic Educational Association," 216–236; John Whitney Evans, *The Newman Movement*, 32–41.

63. Plough, "Catholic Colleges and the Catholic Educational Association," citing a letter from Conway, 220.

64. Evans, *The Newman Movement*, 32–35.

65. Francis B. Cassilly, "Catholic Students at State Universities," *The Ecclesiastical Review* XXXIV, no. 2 (February 1906), 113–20.

66. Austin, *A Century of Religion*, 17; Evans, *The Newman Movement*, 3–31.

67. Hengell, "The Catholic Mission at the University of Wisconsin," 98.

68. Plough, "Catholic Colleges and the Catholic Educational Association," 225–35.

69. Curran, *A History of Georgetown University, Volume 2*, especially pp. 87 and 220, and Curran, *A History of Georgetown University, Volume 3: The Rise to Prominence 1964–1989* (Washington, DC: Georgetown University Press, 2010), especially p. 8.

70. See John E. Riley, *From Sagebrush to Ivy: The Story of Northwest Nazarene College, 1913 to 1988* (Nampa, ID: Nazarene Publishing House, 1988), see especially p. 14.

71. Timothy L. Smith, *Called Unto Holiness: The Story of the Nazarenes: The Formative Years* (Kansas City, MO: Nazarene Publishing House, 1962), 11–26.

72. Smith, *Called Unto Holiness*.

73. See Smith, chap. 1–9, pp. 11–281.

74. *Nampa Leader-Herald*, August 5, 1913, cited in Riley, *From Sagebrush to Ivy*, 48.

75. Riley, *From Sagebrush to Ivy*, 36–45; Robert A. Murphy and Yolanda Murphy, "Northern Shoshone and Bannock," in *Handbook of North American Indians: Great Basin, Volume 11*, ed. Warren L. d'Azevedo (Washington, DC: Smithsonian Institution, 1986) 284–307, downloaded June 3, 2021.

76. Smith, *Called Unto Holiness*, 272–83.

77. Smith, *Called Unto Holiness*, 283–89.

78. Smith, *Called Unto Holiness*, 55, 62.

79. Riley, *From Sagebrush to Ivy*, 44–65.

80. Smith, *Called Unto Holiness*, 288–289; Riley, *From Sagebrush to Ivy*, 225–27.

81. Mary Preston, "Mount Holyoke's Part in Social, Religious and Philanthropic Movements as a College," in *Mount Holyoke College: The Seventy-Fifth Anniversary* (South Hadley, MA: Mount Holyoke College, 1913), 65–70.

82. Fidella Fisk, *Recollections of Mary Lyon with Selections from Her Instructions to the Pupils in Mt. Holyoke Female Seminary* (Boston: American Tract Society, 1866), 98, 115.

83. Fisk, *Recollections of Mary Lyon*, 89, 108–109; Turpin, *A New Moral Vision*, 49–57.

84. Devon A. Mihesuah, *Cultivating the Rosebuds: The Education of Women at the Cherokee Female Seminary, 1851–1909* (Urbana: University of Illinois Press, 1993), 26–32.

85. Andrea L. Turpin, "Memories of Mary: Interpretations of the Founder in the Secularization Process of Mount Holyoke Seminary and College," *Perspectives on the History of Higher Education* 28 (2011): 33–61.

86. Turpin, "Memories of Mary," 40–48.

87. Helen Barnetson Calder, "Mount Holyoke's Part in the Missionary Movement," in *Mount Holyoke College: The Seventy-Fifth Anniversary* (South Hadley MA: Mount Holyoke College, 1913), 71–75; Turpin, "Memories of Mary," 51–53.

88. Louise Porter Thomas, *Seminary Militant: An Account of the Missionary Movement at Mount Holyoke Seminary and College* (Portland, ME: Southworth-Anthoesen Press, 1937), 107, cite in Turpin, "Memories of Mary," 54. See also Turpin, "Memories of Mary," 52–56; https://www.mtholyoke.edu/about/history, downloaded June 9, 2021, and https://www.mtholyoke.edu/student-experience/community-and-belonging/religion-and-spirituality, downloaded March 28, 2023.

CHAPTER FOUR: Campus Religion and the Fracturing of American Religion, 1925–1945

1. Winton U. Solberg, "The Early Years of the Jewish Presence at the University of Illinois," *Religion and American Culture: A Journal of Interpretation* 2, no. 2 (Summer 1992): 215–45, especially 228. The Solberg article is a goldmine of information on the earliest years of Hillel based on wide-ranging unpublished resources. Sadly, there is no scholarly study of Hillel itself, a surprising lack in the history of American higher education and religious life.

2. "Iniquitous Champaign on a Sunday," *Daily Illini*, February 19, 1920, 4; Thomas Arkle Clark, "The Reason for a 'Champaign Sunday,'" *Daily Illini*, February 21, 1920, 4, both cited in Harold S. Wechsler and Steven J. Diner, *Unwelcome Guests: A History of Access to American Higher Education* (Baltimore: Johns Hopkins University Press, 2021), 106.

3. Wechsler and Diner, *Unwelcome Guests*, 227–228.

4. Independent Order of B'nai B'rith, *Proceedings*, Twelfth General Convention, April 20–23, 1925, 28.

5. Lee J. Levinger, "The Jewish Student in America: A Study Made by the Research Bureau of the B'nai B'rith Hillel Foundations," typewritten manuscript issued by B'nai B'rith, 1937, 2; Alfred Jospe, "Jewish College Students in the United States," *The America Jewish Year Book* 65 (1964), The American Jewish Committee, 131–45, see 132–33; https://www.jstor.org/stable /23602980, downloaded December 19, 2020; see also Wechsler and Diner, *Unwelcome Guests*, especially 45–49.

6. Solberg, "The Early Years of the Jewish Presence," 215–26.

7. Solberg, "The Early Years of the Jewish Presence," 217, 229–30. Solberg's otherwise excellent article on the Jewish presence at the University of Illinois is wrong when he says, "In the early twentieth century, the University of Illinois pioneered in encouraging the growth near the campus of religious foundations that provided religious worship and courses in religion for graduation credit." As we saw in chapter 2, Wisconsin's Van Hise was actually the leading exponent of an approach to religion tried in many places that avoided any church–state conflicts and avoided new expense for the universities.

8. David Mislin, "One Nation, Three Faiths: World War I and the Shaping of 'Protestant-Catholic-Jewish' America," *Church History* 84, no. 4 (December 2015): 828–62.

9. Solberg, "The Early Years of the Jewish Presence," 228–31; B'nai B'rith, *Proceedings*, 35. See also Benjamin M. Frankel, "Attracting College Youth to the Synagogue," Central Conference of American Rabbis, *Yearbook* 35 (1925), 326–28.

10. Hillel International History of Hillel, "Hillel Timeline," https://www.hillel.org/about /hillel-story, downloaded June 25, 2021.

11. Independent Order B'nai B'rith, *Proceedings*, Twelfth General Convention, Atlantic City, New Jersey, April 20–23, 1925, 28–31.

12. B'nai B'rith, *Proceedings*, 85–100; Solberg, "The Early Years of the Jewish Presence," 234.

13. Solberg, "The Early Years of the Jewish Presence," 234–37; Abram L. Sachar, *A Host at Last* (Boston: Little, Brown and Company, 1976), 24–25; Edward E. Grusd, "Converting Jews to Judaism," *National Jewish Monthly* (November 1939): 72.

14. Levinger, "The Jewish Student in America," 16, 55.

15. Grusd, "Converting Jews to Judaism," 72–75.

16. Hillel International History of Hillel, "Hillel Timeline."

17. Gilbert Klaperman, *The Story of Yeshiva University: The First Jewish University in America* (New York: Macmillan, 1969), 3

18. Klaperman, *The Story of Yeshiva University*, 17, 48–49, 120, 131, 141, 149–51, 161; see also

the more recent Jeffrey S. Gurock, *The Men and Women of Yeshiva: Higher Education, Orthodoxy, and American Judaism* (New York: Columbia University Press, 1988).

19. Harry Fischel, *Forty Years of Struggle for a Principle* (New York: Bloch Publishing, 1928), 12, cited in Klaperman, *The Story of Yeshiva University*, 7; *Hester Street*, released by Midwest Films, 1975.

20. George M. Marsden, *The Soul of the America University: From Protestant Establishment to Established Nonbelief* (New York: Oxford University Press, 1994), 362–63.

21. David R. Contosta, "The Philadelphia Story: Life at Immaculata, Rosemont, and Chestnut Hill," chap. 6 in *Catholic Women's Colleges in America*, ed. Tracy Schier and Cynthia Russett (Baltimore: Johns Hopkins University Press, 2002), 123–60.

22. Linda Gordon, *The Second Coming of the KKK: The Ku Klux Klan of the 1920s and the America Political Tradition* (New York: W. W. Norton, 2017), 86, 91, 100–104.

23. See Douglas M. Sloan, *Faith & Knowledge: Mainline Protestantism and American Higher Education* (Louisville, KY: Westminster John Know Press, 1994), viii–ix.

24. Adam Laats, *Fundamentalist U: Keeping the Faith in American Higher Education* (New York: Oxford University Press, 2018), 13. The full quotation says the "fundamentalists became the latest and most successful religious leaders." I omitted the "most successful" because it seems to me that Catholics were arguably a more successful hold-out with the modern academic revolution until World War II.

25. Thomas D. Snyder, *120 Years of American Education: A Statistical Portrait* (Washington, DC: National Center for Education Statistics, 1993), 64–66.

26. Robert T. Handy, "The American Religious Depression, 1925–1935," *Church History* 29 (March 1960): 3–16; Marsden, *The Soul of the American University*, 363. See Wechsler and Diner, *Unwelcome Guests.*

27. Paula S. Fass, *The Damned and the Beautiful: American Youth in the 1920s* (New York: Oxford University Press, 1977), 13, 20.

28. S. K. Ratcliffe, "The License of the Youngsters," *Century Magazine* 102 (1921): 392, cited in Fass, *The Damned and the Beautiful*, 43.

29. Katharine Fullerton Gerould, "Reflections of a Grundy Cousin," *Atlantic Monthly* 126 (1920): 158–163. I am grateful to Paula Fass for pointing me to this article.

30. See Marsden, *The Soul of the American University*, 357–358. See also John Whitney Evans, *The Newman Movement: Roman Catholics in American Higher Education, 1883–1971* (Notre Dame, IN: University of Notre Dame Press, 1980). Ironically, there is no major academic study of Hillel, but see Irving Leonard Slade, "An Introductory Survey of Jewish Student Organizations in American Higher Education" (EdD dissertation, Teachers College, Columbia University, 1966).

31. D. G. Hart, *The University Gets Religion: Religious Studies in American Higher Education* (Baltimore: Johns Hopkins University Pess, 1999), 9–101.

32. Paul Ritterband and Harold S. Wechsler, *Jewish Learning in American Universities: The First Century* (Bloomington: Indiana University Press, 1994), 85–91.

33. Robert T. Handy, "The American Religious Depression, 1925–1935," *Church History* 29 (March 1960): 3–16; Will Herberg, *Protestant-Catholic-Jew: An Essay in American Religious Sociology* (Garden City, NY: Doubleday & Co., 1955), 139; Joel A. Carpenter, "Fundamentalist Institutions and the Rise of Evangelical Protestantism, 1929–1942," *Church History* 49 (March 1980): 62–75; Marsden, *The Soul of the American University*, 363. See also Wechsler and Diner, *Unwelcome Guests.*

34. Robert T. Handy, "The American Religious Depression, 1925–1935," *Church History* 29 (March 1960), 3–16; John Schmalzbauer and Kathleen A. Mahoney, *The Resilience of Religion in*

American Higher Education (Waco, TX: Baylor University Press, 2018), see especially pp. 97–110. Snyder, *120 Years of American Education*; Martin E. Marty, *The Noise of Conflict, 1919–1941* (Chicago: University of Chicago Press, 1991), 281–96; Evans, *The Newman Movement*; "Inter-Varsity and IFES History," https://intervarsity.org/about-us/intervarsity-and-ifes-history, downloaded December 28, 2018.

35. L. Gordon Tait, "Evolution: Wishart, Wooster, and William Jennings Bryan," *Journal of Presbyterian History* 62, no. 4 (Winter 1984), 306–21, see especially p. 314.

36. *Memoirs of Charles Frederick Wishart* (typed manuscript in the archives of the College of Wooster), cited in Tait, "Evolution," 308.

37. *Dedication of the University of Wooster, and Inauguration of the President, September 7th, 1870* (Wooster, OH: Republican Steam Book and Job Press, 1870), 18–21, cited in Tait, "Evolution," 308–309. See also, "The College of Wooster," Ohio History Central, https://ohiohistory central.org/w/College_of_Wooster, downloaded June 17, 2021.

38. Horace Nelson Mateer, *Evolution and Christianity* (Wooster, OH: Herald Printing Company, 1905), see especially pp. 1 and 20; "Dr. Mateer, 84, Dies Today at Family Home," *Wooster Daily Record*, Wooster, Ohio, June 10, 1939. I am especially grateful to Denise Monbarren, special collections librarian at the College of Wooster, for her help with this material.

39. Chares F. Wishart, "The Mustard Seed and the Tree," sermon at the Second Presbyterian Church of Chicago, in *The Unwelcome Angel* (Philadelphia: Westminster Press, n.d. [probably around 1919–1920]), 225–26.

40. Lucy Lilian Notestein, *Wooster of the Middle West, Volume Two, 1911–1944* (Kent, OH: Kent State University Press, 1969), 195, 265–67.

41. Tait, "Evolution," 312.

42. Tait, "Evolution," 313. See *The Presbyterian*, April 5, April 19, May 31, and July 26, 1923, for a longer discussion of the issue; Notestein, *Wooster of the Middle West*, 266.

43. *The Daily Illini*, May 26, 1922. See also Fass, *The Damned and the Beautiful*, 358.

44. Notestein, *Wooster of the Middle West*, 201–3, 252–55.

45. "Wooster Adventure in Education," *The College of Wooster Bulletin*, December 1, 1945, https://cdm15963.contentdm.oclc.org/digital/collection/p15963coll17/id/68/rec/131, downloaded January 5, 2022.

46. See College of Wooster website, especially www.wooster.edu/offices/marketing/news -archive/2014/december/safe space, accessed June 25, 2021.

47. Michael S. Hamilton, "The Fundamentalist Harvard: Wheaton College and the Continuing Vitality of American Evangelicalism, 1919–1965" (doctoral dissertation, University of Notre Dame, October 1994), 29. As the following endnotes indicate, the Hamilton dissertation is by far the best source on the history of Wheaton College.

48. See, for example, Jon Barnard, *From Evangelicalism to Progressivism at Oberlin College* (Columbus: Ohio State University, 1969).

49. Hamilton, "The Fundamentalist Harvard," 29–31. See also Laats, *Fundamentalist U*, especially 24–30.

50. Hamilton, "The Fundamentalist Harvard," 30–37.

51. http://wheaton.edu/college-presidents/j—oliver-buswell, downloaded June 19, 2021; Hamilton, "The Fundamentalist Harvard," 30–31, 50–53.

52. Hamilton, "The Fundamentalist Harvard," 84.

53. Hamilton, "The Fundamentalist Harvard," 84–95.

54. Billy Graham, *Just As I Am* (San Francisco: Harper/Zondervan, 1997), 39–41, 62–71.

55. Hamilton, "The Fundamentalist Harvard," 64–78, see Emeline Buswell quotation, p. 70; http://wheaton.edu/college-presidents/j—oliver-buswell, downloaded June 19, 2021.

56. Hamilton, "The Fundamentalist Harvard," 30, 78–83; http://wheaton.edu/about-wheaton /why-wheaton/history, downloaded June 10, 2021; Wheaton College website, wheaton.edu, accessed June 23, 2021.

57. James Riley Montgomery, Stanley J. Folmsbee, and Lee Seifert Greene, *To Foster Knowledge: A History of the University of Tennessee, 1794–1970* (Knoxville: University of Tennessee Press, 1984), 3–5.

58. Montgomery, Folmsbee, and Greene, *To Foster Knowledge*, 7–10.

59. Montgomery, Folmsbee, and Greene, *To Foster Knowledge*, 40–64.

60. Montgomery, Folmsbee, and Greene, *To Foster Knowledge*, 153, 376–77.

61. Montgomery, Folmsbee, and Greene, *To Foster Knowledge*, 65–170.

62. Montgomery, Folmsbee, and Greene, *To Foster Knowledge*, 171–72, 212, 377–79; Fass, *The Damned and the Beautiful*, 45.

63. James W. Gardner, F. H. Hodder, Edward H. Kraus, H. H. Millis, Edward S. Thurston, and H. F. Goodrich, "Report on the University of Tennessee," *Bulletin of the America Association of University Professors* 10, no. 4 (April 1924): 21–69, downloaded June 10, 2021 (hereinafter "AAUP Report"); Montgomery, Folmsbee, and Greene, *To Foster Knowledge*, 186–87.

64. "AAUP Report," 21–28.

65. "AAUP Report," 30, 32, 67.

66. For Bryan quotations and a discussion of the role of religious leaders in the anti-evolution campaign in the above three paragraphs, see Edward J. Larson, *Summer for the Gods: The Scopes Trial and America's Continuing Debate Over Science and Religion* (New York: Basic Books, 1997), 41–48.

67. For background on the Butler Bill in Tennessee, see Edward J. Larson, *Summer for the Gods*, 41–59.

68. There are many accounts of the Scopes Trial, but the best and most thorough is Larson's *Summer for the Gods*.

69. Montgomery, Folmsbee, and Greene, *To Foster Knowledge*, 189.

70. Montgomery, Folmsbee, and Greene, *To Foster Knowledge*, 190–94, 202–12, 228–29, 267–69, 278–79, 392, 397–407; https://www.utk.edu/aboutut/numbers/ and https://news.utk .edu/2019/05/02/a-place-to-belong-ut-campus-ministries/, downloaded July 8, 2021.

71. Mike Wallace, *Greater Gotham: A History of New York City from 1898 to 1919* (New York: Oxford University Press, 2017), 374–75.

72. Wallace, *Greater Gotham*, 374, 375; Irving Howe, *World of Our Fathers: The Journey of East European Jews to America and the Life They Found and Made* (New York: New York University Press, 1976), 280–86.

73. See my *Preparing America's Teachers: A History* (New York: Teachers College Press, 2007), 154–164; see also Katherina Kroo Grunfeld, "Purpose and Ambiguity: The Feminine World of Hunter College, 1869–1945" (EdD dissertation, Teachers College, Columbia University, 1991).

74. Wallace, *Greater Gotham*, 374; Howe, *World of Our Fathers*, 270–71, 281.

75. Harold S. Wechsler, *The Qualified Student: A History of Selective College Admission in America* (New York: Routledge, 1977, 2017), xiv, 139–63.

76. Wallace, *Greater Gotham*, 373–374; Wechsler and Diner, *Unwelcome Guests*, 76.

77. Sydney C. Van Nort, *The City College of New York* (Charleston, SC: Arcadia Publishing, 2007), 47–51; Howe, *World of Our Fathers*, 280–86; Hasia Diner, professor of American Jewish History, personal communication, July 5, 2021.

78. Snyder, *120 Years of American Education*, 65; Wallace, *Greater Gotham*, 374.

79. https://www.cuny.edu/about/history/, downloaded July 10, 2021.

CHAPTER FIVE: A Postwar Boom in Religion and Higher Education, 1945–1960

1. "Jo Ann Gibson Robinson," *King Encyclopedia*, The Martin Luther King, Jr. Research and Education Institute, Stanford University, https://kinginstitute.stanford.edu/encyclopedia /robinson-jo-ann-gibson, downloaded July 21, 2021; "Jo Ann Robinson," *Encyclopedia of Alabama*, http://encyclopediaofalabama.org/article/h-3124?printable-true, downloaded July 21, 2021; Taylor Branch, *Parting the Waters: America in the King Years, 1954–1963* (New York: Simon & Schuster, 1988), 131–36; Jo Ann Gibson Robinson with David J. Garrow, *The Montgomery Bus Boycott and the Women Who Started It: The Memoir of Jo Ann Gibson Robinson* (Knoxville: University of Tennessee Press), 53. There is some debate about whether Robinson or E. D. Nixon of the NAACP first proposed the boycott but, in any case, Robinson's leaflet launched it.

2. "Jo Ann Gibson Robinson," *King Encyclopedia*; "Jo Ann Robinson," *Encyclopedia of Alabama*; Martin Luther King Jr., *Stride toward Freedom* (New York: Harper and Brothers, 1958).

3. Thomas D. Snyder, ed., *120 Years of American Education: A Statistical Portrait* (Washington, DC: National Center for Educational Statistics), 75.

4. If one looks in the index of major histories of American higher education for references to religion, religious studies, or chaplaincy, one will find many for the nineteenth century but virtually none for the post–World War II world. And if one looks at major histories of the religious revival of the 1950s for references to higher education, there are a few references to seminaries but virtually none to undergraduate education or research universities in general. See, for example, Roger L. Geiger, *American Higher Education since World War II: A History* (Princeton, NJ: Princeton University Press, 2019) or John R. Thelin, *A History of American Higher Education* (Baltimore: Johns Hopkins University Press, 2011), or on the other hand Martin E. Marty, *Modern American Religion: Under God Indivisible, 1941–1960* (Chicago: University of Chicago Press, 1996) or Jon Butler, Grant Wacker, and Randall Balmer, *Religion in American Life: A Short History* (New York: Oxford University Press, 2003); Robert S. Ellwood, *The Fifties Spiritual Marketplace: American Religion in a Decade of Conflict* (New Brunswick, NJ: Rutgers University Press, 1997).

5. Thelin, *A History of American Higher Education*, 260–61. See also Richard M. Freeland, *Academia's Golden Age: Universities in Massachusetts, 1945–1970* (New York: Oxford University Press, 1992).

6. Thelin, *A History of American Higher Education*, 262–68. See also Ira Katznelson, *When Affirmative Action Was White: An Untold History of the Racial Inequality in Twentieth Century America* (New York: W. W. Norton, 2006).

7. Thelin, *A History of American Higher Education*, 268–71.

8. Thelin, *A History of American Higher Education*, 277–80; See also Geiger, *American Higher Education*, 75–80, 94–98.

9. Douglas M. Sloan, *Faith and Knowledge: Mainline Protestantism and American Higher Education* (Louisville, KY: Westminster John Knox Press, 1994), 97.

10. Sloan, *Faith and Knowledge*, 97–101.

11. Frederick Houk Borsch, *Keeping Faith at Princeton: A Brief History of Religious Pluralism at Princeton and Other Universities* (Princeton, NJ: Princeton University Press, 2012), 24; Eva Walton Kendrick, "Hodding Carter III," *Mississippi Encyclopedia*, http://mississippiencyclopedia .org/entries/hodding-carter-iii, downloaded August 17, 2021.

12. Billy Graham, *Just as I Am: The Autobiography* (San Francisco: Harper/Zondervan, 1997), 143, 146, 47, 157.

13. Graham, *Just as I Am*, 143–48, 163, 314.

14. Robert D. Putnam and David E. Campbell, *American Grace: How Religion Divides and Unites Us* (New York: Simon & Schuster, 2010), 86; Ellwood, *The Fifties Spiritual Marketplace*, 1–5.

15. Ellwood, *The Fifties Spiritual Marketplace*, 6–9; see also Henry Louis Gates Jr., *The Black Church: This Is Our Story, This Is Our Song* (New York: Penguin Press, 2021), 103–107, 110–15.

16. Ellwood, *The Fifties Spiritual Marketplace*, 10–19.

17. *Time*, March 8, 1948, and March 16, 1959.

18. Ellwood, *The Fifties Spiritual Marketplace*, 9, 11, 56–57. Miller quotation from William Lee Miller, "The 'Religious Revival' and American Politics," in *Piety Along the Potomac: Notes on Politics and Morals in the Fifties* (Boston: Houghton Mifflin, 1964), 125–26, cited on p. 11 in Ellwood, *The Fifties Spiritual Marketplace*.

19. See D. G. Hart, *The University Gets Religion: Religious Studies in American Higher Education* (Baltimore: Johns Hopkins University Press, 1999), 113; Butler, Wacker, and Balmer, *Religion in American Life*, 374, 380.

20. For much more on the "search for normalcy," in these years, see David Halberstam, *The Fifties* (New York: Random House 1993); Elaine Tyler May, *Homeward Bound: American Families in the Cold War Era*, rev. ed. (New York: Basic Books, 2008).

21. For the Cold War, see John Lewis Gaddis, *The United States and the Origins of the Cold War, 1941–1947* (New York: Columbia University press, 1972); Thomas G. Paterson, ed., *Cold War Critics: Alternatives to America Foreign Policy in the Truman Years* (Chicago: Quadrangle Books, 1971); and Richard Hofstadter, *The Paranoid Style in American Politics and Other Essays* (Cambridge, MA: Harvard University Press, 1996).

22. Butler, Wacker, and Balmer, *Religion in American Life*, 374, 380.

23. Taylor Branch, *Parting the Waters: America in the King Years, 1954–1963* (New York: Simon & Schuster); Isabel Wilkerson, *The Warmth of Other Suns: The Epic Story of America's Great Migration* (New York: Random House, 2010). See also Gates, *The Black Church*.

24. Douglas M. Sloan, *Faith and Knowledge: Mainline Protestantism and American Higher Education* (Louisville, KY: Westminster John Knox Press), 35–47. Brown quote from Kenneth Irving Brown, *Not Mind Alone: Some Frontiers of Christian Education* (New York: Harper & Brothers, 1954), 18.

25. Sloan, *Faith and Knowledge*, vii, 43–47.

26. Sloan, *Faith and Knowledge*, 37, 45, 150–211; Bell quotation from Bernard Iddings Bell, *Crisis in Education* (New York: McGraw-Hill Book Co., 1949), 152–53, cited in Sloan, *Faith and Knowledge*, 37.

27. Hart, *The University Gets Religion*, 96; Sloan, *Faith and Knowledge*, 38; See R. H. Edwin Espy, *The Religion of College Teachers* (New York: Association Press, 1951), 151.

28. Hart, *The University Gets Religion*, 109–11. See also Harvard University, *General Education in a Free Society* (Cambridge, MA: Harvard University, 1945). Hart offers far more detail on the debates about the place of religious studies in the postwar world than can be provided here.

29. Frederick Houk Borsch, *Keeping Faith at Princeton: A Brief History of Religious Pluralism at Princeton and Other Universities* (Princeton, NJ: Princeton University Press, 2012), 8–10.

30. Hart, *The University Gets Religion*, 109–12, 131; Borsch, *Keeping Faith at Princeton*, 12.

31. Albert C. Outler, "The Chaplain's Ministry in Building Religious Foundations for Higher Education," in *New Directions for Religion in Higher Education: A Report of the First National Conference of College and University Chaplains and Directors of Religious Life* (New Haven, CT: Yale Divinity School, 1948), 20–21. See quotations and discussion in Sloan, *Faith and Knowledge*, 38 and Seymour A. Smith, *The American College Chaplaincy* (New York: Association Press, 1954), 1–2.

32. Smith, *The American College Chaplaincy*, 2–3. See also Merrimon Cuninggim and

Luther A. Weigle, *The College Seeks Religion: Yale Studies in Religious Education, vol. 20* (New Haven, CT: Yale University Press, 1947), especially p. 1.

33. Robert W. Lynn, "A Ministry on the Margin," in *The Church, the University, and Social Policy: The Danforth Study of Campus Ministries*, vol. II, ed. Kenneth Underwood (Middletown, CT: Wesleyan University Press, 1969), 22–23.

34. Phillip E. Hammond, "The Radical Ministry," in *The Church, the University, and Social Policy: The Danforth Study of Campus Ministries*, vol. II, ed. Kenneth Underwood (Middletown, CT: Wesleyan University Press, 1969), 6; John Whitney Evans, *The Newman Movement: Roman Catholics in American Higher Education, 1883–1971* (Notre Dame, IN: University of Notre Dame Press, 1980), 99; Jeff Rubin, *The Road to Renaissance, 1923–2002: Hillel* (n.d.), 10.

35. Smith, *The American College Chaplaincy*, 40–42; John Schmalzbauer and Kathleen A. Mahoney, *The Resilience of Religion in American Higher Education* (Waco, TX: Baylor University Press, 2018), 76; Phillip E. Hammond, *The Campus Clergyman* (New York: Basic Books, 1966), 111–15.

36. Sloan, *Faith and Knowledge*, 75–77; Hammond, "The Radical Ministry," 7, 42–44; see also Kenneth Underwood, ed., *The Church, the University, and Social Policy: The Danforth Study of Campus Ministries*, vol. II (Middletown, CT: Wesleyan University Press, 1969), 7.

37. Sloan, *Faith and Knowledge*, 75–76.

38. Hammond, "The Radical Ministry," 8–13, Evans, *The Newman Movement*, 100.

39. Butler, Wacker, and Balmer, *Religion in American Life*; Ellwood, *The Fifties Spiritual Marketplace*; Snyder, *120 Years of American Education*; Schmalzbauer and Mahoney, *The Resilience of Religion*, 103–5; H. Richard Niebuhr, *The Purpose of the Church and Its Ministry* (New York: Harper & Row, 1956), 50.

40. Howard Thurman, *Jesus and the Disinherited* (Boston: Beacon Press, 1976, originally 1949); Albert J. Raboteau, *American Prophets: Seven Religious Radicals & Their Struggle for Social and Political Justice* (Princeton, NJ: Princeton University Press, 2016), 95–117.

41. Borsch, *Keeping Faith at Princeton*, 1,11–12, 16–19. See also the discussion of college chapels in chapter 2 and Margaret M. Grubiak, *White Elephants on Campus: The Decline of the University Chapel in America, 1920–1960* (Notre Dame, IN: University of Notre Dame Press, 2014).

42. Keith Hunt and Gladys Hunt, *For Christ and the University: The Story of InterVarsity Christian Fellowship of the U.S.A./1940-1990* (Downers Grove, IL: InterVarsity Press, 1991), 86–94

43. Hunt and Hunt, *For Christ and the University*, especially 141, 163, 209; Schmalzbauer and Mahoney, *The Resilience of Religion*, 106–8.

44. Schmalzbauer and Mahoney, *The Resilience of Religion*, 108–12.

45. Sloan, *Faith and Knowledge*, 112, citing Reinhold Niebuhr, *The Contribution of Religion to Cultural Unity*, Hazen Pamphlets, 13 (n.p., 1945) 3rd impression, 1950, 10.

46. Abram L. Sachar, *A Host at Last* (Boston: Little, Brown, and Co., 1976), 11–30, Niles quotation on p. 25.

47. Sacher, *A Host at Last*, 27–30.

48. Sacher, *A Host at Last*, 28–29.

49. Nancy Diamond, "The 'Host at Last': Abram Sachar and the Establishment of Brandeis University," *Perspectives on the History of Higher Education* 28 (2011): 223–52, see especially 228–30.

50. Diamond, "The 'Host at Last,'" 227.

51. Ethan Schrum, "Clark Kerr's Early Career, Social Science, and the American University," *Perspectives on the History of Higher Education* 28 (2011): 193–222.

52. Roger L. Geiger, *American Higher Education since World War II: A History* (Princeton,

NJ: Princeton University Press, 2019), 56–59; David F. Labaree, *A Perfect Mess: The Unlikely Ascendancy of America Higher Education* (Chicago: University of Chicago Press, 2017); "A Master Plan for Higher Education in California, 1960," in Wilson Smith and Thomas Bender, ed., *American Higher Education Transformed, 1940–2005: Documenting the National Discourse* (Baltimore: Johns Hopkins University Press, 2008), 97–100.

53. Geiger, *American Higher Education*.

54. See Geiger, *American Higher Education since World War II*, 139–48.

55. See Clark Kerr, *The Uses of the University* (Cambridge, MA: Harvard University Press, 1963). See especially pp. 53–58.

56. Religious Studies, UC Santa Barbara, "History of the Department," http://www.religion .ucsb.edu/history-of-the-department/, downloaded July 26, 2021.

57. John S. Hadsell Westminster House collection, GTU 2006-7-02 Graduate Theological Union Archives, Berkeley, CA, https://oac.cdlib.org/findaid/ark:/13030/kt5g5033q9/entire_text/, downloaded January 4, 2022; Harry Lees Kingman Paper, BAC-MSS 76/173 c. The Bancroft Library, University of California, Berkeley, special thanks to my NYU colleague Robby Cohen for pointing me to these papers; https://oac.cdlib.org/findaid/ark:/13030/tf98700756/entire _text/, downloaded January 4, 2022; Keith Chamberlain, "The Berkeley Free Speech Movement and the Campus Ministry," in *The Free Speech Movement: Reflections on Berkeley in the 1960s*, ed. Robert Cohen and Reginald E. Zelnik (Berkeley: University of California Press, 2002), 357–61; for other campuses, see http://www.urcatucla.com/history/ and https://studentaffairs .ucdavis.edu/about-us/committees/religious-council, both downloaded January 4, 2022; Judith Kerr Graven, *Project India: How College Students Won Friends for America, 1952–1969* (Minneapolis, MN: Mill City Press, 2014), 1–2.

58. W. David Baird, *Quest for Distinction: Pepperdine University in the 20th Century* (Malibu, CA: Pepperdine University Press, 2016), 17–26; Pepperdine University, "History," www.peper dine.edu/about/pepperdine/history, downloaded August 23, 2021. The Baird history of Pepperdine is one of the best college histories available. It is meticulously researched and makes no effort to cover up difficult moments in the school's past.

59. Gary Holloway and Douglas A. Foster, *Renewing God's People: A Concise History of Churches of Christ* (Abilene, TX: Abilene Christian University Press, 2001/2006), 11, 94–98.

60. Baird, *Quest for Distinction*, 3–9; Pepperdine University, "History"; Holloway and Foster, *Renewing God's People*, 65–66, 102–4.

61. *Los Angeles Times*, August 25, 1940, "Pepperdine Progress Told," D7; Baird, *Quest for Distinction*, 33–36, 49–50.

62. *Los Angeles Times*, February 15, 1951, "Pepperdine Says He's Penniless Now," 5.

63. Baird, *Quest for Distinction*, 65–68.

64. The crisis over what it meant to stay true to the Christian faith, as interpreted in the Church of Christ, in the late 1940s and early 1950s, is well described in the thoughtful and balanced chapter 6 by Baird, *Quest for Distinction*, 71–83. All direct quotes in these paragraphs are from this chapter.

65. *Los Angeles Times*, April 17, 1958, "Pepperdine Losing 17 from Teaching Faculty," A5; Baird, *Quest for Distinction*, 110–11.

66. Baird, *Quest for Distinction*, 119–43.

67. https://www.pepperdine.edu/; Baird, *Quest for Distinction*, 152–95.

CHAPTER SIX: The Long Sixties

1. Warren Goldstein, *William Sloane Coffin, Jr.: A Holy Impatience* (New Haven, CT: Yale University Press, 2004); Warren Goldstein and Donna Schaper, "The Rise and Fall of 1960s University Chaplaincy: William Sloane Coffin, 'Heroic' White Guys and the Disestablishment

of American Public Religion," *The Luce Lectures on the Changing Role of Chaplains in American Higher Education*, New York University, April 10, 2018. T. D. Snyder, ed., *120 Years of American Education: A Statistical Portrait* (Washington, DC: US Department of Education, Office of Educational Research and Improvement, National Center for Educational Statistics, 1993).

2. Goldstein, *William Sloane Coffin, Jr.*

3. Goldstein, *William Sloane Coffin, Jr.*, 34, 71–75, 96–103; for Reinhold Niebuhr, see Richard Wightman Fox, "Reinhold Niebuhr," *American National Biography*, published online, February 2000, downloaded August 29, 2021.

4. Goldstein, *William Sloane Coffin, Jr.*, 104–7.

5. Taylor Branch, *Parting the Waters: America in the King Years, 1954–1963* (New York: Simon and Schuster, 1988), 412–30; Goldstein, *William Sloane Coffin, Jr.*, 111–28.

6. Robert Kaiser "Coffin Addresses 300 on Church, Civil Rights," *Yale Daily News*, clipping, no date but probably 1962, from the papers of the late Jesse Lemisch, courtesy of Robert Cohen. I am very grateful to my NYU colleague Robby Cohen for sharing this material with me.

7. Goldstein, *William Sloane Coffin, Jr.*, 130–33, 141.

8. Goldstein, *William Sloane Coffin, Jr.*, 148–50, 161–62.

9. Goldstein, *William Sloane Coffin, Jr.*, 183–86, 190–92, 203, 206, 220–21.

10. Goldstein, *William Sloane Coffin, Jr.*, 252, 270–71.

11. Goldstein, *William Sloane Coffin, Jr.*, 222.

12. Goldstein, *William Sloane Coffin, Jr.*, 252–61, 270–73, 284ff.

13. Bob Abernethy, "William Sloane Coffin," March 16, 2007, *Religion & Ethics News Weekly*, PBS, https://www.pbs.org/wnet/religionand ethics/2007/03/16/august-27-2004-william-sloane -coffin, downloaded September 2, 2016; Goldstein, *William Sloane Coffin, Jr.*, 222–23.

14. Seymour A. Smith, *The American College Chaplaincy* (New York: Association Press, 1954), 10–11, 40–43.

15. Faiyaz Jaffer, "A Minority of a Minority: The Shia Muslim Student Experience on American College Campuses" (EdD dissertation, New York University, 2022), 13–14; https:// berkleycenter.georgetown.edu/people/yahya-hendi; Vineet Chander, "Hindus in Higher Ed: Chronicling a History of Organized Hindu Meaning-Making on American College and University Campuses" (EdD dissertation, New York University, 2023), 132 and 186.

16. Smith, *The American College Chaplaincy*, 10–11, 40–43; Phillip E. Hammond, "The Radical Ministry," in *The Church, The University, and Social Policy: The Danforth Study of Campus Ministries*, vol. II, Working and Technical Papers, ed. Kenneth Underwood (Middletown, CT: Wesleyan University Press, 1969), 6; John Whitney Evans, *The Newman Movement: Roman Catholics in American Higher Education, 1883–1971* (Notre Dame, IN: University of Notre Dame Press, 1980), 168; John Schmalzbauer and Kathleen A. Mahoney, *The Resilience of Religion in American Higher Education* (Waco, TX: Baylor University Press, 2018), 115.

17. Howard L. Daughenbaugh, "Campus Ministry in the 60s and 70s: Context and Observations," in *Campus Ministry Memoirs: The Way It Was, 1964–2014*, ed. Betsy Alden (n.p., National Campus Ministry Association, 2014), 66–74. See also Schmalzbauer and Mahoney, *The Resilience of Religion*, 103–8; Robert S. Ellwood, *The Fifties Spiritual Marketplace: American Religion in a Decade of Conflict* (New Brunswick, NJ: Rutgers University Press, 1997), 145–46.

18. Dorothy C. Bass, "Revolutions, Quiet and Otherwise: Protestants and Higher Education during the 1960s," in *Caring for the Commonweal: Education for Religious and Public Life*, ed. Parker J. Palmer, Barbara G. Wheeler, and James W. Fowler (Macon, GA: Mercer University Press, 1990), 221–22, quotation from Gustafson, p. 335.

19. "History of the Department—Religious Studies," University of California Santa Barbara, http://religion.ucst.eu/history-of-the-department/, downloaded July 26, 2021. Note, the author was a student at UCSB 1966–1970 and took several courses in the department.

20. United States Supreme Court, *Abington School District v. Schempp*, 374 U.S. 203 (1963); D. G. Hart, *The University Gets Religion: Religious Studies in American Higher Education* (Baltimore: Johns Hopkins University Press, 1999), 200–201.

21. Hart, *The University Gets Religion*, 193–95, 223–29. See also Paul Ramsey and John Frederick Wilson, *The Study of Religion in Colleges and Universities* (Princeton, NJ: Princeton University Press, 1970).

22. Schmalzbauer and Mahoney, *The Resilience of Religion*, 103–4; Alden, *Campus Ministry Memoirs*, 4–5.

23. Schmalzbauer and Mahoney, *The Resilience of Religion*, 103.

24. Bass, "Revolutions, Quiet and Otherwise," 215–17.

25. Peter L. Berger, *The Noise of Solemn Assemblies: Christian Commitment and the Religious Establishment in America* (Garden City, NY: Doubleday & Co., 1961) and Harvey Cox, *The Secular City* (New York: Macmillan, 1965); Goldstein, *William Sloane Coffin, Jr.*, and Warren Goldstein and Donna Schaper, "Luce Lecture on College Chaplaincy," New York University, April 10, 2018. *120 Years of American Education: A Statistical Portrait.*

26. Bass, "Revolutions, Quiet and Otherwise," 217–21.

27. Goldstein, *William Sloane Coffin, Jr.*; Goldstein and Schaper, "Luce Lecture"; Bass, "Revolutions, Quiet and Otherwise," 207–26; Snyder, *120 Years of American Education: A Statistical Portrait.* (The Bass chapter is by far the most careful and nuanced overview of the fate of college chaplaincy in the late 1960s.)

28. Keith Hunt and Gladys Hunt, *For Christ and the University: The Story of InterVarsity Christian Fellowship of the U.S.A./1940–1990* (Downers Grove, IL: InterVarsity Press, 1991), 236–64, Alexander quote on p. 245.

29. See Taylor Branch, *Parting the Waters: America in the King Years, 1954–1963* (New York: Simon and Schuster, 1988), 271–78.

30. Peter Dreier, "'A Totally Moral Man': The Life of Nonviolent Organizer Rev. James Lawson," in *The 100 Greatest Americans of the 20th Century: A Social Justice Hall of Fame*, ed. Peter Dreier (New York: Bold Type Books, 2012), 347–52; Branch, *Parting the Waters*, 271–74, 278–80.

31. Robert Cohen, *Freedom's Orator: Mario Savio and the Radical Legacy of the 1960s* (New York: Oxford University Press, 2009), 1–7, 41, 52–55. Interview later in life with Mario Savio reported on p. 41. I am especially grateful to my NYU colleague Robby Cohen for calling this aspect of Savio's life and thought to my attention and for his support of this project.

32. Susan Brownmiller, *In Our Time: Memoir of a Revolution* (New York: Dell, 1999), 11–17.

33. Brownmiller, *In Our Time*, 11–17.

34. Carol Christ, *Diving Deep and Surfacing: Women Writers on Spiritual Quest* (Boston: Beacon Press, 2nd ed., 1985), pp. xxvii–xxviii.

35. Susan Yarrow Morris, "Backing into a Calling and the Ripple Effect!" in *Campus Ministry Memoirs: The Way It Was, 1964–2014*, ed. Betsy Alden (n.p., National Campus Ministry Association, 2014), 253–56.

36. Diane Kenney, "A Particular Career in Campus Ministry," in *Campus Ministry Memoirs: The Way It Was, 1964–2014*, ed. Betsy Alden (n.p., National Campus Ministry Association, 2014), 225–41.

37. Donald G. Shockley, "An Examined Life," in *Campus Ministry Memoirs: The Way It Was, 1964–2014*, ed. Betsy Alden (n.p., National Campus Ministry Association, 2014), 141–43 and Donald G. Shockley, *Campus Ministry: The Church Beyond Itself* (Louisville, KY: Westminster/John Knox Press, 1989), 1, 5–6, and Author Biography on used book sites such as World Books.

38. Shockley, *Campus Ministry*, 1, 5–6, 37, 59, 101.

39. David Duncombe, "An Experiment in Evaluation of Faith and Life Communities," in *The Church, The University, and Social Policy: The Danforth Study of Campus Ministries*, vol. II, Working and Technical Papers, ed. Kenneth Underwood (Middletown, CT: Wesleyan University Press, 1969), 146.

40. *SCENE*, the newsletter of the University Christian Foundation, September 1, 1966, Box 6, Folder 5, and Richard Nutt, "Review of Program Goals and Purpose of UCF," 1967, Box 3, Folder 1, both in Records of the University Christian Foundation, RG.39.3. Special Collections, New York University Bobst Library.

41. N. J. Demerath III and Kenneth J. Lutterman, "The Student Parishioner: Radical Rhetoric and Traditional Reality," *The Church, The University, and Social Policy: The Danforth Study of Campus Ministries*, vol. II, Working and Technical Papers, ed. Kenneth Underwood (Middletown, CT: Wesleyan University Press, 1969), 139; Phillip E. Hammond, *The Campus Clergyman* (New York: Basic Books, 1966), 113.

42. Shockley, *Campus Ministry*, 1 and 101; Bass, "Revolutions Quiet and Otherwise," 214; Evans, *The Newman Movement*, 160.

43. Gerald McKevitt, *The University of Santa Clara: A History, 1851–1977* (Stanford, CA: Stanford University Press, 1979), 7, 48–53, 325. Some universities are blessed to have well-written, critical histories. Most do not. McKevitt's is one of the best. See also the more recent George F. Giacomini Jr. and Gerald McKevitt, *Serving the Intellect, Touching the Heart* (Santa Clara, CA: Santa Clara University, 2000), 1, 20–21.

44. McKevitt, *The University of Santa Clara*, 55–58, 120–25; Giacomini and McKevitt, *Serving the Intellect*, 20–21.

45. Susan A. Ross, "It's Been 50 Years since Most Jesuit Colleges Went Co-ed. But Have They Truly Embraced Their Female Students?," *America: The Jesuit Review*, September 20, 2021; McKevitt, *The University of Santa Clara*, 284–85, 297.

46. McKevitt, *The University of Santa Clara*, 293–94.

47. Gerard Campbell, April 9, 1967, cited in Robert Emmett Curran, *The History of Georgetown University, vol. 3: The Rise to Prominence, 1964–1989* (Washington, DC: Georgetown University Press, 2010), 3.

48. McKevitt, *The University of Santa Clara*, 292–97.

49. Giacomini and McKevitt, *Serving the Intellect*, 227–39, Terry quotation, p. 231. See also McKevitt, *The University of Santa Clara*, 299–305.

50. Giacomini and McKevitt, *Serving the Intellect*, 239, 249.

51. See https://www.scu.edu/aboutscu, downloaded April 12, 2023; McKevitt, *The University of Santa Clara*, 297–99.

52. William H. Hildebrand, *A Most Noble Enterprise: The Story of Kent State University, 1910–2010* (Kent, OH: Kent State University Press, 2009), 1–13, 67, 79–81.

53. Thomas M. Grace, *Kent State: Death and Dissent in the Long Sixties* (Amherst: University of Massachusetts Press, 2016), 13–18, 102–5.

54. Hildebrand, *A Most Noble Enterprise*, 91; "Keeping Faith: A History of the Episcopal Church, Kent, Ohio" (typewritten manuscript), www.christchurchkent.org, downloaded October 4, 2021, p. 24.

55. Kent State University, General Catalog, 1969–1971 from the archives of Kent State University, Special Collections, Kent State University Libraries. Special thanks to Kate Siebert Medicus of the Special Collections department who was extraordinarily helpful in finding material in the archives.

56. Grace, *Kent State*, 24–30; Hildebrand, *A Most Noble Enterprise*, 106–8.

57. Grace, *Kent State*, 13, 102–5.

58. Grace, *Kent State*, 219–30.

59. Barbara Child, Oral History, recorded April 16–17, 2020, Kent State Shootings: Oral Histories, Archives, Kent State University Libraries.

60. Anne Andrews, Oral History, December 3, 2019, Kent State Shootings: Oral Histories, Archives, Kent State University Libraries.

61. Nancy K. Bristow, *Steeped in the Blood of Racism: Black Power, Law and Order, and the 1970 Shootings at Jackson State College* (New York: Oxford University Press, 2020), 19.

62. "Jackson State University," *Mississippi Encyclopedia*, https://mississippiencyclopedia.org /entries/jackson-state-univereity/downloaded August 27, 2021.

63. Bristow, *Steeped in the Blood of Racism*, 25–32, 38–39, 45.

64. Bristow, *Steeped in the Blood of Racism*, 66–70. See also the earlier Tim Spofford, *Lynch Street: The May 1970 Slayings at Jackson State College* (Kent, OH: Kent State University Press,

65. Bristow, *Steeped in the Blood of Racism*, 1–5, 71–82.

66. Spofford, *Lynch Street*, 154–56; "The Report of the President's Commission on Campus Unrest including Special Reports: The Killings at Jackson State, The Kent State Tragedy" (New York: Arno Press, 1970); Peter Davies and the Board of Church and Society of the United Methodist Church, *The Truth about Kent State: A Challenge to the American Conscience* (New York: Farrar Straus Giroux, 1973), vii–viii, 217–20.

67. Bristow, *Steeped in the Blood of Racism*, 161, 183–84.

68. Hildebrand, *A Most Noble Enterprise*, 192–193, 200–205, Bristow, *Steeped in the Blood of Racism*, 170–171; Kent State University Summer 1977 Bulletin, Undergraduate Catalog, 1977–1978.

69. https://www.jsums.edu/studentlife/religious-council/, https://kentstatelutherhouse.org; kentucc.org, https://www.kent.edu/downtown-kent/religion, and kent.campuslabsw.com /engage/organizations/latenightchristianfellowship/, all downloaded October 8, 2021.

70. https://www.cnn.com/2016/01/23/politics/donald-trump-shoot-somebody-support /index.html, downloaded October 11, 2021; Jacob Pankow, "Christianity Is Under Tremendous Siege: A Case Study on Donald Trump, Dordt University, and Dutch Evangelicals" (unpublished paper, New York University, December 15, 2020). I am very grateful to Mr. Pankow for a brilliant paper and for calling my attention to the importance of Dordt College in the conservative evangelical world.

71. http://www.dordt.edu/about-dordt/college history, downloaded October 11, 2021; James Tunstead Burtchaell, *The Dying of the Light: The Disengagement of Colleges and Universities from Their Christian Churches* (Grand Rapids, MI: W. B. Eerdmans, 1998), 785–89; B. J. Haan, *A Zeal for Christian Education: The Memoirs of B. J. Haan* (Sioux Center, IA: Dordt College Press, 1992), 23–24. For 2024 update, see, https://www.siouxlandproud.com/news/your-local -election-hq/dordt-university-cancels-trump-rally-in-sioux-center/, downloaded October 10, 2024.

72. Mike Vanden Bosch, *A History of Dordt College: The B. J. Haan Years* (Sioux Center, IA: Dordt College Press, 1990), 54, 57, 91.

73. Vanden Bosch, *A History of Dordt College*, 89–90.

74. Burtchaell, *The Dying of the Light*, 786–89.

75. Vander Bosch, *A History of Dordt College*, 112, 119–20, 137; Burtchaell, *The Dying of the Light*, 789, 795.

76. Vander Bosch, *A History of Dordt College*, 121–23; Burtchaell, *The Dying of the Light*, 795–99.

77. Burtchaell, *The Dying of the Light*, 795–99, 803–9. See also Adam Laats, *Fundamentalist U: Keeping Faith in American Higher Education* (New York: Oxford University Press, 2018).

78. Haan, *A Zeal for Christian Education*, 153–91; Vander Bosch, *A History of Dordt College*, 241.

CHAPTER SEVEN: A Second Religious Depression on Campus, 1980–2000

1. See https://spu.edu/~/media/academics/school-of-theology/documents/brenda-salter -mcneil-CV.ashx, downloaded October 23, 2021.

2. Brenda Salter McNeil, *A Credible Witness: Reflections on Power, Evangelism and Race* (Downers Grove, IL: InterVarsity Press, 2008), 46, 70–71, 92, 99–100, 108–10, 116–17.

3. "InterVarsity Black Campus Ministries," http://bcm.intervarsity.org/history-0, downloaded October 17, 2021; Keith Hunt and Gladys Hunt, *For Christ and the University: The Story of InterVarsity Christian Fellowship of the U.S.A./1940–1990* (Downers Grove, IL: InterVarsity Press, 1991), 115–17.

4. Hunt and Hunt, *For Christ and the University*, 16–17.

5. Hunt and Hunt, *For Christ and the University*, 55, 381.

6. Hunt and Hunt, *For Christ and the University*, 152, 163, 205–64; John Schmalzbauer and Kathleen A. Mahoney, *The Resilience of Religion in American Higher Education* (Waco, TX: Baylor University Press, 2018), 106–7. See also https://intervarsity.org/about-us/intervarsity -and-ifes-history, downloaded October 24, 2021.

7. Schmalzbauer and Mahoney, *The Resilience of Religion*, 106; https://intervarsity-org/our -ministry, downloaded October 24, 2021.

8. Elizabeth Dias, "Top Evangelical College Group to Dismiss Employees Who Support Gay Marriage," *Time*, October 6, 2016; Hunt and Hunt, *For Christ and the University*, 116–17.

9. Robert D. Putnam and David E. Campbell, *American Grace: How Religion Divides and Unites Us* (New York: Simon & Schuster, 2010), 104–6.

10. John G. Turner, *Bill Bright and Campus Crusade for Christ: The Renewal of Evangelism in Postwar America* (Chapel Hill: University of North Carolina Press, 2008), 119–29, 208–15. See also Laurie Goodstein, "Campus Crusade for Christ Is Renamed," *New York Times*, July 20, 2011.

11. Schmalzbauer and Mahoney, *The Resilience of Religion*, 106–12; interview with Amy Wilson, May 31, 2023.

12. Dean M. Kelley, *Why Conservative Churches Are Growing* (New York: Harper & Row, 1972, rev. ed. 1977). See especially the 1977 "Preface to the Paperback Edition," viii–xi.

13. Betsy Alden, *Campus Ministry Memoirs: The Way It Was, 1964–2014* (n.p., National Campus Ministry Association, 2014), 72 and 105.

14. Timothy J. Hallett, "Eating the Seed Corn: The Abandonment of Campus Ministry," in *Disorganized Religion: The Evangelization of Youth and Young Adults*, ed. Sheryl A. Kujawa (Boston: Cowley Publications, 1998), 167–73.

15. Warren Goldstein and Donna Schaper, "Luce Lecture," New York University, April 10, 2018; Hallett, "Eating the Seed Corn," 167.

16. Goldstein and Schaper, "Luce Lecture"; Hallett, "Eating the Seed Corn," 167; Thomas C. Reeves, *The Empty Church: Does Organized Religion Matter Anymore?* (New York: Simon & Schuster, 1996), 2; Putnam and Campbell, *American Grace*.

17. Jane S. Gould, "On Engineers and Evangelism," in *Disorganized Religion: The Evangelization of Youth and Young Adults*, ed. Sheryl A. Kujawa (Boston: Cowley Publications, 1998), 156–66.

18. Alden, *Campus Ministry Memoirs*, 106–18 and 177–79.

19. Putnam and Campbell, *American Grace*, 107.

20. Schmalzbauer and Mahoney, *The Resilience of Religion*, 113–115.

21. Schmalzbauer and Mahoney, *The Resilience of Religion*, 115.

22. Lucy A. Forster-Smith, *College & University Chaplaincy in the 21st Century* (Woodstock, VT: Skylight Paths, 2013), 314–16.

23. James M. Gustafson, "The Study of Religion in Colleges and Universities: A Practical Commentary," in *The Study of Religion in Colleges and Universities*, ed. Paul Ramsey and John F. Wilson (Princeton, NJ: Princeton University Press, 1970), 330–38, cited in and discussed in D. G. Hart, *The University Gets Religion: Religious Studies in American Higher Education* (Baltimore: Johns Hopkins University Press, 1999), 226–27.

24. Ray L. Hart, "Preface," *Journal of the American Academy of Religion* 53, no. 4, 75th Anniversary Meeting of the American Academy of Religion (December 1985): 549–53, downloaded from *JSTOR* October 28, 2021. See also D. G. Hart, *The University Gets Religion*, 193–96.

25. Table of Contents, and Susan Thistlethwaite, "Settled Issues and Neglected Questions: How Is Religion to Be Studied?," *Journal of the American Academy of Religion* 62, no. 4 (Winter 1994): 1037–45, *JSTOR*, downloaded October 28, 2021.

26. John Schmalzbauer, "American College Students Have Not Given Up on the Meaning of Life," in *A Student's Search for Meaning: Reflections on the Intersections of College Chaplaincy, Liberal Arts and the University*, ed. Melissa Carter, James W. Fraser, Chelsea Garbell, and Amy Wilson (London: Ethics International Press, 2023), 113.

27. D. G. Hart, *The University Gets Religion*, 227–38.

28. E. Ann Matter, "The Academic Culture of Disbelief: Religious Studies at the University of Pennsylvania," *Method & Theory in the Study of Religion* 7, no. 4 (1995, Special Issues: Pathologies in the Academic Study of Religion: North American Institutional Case Studies): 383–92. *JSTOR*, downloaded October 28, 2021. See also the discussion in D. G. Hart, *The University Gets Religion*, 235–37.

29. Gary Lease, "The Rise and Fall of Religious Studies at Santa Cruz: A Case Study in Pathology, or the 'Rest of the Story,'" *Method & Theory in the Study of Religion* 7, no. 4 (1995, Special Issues: Pathologies in the Academic Study of Religion: North American Institutional Case Studies): 305–24. *JSTOR*, downloaded October 28, 2021.

30. "Editorial," *Method & Theory in the Study of Religion* 7, no. 4 (1995, Special Issues: Pathologies in the Academic Study of Religion: North American Institutional Case Studies): 295–96. *JSTOR*, downloaded October 28, 2021.

31. D. G. Hart, *The University Gets Religion*, 231.

32. https://www.dinecollege.edu/about_dc/educational-philosophy, downloaded October 30,2021; Vincent Werito, "Understanding Hózhó to Achieve Critical Consciousness: A Contemporary Diné Interpretation of the Philosophical Principles of Hózhó," in *Diné Perspectives: Revitalizing and Reclaiming Navajo Thought*, ed. Lloyd L. Lee (Tucson: University of Arizona Press, 2014), 25–26.

33. Werito, "Understanding Hózhó to Achieve Critical Consciousness," 25–28; Paul Tillich, *The Dynamics of Faith* (New York: Harper & Row, 1957), 5.

34. Paul Boyer, *Capturing Education: Envisioning and Building the First Tribal Colleges* (Pablo MT: Salish Kootenai College Press, 2015), 93; https://www.dinecollege.edu/about_dc/history/, downloaded October 30, 2021.

35. Boyer, *Capturing Education*, 7–8, 14–16.

36. Boyer, *Capturing Education*, 2–7, 23–27.

37. Boyer, *Capturing Education*, 91–102.

38. David Gipp, "The Tribal College Approach to Spirituality," https://facultyresourcenetwork.org/publications/spirituality-and-highereducation, downloaded November 2, 2021.

39. Larry W. Emerson, "Diné Culture, Decolonization, and the Politics of Hózhó," in *Diné Perspectives: Revitalizing and Reclaiming Navajo Thought*, ed. Lloyd L. Lee (Tucson: University of Arizona Press, 2014), 62–67.

40. Charles Dorn, "To Meet the Training and Retraining Needs of Established Business," in

For the Common Good: A New History of Higher Education (Ithaca, NY: Cornell University Press, 2017), 200–225.

41. See Dorn, "To Meet the Training and Retraining Needs," 200. But see also Kevin James Dougherty, *The Contradictory College: Then Conflicting Origins, Impacts, and Futures of Community College* (Albany: State University of New York Press, 1994) and Seven Brint and Jerome Karabel, *The Diverted Dream: Community Colleges and the Promise of Educational Opportunity in America, 1900–1985* (New York: Oxford University Press, 1989).

42. https://humanities.unc.edu/ck12/the-warren-a-nord-teachers-seminars/, downloaded October 29, 2021.

43. Warren Nord, "Does God Make a Difference? Taking Religion Seriously in Our Schools and Universities, an Excerpt," published in *Religion & Education*, 38, no. 1 (March 2011): 3–23, subsequently published as Warren Nord, *Does God Make a Difference?: Taking Religion Seriously in Schools and Universities* (New York: Oxford University Press, 2010). Both the article and the book were published after Nord's death in July 2010. For the last quotations, see the earlier work, Warren Nord, *Religion and American Education: Rethinking a National Dilemma* (Chapel Hill: University of North Carolina Press, 1995), 2–5. Nord had been making the same basic argument in lectures and presentations and in print throughout his long tenure at UNC.

44. David L. Weaver-Zercher, "Visions in Conflict: The Department of Religion at the University of North Carolina, 1947–1960," *North Carolina Historical Review* LXXXIV, no. 4 (October 2002): 393–96.

45. https://www.unc.edu/about/history-and-traditions, downloaded October 29, 2021, and https://religion.unc.edu/about/about-the-department, downloaded October 30, 2021; Weaver-Zercher, "Visions in Conflict," 396.

46. Weaver-Zercher, "Visions in Conflict," 399–401.

47. L. O. Kattsoff, "The Priesthood of the Scholar," *The Christian Scholar* 39, no. 3 (September 1956): 169–72; D. G. Hart, *The University Gets Religion*, 177–93.

48. Weaver-Zercher, "Visions in Conflict," 404–10.

49. Personal communication with Carl W. Ernst, November 8, 2021. I am especially grateful to Professor Ernst for sharing his recollections and a copy of the agenda for the November 3–4, 1995, religious studies department retreat.

50. D. G. Hart, *The University Gets Religion*, 223–34; https://religion.unc/about, downloaded October 30, 2021.

51. Manuel Wortman, "Change," and Jan Rivero, "The Space and Time for Holy Hospitality," in *Campus Ministry Memoirs: The Way It Was, 1964–2014*, ed. Betsy Alden (n.p., National Campus Ministry Association, 2014), 245–47, 290–95, respectively.

52. Personal email communication with John Rogers, executive director, Presbyterian Collegiate Ministries of North Carolina, November 8, 2021. I am deeply grateful to Rev. Rogers for providing detailed historical memories of a time, not long ago, but from which virtually no written records remain; Donald Boulton obituary, Pugh Funeral Home, July 31, 2021.

53. Harold S. Wechsler, "Brewing Bachelors: The History of the University of Newark," *Paedagogica Historica* 46, no. 1–2 (February–April 2010): 229–49.

54. Wechsler, "Brewing Bachelors," 248; email communication from Elizabeth Norman, November 10, 2021.

55. https://www.newark.rutgers.edu/histor, downloaded January 10, 2022; *Encore*, the student yearbook, 1984, pp. 199 and 208, 1992, p. 41. Special thanks to Angela Lawrence, the Rutgers-Newark archivist, for making this material available.

56. Newman Catholic Campus Ministry, ca. 1992; Robert Wiener, "Daner Remembered as 'Quintessential Mensch,'" *New Jersey Jewish News*, November 24, 2010; John Faulstich Obituary, *Newark Star-Ledger*, September 6, 2017; telephone conversation with Professor Norman Samuels,

November 29, 2021. I am especially grateful to Professor Samuels for his detailed reflections on religion during his years as Rutgers University–Newark chancellor.

57. Newark course catalog, 1986–1988, 106–108; Newark course catalog, 1992–1994, 107–109. From the RU-N Archives.

58. https://www.newark.rutgers.edu/history; www.newark.rutgers.edu/diversity-timeline, downloaded November 11. 2021. Telephone conversation with Steven Diner, November 11, 2021; https://www.newark.rutgers.edu/Diversity, downloaded January 11, 2022.

CHAPTER EIGHT: Resurgence and Difference after 9/11, 2001–2021

1. "U. to Hire First Full-Time Hindu, Muslim Chaplains," March 31, 2008; "University Appoints Hindu and Muslim Chaplains," July 30, 2008; "New Muslim, Hindu advisers seek to mentor," September 14, 2008, in *The Daily Princetonian*, downloaded November 27, 2021; seminar with Union Theological Seminary students, Judson Memorial Church, New York, NY, March 10, 2023.

2. Frederick Houk Borsch, *Keeping Faith at Princeton: A Brief History of Religious Pluralism at Princeton and Other Universities* (Princeton, NJ: Princeton University Press, 2012), 2, 9–10, 16, 19, 56–57, 61, 65, 97.

3. "Hindus Light Up Chapel for Diwali Week," *The Daily Princetonian*, November 2008, downloaded November 27, 2021.

4. Faiyaz Jaffer, "A Minority of a Minority: The Shia Muslim Experience on American College Campuses" (EdD dissertation, New York University, 2022); Vineet Chander, "Hindus in Higher Ed: Chronicling a History of Organized Hindu Meaning Making on American College Campuses" (EdD dissertation, New York University, 2023); personal communication with Faiyaz Jaffer, July 10, 2023.

5. Vineet Chander, "Hindus in Higher Ed: An Incomplete History of Hindu Student Organizing on American College and University Campuses" (unpublished paper, New York University, 2020), 3–4. See also Amy Bhatt, Nalini Iyer, and Deepa Banerjee, *Roots and Reflections: South Asians in the Pacific Northwest* (Seattle, WA: University of Seattle Press, 2013).

6. Faiyaz Jaffer, "The History & Future of Muslim Student Engagement in American Higher Education" (unpublished paper, New York University, 2020); Geneive Abdo, *Mecca and Main Street: Muslim Life in America after 9/11* (New York: Oxford University Pres, 2006), 194–98.

7. Jaffer, "The History & Future of Muslim Student Engagement," 3, 9. See also https://absanetwork.com and Alyssa N. Rockenbach, Matthew J. Mayhew, Nicholas A. Bowman, Shauna M. Morin, and Tiffani Riggers-Piehl, "An Examination of Non-Muslim College Students' Attitudes Toward Muslims," *The Journal of Higher Education* 88, no. 4 (2017): 479–504.

8. Chander, "Hindus in Higher Ed," 5–15; Himanee Gupta-Carlson, *Muncie, India(na): Middletown and Asian America* (Champagne: University of Illinois Press, 2018).

9. Chander, "Hindus in Higher Ed," 15–20; Harvard University, Pluralism Project, "Hindu Revival on Campus," 2020.

10. Janet M. Cooper Nelson, "Foreword," in *College & University, Chaplaincy in the 21st Century*, ed. Lucy A. Foster-Smith (Woodstock, VT: Skylight Paths Publishing, 2013), xii.

11. John Schmalzbauer and Kathleen A. Mahoney, *The Resilience of Religion in American Higher Education* (Waco, TX: Baylor University Press, 2018), 1–3.

12. Schmalzbauer and Mahoney, *The Resilience of Religion*, 7.

13. Rockenbach et al., "An Examination of Non-Muslim College Students' Attitudes Toward Muslims," 479–481.

14. Chris Hawley, "NYPD Monitored Muslim Students All over the Northeast," Associated Press, December 20, 20016; Ryan Devereaux, "Muslim Student Monitored by the NYPD: 'It Just

Brings Everything Home,'" *The Guardian*, February 22, 2012; Jaffer, "The History & Future of Muslim Student Engagement," 4–6; Schmalzbauer and Mahoney, *The Resilience of Religion*, 119.

15. Shenilla S. Khoja-Moolji, "An Emerging Model of Muslim Leadership: Chaplaincy on University Campuses," The Pluralism Project, Harvard University, April 2011, see especially pp. 12 and 16.

16. Schmalzbauer and Mahoney, *The Resilience of Religion*, 17–18, 120–21, 130–31.

17. Elizabeth Redden, "Chabad Grows Its Presence on College Campuses," *Inside Higher Ed*, January 7, 2022.

18. Redden, "Chabad Grows Its Presence."

19. Emma Goldberg, "New Chief Chaplain at Harvard? An Atheist," *New York Times*, August 26, 2021; Nick Paumgarten, "Reputation Economy," *The New Yorker*, September 20, 2021.

20. Schmalzbauer and Mahoney, *The Resilience of Religion*, 117–18; Michelle Hiskey, "New Emory Chaplains Appointed to Serve University's Religious Diversity," March 17, 2021, https://news.emory.edu/features/2021/03/osrl-chaplains/index.html, downloaded December 4, 2021.

21. https://csumb.edu/hws/campus-chaplaincy-spiritual-support/ and https://www.bsu.edu/calendar/events/admissions/welcome-week/2021/0820-religious-advisors, and https://multicultural.ufl.edu/resources/cmc/, downloaded December 6, 2021.

22. Tom Perrin, "One Way to Make College Meaningful," *New York Times*, February 3, 2019.

23. Schmalzbauer and Mahoney, *The Resilience of Religion*; John Schmalzbauer, "The Evolving Role of the College and University Chaplaincy: Findings from a National Study," paper presented at the NetVUE Chaplaincy Conferences, 2014; Lucy A. Forster-Smith, *College & University Chaplaincy in the 21st Century: A Multifaith Look at the Practice of Ministry on Campuses Across America* (Woodstock, VT: Skylight Paths Publishing, 2013); Lucy A. Forster-Smith, *Crossing Thresholds: The Making and Re-Making of a 21st Century College Chaplain* (Eugene, OR: Cascade Books, 2015).

24. Forster-Smith, *College & University Chaplaincy*, v–vii, xi–xii, 45–46.

25. I am especially grateful to Sara Aeder, "An Overview of Select Research Conducted about Jewish Students on College Campuses, 1950–2020," unpublished paper, New York University, December 2020; see also Irving Greenberg, "Jewish Survival and the College Campus," *Judaism* 13, no. 3: 260; Leon A. Feldman, *The Personality of the Jewish College Student: A Portrait*, paper presented at the YIVO Social Science Circle, New York, June 6, 1956, cited in Aeder, "An Overview of Select Research," 3.

26. Jennifer Medina and Tamar Lewin, "Campus Debates on Israel Drive a Wedge between Jews and Minorities," *New York Times*, May 9, 2015; Aeder, "An Overview of Select Research."

27. Aeder, "An Overview of Select Research," 5–8; Amy L. Sales and Leonard Saxe, "Particularism in the University: Realities and Opportunities for Jewish Life on Campus," https://avichai.org/wp-content/uploads/2010/06/Jewish-Life-on-Campus.pdf; Barry A. Kosmin and Ariela Keysar, "National Demographic Survey of American Jewish College Students," Trinity College, 2015, http://www.jewishvirtuallibrry.org/jsource/antisemitism/trinityantisemitismreport.pdf, both downloaded December 17, 2020; Matthew J. Mayhew, Nicholas A. Bowman, A. N. Rockenbach, B. Selznick, and Tiffani Riggers-Piehl, "Appreciative Attitudes Toward Jews among Non-Jewish US College Students," *Journal of College Student Development* 59, no. 1 (2018): 71–89; Aeder's research has provided the basis of nearly all this material on Jewish students on college campuses.

28. Elizabeth Redden, "Iowa Pays Nearly $2 Million in Christian Student Group Suits," *Inside Higher Education*, December 8, 2021; Vanessa Miller, "University of Iowa Ordered to Pay Nearly $2m in Faith Based Student Org Lawsuits," *The Gazette* (Cedar Rapids, IA), December 6,

2021, https://www.thegazette.com/higher-education/university-of-iowa-ordered-to-pay-nearly
-2m-in-faith-based-student-org-lawsuits/, downloaded December 8, 2021.

29. Russell T. McCutcheon, *The Discipline of Religion: Structure, Meaning, Rhetoric* (London: Routledge, 2003), 5–6; Robert A. Orsi, "Fair Game," *Bulletin of the Council of Societies for the Study of Religion* 33, no. 3–4 (2004): 87–89; Robert T. McCutcheon, "'It's a Lie. There's No Truth in It! It's a Sin!' On the Limits of the Humanistic Study of Religion and the Costs of Saving Others from Themselves," *Journal of the American Academy of Religion* 74, no. 3 (September 2006): 720–51. I am grateful to Professor Angela Zito for calling my attention to this debate.

30. https://www.bsu.edu/academics/collegesanddepartments/philosophy-religious-studies
/academic-programs/bachelors-religious-studies, https://arts-sciences.und.edu/academics
/philosophy-religion/index.html, and https://www.religion.ucsb.edu/people/faculty/, all downloaded December 7, 2021.

31. Shelby Kearns, "Our Religious Studies Programs Are in Trouble. Here's What We Miss Out on If We Don't Save Them," *America*, April 16, 2021. See, for example, a June 10, 2018, blog by Justin Lane, a regular blogger on *Medium*, https://justin-lene-eddium.com/changes-in
-religion-departments, downloaded December 8, 2021.

32. https://www.insidehighered.com/news/2009/12/21/religious-revival; see also Robert B. Townsend, "A New Found Religion? The Field Surges among AHA Members," American Historical Association, *Perspectives on History*, December 1, 2009, at http://blog.historians.org
/news/823/aha-membership-grows-modestly-as-history-of-religion-surpasses-culture.

33. Laura Levitt, "Proceedings of the Sixth Biennial Conference on Religion and American Culture, Indianapolis, IN, June 2019, 65.

34. Matthew Hedstrom, "Proceedings of the Fifth Biennial Conference on Religion and American Culture, Indianapolis, IN, June 2017, 6–7.

35. Rudy V. Busto, "Proceedings of the Sixth Biennial Conference on Religion and American Culture, Indianapolis, IN, June 2019, 62.

36. "About CCCU," https://www.cccu.org/members_and_affiliates/, downloaded November 26, 2021; Concordia University Chicago, "About Us," https://cuchicago.edu/about-us, downloaded November 26, 2021.

37. For a list of CCCU Institutions, see https://www.cccu.org/about/#heading-our-history, downloaded November 26, 2021.

38. Scott Jaschik, "2 Colleges Leave Christian College Group to Avoid Split Over Gay Marriage," *Inside Higher Education*, September 22, 2015. See also https://www.okwu.edu/, downloaded December 12, 2021.

39. https://iace.education.

40. Elizabeth Redden, "Survey Finds LGBTQ+ Students Attending Religious Colleges Struggle with Belonging," *Inside Higher Education*, March 15, 2021; Elizabeth Redden, "LGBT Students Sue Education Department over Title IX Religious Exemption," *Inside Higher Education*, April 6, 2021; Council for Christian Colleges & Universities, "CCCU Statement on *Hunter v. Department of Education* Lawsuit," April 1, 2021, in https://www.cccu.org/news-updaes/cccu
-statemet-lawsuit-filed-department-eduction/, downloaded November 23, 2021.

41. Bobby Ross Jr., "Closing Doors: Small Religious Colleges Struggle for Survival," Religious News Service, November 20, 2017, https://religiousnewscom/2017/11/20/closing-doors
-small-religious-colleges-strubble, downloaded December 8, 2021; Scott Jaschik, "Ohio Valley University Will Close," *Inside Higher Education*, December 8, 2021.

42. Tanya Storch, "Buddhist Universities in the United States of America," *International Journal of Dharma Studies* 1, no. 4 (2013): 1–16, http://www.internationaljournalofdharma
studies.co./contents/1/1/4, downloaded December 13, 2021; Naropa University, "History of

Naropa," https://www.naropa.edu/about-naropa/history-of-naropa, downloaded December 11, 2021.

43. Zaytuna College, "About," https://zaytuna.edu/about, downloaded December 13, 2021; Mohammed Khaku, "Islamic Studies Graduate School Opens in the Valley," *Lehigh Valley Press*, September 24, 2015.

44. Hindu University of America, http://www.hua.edu/about/heritage/, downloaded December 12, 2021; Storch, "Buddhist Universities in the United States of America," 2.

45. https://liberty.edu/aboutliberty/index.cfm?PID-33803 downloaded December 17, 2021. See also Adam Laats, *Fundamentalist U: Keeping the Faith in American Higher Education* (New York: Oxford University Press, 2018), multiple references.

46. Jerry Falwell Sr., *An Autobiography, The Inside Story* (Lynchburg, VA: Liberty House Publishers, 1997), 388; Laats, *Fundamentalist U*, 237–39; Jimmy Carter, *White House Diary* (New York: Farrar, Straus and Giroux, 2010), 469; Susan Harding, *The Book of Jerry Falwell: Fundamentalist Language and Politics* (Princeton, NJ: Princeton University Press, 2001), 95, 98–99, 112, 120; Glenn H. Utter and James L. True, *Conservative Christians and Political Participation: A Reference Handbook* (Santa Barbara CA: ABC Clio, 2004), see especially pp. 66–70.

47. Virginia Lieson Brereton, *Training God's Army: The American Bible School, 1880–1940* (Bloomington: University of Indiana Press, 1990), xviii.

48. Elizabeth Redden, "Liberty President Stated Goal of 'Getting People Elected,'" *Inside Higher Education*, October 28, 2021.

49. Laats, *Fundamentalist U*, 242–43, 257–66.

50. "Read President Trump's Liberty University Commencement Speech," *Time*, May 13, 2017, https://time.com/4778240/donald-trump-liberty-university-speech-transcript, downloaded December 19, 2021.

51. Laats, *Fundamentalist U*, 254–57.

52. https://liberty-edu/aboutliberty/index.cfm?PID=6907 and https://www.liberty.edu/arts-sciences/creation-studies/, both downloaded December 21, 2021.

53. https://cbmw.org/about/danver-statement, downloaded December 17, 2021.

54. https://cbmw.org/about/danver-statement and https://cbmw.org/nashville-statement/, both downloaded December 17, 2021.

55. Bob Smietana, "Bible Teacher Beth More, Splitting with Lifeway, Says, 'I Am No Longer a Southern Baptist,'" *Religious News Service*, March 9, 2021, downloaded December 19, 2021; Hannah Anderson, "Complementarians Aren't Inherently Patriarchal," *Christianity Today*, May 25, 2021; Rebecca Hopkins, "Questions Continue for Women in Complementarian Churches," *Christianity Today*, December 21, 2020; Matthew 15:9.

56. Elizabeth Redden, "Liberty under Scrutiny for Its Handling of Sexual Assault," *Inside Higher Education*, November 19, 2021.

57. https://www.cbeinternational.org/resource/article/mutuality-blog-magazine/3-ways-egalitarian-theology-opposes-abuse; Jeff Brumley, "Du Mez Sees Link between Sexual Abuse Coverup and Complementarian Theology," *Baptist News*, June 11, 2021, both downloaded December 22, 2021. See also Kristin Kobes Du Mez, *Jesus and John Wayne: How White Evangelicals Corrupted a Faith and Fractured a Nation* (New York: W. W. Norton, 2020).

58. Laats, *Fundamentalist U*, 272–73.

59. https://www.liberty.edu/index.cfm?PID=6908 and https://www.liberty.edu/students/wp-content/uploads/sites/89/2021/09/LW-11.29.2021-OCL-COMPLETE.pdf, both downloaded December 22, 2021.

60. "A History of the University of Nevada, Reno," https://www.unr.edu/about/history, downloaded December 4, 2021; Jay S. Bybee, "Of Orphans and Vouchers: Nevada's 'Little Blaine

Amendment' and the Future of Religious Participation in Public Programs," *Scholarly Works* 354 (2002), https://scholars.law.unlv.edu/facpub/354, downloaded December 27, 2021.

61. Jan Tors, "Hindu Baccalaureate Service Revives Ancient Traditions," The Pluralism Project, April 20, 2009, https://pluralism.org/news/hindu-baccalaureate-service-revives -ancient-traditions/, downloaded December 4, 2021.

62. Annie Flanzraich, "Diverse Panel to Discuss Women's Leadership in Religious and Spiritual Life," *Nevada Today*, February 5, 2020, downloaded December 4, 2021.

63. University of Nevada, Reno, University Catalog 2021–2022, "Religious Studies, Minor," https://catalog.unr.edu/preview_program.php?catoid=47&poid=129370&returnto=64419, downloaded December 28, 2021.

64. https://www.usc.edu/we-are-usc/the-university/facts-and-stats/, downloaded October 11, 2024.

65. https://about.usc.edu/history/ and https://www.laalmanac.com/population/p002.php, both downloaded Decembers 23, 2021.

66. Timothy Smith, *Called Unto Holiness: The Story of the Nazarenes: The Formative Years* (Kansas City, MO: Nazarene Publishing House, 1962), 50, 99, 104–106, 139.

67. Steven B. Sample [USC president], "The University of Southern California at 125: Inventing the Future Since 1880," https://about.usc.edu/steven-b-sample/speeches/address-to -the-newcomen-society-of-the-united-states/; see also https://about.usc.edu/president/ (both downloaded December 23, 2021).

68. https://about.usc.edu/history/#4795 and https://orsl.usc.edu/, both downloaded December 23, 2021.

69. https://crcc.usc.edu/about/, downloaded December 26, 2021.

70. https://dornsife.usc.edu/religion/, downloaded December 26, 2021.

71. https://orsl.usc.edu/, downloaded December 24, 2021; Schmalzbauer and Mahoney, *The Resilience of Religion*, 18; John Dart, "Rabbi Names USC Dean of Religious Life," *Los Angeles Times*, August 31, 1996.

72. For USC religious directors, see https://orsl.usc.edu/organizations/interest/directors association/ and for school talks, see "What Matters to Me and Why," Office of Religious & Spiritual Life, USC, https://orsl,usc.edu/programs/matters/, downloaded November 26, 2021.

73. Rosanna Xia, "Most College Head Chaplains Are Christian. At USC, a Hindu Leads the Way," *Los Angeles Times*, April 3, 2017, downloaded December 26, 2021; see also Varun Soni and Jem Jebbia, "Beyond Crisis: A Prophetic Vision for Chaplaincy in the 21st Century," 126–40 in Melissa Carter, James W. Fraser, Chelsea Garbell, and Amy Wilson, *A Student's Search for Meaning: Reflections on the Intersections of College Chaplaincy, Liberal Arts and the University* (Cambridge: Ethics International Press, 2023).

Afterword

1. Linda A. Livingstone, "Presidential Perspective: Baylor Achieves R1 Status," December 16, 2021, https://www.baylor.edu/president/news.php?action=story&story=225927, downloaded December 30, 2021.

2. Donald D. Schmeltekopf, *Baylor at the Crossroads: Memoirs of a Provost* (Eugene, OR: Cascade Books, 2015), vii–viii, 70–73, 92–98. I am grateful to Andrea Turpin, professor of history at Baylor, for calling my attention to this development and its importance to the Baylor community.

3. https://www.baylor.edu/mediacommunications/news.php?action=story&story=225929, downloaded February 3, 2023. See also Kate McGee, "Baylor University Stirs Anger and Confusion as It Opens the Door for First LGBTQ Student Group," *Texas Tribune*, July 9, 2021, https://www.texastribune.org/2021/07/09/baylor-university-lgbtq-student-group/.

4. Schmeltekopf, *Baylor at the Crossroads*, 22, 108–9, 112–23; Emma Whitford, "Baylor Will Consider LBGTQ Student Group," *Inside Higher Education*, July 13, 2021.

5. Arthur Levine and Scott Van Pelt, *The Great Upheaval: Higher Education's Past, Present, and Uncertain Future* (Baltimore: Johns Hopkins University Press, 2021).

6. Roosevelt Montas, *Rescuing Socrates: How the Great Books Changed My Life and Why They Matter for a New Generation* (Princeton, NJ: Princeton University Press, 2021), 2. See also Melissa Carter, James W. Fraser, Chelsea Garbell, and Amy Wilson, ed., *A Student's Search for Meaning: Reflections on the Intersection of College Chaplaincy, Liberal Arts, and the University* (Cambridge, UK: Ethics International Press, 2023).

7. Muslim Public Affairs Council, https://www.mpac.org/statement/statement-of-support -for-art-professor-fired-from-hamline-university/, downloaded January 17, 2023.

8. Jonathan Zimmerman, "Academic Freedom Trumps Harm, but Forgiveness Beats Vengefulness," *Times Higher Education*, February 3, 2023.

9. Ronald J. Daniels, *What Universities Owe Democracy* (Baltimore: Johns Hopkins University Press, 2021), see 95–100; Jennifer Rubin, "Opinion: Trump Idolatry Has Undermined Religious Faith," *Washington Post*, December 30, 2021; Montas, *Rescuing Socrates*, 2–3.

10. Warren Nord, "Does God Make a Difference? Taking Religion Seriously in Our Schools and Universities, an Excerpt," *Religion & Education* 38, no. 1 (March 2011): 22.

Index

About the Author

James W. Fraser is Professor Emeritus of History and Education at New York University. He is the author or editor of more than a dozen books including *Between Church and State: Religion in Public Education in a Multicultural America* (second edition, Johns Hopkins University Press, 2016) and *Teaching Teachers: Changing Paths and Enduring Debates,* with Lauren Lefty (Johns Hopkins University Press, 2019). His colleagues elected him as president of the History of Education Society for 2013–2014. He is also an ordained minister, and from 1986 to 2006 he was Pastor of Grace Church (Episcopal and United Church of Christ) in East Boston, Massachusetts. He has four grown children and six grandchildren and lives with his wife, Katherine Hanson, and their dogs Ava and Tamala near Cape Cod in Massachusetts. He can be reached at jwf3@nyu.edu.